THE
BARCLAYS
OF
NEW YORK

WHO THEY ARE
AND
WHO THEY ARE NOT

AND
SOME OTHER BARCLAYS

R. Burnham Moffat

HERITAGE BOOKS
2012

HERITAGE BOOKS

AN IMPRINT OF HERITAGE BOOKS, INC.

Books, CDs, and more—Worldwide

For our listing of thousands of titles see our website
at
www.HeritageBooks.com

A Facsimile Reprint
Published 2012 by
HERITAGE BOOKS, INC.
Publishing Division
100 Railroad Ave. #104
Westminster, Maryland 21157

— Publisher's Notice —
In reprints such as this, it is often not possible to remove blemishes from
the original. We feel the contents of this book warrant its reissue despite
these blemishes and hope you will agree and read it with pleasure.

International Standard Book Numbers
Paperbound: 978-0-7884-1925-6
Clothbound: 978-0-7884-9149-8

TO

ALEXANDER BARCLAY, Esq.

OF

St. Paul, Minnesota

CONTENTS.

Contents.

THE following pages have grown out of the author's search for the ancestry of his great grandfather, THOMAS BARCLAY, of St. Mary's County, Maryland. The interesting matter that came to his notice during the course of that search invited frequent digressions from his own line, until his notes were charged with a variety of material which he felt should be preserved in some permanent form. He accordingly determined to print privately and at his own expense what appears in the following pages; but so many requests have come to him for copies of the book that he has recently decided to place it upon the market at somewhat less than cost, and thus make it readily accessible to all who care for it.

He is conscious that in a work of this kind, to which he has been able to give only his leisure hours, errors are bound to creep in,—particularly in tables of descent where it is sought to make a record of precise dates of birth, death and marriage; and he earnestly invites the correction of errors and the supplying of omitted names and dates.

He wishes, too, to express his thanks to the many who have aided him with the material used, and in particular to express his appreciation of the courtesy shown him by Mr. ROBERT H. KELBY, the librarian of the New York Historical Society, by Mr. BEALE, the Register of the Friends Records in Eustace Street, Dublin, and by the Officials of the Record Office in Dublin.

NEW YORK, January 2, 1904.

R. B. M.

PART I.

A TRADITION has been seriously entertained by many of the descendants of Rev. Thomas Barclay, the first rector of St. Peter's at Albany, that they are of Ury stock. Their ancestor, the Rev. Thomas, they assert, was the son of John Barclay of Ury who settled in East New Jersey in 1684, married (according to the tradition) one "Cornelia Van Schaick," and died there in 1731,—the issue of such union being the same Thomas Barclay who in 1708 appeared as a catechist among the Indians on the upper Hudson, and subsequently became more widely known as the first rector of St. Peter's at Albany.

The public and private records, the old letters and the documents which have come to the notice of the writer in tracing his own line of descent, have borne such convincing testimony to the inaccuracy of the tradition that he has felt impelled to lay before those who may be interested the facts which in his judgment wholly disprove the claim that Rev. Thomas Barclay of St. Peter's was of the Ury family.

John Barclay, who settled in East New Jersey in 1684, was the second son of Col. David Barclay of Ury. The father had served with distinction in the Thirty Years War as a follower of Gustavus Adolphus, and had borne arms in the civil wars at home. On December 24th, 1647, he married Lady Katharine Gordon, known as the "White Rose of Scotland," and about a year later (in 1648) purchased from William, Earl of Mareschal, the estate of *Ury* in the County of Kincardine, Scotland. In 1679, under charter from the crown, this estate and some neighboring estates which were also owned by Col. David, were united into the "Barony of Ury." Until some time preceding the purchase of Ury and for a period of more than five hundred years, the family had owned and been identified with the estate of Mathers; but through financial stress Col. David Barclay's father had been forced to part with this ancient holding, and the family later became more widely known as the "Barclays of Ury," although sometimes designated as "of Mathers and Ury."

In 1666 Col. David joined the Society of Friends and as a consequence was subjected to persecution, imprisonment and frequent indignities. He is described "as proper tall a person-" age of a man as could be seen among thousands. His hair " white as the flax, but quite bald upon the top of his head, which " obliged him to wear commonly a black satin cap under his hat." He died in 1686 and was buried near Ury on the 12th of October of that year.[1]

Three sons and two daughters were born to Col. David Barclay, and Lady Katharine Gordon, his wife:

ROBERT, born 1648, the "Apologist;"

LUCY, died 1686, unmarried;

JEAN, married Sir Ewen Cameron, of Lochiel;

JOHN, born 1659, who migrated to East New Jersey; and

DAVID, his youngest son, who died at sea, unmarried.

The migration of John Barclay to America was doubtless due, in part at any rate, to the life appointment of his older brother, Robert, as governor of the then proprietary province of East New Jersey. Robert did not come out to America, nor did John come out as his deputy; but, in the earlier days of his residence in the province, John Barclay was prominent in its affairs and seems, so long as he remained an orthodox Quaker, to have stood in close relations with his family in Scotland. With the change of faith, however, which we read of within the few years following his settlement at Perth Amboy, an estrangement from his family followed (for religious tolerance was but little known in those days, and as little among the Quakers as among others), and John Barclay seems soon to have lost that influence and prestige which his birth and family connections would naturally have secured for him and for his descendants.

The part he played in the affairs of the province may perhaps be the better appreciated if the relation of the province to the mother country be made plain at the outset.

It was on August 27, 1664, that the English captured New Amsterdam from the Dutch; but even prior to such capture, and

---

[1]GENEALOGICAL ACCOUNT OF THE BARCLAYS OF URIE, London; John Herbert, 1812.

in confident anticipation thereof, King Charles II had granted the entire province to his brother James, Duke of York, and he in turn had divided the territory so granted and had conveyed to Lord John Berkeley and to Sir George Carteret all that portion of the province which was bounded on the east by the Hudson River, on the west by the Delaware River, and on the north by a line drawn from river to river at about the 41st parallel of latitude. Both Lord John Berkeley (who was a brother of Sir William Berkeley, more widely known as the Governor of Virginia from 1660 to 1677), and Sir George Carteret had been distinguished and steadfast loyalists during the civil wars; and out of compliment to Carteret, who as Governor of the little island of Jersey in the British Channel had been the last commander during such wars to lower the royal flag, the tract so granted was named *New Jersey*.

In the year following the capture of New Amsterdam, Philip Carteret, a kinsman of Sir George, was granted a governor's commission and sailed for the province accompanied by a number of colonists. He landed at the spot soon afterwards called *Elizabethtown,* in honor of Lady Carteret, and there he established the seat of government.

The Dutch recaptured the province in 1673; but upon the conclusion of peace on February 9th, 1674, the English title to the soil was finally recognized and New Jersey reverted to its English proprietors. Lord John Berkeley, however, retained his share of the province for scarcely thirty days after the conclusion of peace. On March 18th, 1674, he sold his entire undivided interest in the province for the sum of £1,000, to one John Fenwick, a Quaker, who acquired such interest for himself and for another Quaker, named Edward Billings. Two years later, in July, 1676, Carteret and Fenwick agreed upon a formal partition of their holding, and an imaginary line was thereupon drawn from the shore of the ocean at Little Egg Harbor to the northwestern corner of the province. The portion lying to the northerly and easterly of this line, thereafter known as *East New Jersey,* became the separate property of Carteret, while the remaining portion, subsequently known as *West New Jersey,* was divided between its Quaker proprietors. Our interest in this sketch is centred in the first-mentioned portion.

Philip Carteret, on behalf of his kinsman, Sir George, re-sumed the administration of the government of East New Jersey, and such tract being regarded as a separate province, was divided into four counties, Bergen, Essex, Middlesex and Monmouth. Somerset County was the next created,—in 1688.

Sir George Carteret lived but a few years after the establish-ment of East New Jersey, and upon his death left the entire province to the trustees of his estate. They offered it for sale, and in 1682 it was purchased by a company of twelve Quakers, of whom William Penn is now the most widely known. These twelve purchasers associated with themselves twelve others, most of whom, but not all, were both Scotchmen and Quakers, and the twenty-four proprietors, for further assurance, obtained from the Duke of York on the 13th of March, 1683, a new patent of the province, issued directly to themselves. The early history of the province was marked with no little friction between those who administered its affairs on behalf of the proprietors and those who sought to do so on behalf of the Crown; and finally and in 1702 the government of the province was duly ceded by the pro-prietors to the Crown.

Among the twenty-four proprietors to whom the patent of March 13th, 1683, was issued as above mentioned, was *Robert Barclay,* the eldest son of Col. David Barclay and Lady Kath-arine Gordon. It is he who has added the greatest lustre to the Barclay name, through his famous "Apology for the True Chris-tian Divinity" which he wrote, and in 1675, when but twenty-seven years of age, presented to King Charles II. Although chosen by the proprietors to be governor of the province for life, Robert Barclay never came to America, but entrusted the actual administration of its affairs to one Gawen Laurie, whom he ap-pointed to the office of deputy governor. The younger brothers, however, John and David, both came to the province, unmarried. David died at sea on his second voyage out, while John, very shortly after his arrival, settled in Perth Amboy, where he died in 1731.

What has thus far been written is conceded by all. It is here that the tradition referred to, on the one hand, and the pub-lic and private records to be cited below, on the other hand, bear widely divergent testimony. The *tradition* is best told, perhaps, in the words of Mr. George L. Rives, in his work entitled "Correspondence of Thomas Barclay" (New York: Harper & Brothers, 1894), wherein he has edited sundry letters of the first British Consul General in New York, who was a grandson of Rev. Thomas Barclay of Albany.

"About 1685," writes Mr. Rives, without, however, giving any authority for the selection of such year, "he (John Barclay) " married a lady whose name alone is sufficient evidence of her " descent. She was *Cornelia Van Schaick*" (citing HOLGATE'S AMERICAN GENEALOGIES, published 1851, where not even the suggestion of an authority for such alleged marriage is given), "a " member, it would seem, of the extensive Van Schaick family of " Albany." Mr. Rives then refers to John Barclay's conversion to the Church of England as having occurred prior to 1702, and states that an English clergyman, Rev. Thorowgood Moore, had officiated in Perth Amboy sometime between 1702 and 1707, and that, prior to his appearance in Perth Amboy, Mr. Moore had been a missionary at Albany and among the Indians.

"We may well suppose," Mr. Rives thereupon argues, "that " he (Moore) did not fail when he found a likely young man " with a vocation for the ministry, to urge the noble work that " might be done on the wild frontier about the head waters of " the Hudson River. Whether Mr. Moore did indeed find such " a young man at Perth Amboy, and whether he did influence the " course of his career, must remain a conjecture; *but certain it is,*" Mr. Rives asseverates, *"that Thomas Barclay, a son of John Bar-*" *clay, went early in the eighteenth century to England,* took " orders, and was in due time sent, in his turn, by the Society as " Missionary at Albany and among the Indians. He seems to " have reached Albany in 1707 or 1708."

Mr. Rives next seems to think that the fact that the church at Albany bore the same name as the church at Perth Amboy, "St. Peters," is possessed of some significance in view of Rev. Thomas Barclay having been the first rector of the Albany parish. But Mr. Rives has evidently overlooked the fact that the patent was issued for St. Peter's at Albany in 1714, while St. Peter's at Perth Amboy was not chartered until 1718; and the name of the former church, consequently, could hardly have been selected out of any sentimental regard on the part of its rector for the Perth

Amboy parish, which was not even called into being until four years after the establishment of the Albany Church.

Quite apart from what is shown by the records, referred to below, the probabilities are all against the alleged marriage between John Barclay and Cornelia Van Schaick. The Van Schaicks of colonial days were well known. Two separate families of that name were early settlers on the upper Hudson, of one of which Goosen Gerritse Van Schaick was the head, and of the other, Claes Van Schaick.[2] The line of descent from each of these heads is well known, and is available to all who would consult it; yet no such marriage can be found in the records of either line. It is true that a Cornelia Van Schaick, born 1670, is mentioned in those records; but her marriage also is chronicled there as occurring in 1690 to Johannes Pluvier.[3] The only other Cornelia Van Schaick appearing in either line was a daughter of Claes Van Schaick; and she was not born until 1710.

It is hardly probable that if, as has been claimed, John Barclay ever married into this family, all knowledge of such fact would have escaped the students of the Van Schaick genealogy, when we consider not only the prominence of the family from which John Barclay came, but also the prominence of Rev. Thomas Barclay (who by the same tradition is claimed to have been his son), and the subsequent social distinction of many of Rev. Thomas Barclay's descendants.

Nor is it likely that such a marriage would have occurred unnoticed at a time when the feeling between those of differing religious views was as bitter as we know it to have been toward the close of the 17th century. The Van Schaicks were closely identified with the Dutch Church of the day, and John Barclay up to 1692, certainly, was a prominent and earnest Quaker. If any such marriage occurred, of which Rev. Thomas Barclay was (as is claimed) the issue, it could hardly have occurred later than 1687; for in 1708 Rev. Thomas Barclay had taken orders in the established church and was engaged in his mission at Albany. He must certainly have been at least twenty-one years of age when ordained; and even were he ordained at once upon attaining

[2] See Genealogy First Settlers of Albany (Munsell & Co.), pp. 131-133.

[3] See N. Y. Gen. & Biog. Rec., vol. VII, p. 54.

his majority and during the very year in which he came out to Albany, his birth could not have occurred later than 1687. The supposed marriage, therefore, between John Barclay and Cornelia Van Schaick must have occurred, if at all, in or prior to the year 1687.

There is no record of such marriage in any Dutch Church of which the marriage records have been preserved; and neither mention of marriage nor reference to any wife or son of John Barclay can be found in the records of the Quaker meeting which was inaugurated at Amboy on August 3rd, 1686. The original records of that meeting are preserved in Plainfield, New Jersey, the meeting having moved in 1689 from Amboy to Woodbridge, and later to Rahway and thence to Plainfield. Such records show that from 1686 to 1689 (when the records were discontinued until 1704), John Barclay was an active member of the meeting. The marriages of other Friends which occurred during those years were noted, as well as the birth of children to sundry members of the meeting; but no mention is made of John Barclay having married, or of any son having been born to him, nor is there any fact stated from which it could properly be inferred that he was a married man during any portion of those three years. In *Appendix A*, hereunto annexed, will be found sundry extracts from the records of the Amboy Monthly Meeting.

At some time during the fifteen years which intervened between 1689 and 1704, when, as has been stated, the keeping of the records of this meeting was discontinued, John Barclay seems to have left the Society of Friends and gone over to the Church of England. He was undoubtedly influenced to this course by George Keith, by whom, as we shall see below, he had been appointed deputy surveyor of the province in the year 1688. Nor is it at all unlikely that such departure from the testimonies of his father and brother served in some measure to estrange him from his family; for we find that in 1701 his nephew, Robert Barclay, then the head of the family at Ury, appointed others in the province to be his attorneys-in-fact, and that John Barclay from that time forward does not seem to have acted on behalf of any of his Scottish kinsmen.

George Keith was and for many years had been a most ardent preacher among the Quakers; but differing with many of the leaders, whom he publicly charged with deism, he gradually became the head of a sect or faction, and in 1692 was formally disowned by the main body of Friends. In 1694 he went to England and laid his case before the London Yearly Meeting, as a sort of an appeal from Philadelphia. It is said that this is the only instance of such an appeal having been taken. The London Meeting approved the disownment,[4] and shortly thereafter Keith took orders in the Established Church.[5]

John Barclay was undoubtedly a member of the Keithian party; for a careful search of the records of the Woodbridge Monthly Meeting from 1704 (when the keeping of records was resumed) until long subsequently to the year of his death, 1731, fails to disclose the mention of his name. Nor in the register of the births of the children of Friends, which seems to have been most carefully kept by this meeting from 1705 down, was there a single record of a Barclay born; nor in the register similarly kept of the decease of Friends, did the name Barclay occur until as late as 1862.

It is possible and even probable that those members of the Amboy-Woodbridge Meeting who followed Keith from 1689 to 1694, held a monthly meeting of their own and kept their separate records of marriages, births and deaths. In an undated letter to the Society for the Propagation of the Gospel (written probably in England between 1694 and 1702) Keith stated that those of the Quakers in America who had joined him held their separate meetings, and that in 1694 when he sailed for England he left fourteen or fifteen different meetings of his adherents scattered through East and West Jersey and Pennsylvania.[6] One writer states that on the present site of the old Topanemus burying ground (near Marlboro, New Jersey), there stood a Scotch and English Quaker Meeting House, which, through the labors of George Keith, later became the place of worship of the congregation now known as St. Peter's Protestant Episcopal Church of

---

[4] WOODBRIDGE & VICINITY, by Rev. J. W. Dalley: New Brunswick, N. J., 1873, page 62.

[5] See Janney's HISTORY OF THE SOCIETY OF FRIENDS; also Gerard Croese's GENERAL HISTORY OF THE QUAKERS.

[6] See COLLECTIONS OF THE PROTESTANT EPISCOPAL HISTORICAL SOCIETY FOR THE YEAR 1851. New York: Stanford & Swords, publishers.

Freehold, N. J.;[7] and it is stated that John Barclay was one of those interested and active in its erection. The rector of St. Peter's in 1897 informed the writer that no parish records were extant, antedating 1824, although the parish had been chartered as a part of the Colonial Anglican Church in 1731. If such a meeting were in fact held there, it yet remains for someone to locate the records of such meeting, if they still be extant, and to give them to the world. The most diligent inquiry on the part of the writer has failed to discover them.

With the conversion of their leader to the Church of England, the adherents of Keith soon lost their identity as a separate sect; and many of those who had been identified with him in the controversy, followed him into the Established Church. Among such, in all probability, was John Barclay.

In April, 1702, Keith came back to America on a mission tour for the church in which he had been ordained, and remained here until August, 1704. He made many converts and founded numerous societies which subsequently developed into church organizations.

It is believed that most of the meetings of the so-called "Christian Quakers," which he had organized between his disownment in Philadelphia in 1792 and his sailing for England in 1794, became, when not wholly disrupted by his subsequent change of faith, the kernels out of which sundry Baptist churches subsequently grew.

Shortly after his return to England he published, in 1706, a "Narrative" of his "Travels, Services and Successes," which may be found in several of the larger libraries. It has been republished in more readable form in the "Collections of the Protestant Episcopal Historical Society for the year 1851," above cited. Only two extracts from his Narrative, however, are of interest in this sketch. They are as follows:

"1702: Oct. 3, Sunday. I preached at *Amboy* in *East Jersey;* the Auditory was small; My text was *Tit.* 2, 11, 12. But such as were there were well affected; some of them, of my former Acquaintance, and others who had been formerly *Quakers* but were come over to the Church, particularly *Miles Forster* and *John Barclay* (Brother to *Robert Barclay* who published the Apology for the Quakers) the Place has very few Inhabi-

[7]See BRICK CHURCH MEMORIAL, by Rev. Theo. W. Wells: Marlborough, N. J., 1877, page 21.

tants. We were several Days Kindly entertained by *Miles Forster* at his House there."

*   *   *   *   *   *   *   *

"April 26, 1704. I sailed down *Maryland Bay* to Virginia, in Captain *Pulman's* Ship, who very kindly entertained me and Mr. *John Barclay,* my good Friend with me; He, in true Love and Affection, travelled with me from his dwelling House at *Amboy* in *East Jersey,* to *James River* in *Virginia* and he staid with me until he saw me aboard the ship, *June* 8, where we took our Farewell."

The above are the only records that have come to the writer's notice that bear in any way upon John Barclay's change of faith. There is much to be wished for touching the details of that change; but records will doubtless be found hereafter which may establish more clearly his religious associations until the issuing of a charter to St. Peter's Church in Amboy, on the 30th of July, 1718. In and by that charter, John Barclay was constituted junior warden;[8] and, as the vestry records show, he was elected and re-elected warden at the meetings of March 31, 1719; April 18, 1720; April 11, 1721; and March 27, 1722. On September 23, 1728, he was chosen clerk to the corporation of St. Peter's, and on March 31, 1730, was elected vestryman. On April 20, 1731, he was re-elected vestryman; but no further mention of his name is found in the vestry minutes. His death occurred prior to December 31st of that year, as the records of "The General Proprietors of the Eastern Division of New Jersey" bear witness.[9]

While the vestry minutes of St. Peter's at Amboy are preserved, it is a matter of much regret that its earlier *parish* records have been lost; and yet as the church was not established until 1718, it is doubtful whether, even were these parish records extant, they would throw much if any light on the questions that interest us here, namely, the marriage and issue of John Barclay. The records at Perth Amboy of the General Proprietors permit, as it seems to the writer, but a single line of inferences, to wit, that John Barclay was *not* married until somewhere between 1696 and 1699; that his wife's name was *not* Cornelia, but *Katharine;*

---

[8] See original records of the Vestry of St. Peter's Church at Perth Amboy.

[9] Since writing the above, the newspaper notices of John Barclay's death, referred to below, have come to the attention of the writer. From them it appears that he died probably between the 22nd and 29th of April, 1731. His last election as vestryman, therefore, must have preceded his death by a few days only.

that his wife died either in 1702 or in 1703; and that he had but one son whom he named John.

These inferences as to the year of his marriage, as to his wife's Christian name, and as to the time of her death, are drawn from the fact that in all the deeds which are on record as having been executed by John Barclay between 1686 and 1731,—and there are a number of them,—no wife joins with him in a single transfer except in those executed between September, 1696, and March, 1704. During that period three deeds were executed and recorded, the first on December 23rd, 1699, the second on September 12th, 1700, and the third on December 17th, 1701; and in each of them the grantors were "John Barclay, of Amboy, Gentleman, *and Katharine, his wife.*" In a deed executed by him on September 15th, 1696, no wife had joined; and a deed executed on March 14th, 1704, was also, as were all subsequent deeds, executed by John Barclay alone. While the presumption arising from these facts is not conclusive, as proving that somewhere between September 15th, 1696, and December 23rd, 1699, John Barclay married a woman whose Christian name was *Katharine,* and that such wife died somewhere between December 17th, 1701 (the date of the last deed in which she joined), and March 14th, 1704 (the date of the next deed executed by him), the presumption is nevertheless warranted; and until stronger proof to the contrary is adduced, the evidence afforded by these records should be taken as establishing the three facts stated.[10]

The inference as to John Barclay's having a son John, is supported by the record of a deed executed in 1724 to *John Barclay, Jr.,* of Freehold; by the direct statement contained in the record of administration on John Barclay's estate, that "John Barclay, *his son and heir,*" requested that administration should be granted to William Bradford; and by the fact that nearly three years after the grant of such administration, a deed was recorded of a grant of land to "John Barclay of the County of Middlesex."

The following is a brief chronological summary of the records of the General Proprietors of the Eastern Division of

---

[10]Since the above was written, the records of St. Mary's Church at Burlington, West New Jersey, have been examined by the writer. It there appears that on January 6, 1703, *"Catherine Barclay"* was buried at Amboy by Rev. John Talbot. There is no reason to doubt that this was the wife of John Barclay.

New Jersey, in which John Barclay appears either as grantor or as grantee, with a reference to the volumes and pages where such records may respectively be found. There is also noted the record of administration on his estate.

1684 July 10. Deed from ROBERT BARCLAY of Ury, to JOHN BARCLAY his brother, of 500 acres in East Jersey, called "Plainfield." (Referred to in *Liber G.,* p. 97.)

1685 Jan. 18. Patent to JOHN BARCLAY of lands in Plainfield. (Referred to in *Liber D.,* p. 12.)

1686 Mch. 8. Deed from DAVID BARCLAY of Ury, and Robert his eldest son, to JOHN BARCLAY of Amboy.

> *Recites* that DAVID BARCLAY, Sr., gave to his son David, merchant, certain moneys which in the event of said David's dying without issue were to revert to his older brother, Robert; that with those moneys, David, Jr., had bought one-twentieth part of a propriety in the Province of East Jersey, and goods of the value of £150, all of which goods, together with seven or eight servants, he took in August, 1685, on board the ship "America" bound from Aberdeen to East New Jersey; that David died at sea during the voyage; and that the land and property thereupon reverted to Robert, and that Robert with the consent of his father David and out of love and affection for his brother John,

> *Conveys* all said property to JOHN BARCLAY (described as "planter and inhabitant in said province"), on condition that if John should die without issue, everything should revert to Robert, his heirs, executors, &c.

> A part of the expressed consideration for this transfer was the extinguishment by John of a balance due on a bond for 1350 Scotch marks, which Robert had given to John in 1684. (*Liber G.,* p. 108.)

1686 Dec. 20. Proprietors confirm above transfer to JOHN BARCLAY, "in right of DAVID BARCLAY, his late brother." (*Liber B.,* pp. 40 and 42.)

1686 Dec. 29. Endorsed on deed last described was a transfer by JOHN BARCLAY to his brother ROBERT BARCLAY of Ury, of all property thus confirmed to him. No wife joins with JOHN BARCLAY in the transfer. (*Liber B.,* pp. 41 and 42.)

1687 Mch. 1. ROBERT BARCLAY of Ury, confirms to JOHN BARCLAY, a grant of 500 acres. (*Liber B.,* p. 79.)

1687 Nov. 2. In a grant by the proprietors, JOHN BARCLAY appears to be one of the Council of the Deputy Governor. (*Liber B.,* p. 174.)

1688 May 12. The same appears under this date. (*Liber B.,* p. 399.)

1688 Nov. 5. JOHN BARCLAY, described as "of Plainfield" appoints *George McKenzie,* his attorney to collect, &c. (*Liber D.,* p. 14.)

1688 Nov. 7. Deed by JOHN BARCLAY (no wife mentioned), described as "of Plainfield," to *George McKenzie,* of all said Barclay's land in Plainfield. (*Liber D.,* p. 12.)

1690 May 11. Grant by proprietors to JOHN BARCLAY "of Plainfield" of lands on the Raritan River, Middlesex County. (*Liber D.*, p. 169.)

1690 July 19. JOHN BARCLAY (no wife mentioned) "of Plainfield" transfers said lands to *George Willocks*. (*Liber D.*, p. 205.)

1691 June 6. JOHN BARCLAY, in deed of this date, is described as "of Plainfield." (*Liber D.*, p. 305.)

(year uncertain)
May 11. *Andrew Galaway* of Aberdeen, by instrument executed in Aberdeen, appoints as his general agent in the province of East Jersey, "JOHN BARCLAY, second lawful son of Col. DAVID BARCLAY, late of Ury, deceased." (*Liber E.*, p. 17.)

1692 Oct. 17. JOHN BARCLAY on the "17th of the tenth month" appoints *John Reid* a surveyor. (*Liber E.*, p. 40.)

1693 April 1. Administration granted to JOHN BARCLAY on property of *Gawen Lawrie*, "late Governor." (Although here so described, Lawrie was only deputy governor.) (*Liber E.*, p. 139.)

1693 April 22. Deed of gift of 40 acres from *George Allin* of Elizabeth Bounds to JOHN BARCLAY "of County Essex" out of his great love and affection for Barclay. (*Liber E.*, p. 272.)

1693 July 28. Grant of land from proprietors to JOHN BARCLAY. (*Liber E.*, p. 50.)

1693 July 29. Endorsed on deed last described was a transfer of said lands from JOHN BARCLAY to *John Reid*. No wife of Barclay was mentioned. (*Liber E.*, p. 52.)

1696 April 27. Grant of land in Elizabethtown from proprietors to JOHN BARCLAY. (*Liber F.*, p. 48.)

1696 Sep. 15. JOHN BARCLAY transfers above lands to *William Strayhearne*. No wife mentioned in the deed. (*Liber F.*, p. 50.)

1696 Oct. 12. Administration granted to *John Barclay* on property of *John Carrington*, deceased, which his widow, *Margaret Carrington*, had not administered. (*Liber F.*, p. 461.)

MEMO.

1686, Dec. 10. Grant of land by proprietors to *Margaret Carrington* wife of *John Carrington* of Amboy Perth. (*Liber B.*, p. 218.)

1688, Mch. 25. Grant of land by proprietors to *John Carrington*. (*Liber B.*, p. 324.)

1692, Mch. 13. *John Carrington* elected high sheriff of Middlesex County for one year. (*Liber C.* of Commissions, p. 202.)

1695, Oct. 25. Will of *John Carrington*, leaving all his land to his wife, *Margaret Carrington*. (*Liber E.*, p. 235.)

1697 Feb. 26. Deed of "plantation of Plainfield" by McKenzie to JOHN BARCLAY, covering 700 acres in Middlesex County, being the same premises formerly conveyed by Barclay to McKenzie. (*Liber G.*, p. 16.)

1697 Mch. 22. JOHN BARCLAY made trustee for wife of *William Pinhorn* of Bergen. (*Liber B.*, p. 167.)

1697 May 1.   Deed of land in Perth Amboy from proprietors to JOHN BARCLAY. (*Liber F.*, p. 325.)

1697 Dec. 18.   Will of *Margaret Carrington* devising all her lands and tenements to JOHN BARCLAY. (*Liber F.*, p. 460.)

1697 Dec. 27.   ROBERT BARCLAY of Ury, son of Robert the late governor, appoints JOHN BARCLAY one of his attorneys. (*Liber G.*, p. 157.)

1699 Dec. 23.   Deed from "JOHN BARCLAY, of Amboy, Gentleman, and "*Katharine, his wife*," to *John Lainge,* yeoman, of land in Plainfield.

> *Recites* that ROBERT BARCLAY, late of Ury, deceased, did by deed dated July 10th, 1684, sell unto JOHN BARCLAY, his brother, 500 acres of land which with 200 acres that were granted to said JOHN BARCLAY for transporting "said JOHN BARCLAY and his servants into the province," made up the 700 acres "commonly called Plainfield," and that said 700 acres had been mortgaged by JOHN BARCLAY to *George McKenzie* "formerly of New York, now of Barbadoes." (*Liber G.*, p. 97.)

1700 Aug. 30.   Grant by proprietors of land in Monmouth County to JOHN BARCLAY. (*Liber G.*, p. 230.)

1700 Sep. 12.   Deed by JOHN BARCLAY and "*Katharine his wife,*" to *Herman King.* (*Liber G.*, p. 231.)

1701 Sep. 1.   Deed by "ROBERT BARCLAY of Urie, son and heir of ROBERT BARCLAY of Urie" to some third party.

> *Recites* the dates of the original patents, by and to whom granted, the names of the original 12 proprietors, the other 12 to whom they sold half of their holdings, and other historical facts connected with the province of "Nova Cesarea."

> *Recites* the appointment by ROBERT BARCLAY of *John Mollison of Piscataqua* and one *Halconar,* as his attorneys under letter of attorney dated Sept. 1, 1701. JOHN BARCLAY from this time on does not appear to have acted as attorney for his nephew, Robert Barclay of Ury. (*Liber H.*, p. 53.)

1701 Dec. 17.   Deed by JOHN BARCLAY "*and Katharine his wife*" to *William Strayhearne,* planter, of 112 acres in Elizabethtown. Confirms sale of same premises on Sept. 15, 1696. (This is the last deed on record in which JOHN BARCLAY's wife joined.) (*Liber C.*, p. 186.)

1704 Mch. 14.   Deed from JOHN BARCLAY (no wife mentioned) conveying to *John Harrison* land in Amboy in exchange for land in Elizabeth which Harrison conveyed to Barclay. (*Liber K.*, p. 1.)

1707 May 29.   Deed from JOHN BARCLAY of Amboy Perth (no wife mentioned) conveying to *Col. Richard Townley* of Elizabethtown, several tracts amounting in all to about 5,000 acres in Middlesex County, all of which had been conveyed to JOHN BARCLAY the previous day by *Col. Richard Townley* and Elizabeth, his wife. The property had come to Townley's wife through her father. (*Liber C-3,* p. 65—see also, p. 59.)

1712 April 10. Deed from JOHN BARCLAY (no wife mentioned) to *John Reid* "of Hortencie, Monmouth County." (*Liber I.*, p. 437.)

1713 June 22. Deed to JOHN BARCLAY of some 500 acres. (*Liber A*-2, p. 152.)

1715 Sep. 27. Deed from JOHN BARCLAY (no wife mentioned) to one Hodgson, of lot in Amboy. (*Liber C*-2, p. 32.)

1717 June 5. Deed from JOHN BARCLAY (no wife mentioned) to *Henry Ralph*, of land received by will of *Margaret Carrington*. (*Liber A*-2, p. 210.)

1718 May 4. Deed to a ROBERT BARCLAY of Piscataqua. (Who this grantee is, the writer does not know.) (*Liber A*-2, p. 310.)

1719 Mch. 15. Deed to JOHN BARCLAY from Willock, of a lot in City of Amboy. (*Liber C*-2, p. 32.)

1721 Dec. Deed to ROBERT BARCLAY of Piscataqua. (*Liber C*-2, p. 486.)

1723 Mch. 10. Deed from ROBERT BARCLAY of Piscataqua, described as "yeoman." Instead of a signature he made his mark. (*Liber C*-2, p. 514.)

1724 Mch. 28. Deed by JOHN BARCLAY (no wife mentioned) of land in Amboy. (*Liber D*-2, p. 45.)

1724 May 16. Deed from *George Willock* "late of Amboy, now of Philadelphia," to "JOHN BARCLAY, JR." of Freehold, conveying 294 acres. (*Liber D*-2, p. 149.)

1727 May 20. Deed to JOHN BARCLAY and another as executors of one Rudyard. (*Liber E.*, p. 510.)

1729 Nov. 20. Deed to JOHN BARCLAY of land in Amboy. (*Liber K.*, p. 192.)

1729 Dec. 1. Deed of same land to *Evans Drummond* by JOHN BARCLAY (no wife mentioned). (*Liber K.*, p. 193.)

1731 Dec. 31. "Letters of administration granted to *William Bradford*, " principal creditor and administrator of all and singular " the Goods, Chattels, Rights and Credits of JOHN BAR- " CLAY, late of Perth Amboy, deceased, JOHN BARCLAY " his son & heir having requested Administration should " be granted under his hand unto the said *William Brad-* " *ford*. Dated the 31st December, 1731." (*Liber B* of Wills, p. 240.)

In the office of the Secretary of State of New Jersey at Trenton, the grant of administration on John Barclay's estate is also recorded by the following entry:

"*Amboy 31st December, 1731.* Letters of Administration were "granted by the Honble. Lewis Morris Esq, President of his Majestie's "Councill and Commd'r in Chief, unto *William Bradford*, principall Cred- "itor and adm'r of all and Singular the goods, Chattles, Rights and "credits of John Barclay, late of Perth Amboy, Deceased, JOHN BARCLAY "his son & heir having requested adm'n should be granted under his hand "unto the said Wm. Bradford, the said Bradford having duly sworn &c.
before
MICH. KEARNY
Surr."
(*Liber B* of Wills, p. 240.)

And finally in the Records of the Proprietors at Perth Amboy is found the following deed, executed subsequently to John Barclay's death:

1734 April 13. Deed from *Evans Drummond* of 100 acres to "JOHN BAR-CLAY of the County of Middlesex." (*Liber E-*2, p. 189.)

Although a statement of the public offices held by John Barclay, as the same appear from the records of the General Proprietors, cannot bear on either of the questions of his marriage or his issue, the record may nevertheless be of sufficient interest to warrant the taking of space to insert the same here:

1688 Jan.　1.　(1st of the 11th month called January) appointed deputy surveyor by George Keith, who was Surveyor General under commission from the proprietors. (*Liber D.*, p. 56.)

1692 Jan.　7.　Receiver General (*Liber C.* of Commissions, p. 213.)

1692 April 6.　Receiver General (*Liber C.* of Commissions, p. 147), granted in England.

1692 April 6.　Surveyor General (*Liber C.* of Commissions, p. 149.)

1695 Nov. 25.　Deputy Secretary & Register of the Province. (*Liber C.* of Commissions, p. 242.)

1696 May　4.　Commissioner of Court of small debts. (*Liber C.* of Commissions, p. 256.)

1698 Aug.　6.　Register of Court of Chancery. (*Liber C.* of Commissions, p. 286.)

1698 Dec.　1.　Commissioner of Court of small causes. (*Liber C.* of Commissions, p. 288.)

1699 Feb.　5.　Clerk of Court of Common Rights or Supreme or Provincial Court of the Province. (*Liber C.* of Commissions, p. 322.)

1704 June　9.　Receiver General. (*Liber I.*, p. 62.)

1704 June　9.　Ranger General. (*Liber I.*, p. 62.)

1716 Aug.　7.　Surrogate of Eastern Division of Province. (*Liber C.*, p. 21.)

PART II.

A Mistaken Tradition, *Continued.*—Testimony of the Records at
Bury Hill, Surrey.

ANOTHER circumstance that tends strongly to disprove
the tradition of a descent of Rev. Thomas Barclay from
the Barclays of Ury, is the fact that in the early part
of the 19th century a search was made by the family at Bury Hill,
Surrey, for the then living descendants of John Barclay who
migrated to East New Jersey and died there in 1731; and correspondence was had with many of those descendants and they
were recognized as such and their names were recorded in the
family genealogy, whereas the descendants of Rev. Thomas,
although occupying high social position in and about New York,
and although in some instances personally known to those of
the family at Bury Hill who were conducting the search, were
not recognized as descendants of John of East New Jersey and
were *not* recorded in the genealogical plan of the Barclays of Ury.

The search was made and the correspondence had under the
following circumstances:

Robert Barclay, the apologist,—(the elder brother of John
of East New Jersey),—died on October 3rd, 1690, and the estate
of Ury thereupon passed to his eldest son, also named Robert,
who was eighteen years of age at the time. This son, Robert, on
October 9th, 1722, executed a "disposition and deed of entail,"—
(recorded in the register of tailzies in Scotland on February 6th,
1723),—whereby he settled the entire estate, or Barony, of Ury
on (1) Robert Barclay, his eldest son and the heirs male lawfully
to be procreated of his body; failing which, then on (2) David
Barclay, the entailer's second son, and the heirs male of his body;
which failing, then on (3) the heirs male to be procreated of his
own (the entailer's) body; which failing, then on (4) David
Barclay, the entailer's brother, and the heirs male of his body;
which failing, then on (5) John Barclay, the entailer's younger
brother (who had settled in Dublin) and the heirs male of his
body; which failing, then on (6) *John Barclay, the entailer's uncle*

(who had come out to East New Jersey in 1684), and the heirs male of his body; which failing, then on (7) the heirs and assignees of the entailer, generally.

Under such deed of entail the estate passed from Robert Barclay, the entailer, to his son Robert, born 1699, and then, and upon the death of such Robert, to *his* son Robert, born 1731. This son Robert had upon his (second) marriage to Sarah Ann Allardice, taken the name "Allardice" as a part of his own, and the surname of their male descendants, at any rate, thereupon became "Barclay-Allardice." When Robert Barclay-Allardice (born 1731) died, the estate passed under the entail to his oldest son, born 1779, who bore the same name; and it was during *his* ownership that an effort was made to alter the entail by securing to him, in fee simple absolute, a release therefrom of certain portions of the estate which were situated more remotely from the Mansion House of Ury, and substituting therefor certain other lands of a greater rental value and more nearly adjacent to the bulk of the estate, which other lands were already owned in fee by Robert Barclay-Allardice.

A step to be taken towards a release of any part of the entailed estate, was the securing of the consent thereto of Parliament; and accordingly and in 1805 a private bill was passed (indexed among the "Local and Personal Acts," but not officially printed), which will be found among the private bills of 45 George III. A copy of such act is printed in *Appendix B* hereunto annexed.

By this Act of Parliament, leave was granted Robert Barclay-Allardice to apply to the Court of Session in Scotland and under the direction and with the approbation of that Court to settle as a part of the entailed estate, and in all things subject to the terms of the deed of 1722, the lands then owned by him; and it was provided that when such deed of settlement,—or "Settlement of Tailzie," as it was known to the Scotch law,—was duly executed and recorded in the Register of Entails for Scotland, and also in the register of the Court of Session "for preservation," a Charter of resignation should pass and Infeftment be taken "by virtue of the precept of sasine therein contained." The act further provided that at once upon the recording of the deed, the passing of the Charter and the completing of the Infeftment, the specified portion of the entailed estate should thenceforward stand forever released from the limitations contained in the deed of entail of 1722.

From the terms of this act it would seem probable that a reference to the Register of Entails, or to the record of the Court of Session, would disclose the "Settlement of Tailzie," and incidentally the names of the heirs whose contingent rights were cut off by the alteration of the entail. But a search of the Register of Entails from 1723 to 1897 failed to disclose mention of any such deed or settlement, as does a search from 1781 to 1830 of the Sasine Register for Kincardine (the county in which Ury is located) preserved at Stonehaven. So, too, the records of the Court of Session from 1805 to 1835 contain no reference to the matter of any kind whatsoever.

The Register of Deeds at Edinburgh, however, does contain the record of a "Consent and Commission" executed by Robert Barclay-Allardice under date of October 19th, 1805, in which he refers, among other things, to the lands "lately freed from the " fetters of the entail of Ury by an Act passed in the forty-fifth " year of his present Majesty's reign" (recorded Vol. 301, November 20, 1807), thus indicating probably the point of view of those most interested, namely, that where Parliament had once spoken, its authority could not be strengthened by a decree of the Court of Session.

Under date or December 20th, 1821, a Charter of Resignation issued under the great seal (sealed February 21st, 1822), wherein Robert Barclay-Allardice resigned in favor of himself and his heirs, as they existed on July 31st, 1821, certain specified lands, among which were those "erected into the Barony of Ury " by Charter under the Great Seal in favour of Colonel David " Barclay of Ury and his heirs therein mentioned" under date of August 13th, 1679.[1] A resignation of an entailed estate in favor of any person named and his heirs, seems to have had the effect of vesting the fee in such person to the exclusion of those contingently interested in the entail; and when such resignation is confirmed by a charter from the Crown, the entail seems to be most effectively and permanently broken.

---

[1]See REGISTER OF THE GREAT SEAL at Edinburgh, vol. 165, No. 29.

The records contain abundant evidence of the increasing
financial embarrassment which overtook Robert Barclay-Allardice
(or "Capt. Barclay-Allardice," as he was generally known) in
the earlier half of the nineteenth century, and show that on June
21st, 1844, he at length made a transfer of his property in trust
for his creditors.[2] Ten years later and after his death and under
date of November 8th, 1854, his trustees sold his entire estate,
including nearly all of the "Barony of Ury" as erected in 1679,
to Alexander Baird, of Gartsherrie Ironworks, in whose family
the title now stands. As this transfer was effected without the
consent or even citation into Court of any of those who under
the deed of entail of 1722 might have a contingent interest in
the estate, it may be assumed that the entail was deemed of no
effect,—certainly after the passing of the Charter of Resignation
in 1821.[3]

[2] See SHERIFF-COURT BOOKS of Kincardineshire, record of June 1, 1854.

[3] Since making the searches above noted, the writer has been informed by Robert
Barclay-Allardice, Esq., F. S. A., Scot., and Mayor of Lostwithiel, Cornwall,—(a
grandson of the Robert Barclay-Allardice last mentioned in the text),—that in 1820
his grandfather took the opinion of counsel as to whether he was bound by the entail
or could alter the succession at will; and that upon their advising that it was competent for him to change the succession at pleasure, he took steps which resulted in
the issuing on December 20th, 1821, of the Charter of resignation under the great seal
which is referred to in the text. The counsel whose opinions were thus acted upon
were eminent lawyers of the day and both of them Judges of the Court of Session,—
the one Lord Jeffrey (F. Jeffrey) and the other Lord Corehouse (George Cranstoun).
Mr. Barclay-Allardice has courteously sent to the writer a copy of the original memorial
and opinions, which he states have been compared by him personally with the originals
in his custody and are accurate transcripts of the same. They are as follows:

MEMORIAL.

"The memorialist is proprietor of the Estate of Ury, which, by the title
deeds thereof, stands destined to heirs male. His wife lately died, leaving
two daughters on whom he is desirous of settling the above estate, the eldest
to succeed without division. The Estate of Ury stands devised by the present
titles to heirs male, under a Disposition and Deed of Tailzie (which is recorded in the Register of Entails), executed by his great grandfather, Robert
Barclay of Ury, 9th October, 1722.

"If this destination can by no means whatever be defeated, that property, in the event of the memorialist dying without sons, would descend to his
brother; and the memorialist is naturally desirous that it should not go out
of his own family.

"Has the memorialist power under the present investitures of the
Estate of Ury, gratuitously to alter the course of succeession thereby established, and will he be subject to any claim at the instance of the remote heirs
of Tailzie for so doing, and of what nature and to what extent are such
claims to be apprehended?

"A copy of the Deed of Tailzie is sent herewith."

The fact that this was so has proved something of a disappointment, for the writer had hoped to find on some court or other records the names of those whose consent to the breaking of the entail had been deemed essential, and in this way demonstrate still more conclusively that the descendants of Rev. Thomas Barclay were not also the descendants of John Barclay of East New Jersey.

That consents to the release of certain lands from the entail were, shortly prior to the passage of the Act of Parliament above mentioned, obtained from the then living heirs of John Barclay of East New Jersey, is abundantly established by letters which are still preserved at Bury Hill,—the male representation of the Barclays of Mather and Ury having passed after the death of Capt. Barclay-Allardice to the eldest male descendant, then living, of the apologist's second son, David, namely, Charles Barclay (b. 1780) of Bury Hill.

The following chart will serve to make these relationships more clear. It has been abbreviated for the purposes of convenience by the omission therefrom, with few exceptions, of younger sons and of daughters and of the dates of births, deaths and marriages:

Answers.

"I am of opinion that there is no effectual prohibition against altering the order of succession in the Tailzie referred to, and that there is no sufficient resolutive clause to protect even those prohibitions which it does contain. I think, therefore, that the memorialist may alter the order of succession and dispone in favour of his daughters without being liable in damages or otherwise to the heirs of entail.

9th November, 1820.

"F. Jeffrey" (Lord Jeffrey).

"I am of opinion that the memorialist has power under the present investitures to alter the succession of the Estate of Ury and that he will be subject to no claim at the instance of the remote heirs of entail for doing so. The succession may be altered by executing a Procuratory of Resignation in favour of himself and his heirs whatsoever, or such other heirs as he thinks proper to name, and on the Procuratory a Charter and Infeftment ought to be expeded.

28th November, 1820.

"George Cranstoun" (Lord Corehouse).

COL. DAVID BARCLAY
b. 1610
d. 1686

ROBERT BARCLAY
(the apologist)
b. 1648

JOHN BARCLAY
(came to East New
Jersey, in 1684)
(Had issue not shown
on this chart)

DAVID BARCLAY
(died at sea,
unmarried, in 1684)

ROBERT BARCLAY
(the entailer)
b. 1672

ROBERT BARCLAY
b. 1699

ROBERT BARCLAY
(who took the name
of Allardice on the
occasion of his second
marriage)
b. 1731

ROBERT BARCLAY-
ALLARDICE
b. 1779

DAVID BARCLAY
m. 1707, Anne Taylor
1723, Priscilla Freame
(settled in London)

ALEXANDER BARCLAY
b. 1711
d. 1771, at Philadelphia,
where he was Comptroller
of Customs

ROBERT BARCLAY
b. 1751, at Philadelphia
(Owner of the brewery
at Southwark, London,
and founder of the
Bury Hill line

JOHN BARCLAY
(settled in Dublin)
(Had issue not
shown on this
chart)

DAVID BARCLAY
(of Walthamstow,
Essex)

CHARLES BARCLAY
(of Bury Hill)
b. 1780

ARTHUR KETT BARCLAY
(of Bury Hill)
b. 1806

GURNEY BARCLAY
(In 1825 his widow mar-
ried DeLancey Barclay,
son of Col. Thomas
Barclay, British Consul
in New York, who was
a grandson of Rev.
Thomas Barclay)

ROBERT BARCLAY
(of Bury Hill)
b 1837
The present (1903) head
of the house.

REV. CHARLES W. BARCLAY
(of Hertford Heath, Herts)

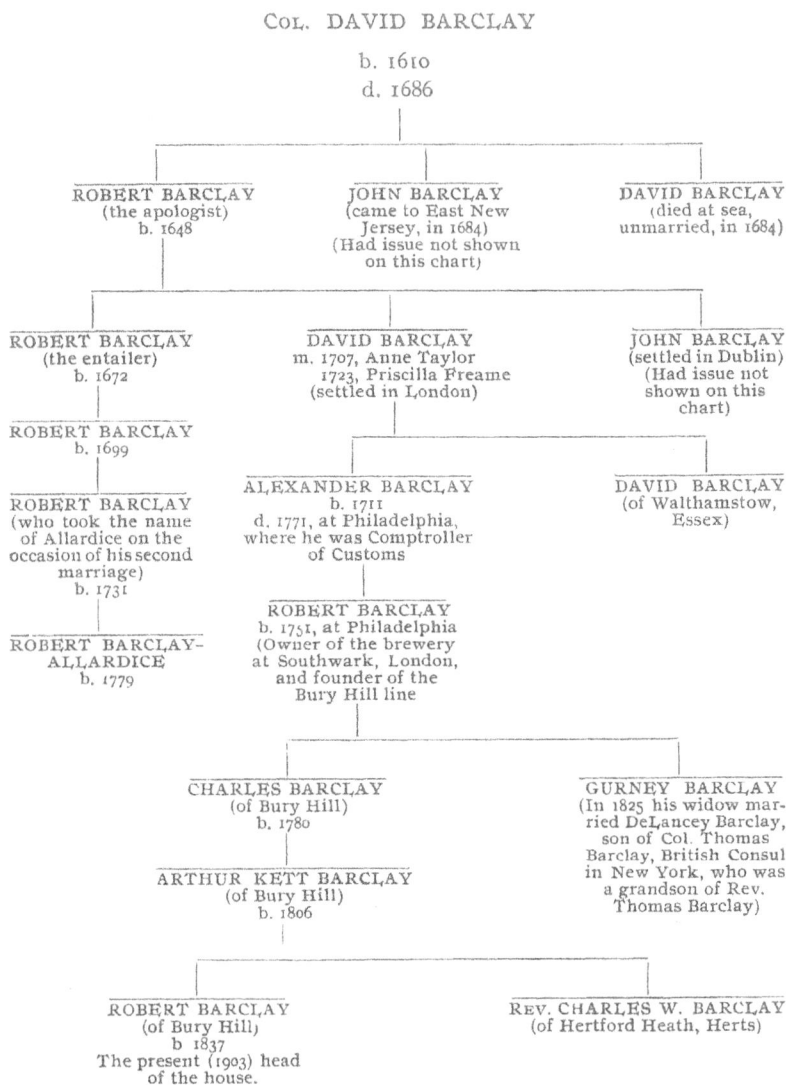

The persons shown in the foregoing chart who took part in
the correspondence to be noted below, were the venerable David
Barclay of Walthamstow, Essex, a grandson of the apologist, and
such David Barclay's nephew, Robert Barclay, the owner of the
great brewery at Southwark which bore his name, and the founder
of the Bury Hill line of Barclays. Robert's father, Alexander

Barclay, (b. 1711), ran quickly through the moneys which were left him by his mother, and then procured an appointment as Comptroller of the Customs at Philadelphia, in which City his son Robert was born in 1751. Robert's life, however, was mainly spent in England where he amassed a considerable fortune, and among other investments purchased some 20,000 acres of coal land on the Susquehanna River in what is now Bradford County, Pennsylvania. This tract is referred to in some of the letters referred to below, photographic copies of the originals of which letters have been furnished me through the courtesy of Rev. Charles Wright Barclay of Little Amwell Vicarage, Hertford Heath, Herts, a brother of the present (1903) head of the house.

As early as 1761, it would seem, and long before any imagined occasion arose for the obtaining of the consents of the heirs of the entail to a modification of the terms thereof, David Barclay, the second son of the apologist, and consequently a nephew of the John Barclay who had settled in East New Jersey in 1684, recognized the John Barclay then living in South Amboy, New Jersey, as a son of his uncle John, and sent to him a gift of £100.

This incident is referred to in the following letter now at Bury Hill written by David Barclay of Walthamstow to his nephew Robert at Park Street, Southwark, London:

Endorsed: DAVID BARCLAY, Walthamstow.
Addressed: ROBERT BARCLAY, Park Street, Southwark.

W. 19/10. 1801 P. M.

DR. NEPHEW—

Since mine sent this morning, I have found three letters from John Barclay viz.

To my Father: Dated perth Amboy 2nd May 1761, in which he writes "I am in the 60th year of my age, I lost my wife 3 yrs. ago and have 5 sons (4 of them married) & 3 daughters" & acknowledged £100—present.

To my Father: Dated Perth Amboy, 20 March 1763 about 440 acres of land of John Falconer's wch he wished to purchase.

To David, John & Robert; Dated South Amboy 20th July 1774 abt. do.

Now it appears that the above John was the son of John the Brother of the Apologist who went to Jersey, & died in 1731, & should be so marked in the plan.

Thy affect   D.B.

William Dillwyn wishes to see the likeness of Dr. Park, so pray bring it with thee. The Pork proved very fine."

Robert Barclay, the nephew, was in this country in 1774, and in that year, at Trenton, met John Barclay the son of the emigrant to East New Jersey, and *his* two sons John and Charles. In their presence, and presumably from information which was afforded by them, he made in his own handwriting a memorandum of the then living descendants of John Barclay, second of that name in New Jersey, with a statement of their respective ages "for mention in the genealogy of our family," as Robert Barclay himself put it. This memorandum, too, is still preserved at Bury Hill and reads as follows:

JNO. BARCLAY, born 1702. Mard. KAT. GORDON, 11 June, 1725.

1 March, 1774.　　　JANE VANDYKE, 1763.

No. 1. DAVID BARCLAY. Born 1st Jan'y, 1727.	ANNE BARCLAY 15 Jan'y, 1729. Married JNO. CRAIGE	No. 2. JOHN. 17 Mch., '31.	No. 3. CHARLES. 14 Feb'y, '33.	No. 4. PETER. 3. Mch., '35.	No. 5. ROBERT. 3 July, '37.	LYDIA. 16 Dec., '39. Married THOS. BROWN.	KATHERINE. 28 Mar, '42. Married DAVID STOUT.
George 21	Saml 22	Richard 9	Marg't 18	Kath.	Lewis 12	James 13	Ann 13
Katherine 18	Archibald 20	Jane 7½	James 16	Deborah } 10	Charles 10	Joseph 11	Elizabeth 11
Hester	Peter 17		John 9½	David }	Kath. 8	John 9	Jno. Barclay 9
Rachel 17			Lydia 8	John	Robert 6	David 7	Lydia 8
Jane 7			David 5		Hanah 4	William 5	David 6
Died 1772.					William 2	Kath. 3	Jesse } Lucy } twins 4½
						Mary 6 mos.	Robert 1½

No. 6. RICHARD. 3d Sept, 1745. Died 1757.

This account I wrote by desire & in the presence of John Barclay, Son, in Mar. 1774, in E. Jersey in the presence of his sons John & Charles.　　ROBERT BARCLAY.

P. S.—Given me for the purpose of mention in the genealogy of our family.　　R. B.

JNO. BARCLAY, born 1659. died 1732.

Another letter addressed to Robert Barclay of Bury Hill is among the papers at Surrey and bears the following endorsement in his handwriting:

"JOHN BARCLAY, New Jersey. Genealogy and letter to purchase 446 acres of ex'ors of D. Falconer".

The letter reads:

Trenton, 16th May, 1774.

Cozin,

My Son Robert Barclay now lives on a tract of land at Matcheponix near Cranberry, in East Jersey containing Four Hundred & Forty Six Acres as by a Survey about the year 1762—the right & title is supposed to be invested in the heirs of David Falconer to whom David Barclay Senr. (Decd) was an Executor. I wish you would learn who they really are and then if their title is quite clear, endeavor to purchase it, giving from fifteen to twenty Shillings per acre—Exch. a 175. The following are the terms of payment I propose, Either to pay one half down & the remainder in a year from the date of the deed, or if that is not accepted, I will have the whole sum paid at the delivery of the deed & this I deem a sufficient Voucher for your proposing the above terms & for the execution of them.

I am your Cozin

JNO. BARCLAY

Prior to the passage of the Act of Parliament above referred to, and manifestly in anticipation thereof, Robert Barclay of Bury Hill and his uncle David Barclay of Walthamstow, addressed the descendants of John Barclay (who came to East New Jersey in 1684) through Phineas Bond, Esq., the British Consul-General at Philadelphia, and requested the execution by them of a deed of consent to the proposed alteration of the entail. The proposed deed was forwarded, together with a genealogical account of the family and other papers which are referred to in the letters that follow. A request was evidently made for detailed information as to the family of each of the grandchildren of John Barclay, the immigrant, for in connection with the signing of the deed of consent separate letters were written by five of the then living grandchildren, of which letters, still preserved at Bury Hill, photographic copies have been furnished through the courtesy of Rev. Charles Wright Barclay, of Hertford Heath. These letters bear pathetic testimony to the rugged experiences which the descendants of this member of the house of Ury had doubtless endured. They are dated on the 8th and 9th of March, 1802, with the exception of the letter from John Barclay (third of that name in New Jersey) which was written from New York under date of March 29th, 1802.

John Barclay's letter, dated March 29th, 1802, is as follows:

New York March the 29 1802

ROBERT BARCLAY,

Dear Kinsman

I Received your letter with pleasure and satisfaction and the other wrightings, the first day of March we met at Cranbery in Jersey as many of us could be colleced and sined the Deeds of Consent which was brought their by Phineas Bond Esqr. from Philadelphia, it is a long time since you was in the Jearses and I have not heard from you sence that time until now. I have inquired of the widdow Scott from London she gave me noe account of the family to be alive but your uncle David and that he had but one Daughter she informed me she was acquined with the famely she is sence dead. But now sence I have heard from you of your Existence wellfair and Prosperity we can keep up and renew our Past aquintence with pleasure and sadisfaction.

My father died February 16 1786 in the Eighty fourth year of his age, I am now 71 years of age and i am well and hearty thrugh Marcy I live with my son en law and Daughter in new York and my wife Likewise My daugther is in a Poor State of helth and has been all winter, My son is settled on a farm too hundred mile from New York and thirty five from Albany In the County of Montgomery and Township of Breadalbane his wifes name is Ruth Jolly of a scots decent they have sons the name of the first John Wesley 10 years old the second David 8 years the third Robert 6 years the forth William Asbary 3 years and a half the fifth Thomas Coke 1 year and a half these are all the Children of my son Richard Barclay he Possesses a Hundred and Twelve Acres of Land and is very induserous and mannages his bisness for the Best I expect he must Learn his Children Trades for the want of Land to settle Them Jean my Daughter has three Children the first a Daughter named Sarah of a dilicate Constitution 11 years old the second Samuel Lee 5 years the third David 1 year and fore months old, Thes are the ofspring of my two Children you saw at my Fathers, My son in law name is Richard Jaques and is of a Reputable famely from the Jearses and has good Naturl and Acquired Abilities and Understands Bisness he occupied a Grocery store these sevrel years past he is going in a nother line of Bisness after the first of May next And now I Conclude with my Respect and Best wishes to all my Relation in Ingleland and scotland and espcsally with Respect to be remembered unto my Kinsman your uncle David Barclay that is in the Decline of Life and as I beleve he can look Back on a well spent Life with pleasure and sadisfaction soe may he continue in the Paths of Virtue that his Last days may be his Best days that when he is done with Time he may Receive the happy Approbation Well done Good and faithfull servant Enter thou into the Joy of thy Lord, Which may be all our happy Lots is the sencer Prayer of your affectionate Kinsman JOHN BARCLAY.

P. S. I send this letter with my worthy friend Thomas Barclay Esqr Consol for the Brittish Nation at New York My Brother Robert is made a list of all the Famely and sent by friend Eirskins

Charles Barclay, the second grandson of the immigrant then living, wrote as follows:

Midlesex County New Jersey March 9 1802

To David & Robert Barclay

Dear Kinsmen

When I Took my Pen in hand to write I did not now how to addres my connecttion so far Distance as for my worthy Kinsman David Barclay uncle to Robert I never saw I hope I shant be forgoten by him by Letters or somethink else I understand by your nefue Robert Barclay Letter you see 74 years of age I have entered 70 years wee both agoing to our Everlasting home if wee Never meet here I hope weel meet in Glory here after I am a Granson of John Barclay died East Jearsey in the year 32 my father John Barclay died in 86 now I am able to follow the plow almost every Day In the summer I have but Two Sones leiving my Son James is a farmmer my son David is a Minister of the Gospel I have Buried one Son named John eadge 13 years and Two Daughters one left 6 Children and the other 4 I have 6 Grandchildren motherless and fatherless lives with me now Wee all in health at present I have never heard of my Kinsman Robert Barclay since my father my Brother Robert and my Self & wife and Sister Stout Dine with him at friend Worllriles in Tren Town Til the Sixt of February when I received your letter Genollegy of our family Deed of Consent by the care of our Friend Phinis Bond on account of Tailed Istate in Urice in Cotchland I was hapy to here of your Weellfaire In this world it seems a greate way of from your connection In America it seems by your letter you and all your connection in England are willing to Exchange Lands I and my three Brothers John Peter & Robert they are all that is Living of our famley males I mean our of Spring is all heartely willing to Comply with our Kinsman Robert Barclay Request. We understand by the Deed of Consent that the Land that is in the Entale rents for more than the Land you are to git in Exchange but wee all hertely willing to comply with your Requst Now I Requst you to rite to me where Robert the Intailer was and what a Kind he was to my Granfather my worthy Kinsman David Barclay seems to want to no in what Sircumstances of Life wee are all in my brother John is a farmer he lives in York State 300 miles from me Peter is a farmer But a poor man Thrue Misfortune Robert is a farmer hes had Ten Children and some of Them is Poore my Sister Leady hes Six Children all Living my Sister Katherine hes had 12 Children all Living and all Grown up they breed like rabbits Now I come to my Self I lost Great Part of my Istate in the Revolution with Grate Briton by the Contenentel money it Depreaceated so that one Bushel of Corn was sold for fifty Dolers Now to my worthy Kinsman David Barclay I hant forgot the acnoledgement your worthy Father David Barclay marchant of London Sent my father Now wee Send you a list of all the ofspring of our Granfather in America males & females for your Perusell I hope you rite to me ivery opportunity to Let me no of your wellfair in this world I nor you wont be Long here wee have lived Three score years & Ten and if to four weel be full of sorrow and pain I give my kind Love to you and all our connection in England my wife is living at 67 years she gives her kind love to you She was a Gordon her granfather came from Scotchland Dear friend you must Excuse my Bad riting and Spelling I Donte rite much———My very Dear Friend Robert Barclay I never Expect to see you in this World I hope you rite to me to let me no how you have made out with the Exchange of lands in Parlement I have Took all the panes in my Power to Anser your Request my Connextion being so far apart it has Cause me a Greate Deal of Trouble but I feel Thankfull I have obliged you, you will have al my Connections Except my Brother Son Richard and my Brother Robert two Two Sons Lewis & John they are so far Distan 300 miles if the are living Now I have our friend P. Bond at my house to Execute the

Bisness Intended he is much of a gentleman I hope you wont forget the Kindness my Connections has Done you in America a Greate many of us is very Poor thrue misfortune Now remember me and my wife kind love to you and your wife that Heirriss Remember me to my Name Sake Charles your Son in Pertikler and all the Rest of your Children Remember me to my Kinsman Evan Barclay my kinsman Whome I nevers herd of Before and Tel him to rite to me Now to Conclude I give my kind Love to you and your Wife and all connection in England——

from your affectionate Kinsman

CHARLES BARCLAY.

To DAVID & ROBERT BARCLAY ALLARDYCE

N. B. Send your letters to the care of P. Bond to George Barclay Son of my Brother David Desed marchant in Second Street in Philadelphia.

Peter Barclay, the next younger grandson, wrote as follows:

March the 8th 1802

State of New Jersey County of Middlesex Township of South Amboy. Kind Kinsman

I inform you that I am in health and all my family at Present thanks be given to God for all his mercies—hopeing these Lines may finde you and your aged uncle and all our connextion in fammily in health also I am the fourth son of John Barclay deceased—and am now in my 68th year of age. I have buryed my first wife—and married a second wife abought fourteen years agoe and have know Issue by her I have one Son John a Carpenter by Trade and one Son Charles a Farmer—they are gone from me and unnone to me where they be at this time I have agreed to sighn the Deed of Concent with the Rest of my brothers and there Sons I have Three Daughters Namely Catherine—Debory & Rachel all married I and all my Children finde it hard geeting a comfortable Living I met with considerable loss at the Time of our Revolution—when you dined with my father and Brothers at Trenton I did not Live near this place—I never hed the happyness to see you but am desires to hold up the family connextion as our forefathers hase don and would Request of you to write me whenever an opportunity offers and direct your letter to the Care of George Barclay merchant in Philadelphia which is my oldest Brother David Barclay Son— I Conclude with remembering my kind Love to you and your aged uncle and kind Kinsman to me

PETER BARCLAY

Robert Barclay, the fourth living grandson, wrote as follows:

March the 8th 1802.

State of New Jersey in the County of Middlesex & Township of South Amboy.

Kind Kinsman

These lines is to inform thee and thy aged uncle—through the mercy of God I am in health and all by numerous family hoping these lines may find thee and all our family connections in health also. I am the youngest son of John Barclay aged now nearly sixty five I was with my father at Trenton at Joseph Whorrels when wee all dined together—Thy aged uncle hase desired to know the ocapations of my Sons my first son Lewis is a Cordwinder—my second son Charles is a farmer—my third son Robert is a cordwinder—my fourth son William is a Carpenter—John my fifth son is a Carpenter—my sixth son Peter is a bricklayer and is singgle yet and lives at home with me—my only daughter Sarah that is living is singgle yet and lives at home with me—I have buryed four Daughters and one Son and I and all my Sons is but low in circumstance wee find it hard geeting a comfortable living I have married a Secon wife in the year 1787 She was brought up in the way of the friends principle—we Received thy letter and other writings in the last of February with great satisfaction to here of thy health and welfare in family and thine aged uncle health also—wee have all agreed to Sighn the Deed of Consent that thee hase requested hoping thee may obtain the estate thereby—wee Being a great Distance apart it is my Desire that thee would write to inform me if thee hase obtained the estate agreeable to thy wishes—it hase been a long time since wee have herd from any of our relations in England—which I expect the Revolution hase been the cause of it wee had a great Deal of Trouble and Losses at that time when thee writes to me direct thy letter to the care of George Barclay in Philadelphia I Conclude with remembering my kind love to thee and thy aged uncle and Kind Kinsman To me.

ROBERT BARCLAY

The next letter was written by a granddaughter, Katherine, who had married one David Stout. It reads as follows:

State of New Jersey, County of Middesex Township of South Amboy,
March 8.
Dear Kinsman this is to inform you throue the Mercy of God I am now Living the Youngest Daughter of my father Your Kinsman John Barclay is now deceased aged 84 he Lived in township of South Amboy I now Live in the same place above men No dout my friend but you recollect me as I was with my father at Trenton to Tea at the house of Joseph Whorls. I have fore Sons and Seven Daughters now Living my first Son named John Barclay a Carpenter 2 Son David a hatter 3 Son Robert Davis a hatter 4 Son Charles Carpenter I have too Daughters that is not married the eldest of the Too is named Charlotte Sophia after the Queen of Grate Britain She Lives in the City of New York hir age is twenty one She is a Milener My husban and I being Loyalists we thought proper to name after the Queen. My youngest daughter named Hannah Lives with hir parants at home. My husband is Living he is aged 68 years I am 60 years old the 17th of this month Dear Kinsman we are all hastening to the World of Spirits I was hapy to hear from you and your aged uncel although I never expect that we shall agin meate in this world it allous me a greate deal of pleasure to think we can Correspond with our kind relations at so grate distance by Letter and althrough I have chaned my yet my affections are still the Same for the family as when with my kind father at home if you right to me direct your letter to the Reverend Abraha Beach of the Episcopal Church in New York or George Barclay philadelphia No more my kind Love and best wishes to your uncel and your self this from your affectionate friend kinswoman

KATHERINE STOUT.

The last in this series of letters which accompanied the signing of the deed of consent was written by Rev. David Barclay, of Bound Brook, a son of Charles Barclay above mentioned. Rev. David Barclay wrote as follows:

Very Dear Kinsman

It is with strange feelings & a heart filled with desire I employ my pen to communicate my thoughts to connexions & Dear kinsman in a distant Nation—Since my birth (tho small) you have visited our family in America, & made an affectionate & parting feast at Trenton March the 16th—1774 —Since that time we have heard no more of you untill the reception of your Letter dated London Oct 31—1801—which came to my fathers hand Jan 27—1802—Accompanied with a Deed of Consent and other papers— The expectations & conjectures on this occasion was big with anxiety, my fathers emotions were so great sleep left him for several nights, on hearing of his forefathers & present friends in Europe—On a visit to my father soon after I had the unexpected & satisfactory opportunity of perusing your letter the sd Deed & other papers, with a letter from Phineas Bond Esqr of Phila. Con Gen &c of the British Nation. The intention and design of all appears to be to procure against the next sitting of Parliament A Deed of Consent signed by all the descendants of my great grandfather John Barclay (or their legal representatives) who is said to have settled in East Jersey & died there in 1732—For the express purpose of enabling Robert Barclay Allardyce to obtain an Act of Parliament to exchange lands in the entail that lay more distant which you say meets the approbation of your excellent uncle David Barclay & all others concerned in your Nation. I doubt not to say that all the descendents of my great grandfather in this country will accede to it; yet permit to say that we do not understand from the writings how it will be our interest & advantage to the entailed estate, when according to the draft of the Deed of Consent the rent of that part of the entailed estate appears to exceed the rents of the lands desired £82 :8 :8, sterling per year Further I would add That we cannot trace the line of descent from Robert Barclay the entailer (notwithstanding the care you have taken to exhibit the same) to the present day or when or from whom it may possibly decnt to us, which you will please to shew in your next as soon as convenient— Yet allow me to affirm that with the greatest chearfulness & alacrity, we all agree in signing the deed of Consent without a dicenting voice, as we doubt not of your probity & friendship, yea it is with inexpressible pleasure we affix our signatures to comply with the desires & interests of our relations in Britain tho we may never reap any fruits It appears from your letter that your aged uncle desires a true list of all our family with their ages occupation & situation in life this I am told to comply with & will be repeated; therefore I shall come to my own family. I am the youngest son as you know of my father Charles Barclay & great grandson of that John Barclay who settled in East Jersey—I am blessed with three living children my first child a daughter is no more Charles Ray Barclay my first son is six years old, Maria Day Barclay is four years old. William Day Barclay my last child is six months old my sons are named after their grandfathers—I am settled twenty-seven miles from my parents at Bound Brook in New Jersey as a Teacher or Embassador of Christ in the Thirty second year of my age. So far advanced in life & so engaged as puts it out of my power to visit Britain tho it hath often been a subject of conversation between me & my father before my marriage & settlement in life—But I think it possible yea probible that some one of our name here will go to Europe to see you all & none more likely than some one of my sons & for my own part I should have no objection if my circumstances should permit—as it would be fraught with improvement to him & I trust satisfaction to you in England—It further appears you desire to have & keep alive a family correspondence, this is very desirable & I shall deem it one of the first & greatest evidences of friendship and without doubt it will be truly agreeable to all our family here in America —I have been in Phia. to see your valued friend P. Bond on our business

& he nas agreed to meet all our connextions tomorrow at Cranberry Town two miles distant from my fathers in order to sign the sd. Deed of Consent & although some of the friends seem to doubt of the propriety yet I presume that wh intention will be develloped to their complet satisfaction—you also wish to know what mode of conveyance will be the most ready & safe I suppose you may enclose back all your letters & commit all your concerns respecting us to P. Bond of Phia. or to his successor—

Dear brethren I differ from you in religious principles (or shall I say in the mode of worship) but I hope and pray we may not in heart & practice—remember me to your worthy uncle David Barclay & to Robert Barclay of Allardyce & to all other unknown kinsmen—my companion joins with me in affectionate reguard to your nearest friend & all other female friends—commending you to God & to the word of his grace which I know is able to save your souls I bid you adieu for the present from your very unworthy friend & kinsman

DAVID BARCLAY

Bound Brook Somerset County, State of New Jersey March the 8—1802. ROBERT BARCLAY Thales Brewery, London.

The suggestion contained in this letter that it was not only possible but "probible" that some one of the sons of this divine might journey to Europe to see the kinsmen there, not unnaturally produced a degree of consternation in the mind of the venerable David Barclay in London. His letter to his nephew Robert Barclay of Bury Hill is ample evidence of such fact. It reads:

Walthamstow 7th of 6th mo. 1802

Dear Nephew

I am pleased to find thou art safely arrived at home, & hope we shall meet soon. By perusing the letters sent thee from our dear relations in America there is some reason to apprehend the communication with them will prove burthensome to thee in particular, as their countryman; from my name sake the parson's intimation, I think it would be prudent to embrace the *first opportunity* to inform him, by no means to send his son to London or to encourage any of our relations to come to a land where by the increased price of everything the heavy taxes & the difficulty of providing for young men, thou has had thoughts of sending some of thy sons to America, & even of coming with them.

I have thought of sending the dear Cousins a present, viz:

ROBERT 71 Gd. son of John.	CHARLES 70 Gd. son of John.	PETER 68 4th son of John.	ROBERT 65 Youngest son of John.

CATHERINE STOUT 60 Youngest Daughter of John.

I think my name sake the parson must not be included because He is only *one* of the sons of Charles, who is only the gd. son of John. But I request thou & Charles will examine all the letters & make more correct my list to bring with you, & as 6th day will be too late for the packet, I submit whether you could not conveniently come on 4th day wch let me know. I shall be willing to divide among them 500 Dollars properly. I have been informed by J. Hibbart that the Richmond, for Philada, will not sail for several weeks, but it will be proper to enquire whether any vessel is going to N York. I shall request thee to answer Charles B's letter to me, & say that I am *infirm* & that I desired thee to write to him. Mention in all thy letters the preference thou gives to America & the heavy taxes &c. paid in England.

By a memorandum of Br. Springalls it appears that My. Wagstaffe's will is in the Tin Box of 108 at ye Anchor, & when that box shall be opened I desire a search may be made in it for a bond of Hartford & Powells for £2000, also for a bond of Evan Barclay & Co. & if at the same time Gibson's letters from 1770 to 1775 could be found, I shall be pleased.

By the copy of M. W.'s will it appears that Ann Sorton is now to have the interest of £1500, 4 per cents, & after her decease, that sum is to be divided among 9 Legatees. Br. S. writes that T. W. reced the dividends on the £500 & remitted to her half yearly.

D.B.

The gifts which David Barclay thus purposed making were duly made, as appears from the following fulsome letter written by Phineas Bond, the British Consul at Philadelphia:

PHILADELPHIA 12 November 1802

My dear Sir:

In compliance with your Request communicated to me by my worthy Friend, my friend Mr. Robert Barclay, I have paid to the five following Persons One Hundred Dollars each, and now inclose their respective Receipts drawn in the Form presented.

Charles Barclay
John Barclay   being the four surviving Sons of John Barclay
Peter Barclay   who died in 1786.
Robert Barclay

also to *Catherine Stout* their Sister;—making together the Sum of Five Hundred Dollars—equal at 168 per cent to £111:12:2 sterling, for which sum I have drawn upon you of this days date at 60 days sight in favour of my Bankers Messrs Child & Co.

From the knowledge I had acquired of these good People in the Intercourse I had had with them, respecting the Deed of Consent executed last Spring, I was satisfied they were so little conversant with matters of Business as to be liable to great Risque in transacting Money Matters, at a *great* Distance, I therefore made it a Point, out of Regard to their Interests, and from motives of personal Respect due to you, to combine this Payment with a Call I had into New Jersey and to see, myself, that your Bounty went into its proper Channel. Upon repairing to Cranberry I had some Expectation of meeting them *all* there; but I was disappointed, as Mr. John Barclay had gone some days before to New York, whither I was obliged to send his Receipt, which will account for the difference of the Dates.

Your kindred received this Mark of Munificence with all the right Feeling of Gratitude which is due to Acts of such uncommon Liberality; and it was a high Gratification to me to observe the Agitation of their

Minds, while they wanted words to express their sense of your Goodness.

I have great Satisfaction in assuring you that they are Persons of good moral Conduct who bear an excellent Reputation in their Neighborhood; two of them Peter & Robert Barclay are not in such good Plight as the others are; but by their Care, Industry and Oeconomy they make out to live tolerably well.

I am happy in this Opportunity of acknowledging the obliging Presents of Books lately transmitted to me, at your Instance, which I consider as a Proof of your Friendship highly flattering to me; *that* in particular which relates to the humane Emancipation of your Slaves in Unity Valley Pen in Jamaica;—an Act which combined with the great Principles you have so long and so zealously endeavor'd to enforce, a practical Observance, by which a prodigious Sacrifice was made, a sacrifice which places the extreme Benevolence of your Heart, and the correct Uniformity of your Judgment, in a most distinguished and exemplary Station.

With Sentiments of the most perfect Respect, I am my dear Sir your very faithful and obedient Servant.

P. Bond.

Although no mention is made in this letter of a gift of aught but money, yet the following memorandum (dated August 5th, 1802,) in Robert Barclay's handwriting, supported as it is by the acknowledgments contained in the letters from John, Charles and Robert of East New Jersey referred to below, would indicate that books as well as money were sent to the American kinsmen. The memorandum is as follows:

BOOKS SENT TO THE BARCLAYS OF JERSEY.

12 Narratives by packet
6 Barclay's poems by the Richmond from R.B.
6 " Apology | to be sent pr next | from
12 Life of R. B. | ship from the Thames | D. B.

To be divided as under

Charles B. 1
John B. 2 to each an apology
Peter B. 3 & life of R.B. in the
Robert B. 4 name of my Uncle Barclay
——— to each 1 Barclay's Poems
George B. and 2 Narratives, in
Phila 5 my name
——— the 6 remaining life of R.B. to be
David B. divided to & among K. Stout and other
of 6 branches in my Uncle's name
Boundbrook

5 Aug. 1802

sent P. Bond

A subsequent memorandum in Robert Barclay's handwriting, which also is preserved at Bury Hill, would indicate that still further gifts were intended for the relatives in New Jersey; but whether or not they were sent the papers that have come into the writer's possession do not show. The memorandum bears date January 15th, 1803, and reads as follows:

1803   Jan'y 15   1803

BARCLAYS OF JERSERY
gift of D. BARCLAY

D BARCLAY directed me to write P. Bond to pay on his Account 150 dollars as follows

to *George,* eldest son   dollars
of David Barclay   50

to *Annie Craige* -   50
to *Lydia Browne* -   50
                        ———
                        150

		Dollars
Charles aged	70	100
John	71	100
Robert.	65	100
Peter	68	100
Catherine		
Stout	60	100
		———
		500

pr P. BOND
100. to each from D B.
Life of R B to each & to D B.
Gift of land to Chas & George sons of Robert at Lycoming.
See Bond's letter.

Three of the recipients of the gifts which were sent in August, 1802, acknowledged the same in letters to Robert Barclay of Bury Hill. The others may have done so, too; but if they did, their letters have not been preserved.

The first of these letters was from Charles Barclay, who wrote as follows:

New Jersey February the 29 1803 Middlesex County.

Dear and most Respectid Kinsman

I Received your Letter Dated August 3 1802 and Like wise from our worthy anchchent and Kinsman David Barclay with a Handsom Present to my famely in America witch wee ought to be Thankfull for you are the only one of all the Blood line of our family that I ever saw in yourope which is a comfort to me I am very unhay to here of your Looseing your valleable Companion but these Changes In this Life will come if any of your Sons should come to America I hope they call upon me or upon my son David Minister of the Gospel at Bown Brook to keep a Correspondence as I am Growing Old and Infirm in my helth I schant stay here long my Wife is in a poor state of Helth at Present there is no Changes in our famley sence I rote you by Death Now I will be hapy to heare from you by Letters your Sitteastion and wellfare when your gone and I am gone my Kinsman in Urope will be a grate ways of Now my hand shakes so I can hearley rite my Son David and I will take it a Great favor if youl git him Baxter's Works. he was a grate Riter it is a books he Vallews much he has sent to Scotland for but Got Dissipointed Now I am in my 71 year of age my Wife is 68 year old and very infirm in her helth wee shant last long in this world my two Sons James and David Desiresed to be Remembered to you and all your Children my wife gives her love to you and to your Children I have Six Granchildren lives with me fatherless and motherles that I have the Care of in my old age.

I Remain your affecshenate Kinsman   CHARLES BARCLAY.

Dont fail to write.

ROBERT BARCLAY Porter Brewer London

The next letter was from the last writer's brother, Robert Barclay, and reads as follows:

State of New Jersey, Middlesex County, Middlesex, March the 14th, 1803
Kinde Kindsman

My Brothers John & Charles Barclay Received a letter from thee by the hand of Phenus Bond Esqr Bearing date the 2th of August 1802—Which Informed us all wee brothers of thy health and well fare which wee was happy to heare—and that wee and our famileyes are in health at Present, which wee are thankfull to Devine Provedence for all his Blessings to us for all his merceys—I am sorry to here of thy Loss of thy worthy Companyon—wee all Received the Money and Books—by the hand of Esqr. Bond that was ordered as a Preasent to us by thy worthy uncle which wee are thankfull to him for his Bennevolent Kindness to us—as wee have acknowledged to him by a family letter sent to him hopeing thee will keep up a Correspondence with thy Poor Kindsfolks here in America—my Two Sons and their familyes moved to the Lands that thee owns on the Suskahannah by Permission of Esqr. Bond and found it so Dissolate and but few Settlers on it they were discouraged and went one hundred miles further to the Lake Country and are settled there and I hope they will geet in a way of liveing in a while hence, but hase it hard times as yet—and so I Conclude—with Remember my love to thy antient uncle David Barclay and thy self and family

From thy affectionate Kindsman

ROBERT BARCLAY.

To ROBERT BARCLAY Porter Brewer

The third letter was from John Barclay and was written from New York some months after his brothers had written the letters above quoted. He wrote as follows:

NEW YORK June the 7th 1804

Dear Cousin

Gratitude inclines me to wright to you to inform you that I am in helth thrugh Mercy and now in the 74 year of my age my Bhrothers and Sisters are in helth at Present Each of us have Receved the Books sence I wrote to you last which we will retain in the Famely And the Money sent to each of us has been laid out to the best advantage by each of us for which Presents we Return our harty Thanks to you and your Worthy Uncle David Barclay I want to hear from you and your Worthy uncle ofner than I can Expect but Gratitude inclines me to keep us a Coraspondence and renew our Relationship I purpose to goe to my sons in a little time and live with him it is beyond Albany Thrty five miles Montgomery County Breadalbane Town I send my Respect and Best wishes to you and Worthy Uncle David My wife is well at Present

I remain your affectionate Kinsman

JOHN BARCLAY

For ROBERT BARCLAY

It is not unreasonable to suppose that if Rev. Thomas Barclay, the first rector of St. Peter's at Albany, had been a son of John Barclay of East New Jersey as is claimed, some memorandum of that fact would have been preserved at Bury Hill, and the signatures of his descendants would have been secured to a deed of consent to the change in the entail at the same time that the deed was being executed by the other descendants of John Barclay as shown above. It is highly improbable that such a descent, had it existed, could have been overlooked. The descendants of Rev. Thomas Barclay, at the time it was thought necessary to obtain the consent of all contingent heirs to a change in the terms of the entail, were widely known and were influential, and had intermarried with members of the most prominent families in New York. The Barclays that *were* recognized, on the other hand, were obscure and for the most part unlettered; and it is practically impossible to imagine that any descent through Rev. Thomas Barclay, if in fact there were one, was unknown to the family at Bury Hill, or if known, would for a moment have been overlooked. The ascertaining of who were the descendants of the apologist's brother John had too important a bearing upon the legal matter then under consideration to permit a mere perfunctory investigation of the line of descent; and it seems to the writer that the unquestioned recognition of John Barclay, Jr., of South Amboy, as the son, and as the *only* son, of the apologist's brother John should be accepted as against an even widely accepted "tradition" to the contrary.

At the time the New Jersey family was engaged in the correspondence above quoted, Col. Thomas Barclay, a grandson of Rev. Thomas, was British Consul-General for the Eastern States of America, resident at New York. He seems to have been acquainted with the John Barclay of New York (third of that name in New Jersey), who wrote one of the foregoing letters, and at the same time was acquainted with the Robert Barclay of Bury Hill, who was so actively interested in securing the consents of the descendants of the apologist's brother John to a change in the terms of the entail. This latter fact is evidenced by the following letters which are still preserved at Bury Hill:

Duplicate   NEW YORK 6th. March 1805
My dear Sir,

You will perceive from a perusal of the inclosed papers,[4] that on my arrival at this place in the year 1799, as His Majesty's Consul General for the Eastern States of America, I adopted the readiest and best means, by applying to Mr. Bond, His Majesty's Consul General at Philadelphia, of obtaining the necessary information of the general duties and forms of the office, and whether there were any and what fees attached to it. In consequence of Mr. Bond's answer that fees might be taken by general consent of the Consuls, or by an application to the Secretary of State and that it was customary elsewhere, I wrote to Lord Grenville, then Secretary of State on the great expence attending living in this country, and that I should presume to take fees of office from Americans and other Foreigners until I received his Lordship's order to the contrary. No countermand has ever been received, and from thence I have with reason concluded his Lordship did not disapprove of the measure.

By a letter which Mr. Merry His Majesty's Minister Plenipotentiary to these States wrote not long since to Mr. Coles, it appeared that he was of the opinion fees could not be taken. You will observe from the copy of my letter to him that I have made him acquainted with my conduct, and the principles on which it was founded. I have reason to believe Mr. Merry will make some representation to prevent the continuance of taking fees. Under this idea, I have by this conveyance written to Mr. Hammond, Under Secretary of State, detailing the particulars and requesting him to lay my letter before Lord Mulgrave for his direction.

I trust you will be of opinion on reading the inclosed that my conduct has been candid and proper, and that the reason urged for Consuls receiving Fees from Foreigners are founded on good grounds. What Mr. Merry's objections may be it is not in my power to anticipate. Americans and other Foreigners in amity with Great Britain have always paid these fees cheerfully, because they are not entitled to require any official act from me gratuitously, and all the other Consuls in this city receive them. These fees, almost without an exception, arise from certificates annexed to Notarial Acts. You will perceive they are simple, and relate only to the Notary Public, and not the Parties who have deposed before him who frequently I do not know, and never see. It is the Notary who applies to me for an attestation that he is duly commissioned, and so scrupulous have I been for some time past, as not to insert in my certificates even the ordinary words, "that faith was due to the notarial act." But it may be objected that in cases where an American citizen covers American property, a certificate of mine to the notarial act, may add some degree of weight to the oath of the exporter. Such an objection cannot require a serious reply.—The officers of His Majesty's Navy when they overhaul a ship and examine her papers, judge from general or particular circumstances independent of the oath of the shipper, the attestation of the notary, or the Consular certificate,—Besides if I am not to certify the notary, the Mayor of this city will do it—So that nothing can be effected by the interdiction.—Under these circumstances it appears to me wonderful that that there can be a shadow of objection to His Majesty's Consuls receiving fees from Foreigners, particularly as the foreign Consuls take fees in all cases from British Subjects.—You will notice what I have said to Mr. Merry on the subject of expenditures, over and above the allowance from Government.—Mr. Wallace His Majesty's Consul for Georgia, died last year, leaving a large family penni-

---

[4] The papers enclosed were letters or copies of letters bearing on the subject of this letter to Robert Barclay.

less—Mr. MacDonogh Consul for Massachusetts who died about a month since has left his family in so distressed a situation, that even the Americans at Boston Philadelpha and New York are making charitable collections for their support.—Is it not distressing to learn the fate of such old servants—My situation is not similar, but it is far from pleasant, with a large family, to reflect, that I am under the necessity to injure the paternal estate of my children to support myself decently, as His Majesty's principal Servant in this city and State.

Will you my dear Sir, on the receipt of this letter wait on Mr. Hammond and converse with him on this subject.—I trust his good sense will point out that I have not acted amiss, and that he will advise His Majesty's Consul may be permitted to take the customary fees from Foreigners. —I once flattered myself that I stood well in the good opinion of Mr. Hammond, and have no reason to suppose he thinks otherwise of me at present—yet I am anxious to have my own interest strengthened by yours and one or two of your friends—To Lord Mulgrave I am wholly unknown.—I trust you will represent me, as you conceive consistent with truth, and add that any extention of Indulgence to my present allowances will be bestowed on a faithful Servant of His Majesty, and at the same time doing you a favor.—I intreat your pardon for soliciting this unpleasant service from you.

Believe me
with truth and regard
Dear Sir
your very faithful and obedient
friend and servant
THO BARCLAY.

Private and Confidential.

New York 9th March, 1805

My dear Sir

The pacquet having been detained for Mr. Merry's despatches, enables me to enclose you a copy of his letter in answer to mine of the 22nd. of February.—I much fear you will be tired of me and the subject, but as I have it much to heart, in vindication of my conduct, and from a conviction that it is sound policy, the Consuls in America should be allowed to take fees of office; permit me to intreat your patience to the following remarks.

Mr. Merry states that one of the reasons which operates against his sanctioning the receiving of fees, is that the custom has not been adopted by Consul General Bond, Consul Hamilton, or any other Consul or Vice Consul in the southern States.—On my arrival in these States in 1799, Mr. Bond suggested to me the propriety and necessity of taking fees of office and it was agreed that a joint application should be made to Lord Grenville—On my return to New York from Philadelphia, Mr. Bond wrote me, that having been several years in office and not having taken fees, it would appear singular for him to apply; but as I had lately been appointed there could be no objection for me to do it.—This letter I cannot lay my hand on; but a copy of his letter marked A, whereof I have sent you a copy is fully expressive of his wishes and sentiments on this subject; and the only reason why Mr. Bond and the Consuls to the Southward have not taken fees, is owing to my not having received expressly an affirmative approbation from Lord Grenville; but which as far as respected myself, required no answer unless his Lordship disapproved of what I had stated to him, I should do, until I received his wishes to the contrary— Thus stands the case for Mr. Bond and the Consuls to the Southward.

When Mr. Merry went to the north of Europe to establish a Consular System, and discovered that Certificates had been granted by a

British Consul for the purpose of showing the neutral quality of Vessels of Merchandize; he acted wisely in suppressing the usage and the fees; because such proceedings were highly improper and dangerous. In this case, was I to hazard an opinion on the person, I should pronounce that the Consul Mr. Merry speaks of, was not a subject of His Majesty, but of the very power in whose favor the certificates of neutral Property were granted—I feel hurt by his naming such a case, on an occasion in which I am personally concerned; because my character civil and military is too well established I should presume, to admit even the possibility of my ever doing an improper act intentionally.

In my former letter I have stated that custom has established here as well as in Europe, Ministerial or Consular declarations necessary to notarial and acts of a similar nature. These are the only species of certificates ever granted by me, save such as are pointed out by Acts of Parliament.   These in no wise touch on the merits, or even notice the affidavit or protest made before the notary.—You will perceive from a copy inclosed of a letter from Vice Admiral Sir Andrew Mitchell Commander in Chief of His Majesty's Ships of War in the American Station, that he and the Admirals in the West Indies, and I suspect now generally elsewhere, understand my certificates perfectly; and so far from their proving injurious, I am convinced they operate by my means to the benefit of the Service.

Mr. Merry is assuredly in an error in opposing the receiving of fees. —On general principles it must be admitted, the better an officer is paid, the less liable will he be to temptation—But recollect I disclaim the Idea that Consul of His Majesty on any occasion would knowingly act in violation of his duty.

I am with sincere regard
dear Sir
Your faithfull friend and Servant

Tho Barclay.

Robert Barclay Esqr.

The style in which the foregoing letters from Col. Thomas Barclay were written, while not bearing with particular strength in either direction, seems rather less consistent with *kinship* than with mere friendship, and may be regarded simply as one of the many straws which point against the correctness of the tradition of a descent of the Rev. Thomas Barclay from Col. David Barclay of Ury or from Col. David's accomplished wife, Lady Katharine Gordon, "the white rose of Scotland."[5]

---

[5]For the ancestry of Lady Katharine Gordon, see *Appendix C* hereto annexed.

PART III.

A Mistaken Tradition, *Continued.*—Testimony of the Records in London.

T HE most convincing proof, however, of the error of the contention that Rev. Thomas Barclay of Albany was the son of John Barclay of East New Jersey, is found in the result of the investigations made by the late Dr. DeLancey H. Barclay of Baltimore, during the last few years of his life. Convinced that the tradition had no basis of fact, Dr. Barclay,—who at the time of his death was the head of the family descended from Rev. Thomas Barclay of Albany,[1]—made personal search in London for information concerning Rev. Thomas Barclay's early life and antecedents.

"The earliest positive and authentic knowledge which we " have of Rev. Thomas Barclay," he writes, "is given to us by the " appearance of his name in the list of students who entered St. " Salvator's College at the University of St. Andrews in Fife, in " the session of 1683-1684. He matriculated at the University " on February 25th, 1684, and was granted the degree M. A. on " June 14th, 1688. His regent's name was Mr. John Mengies, " and the degree was conferred by the Rev. Dr. Alexander Skene, " the Vice-Chancellor of the University. This is all the informa- " tion which is afforded by the records of the University.

"From June 14th, 1688, until May, 1707, a period of nine- " teen years, I have thus far been able to find no reference in any " record I have examined either to his life or to his acts. In " May, 1707, he appears as an applicant for Holy Orders from " the Bishop of London, and in that month was successively or- " dained deacon and priest, as the following extracts taken in " the customary questionable Latin, which are from the Volume " of Ordination,—1675 to 1809,—in St. Paul's Cathedral, London, " will show :—

---

[1] Dr. Barclay's younger brother, CUTHBERT COLLINGWOOD BARCLAY, second of that name, is the present (1903) head of the family.

" '*22 May 1707.* Thomas Barclay, Artimus Magister Coll. Salvetoriaus
" 'quod est Andreapolis in Scotorium, Diacconaliis Ordinem sint ad-
" 'missus

" '*31 May 1707* Thomas Barclay, Art. Mag. Coll. St. Salvatoris nost-
" 'ri quos est Andreapoli in sacrum presbyteratus Ordinum fuit.'

"The proximity of the dates of these two ordinations is evi-
" dence that he was ordained for the colonies, as it was only in
" such case that the rule was waived which required the lapse of
" a year between the taking of orders as deacon and the ordina-
" tion as priest.

" The lapse of nineteen years between his graduation at St.
" Andrews and his ordination in London, it thus far seems im-
" possible to fill. If he entered St. Salvator's in 1683-4 at the
" age of sixteen,—and it is hardly probable that he matriculated
" at a much earlier age,—he would have been twenty when he
" graduated and thirty-nine when he was ordained; and we would
" thus be able to fix the year 1667 or 1668 as the year of his
" birth. He would thus be less than ten years the junior of John
" Barclay, who was born in 1659 and came to East New Jersey
" in 1684.

" On May 31, 1707, the day he took his priestly orders,
" Thomas Barclay signed the Act of Uniformity and was forth-
" with appointed Chaplain of the garrison at Fort Orange, at
" Albany, which had recently been acquired from the Dutch. It
" is probable that he sailed for the colonies within a short time
" after his appointment, for there is evidence of his being in
" Boston in November of the same year. Rev. Thorowgood
" Moore and Rev. John Brooke, two of the missionaries of the
" Society for the Propagation of the Gospel in Foreign Parts,
" sailed from Boston for the mother country in November or
" December, 1707, and were lost at sea. Prior to their sailing
" they made their wills. The will of Thorowgood Moore, which
" was not dated beyond 'November   1707,' recited his in-
" tended departure from America, and was witnessed by four
" clergymen: Samuel Myles, minister of the Chapel at Borden-
" town, N. J.; Thomas Barclay, minister at Albany; Rev. John
" Brooke, of Elizabethtown, N. J.; and Rev. John Talbot, of
" Burlington, N. J. The will of Rev. John Brooke, which was
" undoubtedly made at about the same time, was dated November

"20th, 1707, and thus fixes the date of Rev. Thomas Barclay's
"presence in Boston.[2]

"The next we hear of Rev. Thomas Barclay is his arrival in
"Albany on June 9th, 1708, a considerable part of the intervening
"seven months having possibly been consumed in the journey
"from Boston. From here on for the next thirteen years we
"have many records of his life and work and some indications of
"his personal characteristics."

It was Dr. Barclay's intention to continue the investigations
he had thus commenced, and had his life and health been spared
we would doubtless have known with some degree of certainty
ere this, of which of the many Barclay families of England and
Scotland Rev. Thomas Barclay of Albany was a member. Without feeling at all committed to the point of view, Dr. Barclay inclined somewhat to the belief that Rev. Thomas was a son of Sir
Robert Barclay of Pierston, Ayrshire, Knt., who was created
baronet of Nova Scotia on October 22, 1668.[3] While the fact
that Rev. Thomas matriculated at St. Andrews in Fifeshire might
seem to militate in some degree against this theory, yet the simi-
larity (out of all the recorded Barclay arms) of the arms of the
Barclays of Pierston to those which have come down to the
descendants of Rev. Thomas Barclay of Albany, is the ground
upon which Dr. DeLancey H. Barclay was inclined to rest his
belief that Rev. Thomas was possibly, if not probably, of the
Pierston family. The differing characteristics of the arms of the
Barclays of Mather and Ury and those of the Barclays of Pierston, are pointed out in *Appendix D* hereunto annexed.

One or two letters written by Rev. Thomas Barclay, or by
his wife, to the Society for the Propagation of the Gospel and
sundry extracts from the records of the Society in London,[4]
serve to correct two other errors which are generally accepted as
a part of the "family tradition,"—the one as to the date of Rev.
Thomas Barclay's death and the other as to the number of his
children.

---

[2] For a copy of these wills see Dr. G. M. Hill's HISTORY OF THE CHURCH IN
BURLINGTON, page 74.

[3] See THE PEERAGE, BARONETAGE, AND KNIGHTAGE OF THE BRITISH EMPIRE for
1881, by Joseph Foster. Westminster: Nichols & Sons.

[4] Copies of these letters and records have been kindly furnished by Rev. JOSEPH
HOOPER, M. A., of Durham, Conn., sometime Registrar of the Diocese of Albany.

It has been generally assumed, and published, that Rev. Thomas Barclay died in the year 1722 and had but three children, —Thomas, Henry and Andrew; but the letters quoted below make it clear that he had not only three but four children, and that he was living as late as 1725 and possibly in 1726. The fourth son was undoubtedly John Barclay, Mayor of Albany from 1777 to 1778, who, unlike the rest of his family, was a steadfast patriot throughout the Revolutionary struggle. Further reference will be made to him in Part V below.

The letters to be quoted hereafter show that the closing years of Rev. Thomas Barclay's life were darkened by a mental affliction so grave as to render necessary actual physical restraint, and further show, what is of particular interest in connection with the matters now under search, that as late as 1719 Rev. Thomas had a sister living in England who held his power of attorney for the collection of the yearly stipend due him from the Crown for his services as chaplain of the garrison at Albany. This sister's name, most unfortunately, was not mentioned in the letters, and an examination of the records[5] of the English War Department, through which the stipend was paid, has failed to disclose it; still the fact that he had a sister has played no part whatsoever in the tradition which has regarded Rev. Thomas as the son of John Barclay of East New Jersey, and affords some further proof in support of our charge that the tradition is a false one.

Another circumstance militating in some degree against the accuracy of the tradition, is the fact that Rev. Thomas Barclay's speech was strongly Scotch. In a letter written to the Bishop of London by W. Bennett (probably an officer of the garrison at Albany), dated at New York June 24th, 1726, wherein he asks that a missionary be sent to Albany, he suggests that the clergyman selected be an Englishman as "Mr. Barclay, the late minister, spoke so broad Scotch that it was difficult to understand him."[6]

Until 1716, Mr. Barclay received from the Crown £50 yearly for his services as chaplain to the garrison at Albany, and from the Society for the Propagation of the Gospel another £50 per annum for his services as missionary and catechist at Albany and

---

[5] Made by the late Dr. DeLancey H. Barclay of Baltimore.

[6] See History of St. Peter's Church in the City of Albany by Rev. Joseph Hooper, M. A. Albany: Brandow Printing Co., 1900, page 67.

at Schenectady. For some now unknown reason,—possibly through the influence of those whose enmity Mr. Barclay had incurred,—the allowance by the Society was suddenly discontinued, as is shown by the following extract from the Society's records:

"5th March 1716

"Agreed to by the Society that Mr. Barclay at Albany his salary be withdrawn he having fifty pounds p. ann. allowed him by the Crown."

In an "Account of the Society for the Propagation of the Gospel" published by Rev. Dr. Humphrey in 1730 in London,— an almost contemporaneous record,—it was said:

"It was represented to the Society, that since Mr. Barclay had a salary as chaplain to the garrison at Albany, that, with the voluntary contributions of the people who came to the new church, would be a sufficient maintenance; the Society therefore withdrew his salary."[6]

The withdrawal of this stipend, with the consequent financial embarrassment, seems to have been the first of the troubles which overwhelmed Mr. Barclay and finally resulted in the loss of his mind.

In the Journal of the *Society for the Propagation of the Gospel,* the following entry appears under date of December 5th, 1718:

"It was reported from the Committee that they had read three Letters from Mr. Barclay dated Albany June 28th, and October the 29th 1717 and June the 2nd 1718. Importing that in August 1716 he received the Society's Resolve that his salary should be withdrawn after the 6th of March 1716/7. That as Chaplain to the Garrison of Albany he hath had a Pension of fifty pounds p. ann. from the 25th of March, 1707, which provision being so scanty in that dear Place the late Bishop of London did obtain from the Society an allowance of fifty pounds more yearly as their Missionary and Catechist at Albany and Schenectady which offices he hath discharged to the best of his Power by Catechising the youth and bringing up many hundreds of them in the Worship of the Church of England; that he formed the Congregation of the Mohawk Indians now the cure of Mr. Andrews, and since Mr. Andrews arrival has apply'd himself to the Instruction of the Slaves and has at present above 40 Catechumens, 23 of whom he hath baptized, that for two years and a half past he hath labour'd in building a Church which was opened on the 25th day of November last on which day he preached before a considerable audience who gave a handsome offering, and the day after the Soldiers of the two Independent Companies subscribed fifty pounds towards building a Gallery, that he is in debt for building the said Church 225 lbs. which lies heavy on him having a family of small children and not bread to eat. he humbly prays the Society to take his case into consideration and to continue his allowance since he has no manner of support there but the Pension of Fifty Pounds from the Crown, and so ill paid and Taxes deducted that he cannot possibly subsist himself and family on so small and uncertain an Income. That one half of his allowance from the Government goes for house rent and firewood and the other part after Taxes deducted is not sufficient for clothing, so that nothing remains for food or the education of his children, for which reason and his past services he hopes the Society will not leave him to begg with his family of small children in his *old age* and *declining years*,[1] having spent his all in their service. That Mr. Andrews having come to an Estate by the death of his brother in Virginia talks frequently of leaving his Mohawk Indians, and if that should happen he offers to instruct those Indians for a far less allowance and take care of his flock at Albany too, which may be easily done since the Indians are very often from home: desire's some of the Society's Anniversary Sermons and a few Common Prayer Books, and that, while there is no fort nor Chapel among the Onondagas, the furniture sent over for that Nation (which is in the Governor's hands and which as he is informed is at the disposal of the Bishop of London) may be lent to the Church at Albany since it is (as it were) the Cathedral Church of the Five Nations, they dayly flocking into it, where he do's administer to their Spiritual necessities while at Albany, and has baptized several of their children—sometimes three on one day.

Whereupon the Comm'ee agreed to move the Society to take into consideration that part of his Letter which relates to the Instruction of the Mohawk and other Indians in case Mr. Andrews shall leave them."

Under date of May 25th, 1719, Mr. Barclay wrote to the Secretary of the Society as follows:

"Sir:

By severall Letters I have presumed to lay before the Venerable Society for the Propagation of the Gospel in Foreign Parts, the hardships I lye under since that Illustrious Board has been pleased to withdraw their allowance of fifty pounds per ann. to me as missionary and Catechist at Albany, and to none of my Letters having the honour of any answer; Once more I beg leave with all due deference, to mention only my present circumstances which cry aloud for relief. If want of bread for self and Family (having had but 42 lbs. sterling in two years) in a remote corner of the World where I have no manner of Establishment or perquisite may plead for me: Besides a heavy load of Church Debt; I shall groan under being last Winter thrice arrested within the space of one month, obliged to give what little money I had by me (to pay for my winter provisions) to Lawyers for defending me from close Imprisonment (tho the debt was none of those I stood engaged for) add to this the want of money to pay my House Rent at that very time, though I was not indebted above two quarters Rent Yet my Landlord feed a Lawyer against me, and with Difficulty could I obtain a month's respite, and tho' on the 2nd day of February I paid the next Quarter's Rent, yet on the fifth day of May I had a fresh threatening, and that but for one quarter, and that at a time when I had not one sixpence to buy bread for my family, too little credit can a minister have from his Landlord here; Though the same person who was at that time my Church Warden and has had 97 pounds 10 shillings of house Rent from me from August, 1709: to May last. This is owing to the withdrawing of my salary from the

---

[1] N. B.—John Barclay of East New Jersey, whom the "tradition" regards as the father of Rev. Thomas Barclay, was 59 years of age in 1718. Is it probable that the son was "in his old age and declining years," when the father was but 59?

Society, and the bad payment of my salary from the Crown. I am postponed a whole year's pension from Midsummer, 1713, till Midsummer 1714 as a Debt of the late Queen: and by my sisters last letters (who is my attorney) she acquaints me that she has received but till Christmas, 1717. Soe that at Midsummer next there will be two years and a half due to me from the Government; add to this a Loss I sustained of 62 lbs. 10 s. sterling of the same money from March 25th, 1709 to Midsummer, 1710 by the Fraud of my then attorney; I have had some other Losses besides these mentioned and what the Church is indebted to me which is to the value of 50 lbs. and upwards New York money, this is over and above my own Benefaction of which my wife's before: and all my Travelling charges and Voyages to New York on the Account of building the Church. I might further enlarge on this melancholy subject by telling of the sighs and tears of my poor wife, who while in her Mother's house neither saw nor felt want; the upbraiding of some of her Relations; The bitter sarcasms and bitter Taunts of others who want neither power nor money to supply my wants by themselves or others (especially as to the Church Debts) and tell me that prayer will not doe it: when, alas, I have no means left but tears: for I am not bred to any manual operation (tho' I often wish I had) that may help me to support my family, willingly would I labour three days a week rather than to owe any man one half penny. And tho' I groan under a Double Debt at present both for the Church and the support of my Family, yet I have this comfort I was led into both through necessity and no bad Husbandry. And it is a known truth at Albany that had the intire management of the Building your Church been in my hands, the Fund contributed had been more than enough for that work, but others being joyn'd with me, and I being obliged to Travel severall times to New York for removing the stop illegally put to that work, and that in the King's name by 4 Justices, as well as for gathering subscriptions; stones new wrought in my absence to the value of an hundred pounds for the Beautifying the Fabrick, tho' the guift of his Excellency our governor, out of the King's stores at Albany was sufficient for Finishing the Work. The payment of the workmen during the aforesaid stop for three week's time did likewise increase the charges, and lastly, the makeing of four thousand Bricks for the Beautifying the windows and the Gavel Ends, and after the work was little more than half finished I was left by the Undertakers when the Subscriptions at that time did amount to about six hundred pounds, and five hundred of the six expended and the Church in Debt to the Value of the whole and when I undertook the sole Burthen upon myself on the twelfth of June 1716 the most of the workmen voluntarily offered themselves, soe that though I suffer now a Fraud cannot be charged on me, Since it (is) well known that the Fund was exhausted and I did Build upon Providence and upon the expectation of assistance from Commissary Vesey and Mr. Tenney, the Flower of the English Congregation at New York not having contributed thereto.

"The Reverend Mr. Vesey turned over that trouble on his then Reverend Assistant, and the Reverend Mr. Tenney excused himself first by the Loss he might sustain as to his own Yearly Subscription from the Congregation and since he had the Chaplainship of the Forces, he alledges want of leisure, and that it would ruin his school, the last gave a benefaction of 50 shillings, the first nothing, this I can make evident by both your Letters. I must own that Mr. Commissary did warmly urge Mr Tenney to collect for the payment of the Debts of our Church tho' in vain, but enough of this which I only mention in my own Defence, for I did conceal from our people at Albany as much as I could possible their coldness (I speak the Truth to my Grief) and if I have been too tedious on this ungrateful subject give me leave to say that nothing but the extremity of want could have extorted this from me. I shall not mention one word of my Labours during my Eleven years ministration at Albany only that to magure[8] all Difficulties I slacken not my Diligence, twenty-eight slaves I have Baptized new; and am at present employed in cate-chising the Youth, and in Founding a Latin School, and near 30 white children have I Baptized the last half year, one Indian Child of ten years of age and one of a year old: I say I am at present employed in gathering of a Latin school for one Mr. Willson who arrived here last November from Ireland, a man of sober conversation and has a competent skill in the Latin and Greek Tongues. There are about Seventy Children that attend at the prayers of the Church and are Catechised. I hope the Venerable Society will not be offended at this Trouble which my pinching wants have forced me to. And whenever that Venerable Board shall be pleased to signifie to me by their Secretary to desist and forbear the giving any further Trouble, as in Duty bound I shall submit being well aware That the Society knows best what I doe deserve or what is proper to give to one in my circumstances. And whatever the Issue may be I hope I shall never while I breathe (cease) to have a thankful sense of former favours and heartily pray that God may prosper their Handy-work, and Bountifully Reward their good Works. And being they have been so Instrumentall in turning many unto Righteousness may they shine as bright Starrs for ever and ever.

"S'rs I earnestly beg an answer to this for I have had none to any of my Letters since the withdrawing of my Mission Nov. 6th.

"When I undertook to finish the Church, of the six hundred pounds subscription money five hundred pounds was laid out upon the work and a Debt to the Value of the hundred pounds not paid in.

"I am, S'rs

"Your most humble and most obedient servant,
"THOS. BARCLAY."

So far as the records of the Society show, this letter, though received, was in no wise acted upon; and under date of June 13th, 1721, Mr. Barclay again wrote the Society as follows:

"Sirs

"I beg leave once more to lay the extremity of my case before ye. Venerable Society for the Propagation of the Gospel in foreign parts, which short is this. That by their withdrawing of my allowance of 50 pounds per ann. I am reduced to want of bread for ye pension 50 lbs. which I have from ye Crown when taxes and other dues are paid, does not amount to above 42 lbs. p. annu and that narrow allowance so ill paid that (including one year before the death of ye late Queen) the Government att Michaelmas next will be indebted to me four years salary and how then can I mantain eight in family having no manor of support here and without money or credit never was there any clergyman sent over to this part of ye World reduced to such straits and that did groan under such pressing want, having nothing to feed or cloth my family add to this ye prosecutione I suffer both for the Church Debts and my own, being now obliged to keep within doors not dareing to step abroad on week daies to perform Divine Service, and for a Minister to be confined to his house, being eight in family (as I hinted before) and not a morsel of bread to eat methinks this melancholy Story should stir

---

[8]Evidently a slip of the pen for "maugre."

up Compassion in ye hardest heart far more in ye breasts of ye most Charitable Corporation in the world. Nay I hope their ears will be no longer shut to my sorrowful complaints But that that Venerable body will quickly send relief and restore me to my salary and so prevent my ruin I think I have said enough though I have not recounted the halfe of my sufferings to move compassion. I shall only add That nothing hath be'n wanting on my part, but that as I formerly did so shall I goe on (thro' God's assistance) in my duty both in converting slaves &c. since ye departure of Mr. Andrews, some Indians to the Knowledge of the truth, and I have baptized within a few years between thirty and forty slaves. The Mohock Indians have often desired me to come among y'm but, alas, my low estate will not admit of that expense nor am I able to be hospitable to them as formerly I have been and was my circumstances better I shou'd be capable of doing more good among all sorts of persons. God is my witness I endeavor what I can and wherein I come short God I hope will pardon since I want not ye will but the power—humbly supplicant for an answer from ye Venerable Society. I am Sir Your most humble and afflicted serv't

THOS. BARCLAY."

How this appeal was received may be gathered from the following extract from the Journal of the Society recorded under date of August 18th, 1721:

"Read a letter from the Rev. Mr. Barclay at Albany dated the 13th of June last setting forth his present hard circumstances and praying to be restored to his former salary. Agreed that Mr. Barclay remove either to Rye or Jamaica in New York Government which shall be vacant, with a salary of fifty pounds p. annum if he shall think fit: and in consideration of his very hard circumstances that Ten pounds be given him for his present Relief."

The letter of June 13th, 1721, was the last that Mr. Barclay wrote. Under date of May 22, 1722, his wife wrote the Society as follows:

"Hon'ble Gentlemen

"Whilst it pleaseth Almighty God to suffer my husband Mr. Thos. Barclay to be taken from his family, I his Espouse presume in his behalf to acknowledge the Receipt of your hon'es by a Letter from Mr. Secretary Umphreys dated ye 5th of Sept. last whereby your Honors signifie your having received him to be your Missionary and have appointed him the Choice of removing either to Rye or Jamaica in New York Government which shall be vacant with an alowance of 50 lbs. for his salary a year from ye Hon'ble Society and that I further observe that your pious Consideracons be such as to order him 10 lbs. for his pres't Relief I think never bestowed on one of his function in foreign parts having a wife and four children better y'n on him Wherefore I return unfeigned thanks his laying out his all towards ye finishing of ye Church here (the arrears being considerable and no prospect how to be Refunnded) the delay in paying w'h the Crown allows him, many oppositions he has met on account of ye Church and other misfortunes that have attended him whilst here has in my opinion and apprehension been ye occasion of his present calamity. I pray your honors consider my present circumstances and that you in compassion will continue that salary for his and family's maintenance whilst so being and until ye Almighty God thro' his mercy shall bestow him to his family and able him to officiate on either place where you the Hon'ble Society have appointed him (wch offer was he well am assured he would gladly embrace) and his afflicted wife takes leave with all humility to subscribe herself gratefully to be

Your Honors most humble Serv't
ANNA DOROTEA BARCLAY."

This appeal dated May 22nd, 1722, was laid before a Committee of the Society at a meeting thereof held on February 13th, 1723, as the following extract from its records shows:

"Read a letter from Mrs. Barclay dated Albany, 22nd of May, 1722. And another from the clergy of New York &c. dated July 5th, 1722 setting forth the deplorable circumstances of the Rev. Mr. Barclay (formerly a Missionary from the Society at Albany) and his poor family: that he hath been all along diligent in his cure, and has taken great pains in catechising the Indian Infidels in a place where they are very numerous, but that of late the many misfortunes which have successively attended him have brought him to an outrageous distraction such as has obliged his friends to confine him to a dark room, and in the mean time the small salary which the Governm't in England allow'd him not being paid; his family (a wife and four children) are reduced to extreme Poverty; and praying the Society to consider the deplorable condition he and his family are reduced to, in such manner as shall seem most effectual for their relief. Whereupon the Committee agreed that his case be recommended to the Society as a matter of compassion, and that they be moved to make him such a Gratuity as they shall think proper. Agreed that this matter shall be considered at the next meeting of the Society."

The "relief" so urgently needed and prayed for was finally granted by the Society at its meetings of *March 21st, 1723*, and *April 26th, 1723*, as is shown by the following extracts from the Society's Journal:

"*21st March 1723*. The Society took into consideration the case of the Rev'd Mr. Barclay mentioned in the Minutes of the last Meeting and Agreed that Ten pounds be given him for his present relief.

"*26th of April, 1723*. Upon reading the Report of the Committee representing the case of the Rev. Mr. Barclay: Agreed by the Society that he be allow'd twenty pounds more."

The remaining entries touching this matter in the Society's Journal, which have come to the notice of the writer, are the following:

"*17th July 1724*: Read a letter from Mrs. Dorothea Barclay, wife of the Rev. Mr. Barclay thanking the Society for their charitable gratuity to her in consideration of the deplorable condition of her husband late the Society's Missionary, and praying for a further allowance during his continuing in his present state; and Agreed to referr the consideration thereof to the Society. Ordered that the Secretary make enquiry whether the fifty pounds per annum formerly allow'd to the Rev. Mr. Barclay by the Crown be still continued and paid to him."

"*21st August 1724:* The Secretary acquainted the Board that in pursuance of the Order at last Meeting he has made enquiry and finds that the salary of Fifty pounds p. annum formerly allowed to the Rev. Mr. Barclay by the Crown is still continued and paid to him."

That Mr. Barclay was living as late as July 7, 1725, is evident from a letter written from New York under that date to the Bishop of London by W. Bennett, already referred to, in which he said:

"Mr. Barclay, the minister of the English Church at Albany in this Province, had the mistfortune to lose his senses about four years ago and continues yet in the same unhappy condition. His congregation have waited this long in hopes of his recovery but finding no reason to expect it they are now very desirous of a missionary."[6]

Whether or not Mr. Barclay was living as late as 1726 may or may not be inferred from the following extract from the Journal of the General Assembly of New York:

"October 28, 1726
Afternoon Session

"The Deputy Clerk of the Council, laid before this House, the Petition of ANNA DOROTHY BARCLAY of the City of Albany, to His Excellency, the Council, and the General Assembly setting forth,

"That by Order of the Lord *Cornbury,* the Commissioners of Indian Affairs placed Michael, the Son of Montour, an Indian (who was sent to fetch and bring far Indians to Albany) at Mr Barclay's house, where he was maintained and provided for from the 15th of August, 1708, until the 11th of March, 1712/13;

"Praying it may be taken into Consideration so as that she may be satisfied for the same,

"Which, having been read in Council, was ordered to be carried to this House, and acquaint them that the Demand of the Petitioner appeared to His Excellency and Council to be just, and therefore was recommended by His Excellency, to make provision for satisfying the said Demand;

And the same being read, it was

ORDERED, That the said Petition lie on the Table."

Rev. Thomas Barclay had (subsequently to his arrival in Albany in 1708) married Anna Dorothea, daughter of Captain[9] Andries Drauyer (a Dane by birth, serving in the Navy of the Dutch), and Gerritje Van Schaick, his wife. It is here, possibly, that the name "Van Schaick" found its way into the family tradi-

[9]In the ANNALS OF ALBANY, ANNALS OF SCHENECTADY, etc., he is described as *Captain* Drauyer, although some publications have called him Admiral. The former rank seems the more probable.

tion. The grandmother of Rev. Thomas Barclay's children, on their *mother's* side, was a Van Schaick; and it is not difficult to imagine that in later years the Van Schaick connection might carelessly have come to be regarded as on the father's side instead of on the mother's. It would indeed have been odd had the mother of Rev. Thomas and the mother of his wife both been Van Schaicks, and yet no record of the coincidence have been noted through all these years.

Gerritje Van Schaick was the daughter of Capt. Goosen Gerritse Van Schaick by his second wife, Annatje Lievens. Gerritje was born in 1657 and married Andries Drauyer on January 17th, 1674.[10]

On March 2nd, 1699, Gerritje Van Schaick, wife of Andries Drauyer, joined the Dutch Church in New York on certificate from Copenhagen, and on the same day her husband, described on the Church records (if the English translation be correct) as "Rear Admiral of the King's fleet of Denmark and Norway," joined on a similar certificate. On February 28th, 1700, Johanna Dorothea Drauyer, presumably the future wife of Rev. Thomas Barclay of Albany, likewise joined the Dutch Church in New York, upon confession of faith and belief.[11]

---

[10]See N. Y. Gen. & Biog. Record, vol. II, p. 191.

[11]*Ibid*, vol. VII, p. 56.

PART IV.

The Line of Descent from John Barclay of East New Jersey.

JOHN BARCLAY, second son of Col. David Barclay of Ury and brother of the apologist, died intestate, as we have seen, in 1731 at Perth Amboy, East New Jersey; and administration on his estate was granted to William Bradford,—"John "Barclay, his son and heir having requested administration should "be granted under his hand unto the said William Bradford."[a]

The William Bradford here referred to was undoubtedly the well-known printer who was at that time a resident of Philadelphia.

The following notices of John Barclay's death appeared in THE BOSTON WEEKLY NEWS LETTER of May 6, 1731, and in THE PENNSYLVANIA GAZETTE of April 29, 1731:[b]

From THE BOSTON WEEKLY NEWS LETTER.

"PHILADELPHIA, April 29. Last week died at Amboy, *John Barclay,* Esq., in an advanced Age, a pious man, an excellent Neighbor, and of very great Service to the Publick, but more particularly where he lived, and is very much lamented by all that knew him. He was Brother to *Robert Barclay,* Laird of Ure in the Kingdom of Scotland, the famous Quaker, who wrote *Barclay's Apology.*"

From THE PENNSYLVANIA GAZETTE.

"PHILADELPHIA April 29, From Amboy we hear that last Week died Mr. *John Barclay,* Post master there. He was Brother to the famous *Robert Barclay.*"

John Barclay's wife, Katharine Barclay, had died and been buried at Perth Amboy on January 6, 1703, as appears from the following entry on the records of St. Mary's Church at Burlington, West New Jersey:

"Buried at Amboy N. J. by John Talbot
Jan. 6, 1703—*Catherine Barclay*"

[a]See SECRETARY OF STATE'S OFFICE at Trenton, *Liber B* of Wills, p. 240.
[b]See NEW JERSEY ARCHIVES, vol. XI, first series, p. 243.

That she died on the same day is to be inferred, as it seems to the writer, from the following further entry on the same records:

> "Baptized at Amboy N. J. by John Talbot
> Jan. 6, 1703—*Catherine Barclay*"

The probabilities, in the writer's judgment, are that the Catherine Barclay who was baptized by Mr. Talbot on January 6, 1703, was the same Catherine Barclay whose burial is recorded as above. The apparently unseemly haste of *burying* a convert on the very day of her baptism, militates somewhat against such view; yet it is not at all impossible that the rites of baptism were administered to Catherine Barclay just prior to death and that the funeral was arranged for the same day while Mr. Talbot was still in Amboy, for the probable reason that no other clergyman of the English Church was near at hand or likely soon to be after Mr. Talbot should have proceeded on his way. Moreover, John Barclay, the son, was anywheres from a day to twelve months old when his mother died,[c] and while it

---

[c] Prior to 1752, the year was regarded in England as commencing on March 25th. Occurrences of the period between January 1st and March 25th, therefore, were sometimes noted with mention of both the years in order to avoid the chance of mistake where it was not apparent to which of the calendar years the writer was referring. For example the burial of Katharine Barclay would more properly have been recorded as having taken place on January 6th, 1702/3. And so it is possible that John Barclay, the son,—whose birth is known to have occurred in "1702,"— may have been born even in the eleventh month of that year, according to the old system; and that would mean that he was born in January, 1703, according to the new system.

The confusion out of which the Gregorian or present calendar was evolved, may be partially realized from the following brief historical summary which is taken almost wholly from the Encyclopedia Britannica.

The earliest known Roman year consisted of ten months, or 304 days in all. How the remaining days were disposed of is not known. The year commenced with March, and the present months of July and August were known as *Quintilis* and *Sextiles*. In the reign of Numa two months were added to the year,—January at the beginning and February at the end,—and this arrangement continued until 452 B. C., when the order of the months was changed and February was placed *after* January. The months now consisted of twenty-nine and thirty days alternately, so that the year, 354 days in all, corresponded with the synodic revolution of the moon. An odd number of days, however, were deemed more propitious than an even number, so an extra day was added and the number brought up to 355 days.

Something more than ten days was still needed to make the calendar year coincident with the solar year, so the device was adopted of inserting, every second year, between the 23rd and 24th of February, a new month known as *Mercedonius* consisting, alternately, of twenty-two and twenty-three days. A period of four years would thus contain 1,465 days, making the mean length of the year 366¼ days. To rid the calendar of this extra day, various devices were resorted to which finally resulted in

is possible, it seems hardly probable that the birth of another child, of a daughter Catherine, should have followed his so closely and that she only and not both he and she should have

the intercalation of the necessary number of days being left to the discretion of the pontiffs to whom the care of the calendar was committed; and they in turn quickly abused the power for political ends. By giving to the intercalary month a greater or less number of days, according to their whim, the pontiffs were enabled to prolong the term of a magistracy or hasten the annual elections; and by the time of Julius Caesar the calendar had been thrown into such confusion that the civil equinox differed from the astronomical equinox by fully three months, so that the winter months were carried back into autumn and the autumnal months into summer.

To put an end to these disorders, Caesar abolished the use of the lunar year and of the intercalary months, and decreed that the civil year should be coincident with the solar year, and should consist of 365¼ days, ordaining that every fourth year should have 366 days, and the others 365. The process of change from the one calendar to the other resulted in a year of 445 days known as "the last year of confusion" and the first *Julian* year commenced in 46 B. C.

The year under this system consisted of twelve months, the name *Quintilis* being changed to "July," out of compliment to Julius Caesar. The odd months,—first, third, fifth, etc.,—were given 31 days each, and the even months 30 days each, excepting February, which in common years was given 29 and in every fourth year 30 days.

But when the name of the month *Sextiles* was subsequently changed to "August," out of compliment to Caesar Augustus, the vanity of that monarch would not suffer such month to have a lesser number of days than the month named in honor of his predecessor Julius Caesar, and the calendar was accordingly changed once more so as to give August thirty-one instead of thirty days,—the day thus added being taken from February. This, however, brought into succession three months of thirty-one days each, a result so little to be desired that September and November were summarily reduced to thirty days each and October and December increased to thirty-one.

The calendar year was still too long by one one-hundred-and-twenty-eighth part of a day, so that by A. D. 1582 the vernal equinox had retrograded from the 25th of March to the 11th. Gregory XIII sought permanently to correct this error, and directed that ten days should be altogether suppressed in the then existing calendar, and that thenceforward each year of which the number was divisible by four without a remainder should be a leap year, excepting the centurial years; and that the centurial years should be leap years when divisible by four after omitting the two ciphers. Thus, 1600 was a leap year; but 1700, 1800 and 1900 were common years, while 2000, in turn, will be a leap year,—and so on.

The introduction into Great Britain of the Gregorian Calendar, or "New Style," as it was called, was for a long time successfully opposed by popular prejudice; but the inconvenience of using a different system from that already in use in the greater part of Europe gradually made itself felt, and in 1751 the "New Style" was adopted by Act of Parliament for all public and legal transactions. It was provided in the Act that the day following September 2, 1752, should be accounted the 14th of that month, and the commencement of the legal year was changed from the *25th of March* to the *1st of January.*

In Scotland the new style had been in use since the beginning of 1600,—a fact to be remembered in connection with the Scottish records of events between that period and 1751.

Russia is the only country in which the Julian Calendar or "Old Style" is still employed. A letter addressed in Russia to a correspondent in another country should be dated in both styles, in order to be at once intelligible, as for example, August $\left\{ \begin{array}{l} 8 \\ 20 \end{array} \right.$ or $\left\{ \begin{array}{l} \text{January } 27 \\ \text{February } 8 \end{array} \right.$

been baptized, and that, too, on the day of their mother's funeral.
John Barclay, the husband, as we saw above, had identified himself with the Church of England somewhere between the year
1690 and the recorded visit to Amboy of George Keith in the
year 1703; and it is not unreasonable to suppose that he sought
baptism for his wife on her death-bed and the reading of the
burial service by a clergyman of the established church, while
there chanced to be one still in Amboy, for the English clergymen at that time were simply itinerant through the Jerseys, their
missionary work calling them from place to place.

The son, John Barclay, lived in South Amboy throughout his
life and died there the owner of considerable real estate. His
death occurred on February 16th, 1786, when he was in the 84th
year of his age.[d] This circumstance fixes 1702 as the year of his
birth; besides which, that year is positively stated as the year of
his birth in the memo. made by Robert Barclay of Bury Hill
in 1774, for the purposes of the family genealogy, shown in Part
II above.

Mr. Whitehead, in his "CONTRIBUTIONS TO EAST JERSEY
HISTORY" (published in 1856), says at page 43 that John Barclay,
senior, left but one son John, "of whom nothing is known, excepting that he was alive in 1768 and poor." But the records at
Trenton and at New Brunswick refute the charge of poverty,
unless, indeed, he were "land-poor," as that term has of late
years been understood.

The records of the Old Tennent Church in Monmouth
County, make frequent reference to the son, John Barclay, as
"Capt. John Barclay," and state that he was buried in the old
Topanemus Burying Ground near the present village of Marlborough. He left a will dated May 26th, 1782, which, with a
codicil thereto dated June 9th, 1782, was proved at New Brunswick on December 24th, 1790, and letters testamentary were on
the last mentioned day duly issued to his two sons John and
Robert. A copy of the will and of the codicil as recorded in
the office of the Secretary of State at Trenton in Liber 30 of
Wills at page 502, will be found in *Appendix E* hereunto annexed.

It would have been a difficult task and quite beyond the

---

[d] See letter in Part II above from John Barclay, his son, dated March 29th, 1802.

scope of the present writing to trace the widely diverging lines of descent from John Barclay, second of that name in East New Jersey; but, in the course of the writer's searches along his own line, many dates and circumstances have come to his notice which may be of use to those more directly interested in this particular line of descent from John Barclay of East New Jersey, and he has therefore chronicled them here in the following table of descent which he believes to be reasonably accurate, so far as it goes. The †, appearing after a name in this table, indicates that the writer has no further information at hand concerning such person, or of any possible descent therefrom.

1. **John Barclay,**[2] second son of *Col. David Barclay,*[1] of Ury, and *Lady Katharine Gordon,* his wife; *b* at Ury, Scotland, 1659,[1] and migrated to East New Jersey in 1684; *d* at Perth Amboy, East New Jersey, between April 22nd and April 29th, 1731;[2] *m* (between 1699 and 1702[3]) *Katharine* ————,[3] who died on January 6th, 1702/3.[4]

    (2) *John Barclay,*[3] his only son.[5]

2. **John Barclay,**[3] second of that name in East New Jersey; *b* at Perth Amboy, East New Jersey, 1702;[1, 6] *d* at South Amboy, New Jersey, February 16, 1786;[6] *m* (1) June 11, 1725, *Katharine Gordon,*[1] dau. of *Charles Gordon,*[7] *b* June 14, 1705;[7] *d* October 26, 1757;[7] *m* (2) 1763, *Jane Van Dyke.*[1] (There were no children by the second marriage.)

    (3) *David Barclay.*[4][1]

---

[1]Memo. by Robert Barclay of Bury Hill, made in 1774. See Part II, above.

[2]Obituary notices in THE BOSTON WEEKLY NEWS LETTER of May 6, 1731, and in THE PENNSYLVANIA GAZETTE of April 29, 1731.

[3]Shown by the deeds on record in the office of the Proprietors at Perth Amboy.

[4]Records of St. Mary's Church at Burlington, West New Jersey.

[5]Records of Sec. of State at Trenton, N. J., Liber B of Wills, page 240.

[6]Letter from John Barclay, third of that name in New Jersey, to Robert Barclay of London, dated March 29th, 1802. See Part II, above.

[7]Records of Old Tennent Church, Monmouth County, N. J.: Burials in the old Topanemus Burying Ground.

(4) *Anne Barclay.*[4][1]

(5) *John Barclay.*[4][1]

(6) *Charles Barclay.*[4][1]

(7) *Peter Barclay.*[4][1]

(8) *Robert Barclay.*[4][1]

(9) *Lydia Barclay.*[4][1]

(10) *Katherine Barclay.*[4][1]

(11) *Richard Barclay.*[4][1]

3. **David Barclay,**[4] *b* January 1, 1727;[1] *d* 1772;[1] *m* (License granted) March 3, 1749, *Elizabeth Walker* of Monmouth, New Jersey.[8] (In 1767 they lived "Southward of Brunswick, Middlesex Co.")[9]

    (12) *William Barclay,*[5] *bap* May 19, 1751;[10] *d* prior, probably, to 1774.[1] †

    (13) *George Barclay,*[5][1] *b* 1753;[1] *bap* April, 1753.[10] (In 1802 lived in Philadelphia. Address: 2nd Street.)[11] †

    (14) *Katherine Barclay,*[5] *b* 1756;[1] *bap* January 18, 1756;[7] †

    (15) *Hester*[5][1] (or *Esther*)[7] *Barclay, bap* November 19, 1758.[7] †

    (16) *Rachel Barclay,*[5] *bap* November 22, 1761.[7]†

    (17) *Jane Barclay,*[5][1] *b* 1767.[1] †

4. **Anne Barclay,**[4] *b* January 15, 1729;[1] *d* prior to 1761;[10] *m* (license granted) November 21, 1749,[8] *John Craig,* son of *Archibald Craig,*[10] who died March 6, 1751, aged 72 years.[10]

    (18) *Catharine Craig,*[5] *bap* November 18, 1750;[10] *d* prior, probably, to 1774[1] †

    (19) *Samuel Craig,*[5] *b* 1752;[1] *bap* February 19, 1752.[10] †

---

[8]Records of Sec. of State at Trenton: Marriage licenses.

[9]County Clerk's Office, Middlesex Co., N. J., Liber 6 of Deeds, page 82.

[10]Records of Old Tennent Church: Baptismal records.

(20) *Archibald Craig,*[5] *b* 1754;[1] *bap* April 21, 1754.[10] †

(21) *Peter Craig,*[5] *b* 1757;[1] *bap* May 23, 1756.[10] †

(John Craig, the husband of No. 4 above, took for his second wife, prior to 1761, *Anne Reid,* dau. of *John Reid,* and had by her three children, namely, *Anne Craig, William Craig* and *Mary Craig.*)[10]

5. **John Barclay,**[5] third of that name in New Jersey, *b* March 17, 1731.[1] In 1786 he lived "Southwards of Perth Amboy," his wife probably having died prior to that year.[12]

    (QUERY: Was his wife's name *Catherine Murray?*[13] It is doubtful whether the same John Barclay is here referred to.) In 1802-1804, he lived in New York with his married daughter.[6]

    (22) *Richard Barclay.*[5]

    (23) *Jane Barclay.*[5]

6. **Charles Barclay,**[4] *b* February 14, 1733;[1] *d* September, 1813;[14] *m Rebecca Gordon,* who was *b* 1735, and was living in 1802.[11] (In Charles Barclay's will, dated December 18th, 1810, and proved September 17th, 1813, he describes himself as of "South Brunswick." In this will he mentions his grandchildren *Elizabeth Bayles* and

---

[11]Letter from Charles Barclay to David Barclay of Walthamstow of March 9, 1802. See Part II, above.

[12]County Clerk's Office, Middlesex Co., N. J., Liber 1 of Deeds, p. 800.

[13]See N. Y. Gen. & Biog. Rec., vol. VII, p. 172; vol. IX, p. 82.

[14]From THE COLUMBIAN, New York, Saturday, Sept. 25, 1813: *"Died:* At his residence near Cranbury, in Middlesex County, N. Jersey, CHARLES BARCLAY in the 80th year of his age. He was descended from the ancient and honorable family of the Barclays of Ury, in Scotland; he was the grandson of John Barclay, one of the proprietors and first governor of East Jersey, who was appointed to that station and came over to this country in 1682. Mr. Charles Barclay was fourteenth in descent from Theobald De Berkeley (or, as the name is since spelled, Barclay), who lived in the reign of David the 1st, King of Scotland, who began to reign in the year 1124, and was contemporary with Henry 1st of England, son of the Norman Conqueror. This family has for many centuries been settled on the extensive estates of Mathers and Ury in Scotland. The present head of the family is said to have an income of 20,000 pounds sterling per annum. The family has become numerous, and assumed a level with the independent yeomanry of our country."

Margaret and *Lydia,* but does not state which of his children were the parents of these grandchildren.)[15]

(24) *Margaret Barclay,*[6][1] *b* 1755;[1] *d* prior to 1802, leaving issue.[11] †

(25) *James Barclay,*[5] *b* 1758.[1] In 1802 he was a farmer, having a son named *Charles Barclay.*[6][11] QUERY: Did he marry *Ann Brower?*[16] It is not probable that the same James Barclay is here referred to.

(26) *John Barclay,*[5][1] *b* 1764;[1] *d* 1777.[11] †

(27) *Lydia Barclay,*[5][1] *b* 1766;[1] *d* prior to 1802, leaving issue.[11] †

(28) *David Barclay.*[5]

7.　**Peter Barclay,**[4] *b* March 3, 1735;[1] *d* (Amd'n granted on his estate to *James Voorhees* on April 11th, 1810);[17] *m* twice, the second time in 1788[18] to *Elizabeth Starkey,* dau. of *David Starkey* of South Amboy.[19] QUERY: Was his first wife *Bell Thompson?*[20]

(29) *Katharine Barclay,*[5][1] *m,* prior to 1802[18] *Manuel Quick* (living in Ontario County, N. Y., in 1810.)[21]

(30) *Deborah Barclay,*[5][1]　　*m,* prior to 1802,[18] *Robert Barclay,*[21] No. 38 below. †

b 1764;[1]

(31) *David Barclay,*[5][1]　　*d* prior to 1802.[18] †

(32) *John Barclay,*[5][1] living in New York in 1810.[22] † QUERY: Did he marry *Sarah Logan?*[23]

---

[15]Surrogate's Office, Middlesex Co., N. J., Liber B of Wills, p. 35.

[16]See N. Y. Gen. & Biog. Rec., vol. XIV, p. 40.

[17]Surrogate's Office, Middlesex Co., N. J., Book A of Adm'n, p. 86.

[18]Letter from Peter Barclay to Robert Barclay of London, of March 8, 1802. See Part II, above.

[19]County Clerk's Office, Middlesex Co., N. J., Liber 5 of Deeds, p. 44; *ibid,* p. 236.

[20]See N. Y. Gen. & Biog. Rec., vol. XIV, p. 118.

[21]County Clerk's Office, Middlesex Co., N. J., Liber 8 of Deeds, p. 538.

[22]County Clerk's Office, Middlesex Co., N. J., Liber 8 of Deeds, p. 674.

[23]See N. Y. Gen. & Biog. Rec., vol. XII, p. 35.

(33) *Charles Barclay*,[5][18] *b* subsequently to 1774.[1] †

(34) *Rachel Barclay*,[5][18] *b* subsequently to 1774;[1] *m* prior to 1802.[18] †

8. **Robert Barclay**,[4] *b* July 3, 1737;[1] *bap* Sept. 16, 1737;[10] *d* Aug. 2, 1818;[24] *m* (1) Nov. 2, 1760, *Alice Van Kirk*;[25] *m* (2) 1787,[26] *Miriam* ———,[27] "who had been brought up in the way of the Friends' principles."[26] Letters of administration were granted on the estate of Robert Barclay on May 25th, 1827.[28] (According to family records furnished in 1898 by Henry C. Allen, Esq., of Trenton, N. J.,—No. 97 below,—Robert Barclay was born June 22, 1737; died August 2, 1818, and married October 26th, 1760, *Elsie Van Kirk*, who was born May 28, 1744, and died July 29, 1785.)

(35) *Lewis Barclay*,[5][1] *b* September 8, 1761;[1][24] *bap* October 18, 1761;[10] *d* November 13, 1820.[24] †

(36) *Charles Barclay*,[5][1] *b* February 18, 1764.[1][24] †

(37) *Katherine Barclay*,[5][1] *b* October 31, 1765;[1][24] *d* prior to 1802.[26] †

(38) *Robert Barclay*,[5][1] *b* January 25, 1768;[1][26] *m* prior to 1802 *Deborah Barclay*, No. 30 above.[29] Living in Ontario County, N. Y., in 1810.[29] †

(39) *Hannah Barclay*,[5][1] *b* January 2, 1770;[1][24] *d* prior to 1802.[26] †

(40) *William Barclay*,[5][1] *b* January 9, 1772;[1][24] *m* prior to 1805 *Martha* ———.[30] In 1805 he describes himself as "of Township of South Amboy."[30] †

(41) *John Barclay*,[5] *b* March 9, 1774.[24] †

---

[24]Family records of Henry C. Allen, Esq., of Trenton, N. J.

[25]Records of Christ Church, Shrewsbury, N. J.: Marriages.

[26]Letter from Robert Barclay of East New Jersey to Robert Barclay of London of March 8, 1802. See Part II above.

[27]County Clerk's Office, Middlesex Co., N. J., Liber 7 of Deeds, p. 459.

[28]Surrogate's Office, Middlesex Co., N. J., Book B of Adm'n, p. 35.

[29]County Clerk's Office, Middlesex Co., N. J., Liber 8 of Deeds, p. 538.

[30]County Clerk's Office, Middlesex Co., N. J., Liber 6 of Deeds, p. 146.

(42) *Lydia Barclay*,[5] *b* May 15, 1776;[24] *d* prior to 1802.[26] †

(43) *David Barclay*,[5] *b* September 19, 1778;[24] *d* prior to 1802.[26] †

(44) *Peter Barclay*.[5]

(45) *Sarah Barclay*,[5] *b* July 26, 1783;[24] living unmarried in 1802.[26] †

(46) *Elsie Barclay*,[5] *b* July 24, 1785;[24] *d* March 2, 1788.[24, 26]

9. **Lydia Barclay**,[4] *b* December 16, 1739;[1] *m* *Thomas Brown*.[1] †

(47) *James Brown*,[5][1] *b* 1761.[1] †

(48) *Joseph Brown*,[5][1] *b* 1763.[1]†

(49) *John Brown*,[5][1] *b* 1765;[1] *bap* July 28, 1765.[10] †

(50) *David Brown*,[5][1] *b* 1767;[1] *bap* June 28, 1767.[10] †

(51) *William Brown*,[5][1] *b* 1769;[1] *bap* August 13, 1769.[10] †

(52) *Katharine Brown*,[5][1] *b* 1771;[1] *bap* December 1, 1771.[10] †

(53) *Mary Brown*,[5][1] *b* 1773;[1] *bap* March 13, 1774.[10]†

10. **Katharine Barclay**,[4] *b* March 28, 1742[1] (or March 17, 1742)[31]; *bap* June 13, 1742;[10] *m* November 28, 1760,[32] *David Stout*,[1, 32] *b* 1734,[31] and *bap* (an adult) November 1, 1761.[33] †

(54) *Anne Stout*,[5][1] *b* 1761;[1] *bap* November 1, 1761;[33] married and living in 1802.[31] †

(55) *Elizabeth Stout*,[5][1] *b* 1763;[1] *bap* May 1, 1763;[33] married and living in 1802.[31] †

(56) *John Barclay Stout*,[5] *b* 1764;[1] *bap* December 9, 1764.[33] Living in 1802.[31] †

(57) *Lydia Stout*,[5][1] *b* 1766;[1] married and living in 1802.[31] †

(58) *David Stout*,[5][1] *b* 1768.[1] Living in 1802.[31] †

---

[31]Letter from Katharine Stout to Robert Barclay of London of March 8, 1802. See Part II, above.

[32]Records of Christ Church, Shrewsbury, N. J.: Marriages.

[33]Records of Christ Church, Shrewsbury, N. J.: Baptisms.

(59) *Jessie Stout,*[5][1] ⎫ ⎰ Married and living in
                            ⎪   1802.[31] †
                    ⎬ *b* 1770 ;⎰
(60) *Lucy Stout,*[5][1] ⎪ ⎰ Married and living in
                            ⎭ ⎱   1802.[31] †
(61) *Robert Davis Stout,*[5][1] *b* 1772. Living in
      1802.[31] †
(62) *Charles Stout.*[5] Living in 1802.[31]†
(63) *Charlotte Sophia Stout,*[5] *b* 1781 ;[31] living un-
      married in 1802.[31] †
(64) *Hannah Stout,* living unmarried in 1802.[31] †

11. **Richard Barclay,**[4] *b* September 3, 1745 ;[1] *bap* June 30,
     1745 ;[10] *d* 1757.[1] (An error is manifest either in the
     date of birth or in that of baptism.)

22. **Richard Barclay,**[5] *b* 1765 ;[1] *m Ruth Jolly.*[6] In 1802 they
     were living at Broadalbin in what was then Montgomery
     County, but is now Fulton County, New York.[6]

(65) *John Wesley Barclay,*[6] *b* 1792.[6] †
(66) *David Barclay,*[6] *b* 1794.[6] †
(67) *Robert Barclay,*[6] *b* 1796.[6] †
(68) *William Asbary Barclay,*[6] *b* 1799[6] †
(69) *Thomas Coke Barclay,*[6] *b* 1800.[6] †

23. **Jane Barclay,**[5] *b* 1766 ;[1] *m Richard Jaques.*[6] In 1802
     they were living in the City of New York.[6]

(70) *Sarah Jaques,*[6] *b* 1791[6] †
(71) *Samuel Lee Jaques,*[6] *b* 1797.[6] †
(72) *David Jaques,*[6] *b* 1799.[6] †

28. **David Barclay,**[5] a presbyterian minister,[11] *b* 1770.[1] In
     1802 he lived at Bound Brook, Somerset Co., N. J.[34]

---

[11]Letter from Charles Barclay to David Barclay of London, of March 9, 1802.
See Part II, above. For account of a law-suit in which Rev. David Barclay was the
party plaintiff, see THE TRUE AMERICAN (published at Trenton) of 28 January, 1803.

[34]Letter from David Barclay of New Jersey to Robert Barclay of London, of
March 8, 1802. See Part II, above.

(73) A daughter,[6] *d* prior to 1802.[34] †
(74) *Charles Rea Barclay,*[6] *b* 1796.[34] †
(75) *Maria Day Barclay,*[6] *b* 1798.[34]†
(76) *William Day Barclay.*[6]

44. **Peter Barclay,**[5] *b* March 13, 1781;[24] *m Catharine Van Wickle,*[24] *b* April 12, 1788.[24] In 1810 described himself as "of South Amboy."[22]

     (77) *Simon Barclay.*[6] [24] †
     (78) *George Barclay.*[6] [24]
     (79) *Elsie Barclay.*[6] [24] †
     (80) *Catharine Barclay,*[6] [24] *m* March 23, 1837, *John A. Davison.*[35] †
     (81) *Ann Maria Barclay.*[6]
     (82) *Ida Barclay,*[6] [24] *m* December 14, 1841, *Gilbert S. Denison.*[35] †
     (83) *Augustus Barclay.*[6] [24] †
     (84) *Isaiah Barclay.*[6] [24] †

76. **William Day Barclay,**[6] *b* 1801;[34, 36] *d* 1865.[36]

     (85) *Charles Gordon Barclay.*[7] [36]
     (86) *David Robert Barclay.*[7] [36]
     (87) *William Henry Barclay*[7] (living in 1897 at Beaver, Penn.).[36] †

78. **George Barclay,**[6] *b* November 23, 1809;[37] *d* (Will dated May 26, 1873, proved October 14, 1882);[38] *m* January 18, 1832, *Margaret Duncan.*[35]

     (88) *Isaiah D. Barclay,*[7] of Cranbury, N. J.; sheriff of Middlesex Co. in 1899.[37] †
     (89) *Peter Barclay,*[7] of Monmouth Junction, N. J.,[37] *m* December 16, 1863, *Sarah Ann Hutchinson.*[35] †
     (90) *Isabel D. Barclay,*[7] [37] *m* December 24, 1863, *Isaac S. Mershon.*[35] †

[35]County Clerk's Office, Middlesex Co., N. J., Marriage book.
[36]Family records of William H. Barclay, Esq., of Beaver, Penn.
[37]Family records of Isaiah D. Barclay, Esq., of Cranbury, N. J.
[38]Surrogate's Office, Middlesex Co., N. J., Liber J of Wills, p. 784.

81. **Ann Maria Barclay,**[6] *b* March 28, 1816;[24] *m* October 4, 1837, *Samuel Conover,*[24, 35] *b* January 16, 1809.[24]

> (91) *Catherine A. Conover.*[7, 24]
> (92) *Simon Barclay Conover.*[7, 24] †
> (93) *Augustus Barclay Conover.*[7, 24] †
> (94) *Ida Davison Conover.*[7, 24] †

85. **Charles Gordon Barclay,**[7] *b* 1823 at Uniontown, Penn.;[36] *d* 1897 at Freeport, Penn.[36] †

> (95) *Harry M. Barclay*[8] (living in 1897 at Chicago).

86. **David Robert Barclay,**[7] *b* 1827;[36] *d* 1886.[36] †

> (96) *Robert Barclay,*[8] *M. D., b* 1857 (living in 1898 at St. Louis, Mo.)[36] †

91. **Catherine A. Conover,**[7] *m* April 3, 1886, *Charles Allen.*[24] †

> (97) *Henry C. Allen*[8] (living in 1898 at Trenton, N. J.)[24] †

PART V.

The Dublin Branch of the Barclays of Ury.

ROBERT BARCLAY of Ury, the famous apologist of the Quakers, was born December 23, 1648, died October 3, 1690, and on February 16, 1669, married *Christian Mollison,* who died February 14, 1725. They had nine children, of whom the youngest was *John Barclay, b* October (*i. e.,* 8th mo.) 20th, 1687, who settled in Dublin, and became the head of the Dublin branch of the Barclays of Ury.

In another part of this work the writer has been enabled, through the courtesy of ROBERT BARCLAY ALLARDICE, M.A., F.S.A. (Scot), Mayor of Lostwithiel, Cornwall, to show a considerable portion of the descent from Col. David Barclay of Ury and Lady Katharine Gordon, his wife (Part IX below).

The descent of the Dublin branch of the Ury family, as gathered from the public records in Dublin,—for the family records at Bury Hill afford scant information of those descendants of John Barclay who abjured the testimonies and faith of their fathers,—is as follows:

I. **John Barclay,** the fourth son and youngest child of the apologist, *b* at Ury 20th, 8th mo., 1687;[1] *d* at Dublin 8th, 4th mo., 1751;[1] *bur* Corke St., Dublin, 11th, 4th mo., 1751;[1] *m* (1) 26th, 4th mo., 1709, *Margaret Wilson,*[2] by whom he had no children; *m* (2) 19th, 3rd mo., 1713, *Anne Strettell,*[1] *b* in Dublin 23rd, 12th mo., 1694;[1] *bur* Corke St., Dublin, 21st, 2nd mo., 1771,[1] *dau* of *Amos Strettell* of Dublin, merchant, and of *Experience,* his

[1]Original Register of births, deaths and marriages of Dublin Monthly Meeting, preserved at the Friends' Meeting House, 6 Eustace Street, Dublin, vol. III, pp. 191-192.

[2]"Our Noble and Gentle Families of Royal Descent," by Joseph Foster, 21 Boundary Road, Finchley, London, N. W. This is the only authority for the alleged marriage of John Barclay to Margaret Wilson. In a letter to the writer under date of December 20, 1900, Mr. Foster stated that he *thought* his authority for this marriage was in the Friends' Register at Dublin. But in this he was mistaken.

wife. All the children of John Barclay and of *Anne Barclay,* his wife, were born in Eustace Street, Dublin.[1]

(2) *Experience Barclay.*

(3) *Christian Barclay,* b 16th, 4th mo., 1716;[1] *bur* Corke St., Dublin, 5th, 9th mo., 1719.[1]

(4) *Robert Barclay,* b 19th, 1st mo., 1717/18.[1] †

(5) *Anne Barclay,* b 3rd, 7th mo., 1719;[1] *bur* Corke St., Dublin,[1] date not stated. She was living unmarried in 1758.[3]

(6) *Katherine Barclay,* b 13th, 9th mo., 1720;[1] *bur* Corke St., Dublin, 19th, 9th mo., 1720.[1]

(7) *Patience Barclay,* b 30th, 1st mo., 1721/22;[1] living unmarried in 1754;[4] in 1758;[3] in 1765;[5] and in 1779.[6] †

(8) *John Barclay.*

(9) *Elizabeth Barclay.*

(10) *Jane Barclay,* b 24th, 4th mo., 1729;[1] living unmarried in 1758.[3] †

(11) *Lydia Barclay.*

(12) *Katherine Barclay,* b 3rd, 6th mo., 1734;[1] *bur* Corke St., Dublin, 9th, 8th mo., 1735.[1]

2. **Experience Barclay,** b 12th, 4th mo., 1715;[1] *m* at Dublin 9th, 4th mo., 1738, *James Clibborn,* residing at Moate, County Westmeath, son of *Joshua Clibborn* and *Sarah Clibborn,* his wife.[7] James Clibborn d 21st, 10th mo., 1782;[8, 9] *bur* at Moate 24th, 10th mo., 1782.[9]

---

[3]Will of *Katherine Forbes,* sister of John Barclay (senior), dated February 15, 1758, and proved and recorded in Irish Prerogative Court at Dublin, December 18, 1758.

[4]Will of *Patience Forbes,* another sister of John Barclay (b 1687), dated April 27, 1754, proved in London, July 26, 1757, and proved and recorded in Dublin, August 17, 1757.

[5]Transcript of Memorial of Deed of Annuity from *John Barclay* (junior) to Patience Barclay, spinster, dated November 16, 1765, and registered July 28, 1778, in the Registry of Deeds Office in Henrietta Street, Dublin, vol. 321, page 363. No. 216,798.

[6]Bill of complaint in suit in Irish Equity Exchequer, dated February 20, 1779, between Robert Emmet and others, assignees in bankruptcy of Edward Scriven, plaintiffs, and Anne Barclay and others, defendants.

[7]Transcripts of the registry of births, deaths and marriages of the Dublin Monthly Meeting, preserved at the Friends' Meeting House, 6 Eustace Street, Dublin.

(13) *Joshua Clibborn*, *b* 1746 ;[9] *d* 26th, 3rd mo.,
1751 ;[9] *bur* Corke St., Dublin, 28th, 3rd mo.,
1751.[9]

(14) *John Barclay Clibborn*, *b* 1753 ;[9] *d* 5th, 7th mo.,
1756 ;[9] *bur* at Moate 7th, 7th mo., 1756.[9]

(15) *Joshua Clibborn*, *b* 1755 ;[9] *d* 10th, 1st mo., 1767 ;[9]
bur at Moate 12th, 1st mo., 1767.[9]

(16) *Barclay Clibborn*.

(17) *James Clibborn*, living in 1780 at Warrinstown,
County Down.[8]

(18) *Ann Clibborn*, living 1758 ;[3] *m* John Ogle of the
Falls, County Down, and living in 1780.[8]

(19) *Sarah Clibborn*, living 1758 ;[3] *m John Courtney*
of Waterford, and living in 1780.[8]

8.   **John Barclay**, *b* 18th, 7th mo., 1723 ;[1] *d* October 18, 1768 ;[6]
m "by a priest" 1761, to *Anne Cooper* ;[7] marriage license
dated March 13, 1761 ;[10, 11] *Anne Cooper* was the dau.
of William Cooper of Cooper's Hill, in Shraugh, Queens
County,[12, 13] and of Experience Strettell, his wife.[14]

---

[8]Will of *James Clibborn* of Moate, co. Westmeath, filed with original Prerogative
Wills in record office in the Four Courts, Dublin.
    Will dated: September 29, 1780; proved April 12, 1783; testator died: October
21, 1782. Refers to marriage settlement witth his wife *Experience Barclay*. Also to
marriage settlement of his son *Barclay Clibborn* with Sarah Cooper, dau. of *Experience
Cooper*, widow. Refers to daughter *Ann Ogle*, wife of *John Ogle* of the Falls. co.
Down; to daughter *Sarah Courtney*, wife of *John Courtney* of Waterford; to son
James Clibborn of Warrinstown, co. Down; and to brother *Robert Clibborn*. Appoints
wife and two sons executors. The will was proved by the son *James Clibborn*, who
affirmed as a Quaker.

[9]Transcripts of records of Moate Monthly Meeting preserved at the Friends'
Meeting House, 6 Eustace Street, Dublin.

[10]Will of *John Barclay* (2nd) of the City of Dublin, merchant, filed with original
Prerogative Wills in record office in the Four Courts, Dublin.
    Will dated: September 21, 1767; proved: January 13, 1769. Refers to marriage
settlement with his wife *Anne Barclay*. Refers to son *John Barclay;* to daughters
Anne Barclay, *Wilhelmina Barclay*, *Lucy Barclay* and *Elizabeth Barclay*. Appoints
wife and brother-in-law, *Edward Scriven*, executors.

[11]Irish Prerogative Grant Book. Marriage Licenses.

[12]Will of *William Cooper* of Cooper's Hill, in Shraugh, Queens county, filed with
original Prerogative Wills in record office in the Four Courts, Dublin.
    Will dated: December 6, 1760; proved: January 20, 1761. Refers to eldest son
Edward Cooper, to son *Thomas Cooper*, to wife *Experience Cooper*, to eldest daughter
Lydia Cooper, now Clibborn, "wife of Joshua Clibborn," to daughters *Sarah Cooper*

This marriage, because made outside of the faith, was evidently disapproved by both of the loyal Quaker families and may possibly account for the lack of interest which the Ury family thereafter manifested in the Dublin branch of the Barclays. The following extract from the "Testimonies of Denial," preserved at the Friends Meeting House in Eustace Street, Dublin (vol. II, p. 36, 1756-1789), is interesting in this connection:

> "Whereas, JOHN BARCLAY was educated in profession with us, the People called Quakers, and for some time frequented our Religious Meetings, but hath manifested too little regard for the tender desires and endeavors of his Parents and Friends for his preservation in a demeanor suitable to his profession[15], and of late hath wholly declined the attendance of our Meetings for Worship; and Moreover
>
> "Whereas, He hath lately been married to *Ann Cooper*, a young woman likewise of our profession, without the consent of her mother[16], and contrary to the known rules of our Society,
>
> "We are therefore concerned to signify our DIS-UNITY with the said *John Barclay* and *Ann*, his wife,

and *Anne Cooper*, to daughter-in-law *Sarah Clibborn*, now Cooper, wife of eldest son *Edward Cooper*, and to grandson, *William Cooper*.

The sons Thomas and Edward qualified as executors, and indicated that they were Quakers.

[13]Marriage settlement, dated April 13 and 14, 1761, registered May 5, 1761, in Registry of Deeds Office in Henrietta Street, Dublin (See Transcript of Memorial, vol. 209, p. 416, No. 139,009).

Between *John Barclay* of Dublin City, merchant, of the first part, *Anne Cooper*, daughter of William Cooper of Cooper's Hill in Queens county, deceased, gentleman, of the second part, and *Edward Cooper*, late of Cooper's Hill, aforesaid, gentleman, and *Thomas Cooper* of Craige, County Carlow, gentleman, of the third part.

Witness: Edward Scriven of Dublin City, gentleman, and his clerk Bartholomew Delandre.

[14]Will of *Experience Cooper*, widow, late of Cooper's Hill, Queens county, but now of Dublin, filed with original Prerogative Wills in record office in the Four Courts, Dublin.

Will dated: September 18, 1769; proved: June 8, 1773; testatrix died May 16, 1773; refers to daughter *Lydia Clibborn*, wife of *Joshua Clibborn*, who was a son of *Robert Clibborn*, to daughter *Anne Cooper* (Query: Had not her daughter Anne married *John Barclay* 2nd in 1761?); to her third daughter *Sarah Clibborn* (This was the Sarah Cooper who married *Barclay Clibborn*, nephew of John Barclay 2nd); to son *Edward Cooper*, to testatrix's father *Abel Strettell*, and to her brother *Jonathan Strettell*. Executrices: Two daughters, Lydia Clibborn and Sarah Clibborn, both of whom qualified by affirmation, as Quakers.

[15]John Barclay at this time was upwards of 38 years of age.

[16]This possibly explains why her mother, in her will drawn in 1769, still referred to her daughter as "Anne Cooper."

and Do hereby disown them to be of our Society, untill they manifest a due sense of sorrow for their outrunning, which that they may, and obtain forgiveness of the Almighty, is our sincere desire for them.

"Signed in and on behalf of our Men's Meeting held in Dublin the 22nd, 9 mo., 1761.

Js. Jackson	Aaron Atkinson
Ricd North	J'n Gough
Wm Greenhow	J'n Thacker
Thos Chandlee	Wm Taylor
	Sam Carleton"	

That John Barclay's apostasy was not of sudden growth, may be inferred from the following extract from the Friends Records, entered six years previously ("Dublin Meeting's Proceedings," vol. II, p. 64):

"At a Men's Meeting held in Dublin 22, 7 mo, 1755:

"The young man repeatedly mentioned in the Proceedings of this Meeting to have put off his hat in way of salutation, viz: JOHN BARCLAY was frequently spoken to by the Friends appointed, who represented to him the inconsistency of this practice with our Profession, but hitherto without the desired effect.

"It was therefore thought necessary to make this Record of our care and concern to discourage this practice among us, contrary to the sentiments of Friends from the beginning, who have ever deemed the uncovering the head to be a mark of divine honour or worship paid to Almighty God, and not proper to be given to mortal men,

"And as our faithfull elders were conscienceously concerned to bear their Christian Testimony against this and other instances of the vain honours of this World,

"We being likeminded with them, do hereby signify our DISUNITY with him and all such as deviate from their steps in these cases, as trampling upon that Christian Testimony we desire to maintain."

Formal report was made to the Meeting on the 5th, 5 mo., 1761, that John Barclay and Anne Cooper had been married "by a Priest" ("Dublin Meeting's Proceedings," vol. 12, p. 227), and on the 16th, 6 mo., 1761, the parties concerned made a formal admission of the report, and a testimony of disunity was ordered (*ibid*, p. 233); on the 30th, 6 mo., 1761, the testimony was ordered to be shown them (*ibid*, p. 241); and on the 22nd, 9 mo., 1761, the testimony was signed (*ibid*, p. 249).

Marriage "out of Meeting" was regarded as a serious lapse among the Quakers, as the Proceedings of the Meeting frequently bear witness. A Testimony of Denial, for example, was entered against *Abigail Jaffray* (a cousin of John Barclay's), on 13th, 1 mo., 1784, because of her marriage "by a Priest to a Man not of our Society" (vol. 2, 1756-1789, p. 236) ; and on the 30th, 12 mo., 1784, a similar Denial was signed against *Catherine Jaffray*, sister of Abigail, "for being present at her sister's marriage," etc. (*ibid*, p. 236).[17]

The children of John Barclay (junior) and Anne Cooper were as follows:

- (20) *Anne Barclay, bap* April 20, 1769.[18] Living in 1767[10] and in 1779.[6] †
- (21) *Wilhelmina Barclay.* Living in 1767[10] and in 1779.[6] †
- (22) *John Barclay.* Living in 1767[10] and in 1779.[6] †
- (23) *Lucy Barclay.* Living in 1767 and in 1779.[6] †
- (24) *Elizabeth Barclay.* Living in 1767[10] and in 1779.[6] †

9. **Elizabeth Barclay**, *b* 6th, 2 mo., 1726/7, was *m* "by a priest" 1754.[7] The marriage license, dated May 30, 1754, ran to *Edward Scriven*, of Dublin, gentleman, and *Elizabeth Barclay* of St. Andrews Parish, Dublin City, spinster, and was directed to any cleric of the Established Church.[11] Edward Scriven *d* May 14, 1794.[19]

---

[17]Assignment of a charge of £3,000 on certain stated lands, under will of William Cooper, in favor of his three daughters, shows the relationships of sundry parties mentioned. It is dated March 12, 1770, and registered April 2, 1770. (See Transcript of Memorial in Registry of Deeds Office, Henrietta Street, Dublin, vol. 274, p. 451, No. 180,427.)

The grantors were *Joshua Clibborn* of Dublin City, merchant, and *Lydia Clibborn* al. Cooper, his wife, *James Clibborn* and *Barclay Clibborn* of Moate Grenoge in county Westmeath, gentlemen, *Sarah Clibborn* al. Cooper, wife of said *Barclay Clibborn*, *Edward Scriven* of Dublin City, Esquire, and *Anne Barclay* al. Cooper of Dublin City, widow (which Anne and Edward are executors of the will of *John Barclay* of Dublin, and which Anne, Sarah and Lydia are the three daughters of *William Cooper* of Cooper's Hill in Queens county, gentleman, deceased), and *Thomas Cooper* of Newton, county Carlow.

[18]Parochial Returns of St. Anne's Parish, Dublin, on file in the Record Office.

[19]Will of *Edward Scriven* of Dublin City, Esquire, filed with original Prerogative Wills in record office in the Four Courts, Dublin.

Will dated: March 26, 1782; Proved: June 14, 1794; Testator died May 14, 1794. Refers to wife, *Elizabeth Scriven*, to three sons, *William Barclay Scriven, John Bar-*

This marriage, too, seems to have been the cause of religious disownment if not of family feeling. At a Men's Meeting held in Dublin 11th, 6 mo., 1754, it was reported that ELIZABETH BARCLAY and *Joanna Rooke* (a niece of her mother's[20]) had lately been married "by a priest to men of another Society," etc. (Dublin Meeting's Proceedings, vol. 10, 1750-1754, p. 284), and on the 25th, 6 mo., 1754, *"Elizabeth Scriven* al. Barclay" owned to Friends that she had married without her mother's consent and intended to leave the Society (*ibid,* p. 289). On 6th, 8 mo., 1754, a paper "Concerning Elizabeth Scriven" was considered and directed to be laid before the Quarterly Meeting (*ibid,* p. 298), and on the 20th, 8 mo., 1754, the Quarterly Meeting's recommendation that such paper be publicly read was duly carried out (*ibid,* p. 303). The Testimony of Denial and Disownment is contained in vol. 1 of "Testimonies of Denials," page 525.

In the will of her aunt, Katherine Forbes, dated February 15, 1758,[3] *"Elizabeth Scriven* al. Barclay" was given but five shillings, while substantial bequests were made to her brother John and to her sisters, the stated reason being that she had married without the consent of the testatrix.

On April 25, 1778, a Commission of Bankruptcy was issued against *Edward Scriven* under the Great Seal of Ireland, and from the papers in the proceedings had thereon and in an Equity suit growing out of the same, considerable of the above information has been derived.[6] Edward Scriven died May 14, 1794,[19] and by petition of his son, John Barclay Scriven, as administrator with the will annexed of his estate, sworn to June 28, 1799, it appears that the estate had realized suf-

---

clay Scriven and *Edward Scriven* (a minor), to two unmarried daughters, *Sarah Scriven* and *Elizabeth Scriven,* and to two sons-in-law, *William Glasscock* and *John Macartney.* Executors: Wife and two sons-in-law.

[20]Will of John Barclay (senior) of the City of Dublin, merchant, filed with the original Prerogative Wills in the record office in the Four Courts, Dublin. Dated March 6, 1750. Proved November 20, 1753.

ficient to pay 20 shillings in the pound, and leave a surplus for the bankrupt's family. John Barclay Scriven is described in a deed of 1787 as "Barrister at Law."[21]

The children of Elizabeth Barclay and Edward Scriven were:

(25) *William Barclay Scriven.*[19] †

(26) *John Barclay Scriven,*[19] living in 1799. †

(27) *Edward Scriven,* a minor in 1782.[19] †

(28) *Sarah Scriven.*[19] †

(29) *Elizabeth Scriven.*[19] †

(30) A daughter, *m William Glascock.*[19] †

(31) A daughter, *m John Macartney.*[19] †

11. **Lydia Barclay,** *b* 18th, 2nd mo., 1733;[1] *m* at Dublin 29th, 6 mo., 1753, *Benjamin Alloway* of Dublin;[7] *d* April 29, 1772.[22]

(32) *John Barclay Alloway.*

(33) *Robert Alloway,* living in 1758;[23] *d* prior to 1772.[22] †

(34) *William Alloway.*[22] †

(35) *Mary Alloway, b* after 1758;[23] living in 1772.[22]†

(36) *Benjamin Alloway, b* after 1758;[23] living in 1772.[22] †

Lydia Alloway and her husband, whether their children did or not, seem to have remained members of the Meeting.

---

[21]Marriage settlement, dated August 18, 1787, registered June 3, 1789, in Registry of Deeds Office, Henrietta Street, Dublin (See Transcript of Memorial, vol. 403, p. 463, No. 268,967). Between *John Barclay Alloway* of Dublin City, merchant, of the first part; *John Evans,* the elder, of the same place, Esq., and his daughter *Catherine Evans,* spinster, of the second part; and *John Barclay Scriven,* Barrister-at-Law, and *John Evans,* the younger, of the third part.

[22]Will of Benjamin Alloway of Dublin City, merchant, filed with the original Prerogative Wills, in record office in the Four Courts, Dublin.

Will dated: December 16, 1771. Proved May 2, 1772. Testator died April 29, 1772. Refers to wife, and to four children, *John Alloway, Mary Alloway, Benjamin Alloway* and *William Alloway.*

[23]Will of *Katherine Forbes,* sister of John Barclay, senior, dated February 15, 1758, and proved and recorded in the Irish Prerogative Court at Dublin, December 18, 1758. In this will the testatrix makes substantial bequests "to my niece *Lydia Alloway,* al. Barclay, wife of *Benjamin Alloway*" and "to her sons *Robert, John* and *William Alloway.*"

16. **Barclay Clibborn,** living in Moate in 1765 ;[24] *d* 3rd, 1 mo., 1789 ;[9] *m Sarah Cooper,* dau. of Experience Cooper, widow of William Cooper of Cooper's Hill in County Queens.[14, 17]

    (37) *Ann Clibborn, b* 1772 ;[9] *d* 2nd, 1 mo., 1776 ;[9] *bur* at Dublin 5th, 1 mo., 1776.[9]

33. **John Barclay Alloway,** *b* 1755 ;[25] *d* December 6, 1830 ;[25] *m* 1787,[21] *Catherine Evans* (dau. of *John Evans* of Dublin[21]), *b* 1759 ;[25] *d* October 24, 1830.[25]

The families of Barclay, Strettell, Cooper, Forbes and Jaffray seem so closely allied that the writer has undertaken, wholly from such information as the public records afford, to trace more clearly the relationships between them. The record he presents of children born may be incomplete; but he believes it to be reasonably accurate so far as it goes.

The four daughters of the apologist, and therefore the four sisters of John Barclay (senior) of Dublin, married as follows: *Christian Barclay* married Alexander Jaffray of King's Wells, in Aberdeenshire, Scotland; *Katherine Barclay* married James Forbes; *Patience Barclay* married Timothy Forbes; and *Jean Barclay* married Alexander Forbes. The three Forbes were brothers, being with Dr. Samuel Forbes the sons of one John Forbes, whose estate of Aquorthies lay not far from Ury in Kincardine, Scotland (PENN. MAGAZINE, vol. XXII).

JAMES FORBES, from "Meeting in North Britain," was admitted to the Dublin Meeting on 1st, 1 mo., 1726.[26] He died in

---

[24]Deed of Annuity from *John Barclay* (junior) of Dublin City, merchant, to his sister *Patience Barclay,* of the same place, spinster. In consideration of £400 he grants her an annuity of £30 for the remainder of her life. Witnesses to Patience Barclay's signature: *Barclay Clibborn* of Moate, county Westmeath, gentleman and Peter Layworth of Moate, county Westmeath, clerk. (See Transcript of Memorial, vol. 321, p. 363, No. 216,798, in Registry of Deeds Office, Henrietta Street, Dublin.)

[25]From "Journal of Memorials of the Dead in Ireland," vol. 3, p. 453, Tombstone in St. Anne's Churchyard, Dublin: *John Barclay Alloway* of this city, merchant, died, 6 December, 1830, in his 76th year. *Catherine Alloway,* his wife, died 24 October, 1830, in her 72nd year. *Elizabeth Evans,* her sister, died 21 June, 1837, in her 65th year.

[26]Proceedings of the Dublin Monthly Meeting. Vol. 7, 1724-1733.

1734,[27] leaving a will which was proved in 1735.[28] From a chancery bill filed in 1759 by his widow's executors, it would seem that there were no issue of the marriage.[28] His widow, *Katherine Forbes* al. Barclay, died November 9, 1758,[28] leaving a will in which she seemingly undertook to make a bequest to each of her then living relatives ;[29] and yet a closer study of the will shows that some of her kinsfolk then living were *not* named in the will.

---

[27]Chancery Bill filed April 30, 1759, by *David Barclay* of London City, merchant, William Alloway and Robert Pettigrew, both of Dublin City, merchants, as executors of the will of *Catherine Forbes*, of Dublin City, widow of *James Forbes*, of Dublin City, merchant, against Joseph Tomey, Ellinor Tomey, Peter Tomey and Thomas Constable. Recites that James Forbes died in 1734, leaving a little less than £7,000, which he bequeathed to his widow; that from 1734 to 1751 her affairs were so well managed by her brother, John Barclay of Dublin City, merchant, that at the time of *his* death her fortune had increased to £8,379 well invested in good securities; that she died without issue November 9, 1758; that she had made a will in 1752 after her brother's death, but in 1758 made another when she was at least 80 years old, and very much under the influence of Joseph Tomey, who was her clerk, and Ellinor Tomey, who was her menial servant; that both Joseph Tomey and the testatrix were Quakers, and she looked upon him "as a person of great sanctity;" that by her will of 1752 she left him but £80, while in the second will she left him more than £200, her chaise and pair of geldings, &c., and her furniture, and directed that if her fortune should prove insufficient to pay all legacies in full, each legacy should abate except those to Joseph Tomey, Ellinor Tomey and to testatrix's sister Jane Forbes; that upon getting possession of testatrix's strong box, the executors found securities for £7,925 and cash for £68, and then learned that she had made a present of £500 to Ann Barclay, widow of her brother John Barclay, deceased; and that from her books it appeared that her expenses from 1751 to 1755 averaged yearly £305 : 1 : 10, while from 1755 to 1758 they averaged £393 : 10 : 0. The bill then charges that Joseph Tomey falsified the books which were in his charge, and embezzled securities for debts due to testatrix by Peter Tomey and by Thomas Constable, and asks for appropriate relief.

[28]Will of *James Forbes* of Dublin City, merchant, proved in Irish Prerogative Court.

Will dated November 24, 1727. Proved January 29, 1735. Gives entire estate to wife, *Catherine Forbes* al. Barclay, and makes her sole executrix.

[29]Will of *Katherine Forbes*, proved and recorded in the Irish Prerogative Court at Dublin.

Will dated: February 15, 1758. Proved, December 18, 1758. She leaves bequests as follows:

To her sister *Jane Forbes;* and to the following children of said sister and of her husband *Alexander Forbes*, late of London, deceased; *Alexander Forbes*, only son; *Barbara Forbes, Ann Forbes* and *Katherine Forbes*.

To the following children of her brother-in-law, the late Dr. *Samuel Forbes,* deceased: *Alexander Forbes, Catherine Glester* al. Forbes, his eldest daughter; and *Isabella Hill* al. Forbes.

To the daughter of her brother-in-law, *Timothy Forbes*, deceased, that is to say, to *Catherine Hoope* al. Barclay, wife of James Hoope.

To the following children of her brother *Robert Barclay*, late of Ury, deceased: *Robert Barclay, David Barclay* and *Katherine Barclay*.

To the two daughters of her niece *Mollison Strettell*, that is to say: *Elizabeth Doubleday* and *Prudence Doubleday*.

TIMOTHY FORBES and *Patience Barclay* were married in
1707.[30] The will of the former, dated in 1741, was proved July
15, 1743,[31] and that of the latter dated 1754 was proved in 1757.[32]

To her brother *David Barclay* of London, linendraper, and to two of his children,
namely: *Alexander Barclay*, "now in Pensilvania;" and *Katherine Bell* al. Barclay,
wife of Daniel Bell, Jr., of Tottenham, near London.

To the following children of her brother *John Barclay*, late of Dublin, deceased:
John Barclay, *Experience Clibborn* al. Barclay, wife of James Clibborn of Moate, and
to their children, *Barclay Clibborn*, *James Clibborn*, *Joshua Clibborn*, *Ann Clibborn*
and *Sarah Clibborn; Ann Barclay*, his "second daughter;" *Patience Barclay*, *Jane
Barclay; Lydia Alloway* al. Barclay, wife of Benjamin Alloway, and to their children
Robert Alloway, *John Alloway* and *William Alloway; Elizabeth Scriven* al. Barclay,
another daughter of the same brother, "5 shillings, she having married without my
consent;" and to her sister-in-law, *Anne Barclay*, the widow of her said brother.

To the following children of her sister *Christian Jaffray* and her husband *Alexander Jaffray*, namely: *Robert Jaffray* and his children, *Alexander Jaffray*, *Lydia
Jaffray*, *Christian Jaffray*, *Katherine Jaffray* and *Abigail Jaffray; Gilbert Jaffray*; and
Thomas Jaffray.

To her cousin *David Falconer*.

To the poor Quakers of the Dublin Men's Meeting.

To the poor Quakers of the Quarterly Meeting at Aberdeen, in North Britain.

To sundry servants, including Joseph Tomey and his sister Ellinor Tomey.

To her brother *David Barclay*, the residuary estate.

The will provided that if any dispute concerning the same should arise, it was
not to go before the Men's Meeting.

The executors named were her brother *David Barclay*, or, if he should die, his
son *David Barclay*, also of London, merchant; William Alloway, of Dublin City,
merchant, or, if he should die, his son Benjamin Alloway of the same place; and
Robert Pettigrew of Dublin City, merchant.

[30]Receipt by *John Barclay*, as one of the executors of the will of *Patience
Forbes*, of £400 due from the estate of her deceased husband, Timothy Forbes (See
Transcript of Memorial, vol. 189, p. 419, No. 126,023, in Registry of Deeds Office,
Henrietta Street, Dublin). Dated: November 1, 1757; Registered: November 7, 1757.

Recites Marriage settlement of June 2, 1707, between *Timothy Forbes* of Dublin
City, merchant, of the first part; *Patience Barclay* of London, spinster, of the second
part, and *David Barclay* of London, linendraper, and *John Barclay* of Dublin, merchant, as trustees, of the third part.

Recites that *Patience Forbes* al. Barclay died June 22, 1757, leaving a will wherein she appointed *David Barclay*, *Robert Barclay* and *John Barclay* her executors.

Acknowledges receipt of all moneys due under marriage settlement.

Witnesses: Edward Scriven and another.

[31]Will of *Timothy Forbes*, of Dublin City, filed with the original Prerogative
Wills at the record office in the Four Courts, Dublin.

Will dated: April 30, 1741. Proved July 15, 1743.

Recites wife, *Patience Forbes*; eldest son, *Alexander Forbes*, to whom but 5
shillings are left "on account of his disobedience," etc.; son, *Timothy Forbes* of London, who is forgiven all debts in addition to the £1,200 he had already received;
youngest son, *James Forbes*, who is named as executor and made residuary legatee;
eldest daughter, *Ann Handcock*; daughter, *Sara Handcock*; daughter, *Katherine Hoope*;
brother-in-law, *John Barclay* of Dublin, merchant; the three daughters of his brother
Samuel Forbes, deceased, namely, *Katherine Forbes*, *Isabella Forbes* and *Anna Forbes*;
and grandson, *Timothy Handcock*.

[32]Will of *Patience Forbes* al. Barclay, relict of *Timothy Forbes*, merchant, late of

It would seem from these wills that Timothy Forbes had had issue by a prior wife, but none by his wife Patience Barclay.

ALEXANDER FORBES, who also remained a Quaker, was a merchant of St. Margrat Parish, Lothbury, London, and does not seem at any time to have resided in Dublin. He died May 25, 1740, leaving a widow, *Jean Forbes* al. Barclay, and a number of children surviving him.[33]

ALEXANDER JAFFRAY and *Christian Barclay* had three sons, Robert Jaffray, who settled in Dublin, Gilbert Jaffray and Thomas

---

Dublin, deceased, from the Registry of the Court of Canterbury Prerogative Wills, whereof a copy was filed in the record office in the Four Courts, Dublin.

Will dated: April 27, 1754. Proved in London: July 26, 1757. Proved in Dublin: August 17, 1757.

Recites Marriage settlement of June 2, 1707, above noted. Bequests to her brother, *David Barclay* of London; to her nephew, *Robert Barclay* of Ury; to her great nephews, *Robert Barclay*, junior, *David Barclay* and *Evan Barclay*, sons of said Robert Barclay of Ury; to her nephew, *John Barclay* (junior) of Dublin, merchant; to her niece, *Patience Barclay*, sister of said John Barclay; to *Christian Jaffray*, daughter of Robert Jaffray of Kingswells, Aberdeen, now a merchant in Dublin; to *Eilzabeth Forbes*, wife of Timothy Forbes of London, merchant (Quaere: Was this the wife of the testatrix's son or stepson?); to her sister, *Jean Forbes*, widow of Alexander Forbes, sometime of Aquorthies and late of London, merchant; and makes reference to her son-in-law (step son?) *James Forbes*, as executor of her husband's will.

Appoints as executors, her brother, *David Barclay* of London, merchant; her nephew, *Robert Barclay* of Ury; and her nephew, *John Barclay* (junior) of Dublin, merchant.

The will was written and dated at Springhall, Kincardine, North Britain.

[33]Will of *Alexander Forbes* of London, merchant, filed in the Registry of Canterbury Prerogative Wills, London.

Will dated: 12th, 3rd mo. (May), 1729. Proved June 4, 1740.

Recites that under marriage settlement his wife *Jane Forbes* is entitled to an annuity out of the lands of Aquorthies and Colyhill, in Aberdeenshire, Scotland, which at the time of the settlement was in possesssion of the testator's father, *John Forbes*, but now in his own (Was he the eldest son?) and managed by his sister, *Barbara Forbes*, as his agent.

Refers to his two houses at Dowgate Hill, London, and York Place, Surrey.

Gives residue to his seven children (all minors at the date of the Will), namely, *John Forbes*, the eldest son; *Alexander Forbes*; *Christian Forbes*, the eldest daughter, who subsequently married *William Penn*, grandson of the founder; *Barbara Forbes*; *Ann Forbes*; *Katherine Forbes*; and *Margrat Forbes*.

No witnesses to the will, which, however, was proved by *James Barclay* of St. Dionis, Blackchurch Parish, London (Quaere: Was this the son of *David Barclay* the linendraper?) and *Alexander Forbes* of St. Michael Woodstreet Parish, London, both bankers and both Quakers.

Administration was granted to a creditor. *Barbara Forbes* and *Anne Forbes*, spinsters, renounced their prior right as did *Jane Forbes*, widow, and as guardian of *John Forbes*, *Alexander Forbes* and *Katherine Forbes*, minor children of the testator. The other children, if then living, do not seem to have renounced.

Jaffray.[29]   The son ROBERT JAFFRAY in 1733[34] married *Abigail
Strettell,* a daughter of Abel Strettell, of Dublin.[35]   What the relationship was between this Abel Strettell and the Amos Strettell
whose daughter, Anne Strettell, married John Barclay (senior)
in 1713,[1] is not clear from the records.   Abel Strettell's other
children were: Mary Strettell ;[35] Experience Strettell, who married
William Cooper of Cooper's Hill ;[14, 16] Abel Strettell[36] (junior) ;
and Jonathan Strettell.[14, 36]   Robert Jaffray died about September
20, 1773,[37] leaving a will which was proved a month later,[37] and
his wife, Abigail Jaffray, died in 1788,[38] also leaving a will which
was proved the same year.[38]

[34]Proceedings of the Dublin Monthly Meeting, vol. 7, for 1724-1733.

[35]Marriage settlement dated December 1, 1733, registered December 14, 1733,
in Registry of Deeds office, Henrietta Street, Dublin. (See Transcript of Memorial,
vol. 75, p. 88, No. 52,274.)

Between *Robert Jaffray,* of Dublin City, merchant, of the first part; *Jonathan
Strettell,* of the same place, of the second part; *Abigail Strettell,* spinster, and a
daughter of Abel Strettell of Dublin, merchant, deceased, of the third part. Refers
to another daughter, *Mary Strettell.*

[36]Deed of conveyance, dated October 7 and 8, 1737, and registered December 19,
1737, in the Registry of Deeds office, Henrietta Street, Dublin, in vol. 90, p. 7, No.
62,510.

William Cooper of Shraugh, in county Queens, gentleman, and *Experience
Cooper* al. Strettell, his wife, one of the daughters of Abel Strettell, late of Dublin
City, merchant, deceased; *Robert Jaffray* of Dublin City, merchant, and *Abigail
Jaffray* al. Strettell, his wife, another daughter of said Abel Strettell; *Abel Strettell*
of Ballatore, county Kildare, gentleman, a son of said Abel Strettell; and *Jonathan
Strettell* of Dublin City, merchant, also a son of said Abel Strettell.

Convey to *John Barclay* and *Thomas Strettell, Jr.,* as directed in the will of said
Abel Strettell, a piece of ground 21½ ft. by 19 ft. formerly in the possession of
David Latouche behind the dwelling house of Thomas Strettell in Eustace Street,
and another piece 20 ft. by 11 ft. 4 in. behind the dwelling of one Robert Belling.

[37]Will of *Robert Jaffray* of Dublin City, merchant, filed with the original Irish
Prerogative Wills in the record office in the Four Courts, Dublin.

Will dated: July 5, 1773. Proved: October 20, 1773. Testator "dead a month."
Confirms marriage settlement with wife, *Abigail Jaffray* al. Strettell. Refers to
his only son, *Alexander Jaffray,* to whom he leaves his lands and "Estate of Kingswells in the Freedom of Aberdeen," subject to the charges, &c., recited in the deed
from Aberdeen City to the testator. Refers to his two unmarried daughters, *Katherine Jaffray* and *Abigail Jaffray;* to his daughter, *Lydia Holmes,* wife of John
Holmes; to his daughter *Christian Nicholson,* wife of Thomas Nicholson, describing
her as named for the testator's mother; to his grandchildren, children of his daughter
Christian, *John Nicholson, Abigail Nicholson, Mary Nicholson, Lydia Nicholson,
Robert Nicholson, Christian Nicholson* and *Isabella Nicholson;* to his nephew, *Alexander Jaffray,* son of testator's late brother, Gilbert Jaffray, deceased; to his nephew,
Thomas Jaffray, son of testator's late brother, Thomas Jaffray, deceased, and to his
nieces, *Elizabeth Jaffray* and *Christian Jaffray,* daughters of said Thomas Jaffray,
deceased.

The wife and son were appointed executors, the latter qualifying as a Quaker.

The Cooper connection appears from the records to have been as follows:

WILLIAM COOPER, of Cooper's Hill in Shraugh, county Queens, married *Experience Strettell,* daughter of Abel Strettell of Dublin.[12, 14] Their children were *Edward Cooper,* who married Sarah Clibborn,[12]—(her relationship to the other Clibborns does not appear); *Thomas Cooper,* of Newton, county Carlow, who does not seem to have married up to the year 1770;[12, 17] *Lydia Cooper,* who married Joshua Clibborn, son of Robert Clibborn;[12, 14, 17] *Anne Cooper,* who married John Barclay, junior;[12, 13, 17] and *Sarah Cooper,* who married Barclay Clibborn (son of James Clibborn and Experience Barclay), a nephew of said John Barclay, junior.[6, 17]

The records bear witness to the fact that JOHN BARCLAY (senior) was a man of some degree of commercial importance in Dublin and was of prominence among the Quakers.

The Calendar of Petitions to the Lord Lieutenant of Ireland, or, in his absence, to the Lords Justices of Ireland, which is preserved in the Record Office in Dublin, shows orders granted on the petition of John Barclay, merchant, on March 19, 1741, allowing the export of butter to Newfoundland; on October 16, 1741, allowing the shipment of wheat to Barbadoes; on April 2, 1742, allowing him to send provisions to the ship "Barclay Frigate;" on February 24, 1743, allowing the "Diana" of Dublin to sail with her cargo to Lisbon, etc., etc. On February 13, 1741, he was admitted to membership among the Free Brothers of the Holy Trinity Guild of Merchants.[39]

---

[38]Will of *Abigail Jaffray* of Dublin City, widow, filed with the original Irish Prerogative Wills in the record office in the Four Courts, Dublin.

Will dated: May 19, 1788. Proved: December 10, 1788.

Refers to her son *Alexander Jaffray,* to whom she leaves her house in Eustace Street; to her daughter, *Katharine Jaffray;* to her daughter, *Abigail Hautenville,* and to her children, *Charlotte Hautenville, Robert Jaffray Hautenville* and *Alexander Jaffray Hautenville;* to daughter, *Lydia Holmes;* to her grandchildren, *John Nicholson, Abigail Nicholson, Lydia Bell* (al. Nicholson?), *Isabella Nicholson, Robert Jaffray Nicholson;* to her sons-in-law *Thomas Nicholson* and *Rawdon Hautenville;* to her nieces, *Lydia Clibborn* and *Sarah Clibborn* (daughters of William Cooper and Experience Strettell, his wife); and to her husband's niece, *Christiana Robertson.*

[39]See Wilson's Dublin Directory for 1765.

The records of the Proceedings of the Dublin Monthly Meeting (volumes 7 and 8, covering the years 1724-1742) show that on the 1st, 7 mo., 1724, John Barclay was appointed to act in the securing of more land for the Meeting; on 31st, 6 mo., 1725, he was appointed on a deputation to welcome the new Lord Chancellor, Richard West; on the 15th, 9 mo., 1726, he was on a deputation to the Lord Chancellor concerning rules of the Court of Chancery and the conditions upon which Quakers should be required to affirm; on the 21st, 9 mo., 1729, he was on a deputation from the Quakers to the Lord Lieutenant; on the 21st, 7 mo., 1731, he was on a deputation to present an address to the Duke of Dorset, the new Lord Lieutenant, upon his landing; on the 16th, 4 mo., 1731, he was on the School Committee; on the 13th, 7 mo., 1737, he was on a deputation to draw up an address and present it to the Duke of Devonshire, the new Lord Lieutenant; and he appears to have been on several other deputations and committees.

A number of entries found in volumes 8, 9 and 11 of the Proceedings of the Dublin Monthly Meeting, show that *Anne Barclay* (*b* 1719), daughter of John Barclay, senior, travelled considerably for an unmarried woman of those days. At a Men's Meeting held 21st, 9 mo., 1738, a certificate was received from the Frenchay Monthly Meeting "touching the orderly and agreeable conversation of Anne Barclay who resided there some time."

At a Men's Meeting held 24th, 5 mo., 1744, John Barclay consented, at the request of Elizabeth Shippy and Esther White, "two Public Friends from America," that his daughter Anne Barclay should accompany them in their intended visit to Friends in Scotland and in the North of England; and a "certificate of her orderly conversation" was accordingly granted. On the 28th, 2 mo., 1747, she obtained a certificate to enable her to visit the Meetings of Friends in Munster Province,—a suitable companion offering in the person of one Abigail Watson. On the 21st, 4 mo., 1748, John Barclay made application for a certificate for his daughter Anne Barclay to visit parts of England in company with Abigail Watson, and a certificate was granted accordingly.

At a Men's Meeting held 2nd, 9 mo., 1755, it appeared that Anne Barclay, being then in London, had desired a certificate from the Dublin Meeting, whereupon Robert Clibborn and John Rutty were "desired to make enquiry concerning her conversation

" and clearness in relation to marriage" and to draw a certificate accordingly. There is nothing to show how they decided or whether she ever married.

From these same minutes it appears that in 1731 John Barclay requested of the Meeting a certificate concerning the conversation, etc., of his nephew, David Barclay, who had moved from Dublin to reside at London; and a certificate as to the nephew's conversation "and clearness in regard to marriage" was granted accordingly.

On May 21, 1712, one Benjamin Chetwood and his wife Ann Chetwood, al Ann Eustace, had leased to *Amos Strettell* for a term of three lives, renewable for ever,—the lives selected being those of Robert Strettell, son of Amos Strettell, Jonathan Strettell, son of Abel Strettell, and Joseph Maddock, son of Joseph Maddock—a plot of ground on the West side of Eustace Street, adjoining the Quaker Meeting House;[40] and on the same day a similar lease of the next adjoining plot was made by the same parties to *Abel Strettell*, on the same lives.[41] Amos Strettell built a dwelling house on the parcel thus taken over by him and by instrument dated March 22, 1719, leased the property to John Barclay for the same term.[42] A year later, and by deed dated October 11 and 12, 1720, Amos Strettell conveyed the premises to his son-in-law, John Barclay, "in consideration of 5 s and of " his natural love and affection for his daughter Anne Barclay al. " Strettell, and in fulfillment of a solemn promise made on her " marriage;"[43] and then went into bankruptcy.[44] Prior to this, and by instrument dated June 18, 1718, John Barclay had taken from Benjamin Chetwood a lease of adjacent property on the west side of Eustace Street (whereon it seems that John Barclay built his warehouse), to hold for the lives of John Barclay, the lessee, Thomas Strettell, second son of Amos Strettell, and Robert

---

[40]Transcripts of Memorials in Registry of Deeds Office, Henrietta Street, Dublin, Volume 10, p. 71, No. 3,086, registered July 10, 1712.

[41]*Ibid.* Volume 8, page 395. No. 2,997, registered June 7, 1712.

[42]*Ibid.* Volume 26, page 218. No. 15,262, registered March 24, 1719.

[43]*Ibid.* Volume 29, page 194, No. 16,825, registered October 13, 1720.

[44]Proceedings of Dublin Monthly Meeting. Vol. 1, p. 327. Testimony of Amos Strettell against himself for bankruptcy, dated the 10th day of the 11th month called January, 1720/1.

Jaffray, second son of Alexander Jaffray, of Kings Wells in Aberdeenshire, North Britain,—which Robert Jaffray is described in the record as "then apprentice to said John Barclay,"—with right of renewal forever within six months of the death of each life.[45] These two plots with dwelling house and warehouse seem to have constituted the Barclay homestead in Dublin, and was added to after his death by his son, John Barclay, the second.[46]

Immediately after John Barclay's death and in accordance with instructions contained in his will, his business was continued by his wife and son John under the name of "Ann Barclay & Son:" and it so appears in Wilson's Dublin Directory for the year 1752. The Directories show, however, that in 1762 and 1763, the business was conducted under the son's name, "John Barclay," and at Eustace Street, which was in St. Andrew's Parish. In 1764 the name did not appear in the directory; in 1765, its place of business was at Glasnevin, in Glasnevin Parish; and from 1766 to 1768, inclusive, it was conducted under the name of "John Barclay" in Dawson Street, which was in St. Anne's Parish. In the directories of 1784-5-6 the firm of "Ann Barclay & Sisters," Tea Merchants, were recorded as having their place of business at 18 French Street,—which is now Upper Mercer Street in St. Peter's Parish. The name Barclay does not appear in the directories of 1787-8-9, while in the directories of 1790-1-2, "Barclay & Co.," milliners, are recited as having their place of business at 31 Bolton Street,—in St. Mary's Parish. Whether or not this firm consisted of the daughters of John Barclay, the second, does not definitely appear.

The special interest of the writer in the Dublin branch of the Barclays of Ury, centres in the *Robert Barclay* (grandson of the Apologist, and eldest son of the John Barclay who settled in Dublin, and of Anne Stettrell, his wife), born 19th, 1st mo., 1717/18;[1] for there are some slight circumstances which lean toward the possibility of this Robert having been the father of that *Thomas Barclay* who was born in St. Mary's County, Maryland, on March 18th, 1755.[47] While Thomas Barclay at all times declined,—for

---

[45]Transcripts of Memorials in Registry of Deeds Office, Henrietta Street, Dublin. Volume 22, page 51, No. 11,355, registered June 19, 1718.

[46]*Ibid.* Volume 200, page 349, No. 133,449 registered September 26, 1759.

[47]See Part VI, below.

reasons best known and consistently kept to himself,—to give to his wife or children any information whatsoever concerning his father's family, yet an intimate friend of his earlier days informed his son, Judge Joseph Barclay of Monmouth County, New Jersey, many years after the father's death, that Thomas Barclay was a direct descendant from the Ury family; and he seemed to know whereof he spoke. The possession by Judge Barclay of an old copy of the famous Apology which had come down to him from his father, and the impossibility of a descent from Ury except through this Robert Barclay (*b* 1717/18), complete the very insufficient set of circumstances that make it even possible that the Robert Barclay, whose two sons, John and Thomas, were born in St. Mary's County, Maryland, in the sixth decade of the eighteenth century, was the same Robert Barclay as was born in Dublin on the 19th, 1st mo., 1717/18.

The mystery with which Thomas Barclay surrounded the antecedents of his father Robert, finds a possible counterpart in the complete disappearance from all records concerning the Dublin family,—which seem otherwise to have been very carefully kept (and the records at Bury Hill are much less complete),—of Robert, the Apologist's grandson. It is possible, of course, that Robert Barclay (*b* 1717/18) died young and that his death was not recorded at the Dublin Monthly Meeting; but it is equally possible, and as it seems to the writer more probable, that he did *not* die in childhood but was perhaps disowned in his young manhood because of some religious or moral lapse, or was perhaps believed by his family to have perished, and possibly did perish, in some distant land, so that no record of the fact was made.

The Minutes of Proceedings of the Dublin Monthly Meeting, —which have been carefully searched,—fail to show any testimony of denial or disownment of Robert Barclay, son of John, as they certainly would have done had his family abandoned him because of *religious* lapse; and the criminal records of Dublin County, which have also been searched from 1720 to 1750, contain no reference to his name. It is hardly probable, therefore, that he was disowned because of a *moral* lapse. Yet the fact that no entry of his death appears upon Eustace Street records, is cogent evidence, as it seems to the writer, that he did *not* die in childhood. His father, as we have seen above, was an influential

member of the Dublin Monthly Meeting, and the family deaths
are carefully chronicled on its records both before and after the
year 1750,—the date of the father's will, to be referred to below.
In this connection, note the records of the burials of John Barclay's daughters *Christian Barclay* in 1719, *Katherine Barclay* in
1720, and the second *Katherine Barclay* in 1735; of *John Barclay*
himself in 1751; and of his wife *Anne Barclay* in 1771. Surely
if Robert had died in Dublin in childhood, some mention of his
death or burial would have appeared on these records; and it is
not a violent presumption from the records alone to presume that
he left Dublin in his young manhood for other parts and was
either known or believed by his parents to have died, or was so
wholly lost sight of after a lapse of many years as to have been
regarded as dead by his family.

Be the fact as it may, however, there can be no doubt that
on March 6, 1750, when John Barclay, the father, made his will,
Robert Barclay, his eldest son, was either known or believed by
him to be dead,—or had possibly been disowned. The will was
dated as above and together with two codicils was proved November 20, 1753. The testator mentions his wife *Anne Barclay;* his
son *John Barclay;* his five unmarried daughters *Anne Barclay,
Patience Barclay, Elizabeth Barclay, Jane Barclay* and *Lydia Barclay;* his daughter *Experience Clibborn;* his grandson *Barclay
Clibborn,* son of Experience; and his wife's niece *Joanna Rooke.*
He directs that his business in which his son John is a partner
should be continued under the name of "Anne Barclay and Son,"
for the benefit of his wife, son and unmarried daughters; and he
appoints, as his executors and trustees, his wife *Anne Barclay,*
his son *John Barclay,* his son-in-law *James Clibborn,* and *Robert
Clibborn,* the elder, of Meath Street, Dublin, a brother of said
James Clibborn.

His son *Robert Barclay* is not mentioned in the will or in
either of the codicils.[48]

And finally the following clause of the will seems wholly in-
consistent with a belief on the testator's part that Robert, his son,
was then living:

---

[48]Original Prerogative Will on file in the Record Office in the Four Courts,
Dublin.

" . . . . . To the intent and purpose that my said dear wife shall and may have, receive, take and enjoy to her own use, one full third part of the interest, benefit and produce thereof during her natural life, with full power for her to dispose of the said one-third part of my fortune, either in her lifetime or at her decease, *to and amongst our dear children*[40] in such shares and proportions and at such times as my said dear wife, by deed or will, shall appoint; and for want of such appointment the same to go equally among *all our dear children*[40], share and share alike. . . . . ."

So, too, in the will of John Barclay's sister, *Katherine Forbes* above noted,[29] dated February, 15, 1758, mention is made of all the then living children of John Barclay, *except* Robert; and the conclusion may be fairly drawn that the testatrix either knew or believed that Robert was dead, or possibly,—as seems to have been the fate of most of the kin who abjured the faith of the Friends,—had ceased to regard him as one of the family.

The circumstances thus noted in connection with the possibility of Robert Barclay of Dublin (*b* 1717/18) being the father of John Barclay and of Thomas Barclay of St. Mary's County, Maryland, are too slight and inconsequent to form the basis of a claim, or even of an opinion. They are here set forth in the hope that as time goes on further light may be shed upon both features of the problem.

---

[40]These clauses are not italicised in the will.

PART VI.

Line of Descent from Thomas Barclay of St. Mary's County, Maryland.

THE ancestry of THOMAS BARCLAY (*b* St. Mary's County, Md., March 18, 1755), is by no means clear enough to warrant its being made the basis of a claim, even, much less of an assertion. From family tradition,—an unreliable source at best,—and from statements made by a life-long friend of Thomas Barclay to his son Judge Joseph Barclay (No. 6 below), it would seem that he were of the Ury family; and yet the only member of that family through which such descent could possibly be traced would be *Robert Barclay* of Dublin, son of John Barclay of the same place and grandson of the apologist. Whether this Robert Barclay ever attained manhood or married or had issue, is a matter of conjecture only, as was pointed out in Part V above. No record is preserved either at Dublin or elsewhere (so far as the writer has yet discovered), of anything more than the date and place of this Robert Barclay's birth; and if it be a fact that he came out to America and married and had issue, such fact was unknown to his family or else was ignored by them because of some moral or religious lapse on his part.

Of course it is possible that in his early manhood this Robert Barclay sailed abroad (for his father was interested in shipping and commerce), and was generally believed to have been lost at sea, when such was not the fact; and that for reasons best known to himself he was content that the misapprehension should continue. But be the conjecture what it may, the only *facts* established are that he was born in Dublin 19th, 1st mo., 1717/18, a son of John Barclay and a grandson of the Apologist, and that while records of the births, deaths and marriages (or disownments) of all other members of his family were carefully entered at the Monthly Meeting, no record of any kind was entered concerning this Robert Barclay beyond the record of his birth. The future, let it be hoped, will shed light upon the problem.

Thomas Barclay of St. Mary's County, Md., died in 1804 at Shrewsbury, N. J., and was buried in the graveyard there of Christ Church, of which he had formerly been a vestryman. For some thus far undiscovered reason, he persistently refused even to converse with his wife concerning his father's family, or to answer any queries she put to him with regard thereto; and he left her, as she subsequently told her children, in absolute ignorance of all except that his father's name was Robert, that his mother was an Overton, and that he had had an older brother John.

On July 12, 1776, Thomas Barclay enlisted from St. Mary's County, Md., as a member of the "Flying Camp," and he served throughout the war. In 1779 he was a member of Major Anderson's 3rd Maryland Regiment, which formed a part of Washington's command in New Jersey, and while there he met, and later married, Catherine Williams, the daughter of John Williams of Shrewsbury, whose lands had been confiscated and who was himself then a fugitive because of his adherence to the King. After the war Thomas Barclay made his home in Shrewsbury, and his children all were born there.

His mother,—an Overton,—was possibly *Margaret Overton,* the daughter of William Overton of Hanover County, Va., and Peggy Garland, his wife. There is, however, no certain record of his mother's Christian name or parentage.

The will of his brother John, who died in St. Mary's County, Md., bore date June 12, 1792, and was proved on August 10th of the same year. It would appear from such will that John Barclay never married.

The following is the descent from this Thomas Barclay:

1. **Thomas Barclay,**[1] *b* St. Mary's County, Maryland, March 18, 1755; *d* Shrewsbury, N. J., 1804; *m Catherine Williams, b* August 20, 1760; *d* January 3, 1821.

    (2) *Robert Barclay,*[2] *b* August 4, 1783; *d* 12 June, 1835, *unm.*

    (3) *William Barclay,*[2] *b* September 20, 1785; *d* in Spain. †

    (4) *John Williams Barclay.*[2]

    (5) *George Brinley Barclay.*[2]

(6) *Joseph Barclay.*[2]
(7) *Elizabeth Barclay.*[2]
(8) *Daniel Barclay.*[2]

4. **John Williams Barclay,**[2] *b* Shrewsbury, N. J., February 20, 1788; *d* in New York City; *m* * * *

(9) *Daniel Barclay.*[3]

5. **George Brinley Barclay,**[2] *b* Shrewsbury, N. J. October 3, 1790; *d* New York City, December 27, 1829; *m* at Cranbury, N. J., August 27, 1816, *Abigail Shaw, b* April 16, 1792; *d* September 9, 1871.

(10) *DeWitt Barclay.*[3]
(11) *Alexander Barclay.*[3]
(12) *Elizabeth Virginia Barclay.*[3]
(13) *Annie McChesney Barclay.*[3]
(14) *George Barclay,*[3] *b* May 23, 1827; *d* October 3, 1827.

6. **Joseph Barclay**[2] (Judge), *b* Shrewsbury, N. J., July 10, 1793; *d* Eatontown, N. J., April 15, 1889; *m* (1) at Madison Court House, Va., February 29, 1816, *Mary H. Lee, d* January 2, 1861; *m* (2) at Shrewsbury, N. J., November 20, 1862, *Sarah Maria Allen, b* November 4, 1818; (living 1903).

(15) *William Overton Barclay*[3] (M.D.), *b* April 14, 1817; *d* September 2, 1841, *unm.*
(16) *Caroline Matilda Barclay.*[3]
(17) *Catherine Barclay,*[3] *b* February 20, 1823; *d* October 28, 1825.
(18) *Caroline Amelia Barclay.*[3]

7. **Elizabeth Barclay,**[2] *b* Shrewsbury, N. J., December 25, 1795; *d* Farmingdale, N. J., August 18, 1883; *m* October 30, 1813, *William Van Benthuysen, b* January 20, 1791; *d* 1825.

(19) *Thomas Van Benthuysen,*[3] *d* in childhood at Charleston, S. C. †

(20) *William Van Benthuysen.*[3]

(21) *Joseph Van Benthuysen,*[3] *d* in childhood at New
       York City. †

8. **Daniel Barclay,**[2] *b* Shrewsbury, N. J., January 1, 1802;
    d New York City, January 21, 1845; *m* November 15,
    1836, *Catherine Granger,* dau. of Francis Granger of
    New York, *b* February 22, 1814; *d* February 6, 1872.

    (22) *Catherine FitzAllen Granger Barclay.*[3]

    (23) *George Ann Granger Barclay.*[3]

    (24) *Charlotte Croton Barclay,*[3] *b* October 15, 1843;
          d unm.

    (25) *Mary Louisa Barclay.*[3]

9. **Daniel Barclay,**[3] *b* August 31, 1825; *d* February 2, 1880;
    m (1) at New York, November 22, 1846, *Elizabeth G.
    Eckerson,* *b* November 18, 1828; *d* May 27, 1867; *m* (2)
    at Albany, N. Y., June 8, 1868, *Rebecca Ann Van
    Patton* (widow of Edward S. Barton), *b* December 3,
    1832; (living 1903).

    (26) *Evelyn Barclay,*[4] *b* August 24, 1847; *d* June 19,
          1888. †

    (27) *Emma E. Barclay,*[4] *b* December 25, 1848; *d*
          August 8, 1870. †

    (28) *Harriet J. Barclay,*[4] *b* July 17, 1850; *d* Sep-
          tember 22, 1851.

    (29) *Marana R. Barclay,*[4] *b* June 7, 1853; *d* Decem-
          ber 28, 1889. †

    (30) *Joseph Barclay,*[4] *b* January 26, 1857. †

    (31) *Idin L. Barclay,*[4] *b* February 8, 1862; *d* Janu-
          ary 9, 1879.

    (32) *Daniel John Barclay,*[4] *b* May 24, 1871; *d*
          March 27, 1872.

    (33) *Daniel Barclay,*[4] *b* June 17, 1874. †

10. **DeWitt Barclay**[3] (M.D.), *b* Cranbury, N. J., February
    8, 1818; *d* Monmouth County, N. J., March 21, 1867;
    m at Freehold, N. J., June 20, 1850, *Margaret Augusta
    Baldwin,* *b* September 25, 1830; *d* February 16, 1866.

(34) *Margaret Augusta Barclay.*[4]

(35) *Joseph Barclay,*[4] *b* November 28, 1852; *d* July 18, 1861.

(36) *George Earl Barclay.*[4]

(37) *Harold Philemon Barclay.*[4]

(38) *William DeWitt Barclay.*[4]

(39) *Ellie Baldwin Barclay,*[4] *b* September 29, 1860; d October 16, 1860.

(40) *DeWitt Barclay,*[4] *b* October 28, 1861; *d* February 4, 1862.

(41) *Robert Hard Barclay.*[4]

(42) *Paul Barclay,*[4] *b* February 6, 1866; *d* April 16, 1867.

11. **Alexander Barclay,**[3] *b* Cranbury, N. J., February 10, 1820; *d* Newark, N. J., January 27, 1881; *m* at Newark, N. J., August 12, 1841, *Charlotte Sophia Hard, b* Newtown, Conn., December 26, 1818; *d* Newark, N. J., February 22, 1881.

(43) *William Barclay,*[4] *b* October 15, 1842; *d* April 11, 1843.

(44) *George Barclay,*[4] *b* January 16, 1844; *d* April 15, 1844.

(45) *Charlotte Hortense Barclay,*[4] *b* April 26, 1846; *d* April 13, 1851.

(46) *Augusta Barclay,*[4] *b* October 6, 1848; *d* October 9, 1851.

(47) *Alexander Barclay.*[4]

(48) *Charlotte Sereno Barclay.*[4]

(49) *John DeWitt Barclay,*[4] *b* August 14, 1856; (living 1903) *unm.*

(50) *Thomas Barclay.*[4]

(51) *Guy Barclay,*[4] *b* July 31, 1860; *d* January 21, 1898, *unm.*

(52) *Howard McClellan Barclay,*[4] *b* August 26, 1862; *d* March 13, 1899, *unm.*

12. **Elizabeth Virginia Barclay,**[3] *b* Cranbury, N. J., February 28, 1822; *d* Brooklyn, N. Y., May 26, 1892; *m* at

Newark, N. J., April 15, 1852, *Reuben Curtis Moffat* (M.D.), *b* Ithaca, N. Y., December 11, 1818; *d* Brooklyn, N. Y., August 28, 1894.

(53) *John Little Moffat.*[4]

(54) *George Barclay Moffat.*[4]

(55) *Edgar Vietor Moffat.*[4]

(56) *Ada Moffat.*[4]

(57) *Lillian Moffat,*[4] *b* August 20, 1859; *d* February 11, 1860.

(58) *R. Burnham Moffat.*[4]

(59) *Mabel Moffat,*[4] *b* March 26, 1863; *d* July 30, 1863.

(60) *Willie Partridge Moffat,*[4] *b* and *d* March 21, 1865.

13. **Annie McChesney Barclay,**[3] *b* Cranbury, N. J., February 14, 1825; *d* Newark, N. J., September 18, 1866; *m* at Newark, N. J., May 10, 1848, *Stephen Richards, Jr., b* West Haven, Conn., May 17, 1817; *d* April 4, 1861.

(61) *Anna Elizabeth Richards,*[4] *b* May 15, 1849; (living 1903 West Haven, Conn.), *unm.*

(62) *Emma Elita Richards,*[4] *b* February 22, 1852; *d* June 7, 1854.

(63) *Susan Amelia Richards,*[4] *b* December 6, 1854; *d* June 4, 1871, *unm.*

(64) *Alexander Barclay Richards,*[4] *b* May 11, 1857; (living 1903 at Brooklyn, N. Y.), *unm.*

(65) *Joseph Albert Richards,*[4] *b* September 19, 1859; *d* January 13, 1882, *unm.*

16. **Caroline Matilda Barclay,**[3] *b* Shrewsbury, N. J., May 19, 1819; *d* March 28, 1842; *m* April 17, 1839, *Joseph T. Allen, b* April 18, 1815; *d* February 25, 1889. (He *m* (2) December 21, 1843, Elizabeth Hartshorne, widow of Tembrook White.)

(66) *William Barclay Allen.*[4]

18. **Caroline Amelia Barclay**[3] (born Caroline Amelia Morrison; adopted as a daughter by Judge Barclay and her

name changed by Act of the Legislature of the State of New Jersey of March 9, 1864), *b* April 15, 1850; (living 1903); *m* at Eatontown, N. J., April 22, 1869, *William R. Stevens, b* 8 September, 1845; (living 1903).

(67) *Maud Barclay Stevens.*[4]
(68) *William Barclay Stevens.*[4]

20. **William Van Benthuysen,**[3] *b* New York, January 18, 1819; *d* Farmingdale, N. J., June 30, 1889; *m* (1) at New York October 17, 1843, *Julia A. Fairchild, b* New York, July 10, 1824; *d* Brooklyn, N. Y., February 12, 1866; *m* (2) February 18, 1872, *Louisa Mahala Tirby, b* August 22, 1839; (living 1903).

(69) *Elizabeth Van Benthuysen.*[4]
(70) *Thomas Van Benthuysen.*[4]
(71) *Joseph Barclay Van Benthuysen,*[4] *b* January 17, 1853; (living 1903) *unm.*
(72) *Mary Van Benthuysen,*[4] *b* August 26, 1855; *d* February 1, 1856.
(73) *William Van Benthuysen,*[4] *b* November 21, 1857; *d* December 22, 1877.

22. **Catherine FitzAllen Granger Barclay,**[3] *b* September 21, 1837; *m* at Brooklyn, N. Y., 1854, *Edward Logan.* †
(74) *Edward Daniel Barclay Logan,*[4] *b* January 6, 1856. †

(75) *Georgina Mather Logan,*[4] *b* March 6, 1859. †

23. **George Ann Granger Barclay,**[3] *b* September 13, 1839; *d* April 3, 1892; *m* May 16, 1867, *Christian Van Blarcom, b* July 15, 1831; (living 1903).

(76) *Catherine Elizabeth Van Blarcom.*[4]

25. **Mary Louisa Barclay,**[3] *b* January 15, 1845; *d* June 3, 1877; *m* February 22, 1867, *John H. Boehm.* †
(77) *George M. L. Boehm.*[4] †
(78) *Daniel Barclay Boehm.*[4] †

34. **Margaret Augusta Barclay,**[4] *b* April 10, 1851; *d* Eden Prairie, Minn., August 18, 1878; *m* January 29, 1874, *William Augustus Hankins, b* March 31, 1844; *d* September 25, 1893.

> (79) *George Valentine Hankins,*[5] *b* July 8, 1875; (living 1903), *unm.*

36. **George Earl Barclay,**[4] *b* September 14, 1854; *d* Lennox, South Dakota, February 7, 1899; *m* September 10, 1882, *Harriet Ophelia McCartney, b* December 29, 1863; (living 1903).

> (80) *Margaret Augusta Barclay,*[5] *b* October 14, 1885; (living 1903).
>
> (81) *Roberta Ophelia Barclay,*[5] *b* January 4, 1888; (living 1903).

37. **Harold Philemon Barclay,**[4] *b* October 29, 1856; (living 1903); *m* at Stillwater, Minn., October 18, 1883, *Henrietta Durant, b* October 5, 1857; (living 1903).

> (82) *Durant Barclay,*[5] *b* July 18, 1884; (living 1903).
>
> (83) *Robert Barclay,*[5] *b* May 11, 1886; *d* December 3, 1886.
>
> (84) *Margaret Barclay,*[5] *b* February 14, 1888; (living 1903).
>
> (85) *DeWitt Barclay,*[5] *b* May 16, 1899; (living 1903).
>
> (86) *Marion Barclay,*[5] *b* March 7, 1901; (living 1903).

38. **William DeWitt Barclay,**[4] *b* November 30, 1858; *d* Camden, S. C., December 14, 1893; *m* at Brooklyn, N. Y., February 24, 1887, *May S. Cook,* dau. of Elias Cook of Trenton, N. J., *b* February 28, 1866; *d* Camden, S. C., January 24, 1896.

> (87) *Frances Cook Barclay,*[5] *b* December 15, 1887; *d* August 4, 1888.
>
> (88) *Helen Barclay,*[5] *b* June 22, 1890; (living 1903).

41. **Robert Hard Barclay,**[4] *b* April 8, 1863; (living 1903);
   m at Helena, Montana, April 29, 1891, *Elizabeth Jefferis,*
   b August 4, 1869; (living 1903.) S. P.

47. **Alexander Barclay,**[4] *b* Newark, N. J., April 18, 1852;
   (living 1903 in St. Paul, Minn.) ; *m* at St. Paul, Minn.,
   August 13, 1881, *Effie M. Rogers, b* New York City,
   May 11, 1859; (living 1903).

   (89) *Alexander Barclay,*[5] *b* August 12, 1882; (living
        1903).
   (90) *Gladys Barclay,*[5] *b* June 13, 1886; (living 1903).

48. **Charlotte Sereno Barclay,**[4] *b* Newark, N. J., August 23,
   1854; *d* Newark, N. J., October 18, 1888; *m* Newark,
   N. J., September 13, 1876, *Edward Dickerson, b* Newark,
   N. J., June 11, 1851 ; *d* Newbern, N. C., August 1, 1896.

   (91) *Charlotte Virginia Dickerson,*[5] *b* July 26, 1877;
        (living 1903).
   (92) *Edward Dickerson,*[5] *b* January 23, 1879; *d*
        December 28, 1885.
   (93) *Bertram Dickerson,*[5] *b* September 16, 1880; *d*
        July 31, 1881.
   (94) *Charlotte Hard Dickerson,*[5] *b* February 17,
        1882; *d* January 5, 1886.
   (95) *Alexander Barclay Dickerson,*[5] *b* July 10, 1887;
        (living 1903.)

50. **Thomas Barclay,**[4] *b* Newark, N. J., November 12, 1858;
   (living 1903 at Newark, N. J.) ; *m* Newark, N. J., August 30, 1888, *Constance Marie Beatrice Cadiz* (widow
   of William D. Paterson), *b* Trinidad, W. I., December
   25, 1858; (living 1903).

   (96) *Constance Barclay,*[5] *b* April 27, 1890; (living
        1903).
   (97) *Thomas Barclay,*[5] *b* November 28, 1892; (living
        1903).
   (98) *Helen Barclay,*[5] *b* April 22, 1895; *d* April 22,
        1895.

53. **John Little Moffat**[4] (M.D.), *b* Brooklyn, N. Y., June 14, 1853; (living 1903 at Brooklyn, N. Y.); *m* at Bath Beach, N. Y., April 18, 1893, *Elizabeth Mary Rhodes, b* Antigua, W. I., February 6, 1868; (living 1903).

> (99) *John Little Moffat,*[5] *b* January 21, 1894; (living 1903).
>
> (100) *Helen Moffat,*[5] *b* September 21, 1895; (living 1903).
>
> (101) *Reuben Curtis Moffat,*[5] *b* April 24, 1897; (living 1903).

54. **George Barclay Moffat,**[4] *b* Brooklyn, N. Y., September 29, 1854; (living 1903 in New York City); *m* at Brooklyn, N. Y., October 10, 1888, *Frances Hillard White, b* Brooklyn, N. Y., August 10, 1869; (living 1903).

> (102) *Alexander White Moffat,*[5] *b* June 26, 1891; (living 1903).
>
> (103) *Donald Moffat,*[5] *b* July 18, 1894; (living 1903).
>
> (104) *George Barclay Moffat,*[5] *b* May 16, 1897; (living 1903).
>
> (105) *Frances White Moffat,*[5] *b* November 21, 1899; (living 1903).

55. **Edgar Vietor Moffat**[4] (M.D.), *b* Brooklyn, N. Y., June 20, 1856; (living 1903 at Orange, N. J.); *m* at Brookline, Mass., June 1, 1887, *Edith Wellington, b* Brookline, Mass., May 11, 1858; (living 1903).

> (106) *Harold Wellington Moffat,*[5] *b* November 26, 1888; (living 1903).
>
> (107) *Barclay Wellington Moffat,*[5] *b* July 9, 1890; (living 1903).
>
> (108) *Virginia Moffat,*[5] *b* July 8, 1892; (living 1903).
>
> (109) *Ethel Moffat,*[5] *b* April 21, 1894; (living 1903).
>
> (110) *Constance Moffat,*[5] *b* November 23, 1898; (living 1903).

56. **Ada Moffat,**[4] *b* Brooklyn, N. Y., March 21, 1858; (living 1903, at Germantown, Pa.); *m* Brooklyn, N. Y., No-

vember 17, 1885, *John McLean Lachlan, b* Melbourne, Australia, May 31, 1861; (living 1903). S. P.

58. **R. Burnham Moffat,**[4] *b* Brooklyn, N. Y., January 7, 1861; living 1903 in New York City); *m* at Brooklyn, N. Y., June 5, 1895, *Ellen Low Pierrepont, b* Brooklyn, N. Y., April 15, 1872; (living 1903).

> (111) *Jay Pierrepont Moffat,*[5] *b* July 18, 1896; (living 1903).
>
> (112) *Elizabeth Barclay Moffat,*[5] *b* June 26, 1898; (living 1903).
>
> (113) *Abbot Low Moffat,*[5] *b* May 12, 1901; (living 1903).

66. **William Barclay Allen,**[4] *b* March 6, 1840; *d* July 24, 1874; *m Mary Elizabeth Dangler, d* 1891. †

> (114) *Joseph Barclay Allen,*[5] *b* August 6, 1861; (living 1903), *unm.*
>
> (115) *Edmund Williams Allen,*[5] *b* April 27, 1863; (living 1903), *unm.*
>
> (116) *William Barclay Allen.*[5]
>
> (117) *John Lee Allen,*[5] *b* May 5, 1870; (living 1903), *unm.*
>
> (118) *Eugene Young Allen,*[5] *b* September 11, 1872; *d* December 3, 1876.

67. **Maud Barclay Stevens,**[4] *b* 26 February, 1871; (living 1903 at Eatontown, N. J.); *m* Shrewsbury, N. J., 14 January, 1892, *Harry Campbell, b* 13 June, 1865; (living 1903), S. P.

68. **William Barclay Stevens,**[4] *b* July 16, 1873; (living 1903); *m* June 20, 1892, *Anna Williams* of Trenton, N. J., *b* 28 December, 1872; (living 1903).

> (119) *William Roy Stevens,*[5] *b* March 20, 1893; (living 1903).

69. **Elizabeth Van Benthuysen,**[4] b Monmouth County, N. J., October 2, 1846; (living 1903 at New London, Conn.);

m New York City, January 24, 1869, *Edward Smith, b* Norwich, Conn., October 22, 1833; (living 1903).

- (120) *Edward Lecompte Smith.*[5]
- (121) *Harold Eugene Smith,*[5] *b* February 9, 1877; *d* November 14, 1894.

70. **Thomas Van Benthuysen,**[4] *b* December 26, 1849; (living 1903 at Farmingdale, N. J.); *m* June 18, 1874, *Margaret Logan, b* July 26, 1853; (living 1903).

- (122) *William Van Benthuysen.*[5]
- (123) *Julia Van Benthuysen.*[5]
- (124) *Thomas Van Benthuysen,*[5] *b* December 20, 1878; *d* December 23, 1878.
- (125) *Joseph Van Benthuysen,*[5] *b* December 20, 1878; *d* December 23, 1878.
- (126) *Seth L. Van Benthuysen,*[5] *b* November 9, 1883; (living 1903).
- (127) *Louisa Van Benthuysen,*[5] *b* January 22, 1885; (living 1903).
- (128) *Ellen Van Benthuysen,*[5] *b* June 1, 1888; (living 1903).
- (129) *John L. Van Benthuysen,*[5] *b* May 9, 1890; *d* December 22, 1890.
- (130) *McKinley Van Benthuysen,*[5] *b* March 28, 1893; (living 1903).
- (131) *Harold Van Benthuysen,*[5] *b* March 6, 1895; *d* August 7, 1895.

76. **Catherine Elizabeth Van Blarcom,**[4] *m* December 12, 1880, *Charles S. Hathaway, b* August 16, 1860; (living 1898).

- (132) *Herbert Warren Hathaway,*[5] *b* November 14, 1895; (living 1898).

116. **William Barclay Allen,**[5] *b* August 27, 1865; (living 1903); *m* November 22, 1898, *Charlotte Smith.* †

120. **Edward Lecompte Smith,**[5] *b* June 24, 1873; (living 1903); *m* May 12, 1900, *Louise May Smith, b* December 1, 1875; (living 1903).

> (133) *Harold Edward Smith,*[6] *b* May 15, 1902; (living 1903).

122. **William Van Benthuysen,**[5] *b* June 22, 1875; (living 1903); *m* January 27, 1896, *Agnes Roemer, b* December 17, 1875; *d* June 18, 1900.

> (134) *Lottie Van Benthuysen,*[6] *b* March 18, 1897; (living 1903).

123. **Julia Van Benthuysen,**[5] *b* January 26, 1877; (living 1903); *m* December 12, 1900, *Chester J. G. Stillwell, b* 23 April, 1880; (living 1093).

> (135) *Marguerite Stillwell,*[6] *b* January 3, 1902; (living 1903).

PART VII.

Line of Descent from Rev. Thomas Barclay, the first Rector of St. Peter's Church at Albany.

IT SEEMS to have been generally assumed, although erroneously, that Rev. Thomas Barclay had but three sons,—Thomas, Henry and Andrew. Mr. George L. Rives, in his book already referred to,—"Correspondence of Thomas Barclay" (New York, Harper & Bros., 1894),—states that the sons were Thomas, *Anthony* and Henry, and that *Anthony* married Helena, daughter of Jacobus Roosevelt; but this was undoubtedly a mere clerical error on the part of Mr. Rives. There was no *Anthony* in the family until Rev. Henry Barclay so named his second son, in honor, doubtless, of the boy's maternal grandfather, Col. Anthony Rutgers.[1]

That Rev. Thomas Barclay had *four* children is certain from his wife's letter to the Society for the Propagation of the Gospel, under date of May 22, 1722, quoted in Part II above; and that the fourth child was also a son and bore the name *John,* are the only inferences which it seems to the writer the facts about to be considered will permit.

In the office of the Surrogate of New York County, in Liber 36 of Wills, at page 194, is recorded the will of "John Barclay, mayor of the City of Albany." This will was dated January 30th, 1779, and was proved before the Surrogate of Albany County on June 20th, 1783. It refers to a previous wife of the testator, without naming her; appoints his present wife, *Margaret,* an executrix, and gives to her a life interest in his residuary estate; makes specific bequests to "Charlotte, wife of Coenradt Ten Eyck" and to "Peter Ten Eyck, son of Andries Ten Eyck;" and then, and upon the death of his wife, gives one half of his residuary estate to "the children" (unfortunately not naming

---

[1] See Rev. HENRY BARCLAY's will, proved October 1, 1764, and recorded in the office of the Surrogate of New York County in liber 24 of Wills, at page 498; also, ANDREW BARCLAY's will, proved May 25, 1776, and recorded in the same office in liber 30 of Wills, at page 184.

them) "of my brother Andrew Barclay, *lately deceased,*" and the other half to "the children" (also not naming them) "of my *late* "brother, Henry Barclay, deceased." The records just cited show that Andrew Barclay's will was proved May 25th, 1776, and that Rev. Henry Barclay's will had been proved many years before,—on October 1st, 1764.

It would indeed be a strange coincidence if there were two Barclay families of prominence at that time so closely identified with the City of Albany, in each of which there were three sons named, respectively, Henry, Andrew and John; and the coincidence would be still more marked if the Andrew and the Henry in each of these families had died at about the same time,—the Andrews within a comparatively short time before the month of January, 1779, and the Henrys some years before. The coincidence would be too extraordinary for acceptance without further circumstances to support it; and it seems to the writer that as Mrs. Barclay's letter of May 22, 1722, conclusively establishes that Rev. Thomas Barclay had *four* children instead of three, it may reasonably be assumed that the fourth child was a son named John, who subsequently became Mayor of the City of Albany.

The will of John Barclay, Mayor of Albany, makes no mention of any issue who might survive him, and the disposition of his residuary estate, in the manner above pointed out, permits the inference that he died without issue.

Furthermore, the records at Albany show that throughout the revolutionary struggle this John Barclay was an earnest patriot and zealously supported the cause of the colonies.[2] Col. Thomas Barclay (a son of Rev. Henry), on the other hand, and his brothers-in-law, Stephen de Lancey and Beverley Robinson, were ardent loyalists and fought for the King. Although John Barclay, of Albany, evidently did not choose that these differences should sunder the ties of blood, the fact that his name has wholly disappeared from the more or less plastic charts of the family that have come down to the Barclays of to-day, is probably trace-

---

[2]In the NEW YORK JOURNAL AND GENERAL ADVERTISER of September 15, 1777, is a letter of congratulation from *John Barclay,* Chairman of the Committee of the City of Albany, addressed at Albany, under date of August 20, 1777, to George Clinton, "Governor-General and Commander-in-Chief of all the Militia, and Admiral of the "Navy of the State of New York."

able to the bitterness with which the loyalist descendents of Rev. Thomas regarded a "rebel," even of their own kith and kin.

John Barclay was a prominent member, and vestryman, of St. Peter's Church at Albany both before and during the exciting incumbency of Rev. Harry Munro,[3] and seems in all ways to have been a man of strength and of influence in the community. His first wife was *Gerritje Coeymans* (*bap* 21 October, 1722), daughter of Pieter Barentse Coeymans, who had married 5 October, 1713, Elizabeth Greveraad;[4] and his second wife was *Margaret Ten Eyck*. The list of marriage licenses issued out of the Provincial Secretary's office at Albany, shows that on August 28th, 1771, a marriage license was granted to *John Barclay* and *Margaret Ten Eyck*;[5] and the parish records of St. Peter's Church contain an entry that on September 8th, 1771, John Barclay was married "by license." Curiously enough, the parish records do not state to whom he was married.

That John Barclay died before the expiration of his term of office as mayor (it was his only term), is shown by the following extract from the Records of the City of Albany:

"Albany Common Council Chamber 4 March 1779

"The Worshipful *John Barclay* Esq., late Mayor of this City having departed this Life and the honorable Abraham Ten Broeck Esquire having on the 18th day of February last been appointed by the honorable Council of Appointment of this State to succeed the said John Barclay Esq., deceased, in the Chief Magistracy of this City, a Commission of which appointment he produced to the following Members of the Corporation in whose presence he took the oath appointed by Law and was sworn to the due execution of his respective offices * * * * * * *[6]

It would appear from this that he died on February 18th, 1779,—or possibly on the preceding day; but none of the contemporary newspapers which the writer has been able to find, nor indeed any other record, gives definite information as to the date of his death.

Practically nothing is known of Rev. Thomas Barclay's oldest son, *Thomas Barclay*, beyond the fact that he died un-

---

[3] See HISTORY OF ST. PETER'S CHURCH AT ALBANY, by Rev. Joseph Hooper, M. A. Albany: Brandow Printing Co., 1900.

[4] See GENEALOGIES OF FIRST SETTLERS OF ALBANY, Munsell & Co., p. 32.

[5] See MARRIAGE BOOK, vol. XVII, p. 165.

[6] COLLECTIONS OF THE HISTORY OF ALBANY. J. Munsell, 1865. Vol. I, p. 292.

married. At least the statement that he "died unmarried" appears on several of the charts which have come to the writer's notice, and nothing has thus far developed which suggests a doubt as to the accuracy of such statement. Neither the date of his birth nor the date of his death is recorded on any of the charts.

The line of descent from Rev. Thomas Barclay through his other sons, Henry and Andrew, is rather generally known. Yet in many surprising instances absolute ignorance exists of the dates of birth, death or marriage of even comparatively recent descendants of this well-known ancestor. The writer has undertaken,—and it has proved no easy task,—to compile a table, brought down to the present day, of *all* descendants of Rev. Thomas Barclay; and he believes that what follows is substantially correct. The dates, for the most part, have been furnished him from the private records of the various families in the line of descent, and he would be glad to give, upon request therefor, his authority for any name or date which appears in this table. At the same time he would welcome the correction of error and the supplying of any omitted name or date.

The appearance of a † after a name in the table indicates that the writer is without further information concerning such person or his or her possible issue.

1. **Rev. Thomas Barclay,**[1] first rector of St. Peter's Church at Albany; *b* (probably) 1668; *d* (probably) 1725; *m Anna Dorothea Drauyer,* dau. of Capt. Andries Drauyer (a Dane in the Dutch Navy) and Gertrud Van Schaick, his wife.

    (2) *Thomas Barclay.*[2] †
    (3) *Henry Barclay.*[2]
    (4) *Andrew Barclay.*[2]
    (5) *John Barclay.*[2]

3. **Henry Barclay,**[2] the second rector of Trinity Church, New York, *b* 1712;[7] *d* 20 August, 1764;[7] *m* 15 Decem-

---

[7]From New York Mercury of Monday, 27 August, 1764:

"Last Monday Morning" (i. e., August 20) "between three and four o'Clock, departed this Life in the 53d Year of his Age, the Rev'd Mr. Henry Barclay, D. D., Rector of Trinity Church in this City."

ber, 1749,[8] *Mary Rutgers, b* 1723;[9] *d* 8 June, 1788,[9]; dau. of Col. Anthony Rutgers and Hendricke Vander-water, his wife.

> (6) *Thomas H. Barclay.*[3]
> (7) *Anthony Barclay.*[3]
> (8) *Catherine Barclay,*[3] *d unm.* †
> (9) *Cornelia Barclay.*[3]
> (10) *Anna Dorothea Barclay.*[3]

4. **Andrew Barclay,**[2] *b* October, 1719; *d* 19 June, 1775;[10] *m* 14 June, 1737, *Helena Roosevelt, b* 8 October, 1719; *bur* 25 May, 1772,[11] dau. of Jacobus Roosevelt and Catharina Hardenbroek, his wife.

> (11) *Thomas Barclay,*[3] *d unm.*[12] †
> (12) *James Barclay.*[3]
> (13) *Henry Barclay,*[3] *d unm.*[12] †
> (14) *John Barclay.*[3] [13] †

[8]From New York Gazette of Friday, 18 December, 1749:

"On Tuesday evening last" (*i. e.,* December 15) "the Reverend Mr. BARCLAY, Rector of Trinity Church, in this City, was married to Miss RUTGERS, Daughter of the late Capt. Anthony Rutgers."

[9]From The Daily Advertiser of Wednesday, 11 June, 1788:

"On Sunday evening last departed this life in the 66th year of her age Mrs. MARY BARCLAY, relict of the worthy Dr. *Barclay,* formerly Rector of Trinity Church in this City.

"Panegyrics on departed friends are generally said to be 'gilding their dust,' but the hearts of all who knew Mrs. BARCLAY will testify to her worth. From a long and intimate acquaintance with the precepts of christianity, she fulfilled its duties with uniformity and zeal, the reward of which she is now reaping, while her children must deplore the loss of a most tender parent, the poor a chearful contributor and all her acquaintance a pleasing friend."

[10]From Rivington's New York Gazetteer of Thursday, 22 June, 1775:

"On Monday last" (*i. e.,* June 19) "died Mr. ANDREW BARCLAY, an eminent merchant and brother of the Rev. Dr. *Barclay,* late Rector of this Parish, a most worthy and exemplary citizen, universally beloved by all who knew him."

[11]From Year Book of the Holland Society of New York, 1899, p. 143:

"Record of Burials in the Dutch Church, New York. 1772, May 25: Wife " of ANDREW BARCLAY."

[12]See "Smaller New York and Family Reminiscences," by Oscar Egerton Schmidt. Printed privately, New York, 1899. A copy may be found in the library of the Long Island Historical Society, at Brooklyn, N. Y.

[13]In Mr. Schmidt's book, above cited, it is stated that this *John Barclay* married one *Catherine Murray* and had issue; but there does not seem to be authority for such statement. The records of the First and Second Presbyterian churches in the City of New York refer to the marriage of a John Barclay and a Catherine Murray (See Part XI, below); but there is no reason to believe that the John Barclay there referred to was a son of Andrew Barclay and Helena Roosevelt.

(15) *Ann Dorothy Barclay.*3

(16) *Catherine Barclay.*3

(17) *Sarah Barclay.*3

(18) *Ann Margaret Barclay.*3

(19) *Helena Barclay.*3

(20) *Charlotte Amelia Barclay.*3

5. **John Barclay,**2 mayor of the City of Albany 1778--79, *d* (probably) 18 February 1779; *m* (1) *Gerritje Coeymans, bap* 21 October, 1722; dau. of Pieter Barentse Coeymans and Elizabeth Greveraad, his wife; *m* (2) 8 September, 1771, (license dated 28 August, 1771), *Margaret Ten Eyck.* O. S. P.

6. **Thomas H. Barclay,**3 14 *b* 12 October, 1753; *d* 21 April, 1830; *m* 2 October, 1775,15 *Susanna De Lancey, b* 15

14While Col. THOMAS BARCLAY's baptismal name was "Thomas H." he seems in later years to have dropped the middle letter and was generally spoken of as "Col. Thomas Barclay."

He entered the British army in 1776, and in the following February was made Captain in the Loyal American Regiment of New Yorkers. In 1780 he became Major in a corps of light infantry, and served in Virginia and Carolina. While on his way from Charleston to the Chesapeake with despatches from Lord Rawdon to Earl Cornwallis, he was captured by the French fleet but was soon exchanged and rejoined his regiment, with which he remained until it was disbanded in 1783. In the fall of that year he took his family to Nova Scotia and engaged in farming at Wilmot. In 1789 he commenced the practice of law at Annapolis Royal and was soon elected to the Provincial Assembly. For several years he was speaker of the Assembly. In 1792 he was made Lieut.-Colonel of the Royal Nova Scotia Regiment, and in 1793 was made Adjutant-General of the Militia of the Province. In 1796 he was appointed a commissioner for the British under Jay's treaty, and in 1799 was made British Consul-General for the Eastern States of America, resident at New York. He held this office until 1812. In 1814 he was appointed British commissioner under the Treaty of Ghent in which service he continued until 1828, when he retired from the office (N. Y. GEN. & BIOG. REC., vol. IV, page 173).

15Col. *Thomas Barclay* and *John Watts, Jr.,* married sisters. Their wedding was a double one, and is thus described in Rivington's NEW YORK GAZETTEER of Thursday, 5 October, 1775:

"On Monday evening last" (*i. e.,* October 2nd) "were married at Union Hill, "in the borough of Westchester, JOHN WATTS, junior, Esquire, recorder of this city, "to Miss JANE DeLANCEY; and THOMAS H. BARCLAY, Esq., to Miss SUSSANNA De-"LANCEY, daughters of the late Peter DeLancey, Esq.

> " * * * Round their nuptial beds
> Hovering with purple wings, th' Idalian boy
> Shook from his radiant torch the blissful fires
>   Of innocent desires
> While Venus scattered myrtles.''

September, 1754; *d* 2 May, 1837,[16] dau. of Peter De-
Lancey (*b* 10 January, 1708) and Elizabeth Colden (*b*
5 February, 1720), who were married on January 12th,
1733.

(21) *Eliza Barclay.*[4]

(22) *Henry Barclay.*[4]

(23) *DeLancey Barclay.*[4]

(24) *Maria Barclay.*[4]

(25) *Thomas Edmund Barclay.*[4]

(26) *Susan Barclay.*[4]

(27) *Beverley Robinson Barclay,*[4] *b* at Wilmot, Nova
Scotia, 22 December, 1786; *d* 15 January,
1803.[17]

(28) *Anne Barclay.*[4]

(29) *George Cornwell Barclay.*[4]

(30) *Anthony Barclay.*[4]

(31) *Clement Horton Barclay,*[4] *b* at Annapolis, N.
S., 3 August, 1796; *d* 21 August, 1797.

(32) *Cornelia Elizabeth Stewart Barclay,*[4] *b* at New
York, 23 May 1801; *d* 28 June, 1801.

7. **Anthony Barclay,**[3] *b* 1755; *d* 23 August, 1805; *m Anna
Lent,* dau. of James Lent of Long Island.

(33) *Henry Barclay.*[4]

9. **Cornelia Barclay,**[3] *m* (1) 16 June, 1773,[18] *Stephen De-
Lancey; m* (2) *Gen'l Sir Hudson Lowe, K.C.B.*

(34) *Susan DeLancey,*[4] *m Col. William Johnson.* †

---

[16]Records of St. Mark's Church, New York.

[17]From THE WEEKLY MUSEUM of Saturday, 18 January, 1803:

"*Died:* On Wednesday Morning, BEVERLEY ROBINSON BARCLAY, fourth son of
his Britannic Majesty's Consul-General, etc., an amiable and most promising youth."

[18]From THE NEW YORK JOURNAL of Thursday, 17 June, 1773:

"Last Night, at the House of Mrs. Barclay, in this City, was celebrated a Marriage between STEPHEN DELANCEY, Esq., Son of the Hon. Col. Oliver DeLancey, and
Miss BARCLAY, eldest Daughter of the Rev. Doctor *Barclay,* the late revered and beloved Rector of Trinity Church. This amiable Couple have the most rational Prospect
of all the Happiness the marriage State can afford."

10. **Anna Dorothea Barclay,**[3] *b* 21 January, 1755; *d* 11 April, 1806; *m* 21 January, 1778,[19] Lieut.-Col. *Beverley Robinson, b* 8 March, 1754; *d* 6 October, 1816.

> (35) *Beverley Robinson.*[4]
>
> (36) *Susanna Maria Robinson,*[4] *b* 10 August, 1780; *d* 12 August, 1780.
>
> (37) *Henry Clinton Robinson,*[4] *b* 21 March, 1782; *d* (prob.) 31 December, 1804. O. S. P.
>
> (38) *Morris Robinson.*[4]
>
> (39) *Frederick Philipse Robinson.*[4]
>
> (40) *Thomas Barclay Robinson,*[4] *b* 26 September, 1786; *d* 2 June, 1804,[20] *unm.*
>
> (41) *John Robinson.*[4]
>
> (42) *Susanna Philipse Robinson.*[4]
>
> (43) *William Henry Robinson.*[4]
>
> (44) *Cornelia Robinson,*[4] *b* 2 September, 1794; *d* 22 September, 1794.

12. **James Barclay,**[3] *b* 1750; *d* 15 March, 1791;[21] *m* (license dated 21 November, 1772),[22] 24 November, 1772,[23] *Maria van Beverhoudt, b* 1752; *d* 5 July, 1791.[24]

---

[19]From THE NEW YORK GAZETTE of Monday, 26 January, 1778:

"Wednesday last" (*i. e.*, January 21st) "was married at Flushing, Long Island, BEVERLEY ROBINSON, jun., Esq., Lieut.-Col. of the Loyal American Regiment, to the amiable and accomplished Miss NANCY BARCLAY, youngest daughter of the Rev'd Dr. *Barclay,* formerly Rector of Trinity Church in this Place."

[20]From ST. JOHN (N. B.) GAZETTE of Monday, 4 June, 1804:

"On Saturday last" (that is 2 June, 1804) "Ensign (Thomas Barclay) Robinson, son of Hon. Col. Beverley Robinson, returning with a party of men from pursuing some deserters, was drowned near Sandy Point (in the Kennebecasis River, about five miles from St. John) by the upsetting of a canoe. The men saved themselves by swimming to shore."

[21]From the NEW YORK PACKET of Thursday, 17 March, 1791:

"*Died:* On Tuesday morning" (*i. e.*, March 15th) "at his house in Hanover Square, of a lingering illness, Mr. JAMES BARCLAY."

Another paper describes him as "vendue master" in the 42nd year of his age.

[22]See the old Dutch New Testament, formerly belonging to MARIA VAN BEVER-HOUDT, now in the library of the Long Island Historical Society.

[23]Records of TRINITY PARISH, New York.

[24]From the NEW YORK PACKET of Thursday, 14 July, 1791:

"On the 5th instant departed this life, Mrs. MARIA BARCLAY, the widow of Mr. *James Barclay,* in the 40th year of her age, and yesterday her remains were interred in the family vault in Trinity Church Yard.

"She has left nine children to lament the loss of a most affectionate and valuable

(45) *Andrew D. Barclay,*[4] *b* 30 August, 1773.[25] †

(46) *Margaretta Barclay,*[4] *b* 24 September, 1774;[22] *d* 26 December, 1791,[26] *unm.*

(47) *Maria Barclay,*[4] *b* at New Barbadoes Neck, N. J., 19 March, 1776.[22] †

(48) *Helena Barclay,*[4] *b* at New York, 25 October, 1777;[22] *d* 3 November, 1796.[27]

(49) *James Barclay,*[4] *b* at New York, 7 April, 1779;[22] *d* 10 July, 1779.[22]

(50) *Ann Dorothy Barclay,*[4] *b* at New York, 5 November, 1780;[22] *d* 1 July, 1801,[28] *unm.*

---

parent,—the eldest, a youth who lately entered into business to assist his widowed mother, is now become the chief support of the unfortunate orphans; and as he uniformly maintained an unblemished reputation and shewn himself possessed of talents fully adequate to the business he is engaged in, it is not to be doubted but every person of humanity will make a point of encouraging him."

[25]See "Nominations of the Subscribers to the TONTINE COFFEE HOUSE," New York, 1796. A copy may be found in the library of the New York Historical Society.

[26]From NEW YORK DAILY GAZETTE of Thursday, 29 December, 1791:

"*Died:* On Monday, the 26th inst., in the 18th year of her age, Miss MARGARET BARCLAY, the eldest daughter of James and Maria Barclay, deceased, and yesterday her remains were interred in the family vault of Trinity Church, attended by her relations and friends. The affectionate and sympathetic heart which this amiable young woman possessed was too sensibly affected with the loss which the family sustained in the death of their worthy parents, for so delicate a constitution to survive them long. She was truly an example of piety and waited her dissolution with the utmost patience and resignation."

[27]From THE WEEEKLY MUSEUM of Saturday, 12 November, 1796:

"*Died:* On Thursday evening, the 3rd inst., after a long and painful illness, which she bore with uncommon patience and resignation, Miss HELENA BARCLAY (daughter of Mr. James Barclay, deceased), aged 19 years. Her remains were interred in the family vault in Trinity Church Yard, attended by her relations and friends, who sincerely lament the loss of this truly amiable young woman."

[28]From THE SPECTATOR (New York) of Wednesday, 15 July, 1801:

"*Died:* At Newark, the 1st inst., Miss ANN BARCLAY, late of this city, in the 21st year of her age.

"Miss Barclay possessed a most amiable disposition, delicate sensibility, and an heart modest, pure, benevolent and susceptible of the most refined friendship; her manners were polite and engaging, and such were her virtues, good qualities and deportment that she greatly endeared herself to all her friends and acquaintance. She had an high reverence for religion; her practice of it was uniform, sincere and unaffected. In health, it afforded her the sublimest enjoyments and enabled her to sustain a tedious, painful illness with patience, fortitude and entire resignation to the will of Heaven. To her, DEATH had no *Terror!* She beheld its approach not only with serenity, but even with complacency. She spoke with holy rapture of the blessed change she was about to experience, and after having in the most affectionate manner, taken leave of her friends, she literally smiled in Death and left the world with rational, with assured hopes of blessed immortality! To her, then, how import-

(51) *James Barclay*,[4] *b* at New York, 9 December,
        1781;[22] *d* 12 February, 1782.[22]

(52) *Frederick Jay Barclay*,[4] *b* 3 December,
        1782.[22, 25] †

(53) *Catherine Eliza Barclay*.[4]

(54) *Sarah Amelia Barclay*,[4] *b* at New York 22
        April, 1784;[22] *d* 28 September, 1786.[22]
        (Catherine Eliza and Sarah Amelia were
        twins.)

(55) *Johannes van Beverhoudt Barclay*,[4] *b* at New
        York, 5 May, 1785.[22] †

(56) *Juliana Susanna Barclay*,[4] *b* at New York, 6
        May, 1786;[22] *d* 26 May, 1807,[29] *unm.*

(57) *Sarah Amelia Barclay*,[4] *b* at New York, 6 Janu-
        ary, 1788;[22] *d* 22 August, 1788.[22]

(58) *Charlotte Matilda Barclay*,[4] *b* at New York, 12
        April, 1789.[22] †

15. **Ann Dorothy Barclay**,[3] *b* on the Island of Curacoa, 29
     September, 1741; *d* in New York, 7 November, 1795;
     m 16 October, 1750,[39] *Theophylact Bache, b* at Settle,
     Yorkshire, 17 January, 1734/5;[31] came to New York 17

---

ant was *true* RELIGION? And how important to ALL? This Young Lady was a
bright ornament of it, and of her sex has left them an EXAMPLE worthy of imitation!

> "Best Maid, adieu! indulge the falling tear!
> For thee we weep, tho' we have naught to fear!
> Thy virtues charm'd! thy goodness won the heart!
> But, no more to us dost thou joy impart!
> Short was thy life! Torn from our fond embrace!
> We grieve; but submit to the God of grace!
> He saw thee pure, fit for the realms above!
> And call'd thee hence, in mercy and in love!"

[29]From THE WEEKLY MUSEUM of Saturday, 30 May, 1807:
    "*Died:* On Tuesday" (*i. e.,* May 26th) "in the 22nd year of her age, Miss
JULIAN SUSANNAH BARCLAY, daughter of the late Mr. James Barclay." The funeral
was held from the house of Mr. James Bleecker, 86 Water Street.

[30]From Gaines' NEW YORK MERCURY of Monday, 20 October, 1760:
    "Thursday Night last" (*i. e.,* October 16th) "Mr. *Theophilact Bache* of this
City, Merchant, was married to Miss NANCY BARCLAY, Daughter of Andrew Barclay,
of this Place, Merchant, a Lady of great Beauty and Merit, with a handsome Fortune."

[31]*Richard Bache,* the head of the Philadelphia family of that name, was a
younger brother of *Theophylact Bache.* He was born in Settle, Yorkshire, 12 September, 1737; *d* 29 July, 1811; *m* at Philadelphia, 29 October, 1767, *Sarah Franklin,*
b 11 September, 1743; *d* 5 October, 1808, dau. of Benjamin Franklin. (See SMALLER
NEW YORK AND FAMILY REMINISCENCES, by Oscar Egerton Schmidt, above referred
to).

September, 1751; *d* 30 October, 1807. His funeral was held at the house of his son-in-law, Charles McEvers, Jr., Wall Street, near William Street.

(59) *Elizabeth Garland Bache.*[4]

(60) *Helena Bache,*[4] *b* 15 September, 1764;[12] *d* at Flatbush, L. I., 15 December, 1778.[32]

(61) *Mary Bache.*[4]

(62) *Paul Richard Bache.*[4]

(63) *William Bache,*[4] *b* 10 January, 1769;[12] *d* 15 October, 1770.[12]

(64) *Andrew Barclay Bache.*[4]

(65) *Ann Dorothy Bache.*[4]

(66) *William Bache.*[4]

(67) *Sarah Bache.*[4]

(68) *Catherine Bache.*[4]

(69) *Theophylact Bache,*[4] *b* 23 April, 1778;[12] *d* 29 October, 1783.[12]

(70) *Thomas Bache,*[4] *b* 21 May, 1779;[12] *d* at Flatbush, L. I., 20 August, 1779.[12]

(71) *Helena Bache,*[4] *b* at Flatbush, L. I., 18 December, 1780;[12] *d* 28 March, 1802.[33]

(72) *Margaret Amelia Bache,*[4] *b* at Flatbush, L. I., 19 January, 1783;[12] *d* at Flatbush, 30 July, 1783.[12]

(73) *Amelia Matilda Bache,*[4] *b* 7 August, 1784;[12] *d* 24 February, 1785.[12]

16. **Catherine Barclay,**[3] *b* 1744; *d* 7 March, 1808;[34] *m* (license dated 8 November, 1763) 10 November, 1763,[23]

---

[32]From THE ROYAL GAZETTE of Saturday, 19 December, 1778:

"A few days since died, most sincerely regretted, and on Thursday evening was buried in the family vault at Trinity Church Yard, Miss HELENA BACHE, one of the daughters of Theophylact Bache, Esq., of this City."

[33]From THE WEEKLY MUSEUM of Saturday, 3 April, 1802:

"*Died:* On Sunday evening last" (*i. e.,* March 28th) "in the 22nd year of her age, Miss HELENA BACHE, youngest daughter of Theophylact Bache, Esq. Amiable and lovely, her death is regretted by a large circle of friends to whom her endearing qualities were long known, and the value of her acquaintance justly appreciated."

[34]From THE WEEKLY MUSEUM of Saturday, 19 March, 1808:

"*Died:* On the 7th inst., at Yonkers, of a lingering and painful illness, Mrs. CATHERINE VAN CORTLANDT, consort of Augustus Van Cortlandt, Esq., in the 65th year of her age."

Augustus Van Cortlandt, b 3 August, 1728; *d* 20 December, 1823.

(74) *Anne Van Cortlandt.*4

(75) *Helena Van Cortlandt.*4

(76) *James Van Cortlandt,*4 *b* 8 February, 1770; *d* 17 July, 1773.

17.   **Sarah Barclay,**3 *b* 1745;23 *d* 27 July, 1806;35 *m* (license dated) 10 December, 1764, *Anthony Lispenard, b* 1739;23 *bap* 8 December, 1742; *d* 10 September, 1806.36

(77) *Helena Roosevelt Lispenard.*4

(78) *Leonard Lispenard.*4

(79) *Thomas Lispenard,*4 *d* 10 July, 1803,37 *unm.* †

(80) *Anthony Lispenard,*4 *d* 3 January, 1808,38 *unm.*†

(81) *Alice Lispenard,*4 *b* 1781; *d* 9 January, 1836, at the house of her brother-in-law, Alexander L. Stewart, *unm.*

(82) *Sarah Lispenard.*4

18.   **Ann Margaret Barclay,**3 *d* 28 October, 1791;39 *m* 17 November, 1773,40 *Frederick Jay,* brother of the Chief

---

35From THE WEEKLY MUSEUM of Saturday, 2 August, 1806:

"*Died:* In this City, on Sunday" (*i. e.,* July 27th) "Mrs. SARAH LISPENARD, wife of Anthony Lispenard, Esq."

36From THE WEEKLY MUSEUM of Saturday, 13 September, 1806:

"*Died:* On Wednesday morning" (*i. e.,* September 10th) "in the 64th year of his age, after a lingering illness, ANTHONY LISPENARD, Esq.,

37From THE SPECTATOR of Wednesday, 13 July, 1803 (under date of July 11):

"*Died:* Yesterday afternoon" (that is, Sunday, July 10th) "after 48 hours illness, Mr. THOMAS LISPENARD, second son of A. Lispenard, Esq. The friends of the deceased are requested to attend the Funeral at 6 o'clock This Evening, from the house of his father at Greenwich."

See also THE WEEKLY MUSEUM of Saturday, 16 July, 1803; and the records of Trinity Parish, and those of the New York Board of Health.

38From THE WEEKLY MUSEUM of Saturday, 9 January, 1808:

"*Died:* Suddenly, on Sunday evening" (*i. e.,* January 3rd) "between 8 and 9 o'clock, ANTHONY LISPENARD."

39From the NEW YORK WEEKLY JOURNAL of Wednesday, 2 November, 1791:

"*Died:* On Friday morning" (*i. e.,* October 28th) "after a short illness, Mrs. MARGARET JAY, the wife of Mr. Frederick Jay, of this city."

40From Rivington's NEW YORK GAZETTEER of Thursday, 18 November, 1773:

"Last night was married by the Rev. Dr. Auchmuty, Mr. FREDERICK JAY, merchant, of this City, to Miss BARCLAY, daughter of Mr. Andrew Barclay, merchant in Wall Street."

Justice, b 19 April, 1747; d 14 December, 1799. They had no issue. Frederick Jay survived his wife and subsequently married Euphemia Dunscomb, but left no issue.

19. **Helena Barclay,**[3] d 22 April, 1775; m 16 June, 1774,[41] Major *Thomas Moncrieffe,* d 10 December, 1791.[42]

    (83) *Thomas Barclay Moncrieffe,*[4] b April, 1775;[42] d 18 June, 1807,[43] *unm.*

---

[41]From Rivington's New York Gazetteer of Thursday, 16 June, 1774:

"This morning was married at her father's house in Wall Street, by the Rev. Mr. Charles Inglis, Thomas Moncrieffe, Esq. (Major of Brigade upon the American Establishment), to the very amiable Miss Helena Barclay, fifth daughter of Mr. Andrew Barclay, an eminent Merchant of this City. Immediately after the ceremony they sat out for their country retirement, on Long Island."

[42]From the New York Weekly Journal of Wednesday, 14 December, 1791:

"*Died:* On Friday last, suddenly, by the bursting of a blood vessel, Thomas Moncrieffe, Esq., late Major in the British service; and on Sunday evening his remains were interred in Trinity Church Yard, attended by a great number of respectable citizens."

Among the bound pamphlets in the library of the New York Historical Society, is an extremely well written and unusually interesting one entitled Memoirs of Mrs. Coghlan, New York: T. & J. Swords, 1795. The writer, Margaret Coghlan, was the daughter of Major Moncrieffe by a former wife; and in these Memoirs, written at the age of but thirty-three, she tells of the life, crowded to overflowing with unusual incident even for the days of the Revolution, of a spirited girl who was forced by the iron wills of her father and brother, when but fourteen years of age, to marry a man, Lieut. John Coghlan, whom she abhorred and despised. The particular interest of the Memoirs in connection with the Barclay descent is the tribute paid by Mrs. Coghlan to her father's third wife, Helena Barclay.

The father's first marriage was to Margaret Heron, a daughter of the Governor of Annapolis Royal, who was a wife at fourteen and in her grave before she was twenty, leaving two children surviving her, Edward Cornwallis Moncrieffe and Margaret Moncrieffe, the writer of the Memoirs. In 1765, when the brother was five and the sister but three, they were sent by their father to Dublin to be educated, and there they remained until 1772. On October 10, 1764, hardly a year after his first wife's death, Major Moncrieffe had married Polly Livingston, a daughter of Judge Livingston of New York; and in 1770 he came to Dublin with his regiment, the 55th, and brought his wife with him. "The person of this lady," writes Mrs. Coghlan, "was uncommonly forbidding, but her *purse* was irresistible. Young as I was, I did not like my new mother. She had, as I above remarked, the most disagreeable countenance, and, what is worse, she was a stranger to every social virtue and a rigid Presbyterian."

In 1772, the brother and sister returned to New York. The former entered Kings College, while the latter remained under the care of a governess. In January, 1774, their stepmother died childless, at the age of thirty-four, leaving her fortune to her husband, "for in her marriage articles," writes Mrs. Coghlan, "she had reserved to herself the power of disposing of it."

Less than six months after his second wife's death, Mrs. Coghlan continues, her father took to himself another wife, "one of the lovliest of her sex" (Helena Barclay). "In her bosom virtue, honour and conjugal affection were blended; but alas!

20. **Charlotte Amelia Barclay,**3 *b* 13 August, 1759;23 *d* 1
September, 1805; *m* 16 June, 1778,44 *Dr. Richard
Bayley* (who had previously married Catherine Charl-
ton, by whom he had had three children), *b* 1745; *d* 17
August, 1801.

(84) *Catharine Amelia Bayley.*4

---

her fate destined her for an early grave. Ten months after her marriage she died in childbirth of her infant son, my youngest brother, leaving him and myself under the care of her brother-in-law, Mr. Frederick Jay, who was then member of Congress for the province of New York.

"At this time my father was with General Gage, at Boston. Thus I found myself in the midst of republicans in war against the crown of Great Britain,—persecuted on every side, because my father was fighting for the cause of *a king!* At the age of thirteen, I was sent to board at Elizabeth-Town, New Jersey, with the family of an American Colonel, where I was forced to hear my nearest and dearest relations continually traduced."

She states that at the commencement of the war Congress had repeatedly offered her father a command in the Northern army, which was subsequently given to his nephew, General Montgomery; but all such offers were rejected, "and thus," she writes, "we lost the glorious opportunity of adding the laurel of *patriotism* to a name high in the ranks of *military valor,* and perhaps unequalled in military science. No man ever served the British Monarch with more fidelity or fought for him with greater bravery."

Her marriage to Lieut. John Coghlan occurred on February 28th, 1777, and her father died (according to these Memoirs) on December 10th, 1791.

A possibly different conception of the character of Major Moncrieffe's *second* wife may be gathered from the following obituary notice which appeared in Rivington's NEW YORK GAZETTEER of Thursday, January, 13, 1774:

"Last Tuesday night" (that is, January 11, 1774) "at 9 o'clock, MAJOR MONCRIEFFE met with the inexpressible loss of his Lady, Mrs. Moncrieffe, who died in the 34th year of her age, of a consumption; which, leaving her the free use of her reason, gave her the advantage of exhibiting a degree of patience that allowed not a repining word, and an example of such eminent heroism and affection, that it is difficult which most to admire, the undaunted fortitude of the one, or the ardour and tenderness of the other. Mrs. Moncrieffe was the youngest child of James Livingston, Esq., deceased, and has left an only daughter." (The panegyrist evidently thought, though erroneously, that Margaret Moncrieffe was a daughter of the second wife.) "The corpse will be interred on Friday evening in the old Presbyterian Church."

In GAINE'S GAZETTE AND WEEKLY MERCURY of Monday, March 3, 1777, appears the following notice of Margaret Moncrieffe's marriage:

"Last Monday Evening" (that is, February 24, 1777) "Lieut. JOHN COGHLAN, of the 7th, or English Fuzileers, was married by the Rev'd Dr. Auchmuty, to Miss MARGARET MONCRIEFFE, only Daughter to Thomas Moncrieffe, Esq."

43From THE WEEKLY MUSEUM of Saturday, 20 June, 1807:
"*Died:* Suddenly, on Thursday, Mr. THOMAS BARCLAY MONCRIEFFE."

44From THE ROYAL GAZETTE of Saturday, 20 June, 1778:
"Last Tuesday evening was married at Flatbush, by the Rev. Dr. Inglis, Miss CHARLOTTE AMELIA BARCLAY, youngest daughter of the late Mr. Andrew Barclay, merchant, to Mr. RICHARD BAYLEY, Surgeon, of this City."

See also PROVINCIAL SECRETARY OF STATE'S OFFICE, Marriage Book, vol. XXV, p. 104.

(85) *Richard Bayley*.[4]

(86) *Andrew Barclay Bayley*[4] (M.D.), *b* 1783; *d* 13 August, 1811, *unm.*

(87) *Guy Carleton Bayley*.[4]

(88) *William Augustus Bayley*.[4]

(89) *Helen Bayley*.[4]

(90) *Mary Fitch Bayley*.[4]

21. **Eliza Barclay**,[4] *b* at Flatbush, L. I., 3 December, 1776; *d* at Harlem, 21 June, 1817; *m* 16 June, 1796,[45] *Peter Schuyler Livingston, b* 24 September, 1772; *d* 8 July, 1809.

> (91) *Susan Gertrude Livingston*,[5] *b* 24 May, 1797; *d* 20 March, 1801.
>
> (92) *Cornelia Livingston*,[5] *b* 6 April, 1800; *d* 12 March, 1801.
>
> (93) *Ann Livingston*.[5]
>
> (94) *Schuyler Livingston*.[5]
>
> (95) *Thomas Barclay Livingston*.[5]

22. **Henry Barclay**,[4] *b* near Hell Gate, L. I., 27 October, 1778; *d* at Saugerties, 3 January, 1851; *m* 13 August, 1817,[46] *Catherine Watts, b* 24 July, 1782; *d* 17 January, 1851; dau. of Robert Watts. (They adopted the daughter of Catherine Watts' sister). O. S. P.

23. **DeLancey Barclay**,[4] *b* near Hell Gate, L. I., 16 June, 1780; *d* 29 March, 1826;[47] *m* 17 June, 1825,[48] *Mary*

---

[45]From N. Y. JOURNAL & PATRIOTIC REGISTER of Friday, 24 June, 1796:

"*Married:* At West Chester, on Thursday last" (that is, 16 June, 1796) "by the Rev. Mr. Ireland, Mr. PETER SCHUYLER LIVINGSTON to Miss ELIZA BARCLAY, daughter of Col. Thomas Barclay, of Annapolis, N. S.

[46]From COMMERCIAL ADVERTISER of Thursday, 14th August, 1817:

"*Married:* Last evening by the Rev. Mr. Wilkins, at Lady Mary Watts, Mr. HENRY BARCLAY to Miss CATHERINE WATTS, daughter of the late Robert Watts, Esq."

[47]The following memo., written by Col. Thomas Barclay, was copied by his grandson, Walter Channing Barclay, and is still (1903) preserved by the latter's widow, at Stamford, Conn.:

"On the 29 March, 1826, departed this life our beloved son DeLancey Barclay, after an illness of three days. In addition to his being an amiable, correct man and a dutiful, affectionate son and husband, he was one of the most promising and rapidly advancing men in the British army. In the 1st Regiment of Grenadier Guards with the rank of Lieut.-Colonel commanding the King's Own Company upwards of 12

Fairfield (sometimes written *Mary Freshfield*), widow of Gurney Barclay, a descendant of Col. David Barclay, of Ury. They had one son who died shortly after his birth.

24. **Maria Barclay,**[4] *b* near Hell Gate, L. I., 27 June, 1782; *d* at New York, 7 August, 1862; *m* 27 August, 1806,[49] *Simon Fraser.*†

  (96) *Matilda Fraser,*[5] *d* 1849; *m John P. van Rossum.* †

  (97) *Elizabeth Fraser,*[5] *d* 1849; *m William Fyfe.*†

  (98) *Catherine Fraser,*[5] *m Robert Mackie.* †

25. **Thomas Edmund Barclay,**[4] post captain in the Royal Navy, *b* at Annapolis, Nova Scotia, 4 December, 1783, *d* 30 January, 1838;[50] *m* 14 February, 1821, *Catherine Smith Channing,* dau. of Walter Channing. She *m* (2) 4 September, 1840, Albert Summer.[23])

  (99) *Thomas Barclay.*[5]

  (100) *Walter Channing Barclay.*[5]

  (101) *DeLancey Barclay,*[5] *b* 4 April, 1826;[23] *d* 1867 in Chicago, *unm.* †

---

years and aid-de-camp to H. R. H. the Duke of York, Commander-in-Chief. In 1825 he was appointed aid-de-camp to His present Majesty George IV, with the rank of Colonel, and for his gallant conduct at the battle of Waterloo created a Companion of the Bath. His death was universally lamented. To his aged parents and friends his loss is irreparable."

A note by Walter Channing Barclay states that the issue of the marriage of DeLancey Barclay with the widow of Gurney Barclay, was one son, for whom George IV stood godfather and to whom he gave £5,000. The child died within a few days and his parents took over the royal gift. After the death of DeLancey Barclay his widow again married,—her third choice being Dr. Stewart, Dean of Windsor.

[48]From THE NEW YORK GAZETTE of Wednesday, 17 August, 1825:

"*Married:* On the 17th June, in London, Colonel DELANCEY BARCLAY, C. B., Grenadier Guards, aid-de-camp to the King, to Mrs. GURNEY BARCLAY, of Tellingburne Lodge, in the county of Surrey."

[49]From THE WEEKLY MUSEUM of Saturday, 30 August, 1806:

"*Married:* Wednesday evening" (i. e., August 27th) "by the Rev. Mr. Wilkins, at Ann's View, Haerlem, SIMON FRASER, Esq., of Berbice, to Miss MARIA BARCLAY, daughter of the British Consul-General."

[50]From N. Y. COMMERCIAL ADVERTISER of Wednesday, 31 January, 1838:

"*Died* at his residence, 21 Bond Street (New York), January 30, 1838, Capt. THOMAS BARCLAY of the Royal Navy, in his 55th year. An attack of paralysis disordered his mind, and he ascended to the roof from which he fell and died in a few hours."

(102) *Frederic Augustus Barclay,*[5] *b* 24 February, 1828;[23] *d* 9 December, 1828.[16]

(103) *Henry Hotham Barclay,*[5] *b* 29 December, 1829;[23] *d* 17 December, 1855, *unm.*

(104) *Cuthbert Collingwood Barclay.*[5]

(105) A daughter,[5] *b* and *d* 8 September, 1833.[16]

26. **Susan Barclay,**[4] *b* at Wilmot, Nova Scotia, 5 February, 1785; *d* 14 January, 1805;[51] *m* 20 August, 1803,[52] *Peter Gerard Stuyvesant, b* 21 September, 1777; *d* 16 August, 1847. (He *m* (2) 11 May, 1809, Helena Rutherfurd.)

28. **Anne Barclay,**[4] *b* at Wilmot, Nova Scotia, 9 December, 1788; *d* 20 June, 1869; *m* 29 May, 1815,[53] *William Burrington Parsons, b* 3 February, 1794; *d* 25 August, 1869.

(106) *Thomas Barclay Parsons,*[5] *b* 9 March, 1818; *d* 23 March, 1818.

(107) *Ann Mary Parsons,*[5] *b* 3 January, 1820; *d* 8 July, 1820.

(108) *Susan Barclay Parsons.*[5]

(109) *Maria Fraser Parsons,*[5] *b* 27 August, 1824; *d* 28 September, 1825.

(110) *William Barclay Parsons.*[5]

[51]From The Weekly Museum of Saturday, January, 19, 1805:

"Died: On Monday last" (*i. e.,* January 14, 1805) "after a short illness, Mrs. Susan Stuyvesant, wife of P. G. Stuyvesant, Esq., and daughter of Thomas Barclay, Esq., the British Consul-General, in the 20th year of her age; a most amiable woman and much lamented by all who knew her.

"Lament not, friends, her life so soon is o'er;
Her transient stay with mortals here on earth;
For, lo! she's wafted to that peaceful shore
Where angels dwell, to join their heav'nly mirth."

See also the Republican Watch Tower of Wednesday, 16 January, 1805, where the following is appended to the above notice of death:

"The relations and friends of the deceased are requested to attend the funeral from the house of Mr. Stuyvesant, No. 27 Partition Street, to Trinity Church, This afternoon, the 15th inst., at 3 o'clock."

[52]From Evening Post of Monday, 22 August, 1803:

"Married: On Saturday last, at St. Mark's Church, by the Rev. Mr. Harris, P. G. Stuyvesant, Esq., to Miss Susan Barclay, daughter of Thomas Barclay, Esq., his Brittanic Majesty's Consul-General for the Eastern States of America."

[53]From New York Spectator of 15 July, 1815:

"Married, May 29, 1815, by the Rev. John Brady, at his house, William Burrington Parsons, Esq. (late Purser of H. M. Ship *Sylph*), to Miss Ann Barclay, daughter of Col. Barclay."

29. **George Barclay,**[4] (the baptismal name "Cornwell" was dropped), *b* at Annapolis, Nova Scotia, 4 July, 1790; *d* 28 July, 1869; *m* 8 December, 1818,[54] *Louise Matilda Aufrère, b* 17 November, 1792; *d* 15 February, 1868.

    (111) *Matilda Antonia Barclay.*[5]

30. **Anthony Barclay,**[4] *b* at Annapolis, Nova Scotia, 27 September, 1792; *d* at Hartford, Conn., 21 March, 1877; *m* 17 October, 1816,[55] *Ann Matilda Waldburg Glen, b* 1794; *d* 29 October, 1887,[16] dau. of J. Bartholomew Waldburg, of Savannah, Ga.

    (112) *Clarence Waldburg Barclay,*[5] *b* 1818; *d unm.*†

    (113) *Henry Anthony Waldburg Barclay.*[5]

    (114) *Thomas Waldburg DeLancey Barclay,*[5] *b* 1822; *d* 18 May, 1854, *unm.*

    (115) *Anna Matilda Waldburg Barclay.*[5]

    (116) *George A. Frederick Waldburg Barclay.*[5]

    (117) *Frances Elizabeth Colden Waldburg Barclay,*[5] *b* at Savannah, 3 February, 1826; *d* at New York, 3 March, 1836.

    (118) *Anthony Adelbert Ethelston Waldburg Barclay,*[5] *b* at Savannah, 11 August, 1832; *d* at Savannah, 22 May, 1833.

    (119) *Anthony Adelbert Ethelston Waldburg Barclay.*[5]

33. **Henry Barclay,**[4] *b* 3 April, 1794; *d* 21 March, 1863; *m* 13 April, 1842, *Sarah Moore, b* 5 October, 1809; *d* 3 September, 1873, dau of Daniel Sackett Moore.

    (120) *Henry Anthony Barclay.*[5]

    (121) *Fannie M. Barclay.*[5]

    (122) *James Lent Barclay.*[5]

    (123) *Sackett Moore Barclay.*[5]

---

[54]From NEW YORK SPECTATOR of Tuesday, 2 February, 1819:

"*Married:* At Cheltenham, England, on the 8th of Dec., GEORGE BARCLAY, Esq., son of Col. Barclay, to MATILDA, only daughter of Anthony AUFRERE, Esq., of Hoveton Hall, Norfolk."

[55]From NEW YORK SPECTATOR of Wednesday, 23 October, 1816:

"*Married:* On Thursday evening last" (that is, 17 October, 1816), "at Col. Barclay's, by the Rev. Dr. Bowen, ANTHONY BARCLAY, Esq., to Mrs. ANN GLEN."

35. **Beverley Robinson,**[4] *b* 26 May, 1779; *d* 14 August, 1857; *m* 11 September, 1805, *Frances Duer, b* 18 October, 1785; *d* 13 March, 1869.

> (124) *Anna Dorothea Robinson.*[5]
> (125) *Beverley Robinson.*[5]
> (126) *Catherine Robinson.*[5]
> (127) *William Duer Robinson.*[5]

38. **Morris Robinson,**[4] *b* 2 September, 1784; *d* 5 May, 1849; *m* 1 December, 1813, *Henrietta Elizabeth Duer, b* 22 June, 1790; *d* 9 May, 1839.

> (128) *Catherine Alexander Robinson.*[5]
> (129) *Henry Barclay Robinson.*[5]
> (130) *Beverley Robinson,*[5] *b* 28 November, 1817; *d* 25 February, 1829.
> (131) *Susan Philipse Robinson.*[5]
> (132) *Fanny Duer Robinson.*[5]
> (133) *Beverley Morris Robinson,*[5] *b* 23 July, 1824; *d* 1 September, 1825.
> (134) *Harriet Duer Robinson.*[5]
> (135) *Morris Chew Robinson,*[5] [56] *b* 8 March, 1832; *d* 3 November, 1832.

39. **Frederick Philipse Robinson,**[4] *b* 22 September, 1785; *d* 11 May, 1877; *m* 18 September, 1809, *Jane Paddock, b* 9 April, 1789; *d* 4 February, 1871.

> (136) *Anna Dorothea Robinson.*[5]
> (137) *William Henry Robinson.*[5]
> (138) *Beverley Adino Robinson.*[5]
> (139) *George Morris Robinson,*[5] *b* 22 September, 1819; *d* 9 April, 1841, *unm.*
> (140) *Frederick Philipse Robinson,*[5] *b* 4 December, 1822; *d* 19 December, 1887, *unm.*
> (141) *John Robinson.*[5]

41. **John Robinson,**[4] *b* 18 July, 1788; *d* 7 December, 1866; *m* 31 December, 1818, *Eliza Maria Allaire, b* 11 May, 1795; *d* 25 July, 1874.

---

[56]Records of St. Thomas' Church, New York.

.   (142) *Beverley John Robinson,*[5] *b* 21 April, 1820;
          d 24 March, 1821.
    (143) *Henry Barclay Robinson.*[5]
    (144) *Mary Eliza Robinson.*[5]
    (145) *William Beverley Robinson.*[5]
    (146) *Edward Simonds Robinson,*[5] *b* 4 September,
          1829; *d* 27 August, 1831.
    (147) *Anna Dorothea Robinson,*[5] *b* 28 December,
          1831; *d* 6 November, 1836.
    (148) *John Robinson,*[5] *b* 18 December, 1832; *d* 23
          January, 1834.
    (149) *Morris Robinson.*[5]
    (150) *Thomas Barclay Robinson.*[5]
    (151) *Jack DeLancey Robinson.*[5]

42.   **Susanna Philipse Robinson,**[4] *b* 6 February, 1791; *d* 24
      June, 1868; *m* 5 June, 1820,[57] *George Lee, b* 29 March,
      1774; *d* 29 March, 1853. O. S. P.

43.   **William Henry Robinson,**[4] *b* 23 April, 1793; *d* 27
      March, 1848; *m* 1 September, 1827, *Louisa Millidge, b*
      1 October, 1807; *d* 6 March, 1874. O. S. P.

53.   **Catherine Eliza Barclay,**[4] *b* at New York, 22 April,
      1784;[22] *d* 26 February, 1816; *m* 7 September, 1812,[58]
      James Roosevelt, b 10 January, 1760; *d* 6 February,
      1846.[56]

          (152) *Susan Barclay Roosevelt,*[5] *b* 31 July, 1813;
                d unm. †
          (153) *James Barclay Roosevelt,*[5] *b* 1815; *d unm* †

---

[57]From St. John (N. B.) Gazette of 21 June, 1820:
  "Married: On the 5th inst., at the Parish of St. Mary's, by the Rev. James
Sauerville, George Lee, Esq., to Susan, only daughter of the late Hon. Beverley
Robinson."
  See also New York Gazette of 11 July, 1820.

[58]From the New York Evening Post of Wednesday, 9 September, 1812:
  "Married: On Monday" (*i. e.*, September 7th), "in St. John's Church, by the
Rev. Mr. Wyat, James Roosevelt, Esq., to Miss Catherine Eliza Barclay, daughter
of the late Mr. James Barclay, all of this city."

59. **Elizabeth Garland Bache,**[4] *b* 28 December, 1762; *d* 24 August, 1795;[59] *m* 27 September, 1788,[60] *James Bleecker, b* 10 December, 1764; *d* 5 July, 1842.

> (154) *Theophylact Bache Bleecker,*[5] *b* 16 December, 1790; *d* 26 December, 1792.

61. **Mary Bache,**[4] *b* 3 April, 1766;[12] *m* 22 November, 1787,[61] *Charles McEvers, Jr., b* 5 June, 1764; *d* 31 August, 1841. (He *m* (2) 30 September, 1802, Margaret Cooper, dau of Dr. Ananias Cooper of Rhinebeck, N. Y., *b* 5 May, 1775; *d* 11 April, 1863, by whom he had three daughters.)

> (155) *Mary Bache McEvers,*[5] *b* 10 September, 1792; *d* 25 February, 1806.[62]
>
> (156) *Charles McEvers,*[5] *bap* 2 November, 1794;[23] *d* 30 June, 1843, *unm.*
>
> (157) *Bache McEvers.*[5]

62. **Paul Richard Bache,**[4] *b* 6 November, 1767; *d* 4 June, 1801; *m* 1 November, 1792,[23] *Helena Roosevelt Lis-*

---

[59]From AMERICAN MINERVA (New York) of Tuesday, 25 August, 1795:

"*Died:* Yesterday morning, Mrs. ELIZABETH BLEECKER, wife of Mr. James Bleecker, Merchant, of this City. Her remains attended by a numerous train of relatives and friends were this day interred in the family vault, Trinity Church yard.

> "Domestic Peace! she woo'd thy tranquil joys,
> And Kindred Friendship! all her heart was thine;
> Untroubled with a wish to court those scenes,
> Where female vanity delights to shine.
> Maternal tenderness! Connubial love!
> Ye made your purest fire in her combine;
> And bright religion! 'twas thy holy flame,
> Inspir'd her breast with energies divine,
> Taught her with grace to live,—with fortitude resign."

[60]From the DAILY ADVERTISER of Monday, 29 September, 1788:

"Married by the Reverend Mr. Moore, Mr. JAMES BLEECKER, merchant, to Miss BACHE, daughter of Theophylact Bache, Esq."
See also NEW YORK PACKET of Tuesday, 30 September, 1788.

[61]From THE INDEPENDENT JOURNAL of Saturday, 24 November, 1787:

"Married on Thursday evening" (*i. e.,* November 22nd), "by the Rev. Mr. Moore, Mr. CHARLES McEVERS, Jun., to Miss MARY BACHE, daughter of Mr. Theophylact Bache, of this city, merchant."

[62]From THE WEEKLY MUSEUM of Saturday, 1 March, 1806:

"*Died:* On Tuesday morning" (*i. e.,* February 25th) "most sincerely lamented, Miss MARY BACHE McEVERS, eldest daughter of Charles McEvers, Jun., Esq."

penard[4] (No. 77 above), *b* 1766; *d* 14 February, 1799.[63]
(158) *Sarah Barclay Bache.*[5]

64. **Andrew Barclay Bache,**[4] [56] *b* 1 August, 1770; *d* 13 August, 1847; *m* (in London) 21 April, 1798, *Charlotte Phillips, b* 7 January, 1782; *d* 1 October, 1842.

(159) *Andrew Theobold Bache.*[5]
(160) *James Theophylact Bache.*[5]
(161) *Anne Maria Bache,*[5] *b* 16 October, 1802; *d* 4 August, 1804.
(162) *Charlotte Bache.*[5]
(163) *Theophylact Bache,*[5] *b* 7 September, 1806; *d* 15 November, 1808.
(164) *George Perry Bache.*[5]
(165) *Eliza Barclay Bache.*[5]
(166) *Sarah Bleecker Bache.*[5]
(167) *William Satterthwaite Bache,*[5] *b* 3 November, 1817; *d* 21 February, 1892,[64] *unm.*
(168) *Richard T. Bache,*[5] *b* 28 December, 1819; *d* 1829.
(169) *Helen Bache.*[5]
(170) *Catherine Satterthwaite Bache.*[5]

65. **Ann Dorothy Bache,**[4] *b* 31 August, 1771; *d* 27 June, 1814; *m* 18 December, 1790,[65] *Leonard Lispenard*[4] (No. 78 above), *b* 31 August, 1771; *d* 6 September, 1817.

(171) *Ann Dorothy Lispenard,*[5] *b* 31 October, 1791;[23] *d* 2 September, 1808.[66]
(172) *Sarah Amelia Lispenard,*[5] *b* 19 January, 1793.[23] †

[63]From The Weekly Museum of Saturday, 23 February, 1799:
"*Died:* On Thursday, 14th instant, in the thirty-second year of her age, Mrs. Helena Bache, wife of Paul R. Bache of this city, merchant. Her remains were on Saturday interred in the family vault, Trinity Church, attended by her relations, friends and acquaintance."

[64]From Records of St. Michael's Church, New York.

[65]From The New York Weekly Journal of Thursday, 23 December, 1790:
"*Married:* Last Saturday evening" (*i. e.,* December 18th) "Mr. Leonard Lispenard to Miss Nancy Bache."
See also Trinity parish records.

[66]"*Died,* September 2, 1808, after a lingering illness, aged 17 years, Miss Ann D. Lispenard, eldest daughter of Leonard Lispenard, Esq."

(173) *Leonard Lispenard*,[5] *bap* 15 December, 1794;[23] *d* 2 May, 1801.[23]

(174) *Theophylact Bache Lispenard*.[5]

(175) *Sarah Lispenard*,[5] *b* 1 August, 1798;[12] *d* 12 April, 1881,[23] *unm*.

(176) *Helena Bache Lispenard*.[5] [67]

66. **William Bache**,[4] *b* 20 November, 1773; *d* 22 August, 1813; *m Christina Elizabeth Cooper, b* 20 December, 1777;[68] *d* 13 September 1826,[69] dau of Dr. Ananias Cooper of Rhinebeck, N. Y.

(177) *Eliza Ann Bache*.[5]

(178) *Helena Bache*.[5]

(179) *Theophylact Bache*,[5] *b* 17 July, 1806; *d* (drowned off Squan Beach, N. J.) 15 February, 1846,[69, 70] *unm*.

(180) *William C. Bache*,[5] *b* 1812; *d* 29 August, 1833, *unm*.

67. **Sarah Bache**,[4] *b* 25 December, 1774; *d* 16 March, 1852; *m* 25 July, 1796,[71] *James Bleecker, b* 10 December, 1764; *d* 5 July, 1842, who had previously married her sister, Elizabeth Garland Bache, No. 59 above.

---

[87] In addition to the above noted, the records of Trinity Parish contain the following entries:

Buried: 1801, November 1, LEONARD LISPENARD's child, aged 1 yr. 7 mos.

1804, September 2, Mr. LISPENARD's child, aged 10 mos.

1807, February 14,   do.   "   2 yrs.

1808, February 4,   do.   "   1 yr. 6 mos.

The first of these entries, if recorded correctly, can hardly refer to the child of the Leonard Lispenard that married Ann Dorothy Bache, for their daughter, Helena Bache Lispenard, was born 2 January, 1800.

There is also an entry:

Baptism: 1806, December 17, LISPENARD.

[68] From Records of REFORMED CHURCH at Rhinebeck, N. Y.:

JOSEPH CORNELIUS and CHRISTINA ELIZABETH, children of Doctor Ananias COOPER and Elizabeth Decay, born December 20, 1777, and baptized February 7, 1778.

[69] Records of New York City BOARD OF HEALTH.

[70] "The body of THEOPHYLACT BACHE, a passenger on board the '*John Minturn*,' having been received, the funeral will be held on February 26th (1846) from St. Paul's Church."

[71] From THE WEEKLY MUSEUM of Saturday, 30 July, 1796:

"*Married:* On Monday evening last" (*i. e.*, July 25th) "by the Rev. Dr. Moore, Mr. JAMES BLEECKER, merchant, to Miss SARAH BACHE, daughter of Mr Theophylact Bache, merchant, of this City."

(181) *Helena Bleecker.*[5]

(182) *Mary Bleecker.*[5]

(183) *Anthony J. Bleecker.*[5]

(184) *Ann Dorothy Bleecker,*[5] *b* 13 December, 1801; *d* 9 April, 1808.

(185) *Theophylact Bache Bleecker.*[5]

(186) *Catherine Elizabeth Bleecker,*[5] *b* 11 October, 1805; *d* 25 February, 1807.

(187) *Catherine Elizabeth Bleecker,*[5] *b* 16 October, 1807; *d* 19 May, 1809.

(188) *Sarah Bache Bleecker.*[5]

(189) *James Bleecker,*[5] *b* 22 September, 1811; *d* 23 August, 1819.[23]

(190) *Barclay Bleecker,*[5] *b* 19 December, 1814;[23] *d* 4 August, 1826.[56]

(191) *Anna Josepha Bleecker,*[5] *b* 19 August, 1816;[23, 69] *d* 2 March, 1831.[69]

68. Catherine Bache,[4] *b* at Flatbush, L. I., 5 March, 1776; *d* 17 April, 1854; *m* 5 March, 1796,[72] *Thomas W. Satterthwaite, b* 14 November, 1772; *d* 20 May, 1815.

(192) *Thomas Wilkinson Satterthwaite.*[5]

(193) *Catherine Bache Satterthwaite,*[5] *b* 22 March, 1799; *d* 14 November, 1800.

(194) *Ann Dorothy Satterthwaite.*[5]

(195) *William Bache Satterthwaite,*[5] *b* 20 November, 1803; *d* (at sea) *unm.*

(196) *Theophylact Bache Satterthwaite.*[5]

(197) *James Clough Satterthwaite,*[5] *b* 17 June, 1807; *d* 6 June, 1832, *unm.*

(198) *George Satterthwaite,*[5] *b* 2 June, 1809; *d* 25 January, 1811.

(199) *John Blackwood Satterthwaite.*[5]

(200) *Eliza Helena Satterthwaite,*[5] *b* 13 August, 1814; *d* 5 November, 1817.

---

[72]From THE WEEKLY MUSEUM of Saturday, 12 March, 1796:

"Married: On Saturday evening last" (*i. e.,* March 5th) "by the Rev. Dr. Moore, Mr. THOMAS W. SATTERTHWAITE, merchant, to Miss CATHERINE BACHE, daughter of Mr. Theophylact Bache, merchant, of this city."

74. **Anne VanCortlandt,**[4] *b* 18 January, 1766; *d* 31 August, 1814;[73] *m* 17 November, 1785,[74] *Henry White, b* 12 September, 1763; *d* 11 April, 1822.

> (201) *Catherine White.*[5]
>
> (202) *Augustus VanCortlandt White,*[5] *b* 24 January, 1789; *d* 24 February, 1794.
>
> (203) *Henry White.*[5] Lived but a few days †
>
> (204) *Anne White,*[5] *b* 2 September, 1790; *d* 15 December, 1824.
>
> (205) *Helen White.*[5]
>
> (206) *Augustus White*[5] (took the name VANCORTLANDT), *b* 19 June, 1794; *d* 1 April, 1839, *unm.*
>
> (207) *Augusta White.*[5]
>
> (208) *Harriet White,*[5] *b* 11 August, 1797; *d* 5 September, 1864, *unm.*
>
> (209) *Henry White,*[5] *b* 1799; *d* 1802.
>
> (210) *Margaret White,*[5] *b* 1799; *d* September, 1815. (Henry and Margaret were twins.)
>
> (211) *Francena White.*[5] Lived but eight months. †
>
> (212) *Henry White*[5] (took the name VANCORTLANDT), *b* 20 April, 1802; *d* 13 October, 1839, *unm.*
>
> (213) *Francena White.*[5]

75. **Helena VanCortlandt,**[4] *b* 4 January, 1768; *d* 3 April, 1812; *m* 1 February, 1796,[75] *James Morris, b* 1764; *d* 7 September, 1827.

---

[73]From NEW YORK GAZETTE of Saturday, 3 September, 1814:
"*Died:* At Yonkers, on Wednesday last" (that is, 31 August, 1814) "ANN WHITE, wife of Henry White, Esq."

[74]From THE NEW YORK PACKET of Monday, 21 November, 1785:
"On Thursday evening" (*i. e.,* November 17th) "was married by the Rev. Mr. Moore, at Younkers, the seat of Augustus Cortlandt, Esq., Miss ANNE CORTLANDT, eldest daughter of that gentleman, to HENRY WHITE, Junior, Esq., eldest son of Henry White, Esq., formerly a principal merchant in this city, and now residing in London."

[75]From THE WEEKLY MUSEUM of Saturday, 6 February, 1796:
"*Married:* On Monday evening last" (*i. e.,* February 1st) "at Yonkers, by the Rev. Mr. Cooper, JAMES MORRIS, Esquire, to Miss HELEN V. CORTLANDT, daughter of Augustus VanCortlandt, Esquire."

(214) *James Van Cortlandt Morris.*[5]

(215) *Augustus Frederick Morris*[5] (took the name VAN CORTLANDT).

(216) *Catherine Morris.*[5]

(217) *Mary Walton Morris,*[5] *b* 13 September, 1800; *d* 10 December, 1830, *unm.*

(218) *Helen Morris.*[5]

(219) *Ann Morris,*[5] *b* 13 March, 1803; *d* 30 March, 1823, *unm.*

(220) *Jane Urquhart Morris,*[5] *b* 20 October, 1804; *d* 10 August, 1819.

(221) *Richard Lewis Morris.*[5]

(222) *Robert Rutherfurd Morris.*[5]

(223) *Sarah Louisa Morris.*[5]

(224) *William H. Morris.*[5]

(225) *Charlotte Morris.*[5]

77. **Helena Roosevelt Lispenard,**[4] *b* 1766; *d* 14 February, 1799; *m* 1 November, 1792, *Paul Richard Bache*[4] (No. 62 above), *b* 6 November, 1767; *d* 4 June, 1801.

(The issue of this marriage is chronicled above, under: 62, PAUL RICHARD BACHE.[4])

78. **Leonard Lispenard,**[4] *b* 31 August, 1771; *d* 6 September, 1817; *m* 18 December, 1790, *Ann Dorothy Bache*[4] (No. 65 above), *b* 31 August, 1771; *d* 27 June, 1814.

(The issue of this marriage are chronicled above, under: 65, ANN DOROTHY BACHE.[4])

82. **Sarah Lispenard,**[4] *b* 6 September, 1783; *d* 28 October, 1831; *m* 27 January, 1803, *Alexander L. Stewart, b* 31 May, 1775; *d* 29 March, 1838.

(226) *Helen Lispenard Stewart.*[5]

(227) *Lispenard Stewart.*[5]

(228) *Sarah A. Stewart.*[5]

(229) *Mary Jordan Stewart.*[5]

(230) *Eliza Barclay Stewart,*[5] *b* March, 1812; *d* 22 February, 1866, *unm.*

    (231) *Amelia Barclay Stewart,*[5] *b* 6 November, 1814;
        d 14 April, 1826.

    (232) *Matilda Wilson Stewart.*[5]

84. **Catharine Amelia Bayley,**[4] *b* 1779; *d* 22 July, 1805; *m*
    19 June, 1799, *William Craig,*[5] *d* 2 September, 1826. †
    (233) *William Craig,*[5] *d* 21 September, 1821. †
    (234) *Henry Sadler Craig,*[5] *b* 14 July, 1805; *d* 1
        December, 1805.

85. **Richard Bayley,**[4] *b* 7 August, 1781; *d* 29 May, 1815; *m*
    26 October, 1812, *Catherine White*[5] (No. 201 above),
    b 30 November, 1786; *d* 29 September, 1878.
    (235) *Henry White Bayley,*[5] *b* 26 June, 1813; *d* 27
        May, 1816.
    (236) *Ann Margaret Bayley.*[5]

87. **Guy Carleton Bayley**[4] (M.D.), *b* 1786; *d* 7 November,
    1859; *m* 4 November, 1813,[64] *Grace Walton Roosevelt,*
    b 10 February, 1792; *d* 28 March, 1828.[76]
    (237) *James Roosevelt Bayley,*[5] (became the Roman
        Catholic Archbishop of Baltimore), *b* 23
        August, 1814; *bap* (Trinity Church, New
        York) 21 September, 1814;[23] *d* 3 October,
        1877.
    (238) *Richard Bayley.*[5]
    (239) *Guy Carleton Bayley.*[5]
    (240) *William Augustus Bayley.*[5]
    (241) *Maria Eliza Bayley.*[5]

88. **William Augustus Bayley,**[4] *b* 1788; *d* 14 November,
    1817; *m* 3 September, 1811, *Jane Smith.* †
    (242) *William Augustus Bayley,*[5] *b* 16 September,
        1814;[23] *d* at Mobile, Ala., 1836, *unm.*
    (243) *Helen Amelia Bayley,*[5] *b* 3 July, 1816.[23] †

89. **Helen Bayley,**[4] *b* 10 June, 1790; *d* 4 May, 1849;[77] *m*
    31 May, 1814,[23] *Samuel Craig, b* 1782; *d* 9 July, 1830.

---

[76]Inscription on monument by Bayley vault, Van Cortlandt Park, New York.

[77]From the Commercial Advertiser of Saturday, 5 May, 1849:

    "Died: On the 4th inst., in the 58th year of her age, Helen, relict of the late Samuel Craig, Esq., and daughter of the late Dr. Richard Bayley, of this City.

    "The funeral services will be performed at Calvary Church on Sunday next, at

(244) *Henry Sadler Craig.*[5]

(245) *William Craig,*[5] *b* 17 July, 1817.[23] †

(246) *Richard Bayley Craig,*[5] *b* 23 March, 1819;[23] *d* 3 June, 1884, *unm.*

(247) *Charlotte Amelia Craig.*[5]

(248) *William Craig.*[5]

(249) *Helen Elizabeth Craig.*[5]

(250) *Samuel R. Craig.*[5]

90. **Mary Fitch Bayley,**[4] *bap* 16 April, 1796;[23] *d* 7 November, 1830; *m* 18 November, 1817, *Robert Henry Bunch,* *b* 24 October, 1795; *d* 29 September, 1856.

> (251) *Robert Bunch.*[5]
>
> (252) *Charlotte Amelia Bayley Bunch.*[5]
>
> (253) *George Bunch.*[5]

93. **Ann Livingston,**[5] *b* 15 January, 1802; *d* 8 May, 1859; *m* 5 May, 1840, *James Reyburn, b* 1797; *d* 15 July, 1849, O. S. P.

94. **Schuyler Livingston,**[5] *b* 5 April, 1804; *d* 2 December, 1862; *m* (1) 23 May, 1826, *Ann Eliza Hosie, b* 16 May, 1805; *d* 27 June, 1838; *m* (2) 2 January, 1840, *Margaret Maria Livingston, b* 18 December, 1820; *d* 26 February, 1848; *m* (3) 5 September, 1854,[78] *Sarah Grace Carroll, b* 12 June, 1803;[23] *d* 10 January, 1878.

> (254) *Eliza Barclay Livingston,*[6] *b* 20 March, 1827; *d* 29 September, 1830.[16]
>
> (255) *Henry Barclay Livingston.*[6]
>
> (256) *Eliza Glass Livingston.*[6]
>
> (257) *George Barclay Livingston*[6] (U.S.N.), *b* 12 November, 1833; *d* 19 September, 1890, *unm.*

---

2 p. m., to which the relatives and friends are invited. The remains will be interred in the family vault at Yonkers.''

The records of CALVARY CHURCH, New York, state that Mrs. Craig was buried May 6, 1849.

The inscription on the monument by the BAYLEY VAULT in Van Cortlandt Park, New York, erroneously states *11* May, 1849, as the date of Mrs. Craig's death. The monument was erected about 1860, and the faulty date was doubtless inscribed from memory.

[78]Records of GRACE CHURCH, New York.

(258) *Schuyler Livingston,*[6] *b* 21 April, 1836; *d* 14
    June, 1885, *unm.*
(259) *Matilda Corinna Livingston.*[6]

95. **Thomas Barclay Livingston,**[5] *b* 31 July, 1806; *d* 26
    December, 1852; *m* 26 June, 1834, *Mary Livingston
    Kearney, b* 1 October, 1810; *d* 1873; dau. of John Watts
    Kearney. O. S. P.

99. **Thomas Barclay,**[5] *b* 3 June, 1822;[23] *d* 17 June, 1893;
    m 20 January, 1859, *Frances Holme Maghee, b* 23
    January, 1838; *d* 14 September, 1874, dau. of Thomas
    H. Maghee. O. S. P.

100. **Walter Channing Barclay,**[5] *b* 15 January, 1825;[23] *d* 1
    September, 1899; *m* (1) 19 December, 1850,[56] *Grace
    Ann Douglass, b* 20 January, 1825; *d* 8 December, 1863,
    dau. of Richard H. Douglass; *m* (2) 8 December, 1866,
    Serefina B. Smith, b 9 July, 1837; (living 1903), dau.
    of Richard Dimock Smith.

    (260) *Letitia Grace Barclay,*[6] *b* 15 August, 1852; *d*
        8 April, 1879, *unm.*
    (261) *DeLancey Hethcote Barclay.*[6]
    (262) *Walter Channing Barclay,*[6] *b* 29 February,
        1856; *d* 28 February, 1882, *unm.*
    (263) *Catherine Channing Barclay.*[6]
    (264) *Lillian Allardice Barclay,*[6] *b* 20 December,
        1859; *d* 22 May, 1873, *unm.*
    (265) *Cuthbert Collingwood Barclay,*[6] *b* 6 November,
        ber, 1862; (living 1903).
    (266) *Edith Leonora Barclay,*[6] *b* 18 January, 1870;
        (living 1903).

104. **Cuthbert Collingwood Barclay**[5] (Rev.), *b* 10 March,
    1831; *d* 7 February, 1863; *m* 29 January, 1858,[23] *Sarah
    Sophia Schieffelin, b* 22 June, 1834; *d* 5 March, 1886,
    dau. of Richard Lawrence Schieffelin, of New York.
    O. S. P.

108. **Susan Barclay Parsons,**[5] *b* 17 July, 1822; *d* 4 June, 1893; *m* 22 November, 1842, *Montagnie Ward, b* 11 February, 1812; *d* 30 June, 1879.
    (267) *George Barclay Ward.*[6]
    (268) *William deLancey Ward.*[6]
    (269) *Beverley Ward.*[6]
    (270) *Annie Parsons Ward.*[6]

110. **William Barclay Parsons,**[5] *b* 4 September, 1828; *d* 31 December, 1887; *m* 4 November, 1851, *Eliza Glass Livingston*[6] (No. 256 above), *b* 7 September, 1831; (living 1903).
    (271) *Schuyler Livingston Parsons.*[6]
    (272) *William Barclay Parsons.*[6]
    (273) *Harry de Berkeley Parsons.*[6]
    (274) *George Burrington Parsons.*[6]

111. **Matilda Antonia Barclay,**[5] *b* 7 December, 1824; *d* 25 January, 1888; *m* 16 May, 1848, *Francis Robert Rives, b* 16 February, 1822; *d* 16 July, 1891.
    (275) *George Lockhart Rives.*[6]
    (276) *Ella Louise Rives.*[6]
    (277) *Francis Robert Rives.*[6]
    {(278) *Maud Antonia Rives.*[6]
    {(279) *Constance Evelyn Rives.*[6]
    (280) *Reginald William Rives.*[6]

113. **Henry Anthony Waldburg Barclay,**[5] *b* 15 June, 1819;[23] *d* 1 October, 1857; *m* 25 May, 1847,[78]*Cornelia S. Cochrane, b* 10 September, 1825; *d* 10 February, 1890, dau. of Walter Cochrane.
    (281) *Henry A. W. Barclay,*[6] *b* June, 1848; *d* October, 1884, *unm.*
    (282) *Cornelia Cochrane Barclay.*[6]

115. **Anna Matilda Waldburg Barclay,**[5] *b* 1824; *d* 18 May, 1878; *m* (1) 28 February, 1840, *T. Pollock Burgwn,* of North Carolina; *m* (2) 1873, *William Miller, b* 1825; *d* 1881. †
    (283) *Francis M. Burgwn,*[6] *b* 13 June, 1841;[69] *d* 16 June, 1841.[69]

116. George A. Frederick Waldburg Barclay,[5] *b* 1826; *d* 14 November, 1859; *m* 19 April, 1855, *Louisa Carolina Al-Burtis, b* 29 January, 1823; *d* 8 April, 1891.

    (284) *Carolina Alberta Victoria Barclay,*[6] *b* 25 September, 1857; *d* 25 March, 1862.

119. Anthony Adelbert Ethelston Waldburg Barclay,[5] *b* 1834; *d* 29 October, 1887;[16] *m* (1) 21 November, 1855, *Margaret Marshall,* of Savannah, Ga., *b* 1839; *d* 1859; *m* (2) 2 November, 1876, *Fanny Moss Tucker,* of Hartford, Conn., *b* 23 November, 1849; (living 1903). She *m* (2) Joseph Dominici, of Rome, Italy.

    (285) *Mary Marshall Barclay.*[6]

    (286) *Etienne de Lancey Barclay,*[6] *b* 11 November, 1877; *d* 28 February, 1887.

120. Henry Anthony Barclay,[5] *b* 14 December, 1844; (living 1903); *m* 28 October, 1873, *Clara O. Wright, b* 15 May, 1853; (living 1903).

    (287) *Gertrude O. Barclay.*[6]

    (288) *Henry A. Barclay.*[6]

    (289) *Wright Barclay.*[6]

    (290) *Mildred M. Barclay,*[6] *b* 23 December, 1888; (living 1903).

    (291) *Clara Wright Barclay,*[6] *b* 26 February, 1890; (living 1903).

121. Fanny M. Barclay,[5] *b* 16 August, 1846; (living 1903); *m* 7 June, 1864, *William Constable, b* 11 December, 1834; (living 1903). S. P.

122. James Lent Barclay,[5] *b* 5 October, 1848; (living 1903); *m* (1) 19 December, 1876, *Olivia Mott Bell, b* May, 1854; *d* 3 January, 1894; *m* (2) 16 April, 1896, *Priscilla Dixon* (Sloane), *b* 25 February, 1851; (living 1903).

    (292) *Adelaide Mott Barclay.*[6]

123. **Sackett Moore Barclay,**[5] *b* 1 December, 1850; (living 1903); *m* 19 October, 1871, *Cornelia Cochrane Barclay*[6] (No. 282 above), *b* 3 March, 1851; (living 1903).

> (293) *Harold Barclay,*[6] *b* 14 August, 1872; (living 1903), *unm.*
>
> (294) *Robert C. Barclay,*[6] *b* 26 March, 1874; (living 1903), *unm.*
>
> (295) *Beatrice W. Barclay.*[6]
>
> (296) *Ethel N. Barclay.*[6]
>
> (297) *Cornelia Cochrane Barclay,*[6] *b* 22 March, 1892; (living 1903).

124. **Anna Dorothea Robinson,**[5] *b* 24 August, 1806; *d* 20 January, 1876; *m* 18 October, 1826, *William Betts, b* at Santa Cruz, 28 January, 1802; *d* 5 July, 1884.

> (298) *Beverley Robinson Betts.*[6]
>
> (299) *Caroline Betts.*[6]
>
> (300) *William Betts.*[6]

125. **Beverley Robinson,**[5] *b* 25 November, 1808; *d* 16 February, 1876; *m* 15 November, 1836, *Mary Read Jenkins, b* 18 January, 1815; *d* 15 April, 1891.

> (301) *Beverley Robinson.*[6]
>
> (302) *Philip Palmer Robinson.*[6]
>
> (303) *Lydia Potter Robinson,*[6] *b* 18 October, 1841; *d* 21 October, 1843.
>
> (304) *Robert Emmet Robinson.*[6]
>
> (305) *Mary Hubley Robinson.*[6]
>
> (306) *Frederic Philipse Robinson,*[6] *b* 20 July, 1849; *d* 23 March, 1852.
>
> (307) *John Robert Rhinelander Robinson,*[6] *b* 19 September, 1851; *d* 10 March, 1890, *unm.*
>
> (308) *Fanny Duer Robinson.*[6]
>
> (309) *George Duer Robinson,*[6] *b* 12 September, 1855; *d* 24 December, 1860.
>
> (310) *Maud De Lancey Robinson,*[6] *b* 8 April, 1858; *d* 5 December, 1860.
>
> (311) *Walter De Lancey Robinson,*[6] *b* 23 February, 1861; (living 1903), *unm.*

126. **Catherine Robinson,**[5] *b* 12 June, 1810; *d* 3 March, 1872;
m 24 October, 1844, *George Wickham Duer, b* 12 May,
1812; *d* 28 May, 1888.

> (312) *Morris Robinson Duer,*[6] *b* 23 August, 1847;
> *d* 25 April, 1894, *unm.*
> (313) *John Beverley Duer.*[6]

127. **William Duer Robinson,**[5] *b* 7 December, 1811; *d* 2 July,
1876; *m* 3 November, 1874, *Mary Bergh, d* 1882, dau.
of Tunis Bergh.   O. S. P.

128. **Catherine Alexander Robinson,**[5] *b* 28 October, 1814; *d*
27 April, 1883; *m* 30 September, 1835,[79] *Alexander
Slidell* (U.S.N.), *b* 6 March, 1803; *d* 13 September
1848.

> (314) *Ranald Slidell-Mackenzie,*[6] *b* 27 July, 1840; *d*
> 19 January, 1899, *unm.*
> (315) *Alexander Slidell-Mackenzie,*[6] *b* 24 January,
> 1842; *d* 13 June, 1867, *unm.*
> (316) *Harriet Duer Slidell-Mackenzie,*[6] *b* 20 January, 1844; (living 1903).
> (317) *May Slidell-Mackenzie,*[6] *b* 15 January, 1846;
> *d* 10 October, 1856.
> (318) *Morris Robinson Slidell-Mackenzie.*[6]

129. **Henry Barclay Robinson,**[5] *b* 24 April, 1816; *d* 26 December, 1863; *m* (1) 6 November, 1845, *Catherine
Elizabeth Hudson, b* 18 September, 1824;[23] *d* 10 November, 1846; *m* (2) 12 April, 1855, *Marie Antoinette
Winthrop, b* 29 May, 1830;[80] *d* 20 August, 1875.

> (319) *Catherine Elizabeth Hudson Robinson.*[6]
> (320) *Georgiana Winthrop Robinson.*[6]
> (321) *Harriet Duer Robinson*[6] (living 1903).

[79]From New York Gazette of Friday, 2 October, 1835:
"*Married:* On Wednesday evening" (that is, 30 September, 1835) "Alexander
Slidell of the U. S. Navy, to Catherine Alexander, daughter of Morris Robinson."

[80]Records of St. James' Church, New York.

(322) *Morris Robinson,*[6] *b* 8 May, 1859; *d* 14 August, 1859.

(323) *Gertrude Beverley Robinson.*[6]

(324) *Beverley Robinson,*[6] *b* 13 August, 1862; *d* 15 August, 1862.

131. **Susan Philipse Robinson,**[5] *b* 25 November, 1818; (living 1903); *m* 11 November, 1862, *George Mountain Odell* (M.D.), *b* 3 March, 1818; *d* 21 April, 1892. S. P.

132. **Fanny Duer Robinson,**[5] *b* 3 July, 1822; (living 1903); *m* 1 April, 1841, *Edward Jones, b* 3 April, 1812; *d* 8 December, 1869.

(325) *Edward Renshaw Jones.*[6]

(326) *Harriet Duer Jones.*[6]

(327) *Elizabeth Schermerhorn Jones,*[6] *b* 23 May, 1845; (living 1903).

(328) *Morris Robinson Jones,*[6] *b* 16 March, 1847; *d* 31 March, 1849.[23]

134. **Harriet Duer Robinson,**[5] *b* 24 September, 1828; *d* October, 1893; *m* 30 October, 1849, *Albert Gallatin, b* 7 February, 1825; *d* 13 September, 1858.

(329) *Albert Louis Gallatin.*[6]

(330) *James Francis Gallatin,*[6] *b* 2 January, 1853; (living 1903), *unm.*

136. **Anna Dorothea Robinson,**[5] *b* 1 November, 1813; *d* 6 July, 1886; *m* 13 October, 1840, *Thomas Saunders Wetmore, b* 26 November, 1813. †

(331) *Jane Paddock Wetmore.*[6]

137. **William Henry Robinson,**[5] *b* 29 November, 1815; *d* 29 December, 1873; *m* 15 June, 1847, *Mary Paddock, b* 25 November, 1821; (living 1903).

(332) *Mary Robinson,*[6] *b* 5 April, 1848; *d* 11 August, 1849.

(333) *George Morris Robinson.*[6]

(334) *Adelaide Mary Robinson,*[6] *b* 16 September, 1851; (living 1903).

(335) *Jane Robinson,*[6] *b* 2 June, 1853; (living 1903).

(336) *Susanna Maria Robinson,*[6] *b* 23 March, 1855; *d* 13 March, 1858.

(337) *Anna Dorothea Robinson,*[6] *b* 21 September, 1857; (living 1903).

(338) *William Henry Robinson.*[6]

(339) *Mary Robinson,*[6] *b* 2 October, 1862; (living 1903).

138. **Beverley Adino Robinson,**[5] *b* 12 August, 1817; *d* 28 January, 1901; *m* 31 May, 1848, *Anna Maria Thurger,* *b* 4 August, 1827; (living 1903).

(340) *Anna Beverley Robinson.*[6]

(341) *Frederick Philipse Robinson.*[6]

(342) *Mary Maud Robinson.*[6]

141. **John Robinson,**[5] *b* 22 July, 1824; *d* 15 February, 1890; *m* 19 August, 1871, *Mary Hyde Roberts, b* 6 July, 1844; (living 1903). O. S. P.

143. **Henry Barclay Robinson,**[5] *b* 2 June, 1822; *d* 28 March, 1874; *m* 8 January, 1852, *Caroline Betts* (No. 299 above), *b* 17 August, 1831; *d* 22 March, 1903.

(343) *John Beverley Robinson.*[6]

(344) *Annie Morris Robinson.*[6]

(345) *William Betts Robinson,*[6] *b* 29 January, 1857; *d* 29 July, 1857.

(346) *Laurestine Mary Robinson,*[6] *b* 4 April, 1858; *d* 21 January, 1861.

(347) *Henry Barclay Robinson,*[6] *b* 12 September, 1860; *d* at Talcahuano, Chili, 1878, exact date unknown.

(348) *Caroline Alice Robinson.*[6]

(349) *Catherine Beverley Robinson.*[6]

(350) *Frederick DeLancey Robinson,*[6] *b* 16 July, 1867; *d* 20 August, 1891.

(351) *Frances Duer Robinson.*[6]

144. **Mary Eliza Robinson,**[5] *b* 8 April, 1824; *d* 18 November,
      1894; *m* 23 July, 1845, *Samuel James Scovil, b* 8 Au-
      gust, 1816; *d* 3 May, 1883.

      (352) *Mary Eliza Scovil,*[6] *b* 10 June, 1846; *d* 14
             April, 1849.
      (353) *Elizabeth Robinson Scovil,*[6] *b* 30 April, 1849;
             (living 1903).
      (354) *Sophia Allaire Scovil,*[6] *b* 24 June, 1850; *d* 26
             April, 1854.
      (355) *Samuel Scovil,*[6] *b* 16 February, 1852; *d* 1 June,
             1855.
      (356) *Samuel John Scovil.*[6]
      (357) *Morris Scovil.*[6]
      (358) *Arthur Scovil,*[6] *b* 14 April, 1862; *d* 14 Janu-
             ary, 1863.
      (359) *Alice Mary Scovil,*[6] *b* 2 October, 1863; *d* 19
             March, 1868.
      (360) *Henry Barclay Scovil,*[6] *b* 22 October, 1864;
             d 14 April, 1865.
      (361) *Barclay Allaire Scovil,*[6] *b* 21 March, 1867;
             (living 1903), *unm.*

145. **William Beverley Robinson,**[5] *b* 22 June, 1826; *d* 29
      June, 1873; *m* 22 April, 1857, *Sophia Isabella Bliss Dib-
      blee, b* 12 October, 1836; *d* 10 June, 1893.

      (362) *Mary Julia Robinson,*[6] *b* 20 January, 1858;
             d 31 May, 1873, *unm.*
      (363) *Louisa Maria Morrison Robinson.*[6]
      (364) *Sophie Robinson.*[6]
      (365) *William Henry Robinson,*[6] *b* 18 July, 1863;
             d 14 March, 1892, *unm.*
      (366) *Susan Beverley Robinson.*[6]
      (367) *John Rokeby Robinson.*[6]
      (368) *Beverley Robinson.*[6]
      (369) *Cornelia DeLancey Robinson.*[6]
      (370) *Mary Beverley Robinson.*[6]

149. **Morris Robinson,**[5] *b* 22 April, 1835; *d* 22 February, 1890;
      m 22 April, 1873, *Grace Hailes Dibblee, b* 8 May, 1843;
      (living 1903).

(371) *William Beverley Robinson,*[6] *b* 16 February, 1874; (living 1903), *unm.*

(372) *Percy Statham Robinson,*[6] *b* 12 October, 1875; (living 1903), *unm.*

(373) *DeLancey Allaire Robinson,*[6] *b* 14 February, 1887; (living 1903).

150. **Thomas Barclay Robinson,**[5] *b* 27 December, 1838; (living 1903); *m* 17 September, 1868, *Lucy Helen Smith, b* 24 April, 1843; (living 1903).

(374) *Henry Barclay Robinson.*[6]

(375) *Philipse Clinton Robinson.*[6]

(376) *Guy DeLancey Robinson,*[6] *b* 7 December, 1877; (living 1903), *unm.*

(377) *Frederick Gerald Robinson,*[6] *b* 22 July, 1884; (living 1903).

151. **Jack DeLancey Robinson,**[5] *b* 19 June, 1841; (living 1903); *m* 10 October, 1864, *Susan White Hubbard, b* 17 October, 1844; (living 1903).

(378) *Frances Eliza Robinson.*[6]

(379) *Mary DeLancey Robinson,*[6] *b* 3 April, 1867; (living 1903).

(380) *Susan Philipse Dudley Robinson,*[6] *b* 5 May, 1870; *d* 13 January, 1874.

(381) *Francis DeLancey Robinson,*[6] *b* 28 April, 1872; (living 1903), *unm.*

(382) *Cortlandt Allaire Robinson,*[6] *b* 25 September, 1880; living 1903), *unm.*

157. **Bache McEvers,**[5] *b* 11 October, 1798; *d* 15 July, 1851; *m* 15 October, 1825, *Jane Erin Emmet, b* 18 April, 1802; *d* 7 June, 1890, dau. of Thomas Addis Emmet.

(383) *Jeanette Emmet McEvers.*[6]

(384) *Mary Bache McEvers.*[6]

(385) *Addis Emmet McEvers,*[6] *b* 10 April, 1835; *d* 16 August, 1836.

158. **Sarah Barclay Bache,**[5] *b* 26 September, 1793;[23] *d* 24 November, 1859; *m* 11 December, 1811, *Robert Montgomery Livingston, b* 11 June, 1790; *d* 27 January, 1838.

(386) *Eliza Helen Livingston,*[6] *b* 7 December, 1812;
    d 26 February, 1896, *unm.*

(387) *Julia Eliza Montgomery Livingston,*[6] *b* 3
    April, 1814; *d* 30 October, 1827.

(388) *Angelica Livingston,*[6] *b* 5 October, 1815;
    (living 1903), *unm.*

(389) *Sarah Barclay Livingston,*[6] *b* 27 June, 1819;
    d 28 October, 1870, *unm.*

(390) *Richard Montgomery Livingston,*[6] *b* 10 June,
    1824; *d* 1 May, 1899. †

(391) *John Robert Livingston*[6] (Rev.), *b* 28 Au-
    gust, 1829; *d* 11 April, 1878, *unm.*

(392) *Charles Octavius Livingston.*[6]

(393) *Arthur Lispenard Livingston,*[6] *b* 8 October,
    1834; *d* 1 October, 1835.

159. **Andrew Theobald Bache,**[5] *b* 4 May, 1799; *d* 12 November, 1855; *m* 5 July, 1821, *Caroline McVoy, b* 25 August, 1804; *d* 8 January, 1895.

    (394) *Helen Lispenard Bache.*[6]

    (395) *Eliza Bleecker Bache.*[6]

    (396) *Sarah Louise Bache.*[6]

    (397) *Andrew James Bache.*[6]

    (398) *Charlotte L. Bache,*[6] *b* 28 January, 1831; *d* 3
        June, 1840.

    (399) *Catherine P. Bache,*[6] *b* 1 August, 1833; *d* 7
        March, 1844.

    (400) *George Frederick Bache.*[6]

    (401) *Julia Lynch Bache.*[6]

    (402) *Albert Bache,*[6] *b* 23 June, 1843; *d* 29 June,
        1843.

    (403) *William F. Bache,*[6] *b* 23 December, 1846; *d*
        25 August, 1848.

    (404) *Charlotte A. Bache.*[6]

160. **James Theophylact Bache,**[5] *b* 8 December, 1800; *d* 9
August, 1862; *m* 22 February, 1833, *Rosabella True-
man, b* 7 January, 1811; *d* 14 October, 1875.

    (405) *Charlotte Barclay Bache.*[6]

    (406) *John Henry Bache.*[6]

(407) *James Andrew Bache,*[6] *b* 2 February, 1839;
 d 16 March, 1839.

(408) *James Phillips Bache,*[6] *b* 7 February, 1841;
 d 28 October, 1871, *unm.*

(409) *Charles Morton Bache,*[6] *b* 20 June, 1844;
 d 6 June, 1845.

(410) *Sarah Emma Bache,*[6] *b* 13 September, 1846;
 d 24 December, 1876, *unm.*

(411) *William Frederick Bache.*[6]

162. Charlotte Bache,[5] *b* 31 May, 1804; *d* 23 May, 1830; *m*
14 February, 1821, *Francis B. Lynch, b* 3 August, 1797;
d 30 December, 1841.

(412) *Charlotte Lynch,*[6] *d unm.* †

(413) *Mary Lynch,*[6] *m Brien O'Hara.* †

(414) *Julia Lynch,*[6] *m Robert McPherson.* †

164. George Perry Bache,[5] *b* 8 March, 1809; *d* 9 March,
1889; *m* 13 January, 1834, *Eliza Ann Horne, d* prior to
1888, dau. of Dr. George T. Horne. †

(415) *Edgar H. Bache,*[6] *b* 25 April, 1836;[23] *d* 1871. †

(416) *George Perry Bache,*[6] died prior to 1888, aet.
37. †

(417) *John Owen Bache.*[6]

165. Eliza Barclay Bache,[5] *b* 28 October, 1811; *d* 31 July,
1887; *m* 25 April, 1832, *George Frederick Dückwitz,
b* in Bremen, Germany, 28 August, 1804; *d* 29 December, 1868.

(418) *Charlotte Gezina Dückwitz.*[6]

(419) *Arnold Frederick Dückwitz,*[6] *b* 15 October,
1836; (living 1903), *unm.*

(420) *George Theodore Dückwitz,*[6] *b* 17 August,
1839; *d* 23 January, 1900, *unm.*

(421) *Charles Andrew Dückwitz.*[6]

(422) *Eliza Helena Dückwitz,*[6] *b* 5 May, 1843; *d* 14
September, 1872, *unm.*

(423) *Sarah Dückwitz.*[6]

(424) *Mary Louise Dückwitz.*[6]

(425) *Emilie Meta Dückwitz.*[6]

(426) *William Henry Dückwitz.*[6]
(427) *Frances Adele Dückwitz.*[6]
(428) *Kate Isabel Dückwitz.*[6]
(429) *Julia Henrietta Dückwitz,*[6] *b* 16 January, 1856;
    d 16 October, 1898, *unm.*

166. **Sarah Bleecker Bache,**[5] *b* 28 May, 1815; *d* 5 January,
1903; *m* (1) 11 September, 1832, *John Daniel Kleudgen,*
b 14 July, 1809; *d* 14 July, 1847; *m* (2) 7 October, 1852,
Jacob R. Nevius, b 23 January, 1808;[69] *d* 23 December,
1867. O. S. P.

169. **Helen Bache,**[5] *b* 28 February, 1822; *d* 18 October, 1875;
m 29 April, 1852,[23] *William W. Jones* (M.D.), *b* 18
May, 1813; *d* 11 July, 1891. O. S. P.

170. **Catherine Satterthwaite Bache,**[5] *b* 12 October, 1824;
d 23 May, 1866; *m* 28 April, 1857, *Rev. William Rudder,*
b 1822; *d* 29 January, 1880. O. S. P.

174. **Theophylact Bache Lispenard,**[5] *b* 22 April, 1796;[23] *d*
26 August, 1834;[81] *m* 25 September, 1827,[81] *Mary Ann
Reeves, b* 14 November, 1805; *d* 3 April, 1890. (She
m (2) Louis A. Smith).
    (430) *Helen Sophia Lispenard.*[6]
    (431) *Leonard Augustus Lispenard,*[6] *b* 16 May,
        1830;[81] *d* 2 August, 1830.[81]
    (432) *Theophylact Bache Lispenard,*[6] *b* 1 October,
        1831;[81] *d* 28 July, 1832.[81]
    (433) *Julia Ann Sarah Lispenard.*[6]
    (434) *Esther Maria Lispenard.*[6]

176. **Helena Bache Lispenard,**[5] *b* 2 January, 1800;[23] *d* 16 September, 1845; *m* 22 May, 1821,[82] *Augustus A. Nichol-
son* (U.S.M.C.), *b* 1 August, 1800; *d* 18 July, 1855.
    (435) *Somerville Nicholson.*[6]
    (436) *Helen Lispenard Nicholson.*[6]

---

[81]Register of the CHURCH OF SCOTLAND, Quebec, Canada.

[82]"Married, May 22, 1821, Lieut. AUGUSTUS A. NICHOLSON, U. S. Marine Corps,
to Miss HELEN BACHE LISPENARD, daughter of the late Leonard Lispenard."

(437) *Annie Ducachet Nicholson.*[6]
(438) *Augustus Satterthwaite Nicholson.*[6]
(439) *Sarah Bleecker Nicholson,*[6] *b* 28 December, 1832; *d* August, 1833.
(440) *Catherine Satterthwaite Nicholson,*[6] *b* 17 March, 1834; *d* 9 April, 1835.
(441) *Mary Cornelia Nicholson.*[6]
(442) *Henry William Ducachet Nicholson.*[6]
(443) *Julia Barclay Nicholson,*[6] *b* 30 July, 1840; *d* 6 January, 1845.
(444) *Leonard Lispenard Nicholson.*[6]
(445) *Virginia Bache Nicholson,*[6] *b* 12 August, 1845; *d* 19 July, 1846.

177. **Eliza Ann Bache,**[5] *b* 18 October, 1797; *d* at Berlin, Prussia, 10 April, 1874; *m* 14 December, 1815, *John William Schmidt, b* at Weinsiedel, Germany, 11 September, 1781; *d* at Locust Island, New Rochelle (now Starin's Glen Island), 12 August, 1865.
    (446) *Helena E. Schmidt.*[6]
    (447) *Laura Schmidt.*[6]
    (448) *Florentine Theodore Schmidt,*[6] *b* 16 January, 1830;[23] *d* 6 November, 1852, *unm.*
    (449) *Alice Rosalie Schmidt.*[6]
    (450) *F. Leopold Schmidt.*[6]
    (451) *Oscar Egerton Schmidt.*[6]
    (452) *Pauline Schmidt.*[6]
    (453) *Ida M. Schmidt.*[6]

178. **Helena Bache,**[5] *b* 2 November, 1799; *d* 30 April, 1864; *m Samuel Patterson, d* Charleston, S. C., 24 December, 1838. †
    (454) *Mary Alice Patterson,*[6] *b* 10 August, 1838; (living 1903).

181. **Helena Bleecker,**[5] *b* 8 September, 1796; *d* 17 August, 1821; *m* 16 April, 1816, Rev. *Cornelius Roosevelt Duffie, b* 31 March, 1789; *d* 20 August, 1827.
    (455) *Charles William Duffie,*[6] *b* 17 January, 1817; *d* 24 June, 1824.

(456) *Helena Bleecker Duffie*,[6] *b* 20 May, 1817; *d* 17 September, 1886, *unm.*

(457) *Maria Roosevelt Duffie*,[6] *b* 6 December, 1819; *d* 14 March, 1876, *unm.*

(458) *Cornelius Roosevelt Duffie.*[6]

182. **Mary Bleecker,**[5] *b* 11 December, 1797; *d* 5 May, 1882; *m* 19 November, 1835, *Thomas W. Clerke* (a Justice of the Supreme Court of the State of New York), *b* 20 February, 1800; *d* 15 December, 1885. (He had issue, —one son, and a daughter (who died in infancy),—by a former wife.)

    (459) *Sarah Helena Clerke*,[6] *b* 6 June, 1838;[23] *d* 24 October, 1839.

183. **Anthony J. Bleecker,**[5] *b* 20 October, 1799; *d* 17 January, 1884; *m* 24 November, 1824, *Cornelia Van Benthuysen*, *b* 22 February, 1800; *d* 17 August, 1859.

    (460) *John Van Benthuysen Bleecker.*[6]

    (461) *Sarah Bache Bleecker.*[6]

    (462) *Helena Duffie Bleecker*,[6] *bap* 14 August, 1832; *d* in infancy. †

    (463) *James Bleecker.*[6]

185. **Theophylact Bache Bleecker,**[5] *b* 7 January, 1804; *d* 18 August, 1890; *m* 2 December, 1828, *Lydia Bloodgood DeWitt*, *b* 7 June, 1805; *d* 26 April, 1890.

    (464) *Eveleen DeWitt Bleecker*,[6] *b* 16 September, 1829; (living 1903).

    (465) *Anna Josepha Bleecker*,[6] *b* 4 April, 1831; (living 1903).

    (466) *Mary Nottingham Bleecker*,[6] *b* 10 February, 1833; (living 1903).

    (467) *Theophylact Bache Bleecker.*[6]

    (468) *Sarah Bache Bleecker*,[6] *b* 28 June, 1838; (living 1903).

    (469) *Lydia DeWitt Bleecker.*[6]

    (470) *Benjamin DeWitt Bleecker.*[6]

    (471) *Ann Eliza Satterthwaite Bleecker*,[6] *b* 24 October, 1844; *d* 19 May, 1846.

188. Sarah Bache Bleecker,[5] *b* 9 July, 1809; *d* 12 March, 1875; *m* (1) 22 June, 1829, *Theodore Low, b* 1805; *d* 27 November, 1833; *m* (2) 7 November, 1844, *William Pennock Hansford, b* 14 January, 1813; *d* 21 January, 1874.

> (472) *Theodore Low,*[6] *b* 1 May, 1830; [69] *d* 1 May, 1830.[69]
>
> (473) *James Bleecker Low,*[6] *b* 22 June, 1831; *d* 12 August, 1853, *unm.*
>
> (474) *Maria Pennock Hansford.*[6]
>
> (475) *Louis Bleecker Hansford,*[6] *b* 18 December, 1848; *d* 2 August, 1850.

192. Thomas Wilkinson Satterthwaite,[5] *b* 1 October, 1797; *d* 12 November, 1878; *m* (1) at Ayr, Scotland, 6 March, 1826,[83] *Jane Campbell McVitie, b* October, 1803; *d* in Quebec, 11 November, 1826; *m* (2) 1 November, 1837, *Ann Fisher Sheafe, b* 27 July, 1801; *d* 18 March, 1890.

> (476) *Elizabeth Wentworth Satterthwaite.*[6]
>
> (477) *James Sheafe Satterthwaite.*[6]
>
> (478) *Sarah F. Satterthwaite.*[6]
>
> (479) *Thomas E. Satterthwaite.*[6]
>
> (480) *J. Fisher Satterthwaite,*[6] *b* 4 July, 1844; (living 1903), *unm.*

194. Ann Dorothy Satterthwaite,[5] *b* 17 January, 1801; *d* 17 September, 1871; *m* 4 November, 1818, Rev. *Henry W. Ducachet, b* 7 February, 1797; *d* 13 December, 1865.

> (481) *Henry W. Ducachet*[6] (M.D.), *b* 27 June, 1821; *d* 11 October, 1865, *unm.*

196. Theophylact Bache Satterthwaite,[5] *b* 5 August, 1805; *d* 6 June, 1862; *m* 14 April, 1830, *Ann Eliza DeWitt, b* 31 January, 1807; *d* 6 January, 1887. O. S. P.

---

[83]From NEW YORK SPECTATOR of Friday, 5 May, 1826:

"*Married:* At Ayr, Scotland, on the 6th March, THOMAS WILKINSON SATTERTHWAITE, Esq., of Quebec (and formerly of this City), to JANE CAMPBELL McVITIE, daughter of the late Charles McVitie, Cumnock."

199. **John Blackwood Satterthwaite,**[5] *b* 13 June, 1812; *d* 16
    August, 1862; *m* 31 December, 1844, *Ellen Duane, b* 26
    December, 1816; *d* 4 January, 1846.
    (482) *Franklin Satterthwaite.*[6]

201. **Catherine White,**[5] *b* 30 November, 1786; *d* 29 Septem-
    ber 1878; *m* 26 October, 1812, *Richard Bayley*[4] (No.
    85 above), *b* 7 August, 1781; *d* 29 May, 1815.
    (The issue of this marriage are chronicled above,
    under: 85, RICHARD BAYLEY.[4])

205. **Helen White,**[5] *b* 12 November, 1792; *d* 25 May, 1881;
    m 12 September, 1809, *Abraham Schermerhorn, b* 9
    April, 1783; *d* 3 February, 1850.
    (483) *Henry White Schermerhorn,*[6] *b* 31 July, 1810;
        d 28 November, 1811.
    (484) *Augustus VanCortlandt Schermerhorn.*[6]
    (485) *Archibald Bruce Schermerhorn,*[6] *b* 18 Feb-
        ruary, 1814; *d* 27 April, 1861, *unm.*
    (486) *Elizabeth Schermerhorn.*[6]
    (487) *Ann White Schermerhorn.*[6]
    (488) *Helen Schermerhorn.*[6]
    (489) *Cordelia S. Schermerhorn,*[6] *b* 15 March, 1823;
        d 14 May, 1839, *unm.*
    (490) *Catherine Schermerhorn.*[6]
    (491) *Caroline Webster Schermerhorn.*[6]

207. **Augusta White,**[5] *b* 9 July, 1795; *d* 21 August, 1871; *m*
    16 October, 1821, *Edward Newenham Bibby* (M.D.),
    b 23 October, 1791; *d* 24 November, 1882.
    (492) *Anne White Bibby.*[6]
    (493) *Frances Augusta Bibby.*[6]
    (494) *Augustus VanCortlandt Bibby*[6] (took the sur-
        name VANCORTLANDT).
    (495) *Herman Isaac Bibby,*[6] *b* 25 December, 1827;
        d 25 April, 1832.
    (496) *Edward Newenham Bibby,*[6] [84] *b* 24 Septem-
        ber, 1831; *d* 15 August, 1833.

(497) *Henry Warburton Bibby,*[6] *b* 18 August, 1834;
       d 24 August, 1902, *unm.*

213. **Francena White,** [5] *b* 12 September, 1804; *d* 19 August,
       1868; *m* (1) 4 December, 1822, *Henry M. Groshon*
       (M.D.), *b* 15 September, 1796; *d* 18 August, 1828;
       m (2) 4 April, 1832, *John Wolff Meyer, b* 4 April,
       1800; *d* 1 May, 1847.

       (498) *Henry White Groshon.*[6]
       (499) *John Pierre Groshon.*[6]
       (500) *William Francis Groshon.*[6]
       (501) *Henrietta Anne Elizabeth Groshon.*[6]
       (502) *Francena Meyer.*[6]
       (503) *Augustus VanCortlandt Meyer.*[6]

214. **James VanCortlandt Morris,**[5] *b* 19 August, 1796; *d* 1
       January, 1843; *m* 4 February, 1824, *Catherine Charlton
       Post, b* 20 October, 1798;[23] *d* 20 January, 1828, dau. of
       Wright Post, M.D.

       (504) *James Morris,*[6] *b* 14 March, 1825;[78] *d* 29
              January, 1853, *unm.*

215. **Augustus Frederick (Morris) VanCortlandt,**[5] *b* 3 Oc-
       tober, 1797; *d* 18 December, 1859; *m* (1) 10 Decem-
       ber, 1823, *Harriet Munro, b* 21 June, 1798; *d* 10 March,
       1836, dau. of Peter Jay Munro; *m* (2) 3 April, 1839,
       Jane Catherine Maitland, dau. of Robert Maitland. †

       (505) A son,[6] *b* and *d* 4 March, 1825.
       (506) *Augustus VanCortlandt*[6] (M.D.), *b* 30 Au-
              gust, 1826; *d* 23 December, 1884, *unm.*
       (507) *Peter Jay Munro VanCortlandt.*[6]
       (508) *Frederick Morris VanCortlandt,*[6] *b* 5 March,
              1836; *d* 17 March, 1836.

---

[84]The records of the New York Board of Health refer to the death at Greenwich
Village on 9 May, 1828, of E. N. BIBBY aet. 6 mos. born in New York and buried in
Trinity. Mrs. Frances A. Munro (No. 493 above) states that this was *not* a son of
Dr. Edward N. and Augusta Bibby.

So, too, the records of Grace Church, New York, state that on December 23,
1826, ROBERT BIBBY was baptized, son of Edward N. and Augusta Bibby, born January 17, 1826. But Mrs. Munro is authority for the statement that this entry is in-
correct,—there never having been a Robert among her brothers.

216. **Catherine Morris,**[5] *b* 11 June, 1799; *d* 16 July, 1838; *m* 19 April, 1825, *Alexander H. Stevens* (M.D.), *b* 15 September, 1789; *d* 30 March, 1869.

> (509) *Helen Stevens,*[6] *b* 14 January, 1826; *d* 14 March, 1827.
>
> (510) *Catharine Byam Stevens,*[6] *b* December, 1828;[85] *d* 7 July, 1834.[86]
>
> (511) *Alexa Charlotte Stevens.*[6]

218. **Helen Morris,**[5] *b* 20 December, 1801; *d* 26 April, 1852.[86] *m* 30 October, 1823, *Richard Rutherfurd Morris, b* 20 August, 1798; *d* 2 June, 1866; son of Col. Lewis Morris.

> (512) *Helen Morris,*[6] *b* 1825; *d* 30 June, 1874, *unm.*
>
> (513) *Lewis Morris,*[6] *b* 1827; *d* 28 March, 1855, *unm.*
>
> (514) *Anna Elliot Morris.*[6]
>
> (515) *Mary Walton Morris,*[6] *b* 1831; *d* 17 May, 1890, *unm.*
>
> (516) *Charlotte Sophia Percy Morris.*[6]

221. **Richard Lewis Morris**[5] (M.D.), *b* 4 November, 1805; *d* 14 June, 1880; *m* 15 October, 1829, *Elizabeth Sarah Fish, b* 25 May, 1810; *d* 25 March, 1881, dau. of Col. Nicholas Fish.

> (517) *James Morris.*[6]
>
> (518) *Elizabeth Stuyvesant Fish Morris.*[6]
>
> (519) *Nicholas Fish Morris,*[6] *b* 19 June, 1836; *d* 1854, on the sloop-of-war "Albany," Capt. Elbridge T. Gerry, which sailed from Aspinwall 28 September, 1854, and was never heard of again.[87]
>
> (520) *Richard Lewis Morris,*[6] *b* 15 February, 1838; *d* 7 January, 1840.

---

[85]From NEW YORK COMMERCIAL ADVERTISER of Tuesday, 8 July, 1834:
   "Died: At Rockaway, on the 7th inst., of croup, succeeding scarlet fever, CATHERINE BYAM, only child of Dr. Alex. H. STEVENS, aged 5 years and 6 months."

[86]From THE EVENING MIRROR of Wednesday, 28 April, 1852:
   "Died: At her residence at Pelham, Westchester Co., April 26th, in the 51st year of her age, HELEN, the wife of Richard R. MORRIS."

[87]MUNSELL'S EVERYDAY BOOK OF HISTORY AND CHRONOLOGY, Albany: 1858.

(521) *Richard Lewis Morris.*[6]

(522) *Stuyvesant Fish Morris.*[6]

(523) *Helen Van Cortlandt Morris.*[6]

(524) *Charlotte Louisa Morris.*[6]

(525) *Margaret Livingston Morris.*[6]

222. **Robert Rutherfurd Morris,**[5] *b* 15 April, 1807; *d* 5 September, 1881; *m* 12 June, 1834, *Hannah Edgar, b* 16 January, 1815; *d* 7 June, 1850; dau. of William Edgar.

(526) *Katharine Augusta Morris.*[6]

(527) *Cornelia LeRoy Morris,*[6] *b* 1838; *d* 16 March, 1888, *unm.*

(528) *William Edgar Morris,*[6] *b* 22 August, 1843; *d* 13 February, 1875, *unm.*

(529) *Helen Louisa Morris.*[6]

223. **Sarah Louisa Morris,**[5] *b* 16 May, 1809; *d* 23 December, 1831; *m* 10 December, 1828, *Edward Augustus LeRoy, b* 4 March, 1805; *d* 16 January, 1865.

(530) *Helen Van Cortlandt LeRoy.*[6]

(531) *Herman LeRoy,*[6] *b* 1831; *d* 21 February, 1832.

224. **William H. Morris,**[5] *b* 3 August, 1810; *d* 11 February, 1896; *m* (1) 4 December, 1834, *Hannah Cornell Newbold, b* 17 July, 1816; *d* 5 May, 1842; *m* (2) 20 May, 1846, *Caroline Halsted, b* 3 June, 1827; *d* 28 June, 1848; *m* (3) 7 November, 1850, *Ella Birckhead, b* 3 September, 1830; *d* 21 November, 1881.

(532) *James Staats Morris,*[6] *b* 3 March, 1836; *d* 8 August, 1875, *unm.*

(533) *Augustus Newbold Morris.*[6]

(534) *William H. Morris,*[6] *b* 10 September, 1840; *d* 1 May, 1882, *unm.*

(535) *Augusta McEvers Morris.*[6]

(536) *Juliet Birckhead Morris.*[6]

225. **Charlotte Morris,**[5] *b* 4 April, 1812; *d* 2 June, 1838; *m* 10 June, 1836, *Richard Frederick Kemble, b* 22 May, 1800; *d* 22 January, 1888.

(537) *Mary Walton Kemble.*[6] *b* 21 September, 1837; (living 1903).

226. Helen Lispenard Stewart,[5] *b* 28 February, 1805; *d* 31 July, 1848; *m* 1 July, 1823,[88] *James Watson Webb, b* 8 February, 1802; *d* 7 June, 1884. (He *m* (2) 9 November, 1849, Laura Virginia Cram, *b* 2 January, 1826, dau. of Jacob Cram, and had issue: W. Seward Webb, H. Walter Webb, G. Creighton Webb, and others.)

> (538) *Robert Stewart Webb.*[6]
> (539) *Lispenard Stewart Webb,*[6] *b* 25 September, 1825; *d* 26 September, 1828.
> (540) *Amelia Barclay Webb,*[6] *b* August, 1829; *d* 11 October, 1830.[89]
> (541) *Helen Matilda Webb.*[6]
> (542) *Catherine Louisa Webb.*[6]
> (543) *James Watson Webb,*[6] *b* March, 1832; *d* 12 September, 1832.[90]
> (544) *Watson Webb.*[6]
> (545) *Alexander Stewart Webb.*[6]

227. Lispenard Stewart,[5] *b* 9 August, 1809; *d* 12 November, 1867; *m* (1) 4 June, 1834, *Louise Stephanie Salles* (dau. of Laurent Salles), *b* 1814; *d* 21 April, 1837; *m* (2) 22 December, 1847, *Mary Rogers Rhinelander, b* 14 September, 1822; *d* 7 October, 1893.

> (546) *Louise Stephanie Stewart.*[6]
> (547) *Sarah Lispenard Stewart.*[6]
> (548) *William Rhinelander Stewart.*[6]
> (549) *Lispenard Stewart,*[6] *b* 19 July, 1855; (living 1903), *unm.*
> (550) *Mary Rhinelander Stewart.*[6]

---

[88]From NEW YORK SPECTATOR of Tuesday, 8 July, 1823:

"Married: On Tuesday evening" (that is, 1 July, 1823) "by the Rev. Mr. Parkinson, Lieut. JAMES WATSON WEBB, of the 3rd Regt., U. S. Infantry, to Miss HELEN LISPENARD, daughter of Alexander L. STEWART, Esq."

[89]From THE NEW YORK GAZETTE of Tuesday, 12 October, 1830:

"Died: Yesterday afternoon, AMELIA BARCLAY, daughter of James Watson WEBB, aged 14 months.

[90]From THE NEW YORK SPECTATOR of Monday, 17 September, 1832:

"Died: On Wednesday evening" (that is, 12 September, 1832) "JAMES WATSON, infant son of James Watson WEBB, Esq., aged 6 months."

228. **Sarah A. Stewart,**[5] *b* 18 April, 1808; *d* 16 June, 1854; *m* (1) 17 January, 1825,[91] *John B. Skillman, b* at Schoharie, N. Y., 1797; *d* 30 September, 1831; *m* (2) 24 September, 1835, Rev. *Charles Samuel Stewart, b* 16 October, 1795; *d* 14 December, 1870.

> (551) *Lispenard Skillman*[6] (changed his name to STEWART).
>
> (552) *Sarah Lispenard Skillman*[6] (changed her name to STEWART).

229. **Mary Jordan Stewart,**[5] *b* 24 August, 1806; *d* 31 October, 1844; *m* 14 February, 1826,[92] *Stephen Hogeboom Webb, b* 25 September, 1796; *d* 15 February, 1873.

> (553) *Alexander Stewart Webb,*[6] *b* 4 January, 1827; *d* 16 December, 1830.
>
> (554) *Lispenard Stewart Webb,*[6] *b* 26 July, 1828; *d* 13 April, 1890, *unm.*
>
> (555) *Henry Barclay Webb,*[6] *b* 7 June, 1830; *d* 14 April, 1832.
>
> (556) *Eliza Stewart Webb,*[6] *b* 18 February, 1832; *d* 11 February, 1833.
>
> (557) *Mary Stewart Webb,*[6] *b* 6 March, 1834; *d* 27 February, 1893, *unm.*
>
> (558) *Stephania Louisa Webb,*[6] *b* 19 July 1835;. (living 1903). †
>
> (559) *Stephen Hogeboom Webb,*[6] *b* 26 February, 1838; (living 1903), *unm.*
>
> (560) *Virginia Garland Webb.*[6]

232. **Matilda Wilson Stewart,**[5] *b* 6 February, 1816; *d* 8 April, 1856; *m* 24 September, 1838, *Herman C. LeRoy, b* 27 February, 1818; *d* 7 May, 1872.

> (561) *Matilda Stewart LeRoy,*[6] *b* 13 August, 1839; *d* 4 August, 1840.
>
> (562) *Herman Stewart LeRoy.*[6]

---

[91]From THE NEW YORK GAZETTE of Saturday, 29 January, 1825:

"*Married:* On Thursday evening, by the Rev. Mr. Parkinson, JOHN B. SKILLMAN, merchant, to Miss SARAH ANN, daughter of A. L. STEWART, Esq."

[92]From COMMERCIAL ADVERTISER of Wednesday, 15 February, 1826:

"*Married:* Last evening, by the Rev. William Parkinson, Captain STEPHEN H. WEBB, of the U. S. Army, to Miss MARY J., daughter of A. L. STEWART, Esq."

236. Ann Margaret Bayley,[5] *b* 22 September, 1815; *d* 27
August, 1879; *m* 8 July, 1840, *Henry Munro, b* 18 February, 1802; *d* 21 May, 1862.

> (563) *Catherine Munro,*[6] *b* 15 October, 1841; *d* 24
> July, 1890, *unm.*
> (564) *Henry Munro,*[6] *b* 3 October, 1843; *d* 25 June,
> 1845.
> (565) *Peter Jay Munro,*[6] *b* 3 October, 1843; (living
> 1903), *unm.*
> (566) *Margaret White Munro.*[6]

238. Richard Bayley,[5] *b* 25 October, 1816; *d* 7 January, 1852;
m 8 October, 1845, *Mary Dietz, b* 23 July, 1821; *d* 3
January, 1890.

> (567) *Richard Walton Bayley,*[6] *b* 7 July, 1848; *d* 26
> January, 1897, *unm.*
> (568) *Guy Carleton Bayley.*[6]

239. Guy Carleton Bayley,[5] *b* 26 November, 1818; *d* 7 August, 1872; *m* (1) 22 July, 1846, *Lillias Graham, b* 9
March, 1823; *d* 22 February, 1855; *m* (2) 7 July, 1857,
Catherine Murray, b 10 February, 1831; *d* 20 June, 1879.

> (569) *Grace Walton Bayley.*[6]
> (570) *Emma Craig Bayley,*[6] *b* 6 July, 1849; *d* 10
> October, 1851.
> (571) *Carleton James Roosevelt Bayley,*[6] *b* 7 March,
> 1861; *d* 10 May, 1876.
> (572) *Mary Catherine Seton Bayley.*[6]

240. William Augustus Bayley,[5] *b* 16 May, 1821; *d* 8 August,
1870; *m* 8 May, 1845,[50] *Julia Neilson, b* October, 1822;
d 4 March, 1888.

> (573) *James Roosevelt Bayley,*[6] *b* 4 February, 1846;
> *d* 16 September, 1874, *unm.*
> (574) *Neilson Bayley,*[6] *b* 9 March, 1848.[78] †

241. Maria Eliza Bayley,[5] *b* 1 March, 1823; (living 1903);
m 17 November, 1847, *Jacob Boerum Jewett, b* 14 May,
1825; *d* 23 January, 1876.

> (575) *Louisa Brown Jewett,*[6] *b* 17 October, 1848;
> (living 1903).

(576) *Harriet Roosevelt Jewett,*[6] *b* 5 January, 1850;
    (living 1903).

(577) *Augustus Williamson Jewett,*[6] *b* 7 September,
    1851; (living 1903), *unm.*

(578) *Grace Bayley Jewett.*[6]

(579) *Mary Williamson Jewett.*[6]

(580) *Edward Woolsey Jewett,*[6] *b* 27 October, 1858;
    (living 1903), *unm.*

244. **Henry Sadler Craig,**[5] *b* 9 March, 1815;[23] *d* 13 January,
1840; *m* 4 October, 1838, *Catherine Gertrude Schuyler,*
b 15 January, 1818; *d* 8 October, 1887. O. S. P.

247. **Charlotte Amelia Craig,**[5] *b* 23 January, 1821; *d* 20 October, 1884; *m* 18 October, 1853, *Robert Bunch* (No.
251 above), *b* 11 September, 1820; *d* 21 March, 1881.

    (581) *Helen Baldock Bunch.*[6]

248. **William Craig,**[5] *b* 2 April, 1824;[23] *d* 13 February, 1866;
m 11 October, 1860, *Isabella Skerry, b* 9 May, 1838; *d*
22 July, 1863.

    (582) *William Craig,*[6] *b* 4 July, 1863; *d* 10 August,
        1866.

249. **Helen Elizabeth Craig,**[5] *b* 23 October, 1825; (living
1903); *m* 21 July, 1856, *Daniel Blake, b* 31 January,
1803; *d* 10 August, 1872.

    (583) *Robert Bunch Blake,*[6] *b* 23 January, 1861;
        (living 1903), *unm.*

    (584) *Emma Craig Blake.*[6]

    (585) *Helen Bayley Blake.*[6]

250. **Samuel R. Craig,**[5] *b* 31 March, 1828; *d* 14 September,
1903; *m* 14 July, 1866, *Amelia Houston McInnes, b* 3
May, 1846; (living 1903).

    (586) *William A. B. Craig,*[6] *b* 23 April, 1867; *d* 3
        April, 1890, *unm.*

    (587) *Elizabeth Craig.*[6]

    (588) *Daniel Blake Craig,*[6] *b* 25 February, 1871;
        d 24 July, 1874.

    (589) *James Roosevelt Bayley Craig.*[6]

(590) *Henry Armstrong Craig,*[6] *b* 25 July, 1878; (living 1903), *unm.*

(591) *Helen Blake Craig,*[6] *b* 28 April, 1881; (living 1903).

(592) *Emily Louise Craig,*[6] *b* 2 May, 1884; (living 1903).

(593) *Samuel Roland Craig,*[6] *b* 16 November, 1888; (living 1903).

251. **Robert Bunch,**[5] *b* 11 September, 1820; *d* 21 March, 1881; *m* 18 October, 1853, *Charlotte Amelia Craig*[5] (No. 247 above), *b* 23 January, 1821; *d* 20 October, 1884.
(The issue of this marriage is chronicled above, under: 247, CHARLOTTE AMELIA CRAIG[5]).

252. **Charlotte Amelia Bayley Bunch,**[5] *b* 27 May, 1826;[23] *d* 24 January, 1890; *m* 2 June, 1852, *Augustus* (Bibby) *Van Cortlandt*[6] (No. 494 above), *b* 31 July, 1826; (living 1903).

(594) *Augustus Van Cortlandt.*[6]

(595) *Henry White Van Cortlandt,*[6] *b* 15 May, 1858; (living 1903), *unm.*

(596) *Mary Bayley Van Cortlandt,*[6] *b* 3 February, 1860; (living 1903).†

(597) *Robert Bunch Van Cortlandt,*[6] *b* 14 August, 1862; (living 1903), *unm.*

(598) *Edward Newenham Van Cortlandt,*[6] *b* 6 December, 1864; (living 1903), *unm.*

(599) *Oloff de Lancey Van Cortlandt,*[6] *b* 6 February, 1868; *d* 14 April, 1900, *unm.*

253. **George Bunch,**[5] *b* 10 September, 1828; *d* 10 November, 1899; *m* at Caracas, Venezuela, 12 March, 1868, *Charlotte Morres, b* 16 April, 1844; *d* October, 1895.

(600) *Charlotte Bunch.*[6] †

(601) *Robert Bunch,*[6] (living 1903), *unm.* †

(602) *Elena Bunch.*[6] †

(603) *Elisa Bunch,*[6] *d* 1901; *m* 1898, M. Barreda. †

(604) *Adela Bunch.*[6] †

(605) *Yorje Bunch.*[6] †

255. Henry Barclay Livingston,[6] *b* 31 October, 1828; *d* 15 August, 1883; *m* May, 1850, *Julia Rathbone.* †
> (606) *Margaret Maria Livingston,*[7] *b* 25 August, 1852; (living 1903).

256. **Eliza Glass Livingston,**[6] *b* 7 September, 1831; (living 1903); *m* 4 November, 1851, *William Barclay Parsons*[5] (No. 110 above), *b* 4 September, 1828; *d* 31 December, 1887.
> (The issue of this marriage are chronicled above, under: 110, WILLIAM BARCLAY PARSONS[5]).

259. Matilda Corinna Livingston,[6] *b* 26 November, 1842; (living 1903); *m* 21 December, 1865, *Frederic W. Satterlee, b* 1 May, 1840; (living 1903).
> (607) *Carroll Livingston Satterlee,*[7] *b* 3 July, 1866; *d* 17 March, 1875.
> (608) *Frederic Rowland Satterlee,*[7] *b* 24 June, 1869; (living 1903), *unm.*

261. **DeLancey Hethcote Barclay**[6] (M.D.), *b* 19 June, 1854; *d* 9 July, 1900; *m* 19 April, 1888, *Sophia Caroline Saulsbury, b* 19 February, 1864; (living 1903), dau. of Alfred Saulsbury, of Baltimore, Md.
> (609) *Grace Douglass Barclay,*[7] *b* 15 April, 1889; (living 1903).
> (610) *Louise DeLancey Barclay,*[7] *b* 6 January, 1896; (living 1903).

263. **Catherine Channing Barclay,**[6] *b* 19 November, 1857; (living 1903); *m* at Stamford, Conn., 12 November, 1884, Rev. *Thomas Alexander Johnstone, b* 12 March, 1853; (living 1903). S. P.

267. **George Barclay Ward,**[6] *b* 1 January, 1845; (living 1903); *m* 7 April, 1869, *Jane Mary de Pau, b* 10 April, 1848; *d* 17 August, 1886.
> (611) *Jennie de Grasse Ward,*[7] *b* 20 April, 1870; (living 1903).
> (612) *George Clarence Barclay Ward.*[7]
> (613) *Louis deLancey Ward,*[7] *b* 12 August, 1873; (living 1903), *unm.*

268. **William deLancey Ward,**[6] *b* 14 June, 1847; (living 1903); *m* 21 June, 1872, *Emma Liddy Kutschke, b* 27 September, 1848; (living 1903).

> (614) *Elsa Martha Ward,*[7] *b* 19 June, 1873; (living 1903).

269. **Beverley Ward,**[6] *b* 7 June, 1850; (living 1903); *m* (1) 30 January, 1872, *Mary Wool Hastings, b* 31 October, 1852; (living 1903); *m* (2) 26 March, 1892, *Caroline Suckley, b* 13 October, 1861; (living 1903).

> (615) *Susan Hastings Ward.*[7]
> (616) *Beverley Ward,*[7] *b* 17 December, 1873; *d* 16 December, 1897, *unm.*
> (617) *Beatrice Colden Ward,*[7] *b* 7 December, 1883; (living 1903).
> (618) *Caroline DeLancey Ward,*[7] *b* 22 July, 1894; (living 1903).
> (619) *Jane Suckley Ward,*[7] *b* 8 November, 1897; (living 1903).

270. **Annie Parsons Ward,**[6] *b* 11 February, 1852; (living 1903); *m* 29 April, 1875, *Luther Kountze, b* 29 October, 1845; (living 1903).

> (620) *Barclay Ward Kountze,*[7] *b* 27 February, 1876; *d* 29 August, 1901, *unm.*
> (621) *William DeLancey Kountze,*[7] *b* 23 July, 1878; (living 1903), *unm.*
> (622) *Helen Livingston Kountze.*[7]
> (623) *Annie Ward Kountze,*[7] *b* 22 March, 1888; (living 1903).

271. **Schuyler Livingston Parsons,**[6] *b* 12 October, 1852; (living 1903); *m* 13 June, 1877, *Helena Johnson, b* 2 June, 1856; *d* 26 August, 1897.

> (624) *Helena Johnson Parsons,*[7] *b* 8 May, 1878; (living 1903).
> (625) *Evelyn Knapp Parsons,*[7] *b* 26 March, 1881; (living 1903).
> (626) *Schuyler Livingston Parsons,*[7] *b* 28 May, 1892; (living 1903).

272. **William Barclay Parsons,**[6] *b* 15 April, 1859; (living 1903); *m* 20 May, 1884, *Anna DeWitt Reed* (living 1903).

    (627) *Sylvia Caroline Parsons,*[7] *b* 19 November, 1885; (living 1903).

    (628) *William Barclay Parsons,*[7] *b* 22 May, 1888; (living 1903).

273. **Harry deBerkeley Parsons,**[6] *b* 6 January, 1862; (living 1903); *m* 16 December, 1890, *Frances Thompson Walker* (living 1903).

    (629) *Francis Livingston Parsons,*[7] *b* 27 January, 1894; (living 1903).

    (630) *Katharine deBerkeley Parsons,*[7] *b* 2 April, 1897; (living 1903).

274. **George Burrington Parsons,**[6] *b* 4 March, 1863; (living 1903); *m* 14 November, 1891, *Elizabeth Remsen Webb* (No. 991 below), *b* 6 July, 1861; (living 1903). S. P.

275. **George Lockhart Rives,**[6] *b* 1 May, 1849; (living 1903); *m* (1) 21 May, 1873, *Caroline Morris Kean, b* 24 July, 1849; *d* 29 March, 1887; *m* (2) 20 March, 1889, *Sara Whiting, b* 22 June, 1861; (living 1903).

    (631) *George Barclay Rives.*[7]

    (632) *Francis Bayard Rives,*[7] *b* 11 January, 1890; (living 1903).

    (633) *Mildred Sara Rives,*[7] *b* 31 July, 1893; (living 1903).

276. **Ella Louise Rives,**[6] *b* 8 March, 1851; (living 1903); *m* 7 January, 1875, *David King, b* 29 December, 1839; *d* 8 March, 1894.

    (634) *Maud Gwendolen King.*[7]

    (635) *Philip Wharton Rives King,*[7] *b* 12 June, 1879; (living 1903).

277. **Francis Robert Rives,**[6] *b* 28 January, 1853; *d* 7 January, 1890; *m* (1) 29 April, 1879, *Georgia Anna Fellows, d* 4 January, 1880; *m* (2) 25 August, 1887, *Frances Agnes Bininger;* (living 1903). O. S. P.

278. **Maud Antonia Rives,**[6] *b* 17 July, 1855; (living 1903);
m 23 May, 1882, *Walker Breese Smith;* (living 1903).

(636) *Evelyn Smith,*[7] *b* 15 June, 1888; (living 1903).

279. **Constance Evelyn Rives,**[6] *b* 17 July, 1855; (living 1903);
m 24 June, 1884, *John Borland, b* 7 July, 1856; *d* 27
April, 1893.

(637) *Maud Rives Borland,*[7] *b* 14 April, 1886;
(living 1903).

(638) *John Borland,*[7] *b* 15 October, 1887; (living
1903).

(639) *Ella Aufrère Borland,*[7] *b* 25 September, 1889;
(living 1903).

280. **Reginald William Rives,**[6] *b* 18 May, 1861; (living 1903);
m 1 June, 1887, *Mary Caroline Bulkeley* (living 1903).

(640) *Helen Mildred Rives,*[7] *b* 26 May, 1888; (living
1903).

(641) *Reginald Bulkeley Rives,*[7] *b* 9 April, 1890;
(living 1903).

282. **Cornelia C. Barclay,**[6] *b* 3 March, 1851; (living 1903);
m 19 October, 1871, *Sackett Moore Barclay*[5] (No. 123
above), *b* 1 December, 1850; (living 1903).

(The issue of this marriage are chronicled above,
under: 123, SACKETT MOORE BARCLAY.[5])

285. **Mary Marshall Barclay,**[6] *b* 25 July, 1859; *d* 15 February,
1893; *m* 13 October, 1881, *Charles C. Taliaferro,* of Savannah, Ga., *b* 26 June, 1843; (living 1903). He *m*
(2) 18 October, 1895, Mary Wilkinson.

(642) *Frances Armistead Taliaferro,*[7] *b* 22 June,
1882; (living 1903).

(643) *Charles C. Taliaferro,*[7] *b* 22 May, 1883; (living
1903).

(644) *Anthony Barclay Taliaferro,*[7] *b* 22 October,
1884; (living 1903).

(645) *Benjamin Franklin Taliaferro,*[7] *b* 14 February,
1886; *d* 23 September, 1889.

(646) *Catherine deLancey Barclay Taliaferro,*[7] *b*
12 June, 1888; *d* 24 December, 1888.

(647) *Marie C. Taliaferro,*[7] *b* 15 May, 1890; *d* 15
May, 1890.

287. **Gertrude O. Barclay,**[6] *b* 25 July, 1874; (living 1903);
m 29 April, 1901, *Julien Stevens Ulman, b* 1 October,
1865; (living 1903). S. P.

288. **Henry Anthony Barclay,**[6] *b* 13 October, 1875; (living
1903); *m* 18 April, 1901, *Rosalie X. Paul, b* 5 April,
1878; (living 1903).

(648) *Rosalie Paul Barclay,*[7] *b* 17 May, 1903; (living
1903).

289. **Wright Barclay,**[6] *b* 26 March, 1877; (living 1903); *m*
23 June, 1903, *Louise Fontaine Mitchell* (widow of
Nathaniel E. Venable), *b* 31 December, 1869; *d* 26 July,
1903. S. P.

292. **Adelaide Mott Barclay,**[6] *b* 19 November, 1884; (living
1903); *m* 23 September, 1903, *Algernon K. Boyesen, b*
13 October, 1880; (living 1903). S. P.

295. **Beatrice W. Barclay,**[6] *b* 21 December, 1875; (living
1903); *m* 9 October, 1901, *Stockton Beekman Colt, b*
20 March, 1863; (living 1903).

(649) *Stockton Beekman Colt,*[7] *b* 21 July, 1902;
(living 1903).

(650) *Rutger Barclay Colt,*[7] *b* 11 November, 1903;
(living 1903).

296. **Ethel N. Barclay,**[6] *b* 28 May, 1877; (living 1903); *m* 18
July, 1900, *Thornton Chard, b* 29 August, 1873; (living
1903).

(651) *Ethel C. E. Chard,*[7] *b* 22 December, 1901;
(living 1903).

298. **Beverley Robinson Betts**[6] (Rev.), *b* 3 August, 1827; *d*
21 May, 1899; *m* 6 October, 1892, *Emily Henrietta Nis-
bett, b* 1 August, 1840; (living 1903). O. S. P.

299. **Caroline Betts,**[6] *b* 17 August, 1831; *d* 22 March, 1903; *m* 8 January, 1852, *Henry Barclay Robinson*[5] (No. 143 above), *b* 2 June, 1822; *d* 28 March, 1874.
     (The issue of this marriage are chronicled above under: 143, HENRY BARCLAY ROBINSON.[5])

300. **William Betts,**[6] *b* 2 March, 1835; *d* 14 February, 1869; *m* 10 June, 1857, *Isabel Fords Needham, b* 6 October, 1836; (living 1903).
     (652) *Francis Needham Betts,*[7] *b* 11 June, 1858; *d* 3 February, 1859.
     (653) *William Hazen Betts,*[7] *b* 6 November, 1859; *d* 2 October, 1860.
     (654) *Anna Dorothea Betts,*[7] *b* 15 February, 1861; *d* 8 April, 1872.
     (655) *Mary Shaw Betts,*[7] *b* 24 January, 1863; *d* 26 October, 1863.
     (656) *Isabel Fords Betts.*[7]

301. **Beverley Robinson,**[6] *b* 7 January, 1838; *d* 30 May, 1885; *m* 16 March, 1864, *Eliza Gracie King, b* 7 July, 1843; *d* 30 December, 1898.
     (657) *Adeline King Robinson,*[7] *b* 22 March, 1865; (living 1903).
     (658) *Beverley Robinson.*[7]
     (659) *Maud deLancey Robinson.*[7]
     (660) *Rufus King Robinson,*[7] *b* 25 December, 1879; (living 1903), *unm.*

302. **Philip Palmer Robinson,**[6] *b* 3 September, 1839; *d* 30 June, 1889; *m* 21 April, 1875, *Ella Fergusson, b* 7 July, 1853; (living 1903).
     (661) *Frances Duer Robinson.*[7]
     (662) *Ethel Robinson,*[7] *b* 29 October, 1877; (living 1903).

304. **Robert Emmet Robinson,**[6] *b* 19 August, 1843; *d* 3 February, 1903; *m* 6 December, 1871, *Julia Eliza Smith, b* 6 March, 1837; (living 1903).
     (663) *Julia Beverley Robinson.*[7]
     (664) *Beverley William Robinson.*[7]

305. **Mary Hubley Robinson,**[6] *b* 17 April, 1847; (living
1903); *m* 9 July, 1901, *Martin E. Greene, b* 17 April,
1828; (living 1903). S. P.

308. **Fanny Duer Robinson,**[6] *b* 13 August, 1853; *d* 6 March,
1902; *m* 8 February, 1882, *William Hathorn Stewart
Davidge, b* 6 November, 1853; (living 1903).
(665) *Frances Beverley Davidge,*[7] *b* 27 September,
1882; (living 1903).

313. **John Beverley Duer,**[6] *b* 23 April, 1851; (living 1903);
m 5 February, 1894, *Mary Augusta Hamilton* (living
1903). S. P.

318. **Morris Robinson Slidell=Mackenzie,**[6] *b* 5 May, 1848;
(living 1903); *m* 28 August, 1872, *Anna Clarkson Crosby Stevens;* (living 1903). S. P.

319. **Catherine Elizabeth Hudson Robinson,**[6] *b* 27 October,
1846; (living 1903); *m* 17 June, 1879, *William Taylor
Moore, b* 8 October, 1823; *d* 19 May, 1897. S. P.

320. **Georgiana Winthrop Robinson,**[6] *b* 4 March, 1856; (living 1903); *m* 5 January, 1876, *David Abeel Storer, b*
19 July, 1842; *d* 11 October, 1897.
(666) *David Abeel Storer,*[7] *b* 12 January, 1872; *d*
16 January, 1878.
(667) *Ethel Winthrop Storer.*[7]
(668) *Henry Duer Storer,*[7] *b* 5 August, 1881; (living
1903).
(669) *David Abeel Storer,*[7] *b* 8 August, 1885; (living 1903).
(670) *Dorothy Dudley Storer,*[7] *b* 6 July, 1888; (living 1903).

323. **Gertrude Beverley Robinson**[6] (living 1903); *m* 3 June,
1882, *William McA. Motley, b* 24 December, 1848;
(living 1903). S. P.

325. **Edward Renshaw Jones,**[6] *b* 28 January, 1842; *d* 15 April,
1884; *m* 14 November, 1866, *Mary Elizabeth Yates
Baldwin;* (living 1903).

(671) *Edward Renshaw Jones,*[7] *b* 14 June, 1871;
d 18 February, 1896, *unm.*

(672) *Frances Duer Jones.*[7]

(673) *Mabel Irving Jones,*[7] *b* 14 January, 1875; (living 1903).

326. **Harriet Duer Jones,**[6] *b* 30 August, 1843; (living 1903);
m 2 December, 1868, *James Neilson Potter, b* 25 August,
1841; (living 1903).

(674) *Elizabeth Schermerhorn Potter.*[7]

(675) *Henrietta Neilson Potter,*[7] *b* 19 June, 1872;
(living 1903).

(676) *Margaret Renshaw Potter,*[7] *b* 2 September,
1876; (living 1903).

(677) *Katharine Alexander Duer Potter,*[7] *b* 25 September, 1885; (living 1903).

329. **Albert Louis Gallatin,**[6] *b* 19 September, 1850; *d* 12 February, 1880; *m* 2 May, 1876, *Zefita Heyward, d* March,
1896. O. S. P.

331. **Jane Paddock Wetmore,**[6] *b* 18 November, 1841; *d* 18
November, 1868; *m* 23 October, 1863, *William E.
Scovil, b* 3 January, 1843; (living 1903).

(678) *Anna Dorothea Scovil.*[7]

(679) *Frances Marion Scovil.*[7]

(680) *William Thomas Scovil.*[7]

333. **George Morris Robinson,**[6] *b* 29 July, 1850; *d* 3 August,
1895; *m* 25 September, 1889, *Adelaide May Llewellyn.* †

(681) *Beverley William Llewellyn Robinson,*[7] *b* 23
June, 1893; (living 1903).

338. **William Henry Robinson,**[6] *b* 3 September, 1859; (living
1903); *m* 22 February, 1898, *Gertrude Anna Fielders,
b* 29 May, 1871; (living 1903).

(682) *John Philipse Robinson,*[7] *b* 20 September,
1900; (living 1903).

340. **Anna Beverley Robinson,**[6] *b* 29 December, 1850; (living
1903); *m* (1) 6 February, 1884, *George William Marsh,
b* 11 November, 1859; *d* 11 November, 1886; *m* (2)

22 July, 1890, Rt. Rev. *Hollingworth Tully Kingdon,*
Bishop of Fredericton, N. B., *b* 16 April, 1835; (living
1903).

    (683) *Constance Cecil Maud Marsh,*[7] *b* 31 January,
        1885; *d* 15 September, 1902.

    (684) *Violet Anna Beverley Marsh,*[7] *b* 20 August,
        1886; (living 1903).

    (685) *Anna Phillipps Renorden Kingdon,*[7] *b* 10 De-
        cember, 1891; (living 1903).

341. **Frederick Philipse Robinson,**[6] *b* 16 December, 1855;
(living 1903); *m* 2 January, 1889, *Georgina Archer
Gregory;* (living 1903). S. P.

342. **Mary Maud Robinson,**[6] *b* 26 June, 1857; (living 1903);
m 6 February, 1894, *William Henry Bruce-Heath, b* 12
October, 1857; (living 1903). S. P.

343. **John Beverley Robinson,**[6] b 10 June, 1853; (living
1903); *m* 1 July, 1885, *Elizabeth Olmstead, b* 15 February, 1857; (living 1903).

    (686) *Beverley Robinson,*[7] *b* 6 April, 1886; (living
        1903).

    (687) *Elizabeth Robinson,*[7] *b* 6 April, 1886; (living
        1903).

    (688) *Devereux Robinson,*[7] *b* 26 August, 1887; (liv-
        ing 1903).

344. **Annie Morris Robinson,**[6] *b* 10 November, 1855; (living
1903); *m* 4 October, 1878, *James Cooper Wheeler, b* 4
August, 1849; (living 1903).

    (689) *Candace Wheeler,*[7] *b* 16 October, 1879; (living
        1903).

348. **Caroline Alice Robinson,**[6] *b* 3 February, 1863; (living
1903); *m* 23 October, 1888, *Charles T. Matson, b* 16
November, 1860; (living 1903).

    (690) *William Charles Matson,*[7] *b* 26 May, 1890;
        (living 1903).

349. **Catherine Beverley Robinson,**[6] *b* 2 April, 1865; *d* 26 July, 1898; *m* 10 December, 1896, *Beverley Robinson*[6] (No. 368 above), *b* 9 May, 1896; (living 1903). O. S. P.

351. **Frances Duer Robinson,**[6] *b* 4 October, 1873; *d* 25 July, 1898; *m* 16 March, 1895, *David Gregg Metheny.*† O. S. P.

356. **Samuel John Scovil,**[6] *b* 2 May, 1856; (living 1903); *m* 11 October, 1882, *Eliza Adeline Barker, b* 21 May, 1859; (living 1903).
    (691) *John DeLancey Scovil,*[7] *b* 17 March, 1884; (living 1903).
    (692) *Charles Barker Scovil,*[7] *b* 10 November, 1886; (living 1903).
    (693) *Elizabeth Adeline Scovil,*[7] *b* 25 March, 1889 (living 1903).

357. **Morris Scovil,**[6] *b* 19 June, 1860; (living 1903); *m* 12 September, 1888, *Harriet Lavinia DuVernet, b* 18 March, 1866; (living 1903).
    (694) *Morris Allaire Scovil,*[7] *b* 4 July, 1889; (living 1903).
    (695) *Elizabeth Robinson Scovil,*[7] *b* 16 August, 1890; (living 1903).
    (696) *Gertrude Jervis Scovil,*[7] *b* 27 September, 1891; (living 1903).
    (697) *Mary DuVernet Scovil,*[7] *b* 10 January, 1896; (living 1903).
    (698) *Roger Peniston Scovil,*[7] *b* 14 August, 1897; (living 1903).

363. **Louisa Maria Morrison Robinson,**[6] *b* 21 October, 1859; (living 1903); *m* 8 September, 1881, *James Frederick Allison, b* 20 October, 1850; (living 1903).
    (699) *Louise Muriel Allison,*[7] *b* 16 October, 1882; *d* 18 August, 1883.
    (700) *William Beverley Allison,*[7] *b* 22 June, 1884; (living 1903).
    (701) *Mary Gretchen Allison,*[7] *b* 10 January, 1889; (living 1903).

364. **Sophie Robinson,**[6] *b* 8 July, 1861; (living 1903); *m* 12 July, 1888, *Charles deWolfe MacDonald, b* 23 October, 1854; (living 1903).

(702) *Alexander Cameron MacDonald,*[7] *b* 25 May, 1889; *d* 31 March, 1890.

(703) *Joan Allison MacDonald,*[7] *b* 24 May, 1891; (living 1903).

(704) *Charles Beverley Robinson MacDonald,*[7] *b* 8 December, 1893; (living 1903).

(705) *Eleanor Amelia Bliss MacDonald,*[7] *b* 2 September, 1897; (living 1903).

(706) *Donald Cameron MacDonald,*[7] *b* 30 January, 1900; (living 1903).

366. **Susan Beverley Robinson,**[6] *b* 27 March, 1865; (living 1903); *m* 12 April, 1893, *Percy Cunliffe Powys, b* 27 August, 1867; (living 1903).

(707) *Constance Gwendolen Powys,*[7] *b* 24 September, 1894; (living 1903).

(708) *Beverley Cunliffe Powys,*[7] *b* 1 January, 1896; (living 1903).

(709) *Alice Constance Robinson Powys,*[7] *b* 20 June, 1898; (living 1903).

(710) *Margaret Lybbe Powys,*[7] *b* 28 September, 1901; (living 1903).

367. **John Rokeby Robinson,**[6] *b* 18 July, 1867; (living 1903); *m* 12 December, 1893, *Seraph Spurr, b* 12 November, 1870; (living 1903).

(711) *Frederick Rokeby Robinson,*[7] *b* 9 October, 1894; (living 1903).

(712) *Mary Louise Phillis Robinson,*[7] *b* 30 March, 1899; (living 1903).

(713) *John Beverley Robinson,*[7] *b* 17 November, 1902; (living 1903).

368. **Beverley Robinson,**[6] *b* 9 May, 1869; (living 1903); *m* 10 December, 1896, *Catherine Beverley Robinson*[6] (No. 349 above), *b* 2 April, 1865; *d* 26 July, 1898. S. P.

369. **Cornelia DeLancey Robinson,**[6] *b* 20 January, 1871; (living 1903); *m* 7 September, 1892, *John Wilson Young Smith, b* 18 March, 1869; (living 1903).

> (714) *Sarah Marjory Sophia Smith,*[7] *b* 31 March, 1894; (living 1903).

370. **Mary Beverley Robinson,**[6] *b* 22 June, 1873; (living 1903); *m* 5 November, 1898, *Francis Moore Campbell Crosskill, b* 22 November, 1868; (living 1903).

> (715) *Beverley Campbell Crosskill,*[7] *b* 24 August, 1900; (living 1903).

374. **Henry Barclay Robinson,**[6] *b* 13 June, 1870; (living 1903); *m* 8 July, 1896, *Edith May Beer, b* 2 May, 1873; (living 1903).

> (716) *Lucy Florence Barclay Robinson,*[7] *b* 20 May, 1897; (living 1903).

375. **Philipse Clinton Robinson,**[6] *b* 3 September, 1873; (living 1903); *m* 9 January 1901, *Louisa Rainsford Holden, b* 25 May, 1874; (living 1903). S. P.

378. **Frances Eliza Robinson,**[6] *b* 17 August, 1865; (living 1903); *m* 1 June, 1887, *Arthur William Carr, b* 21 December, 1861; (living 1903).

> (717) *Walter deLancey Avis Carr,*[7] *b* 27 October, 1888; (living 1903).
>
> (718) *Constance Mary Carr,*[7] *b* 25 March, 1892; (living 1903).

383. **Jeannette Emmet McEvers,**[6] *b* 12 August, 1826; *d* 22 July, 1884; *m* 21 February, 1850, *Samuel Haight Whitlock, b* 5 September, 1819; *d* 19 May, 1856.

> (719) *William Whitlock.*[7]
>
> (720) *Bache McEvers Whitlock.*[7]

384. **Mary Bache McEvers,**[6] *b* 8 May, 1828; *d* 25 May, 1866; *m* 17 May, 1849, *Edward Cunard, b* 1 January, 1816; *d* 8 April, 1869.

> (721) *Samuel Cunard,*[7] *b* 15 March, 1850; *d* 25 September, 1850.
>
> (722) *Bache Edward Cunard.*[7]

(723)	*Mary McEvers Cunard.*[7]
(724)	*Edward Cunard,*[7] *b* 1 January, 1855; *d* 31 August, 1877, *unm.*
(725)	*Gordon Cunard.*[7]
(726)	*Jeannette Emmet Cunard.*[7]
(727)	*Annie Allen Cunard.*[7]
(728)	*Caroline Margaret Cunard.*[7]

392.	**Charles Octavius Livingston,**[6] *b* 4 October, 1831; (living 1903); *m* 20 November, 1872, *Sarah Elizabeth Ramsey, b* 1 July, 1847; (living 1903).

(729)	*Charles Victor Livingston,*[7] *b* 30 August, 1873; (living 1903), *unm.*
(730)	*Robert R. Livingston,*[7] *b* 16 March, 1878; (living 1903), *unm.*

394.	**Helen Lispenard Bache,**[6] *b* 21 May, 1822; *d* 5 November, 1902; *m* 29 June, 1843, *Andrew Hall, b* 15 November, 1816; *d* 13 October, 1891.

(731)	*Charlotte Louise Hall.*[7]
(732)	*Annie Armstrong Hall,*[7] *b* 26 July, 1847; (living 1903).
(733)	*Helen Bache Hall.*[7]

395.	**Eliza Bleecker Bache,**[6] *b* 20 September, 1823; *d* 28 October, 1855; *m* 11 June, 1845, *John A. Hull.*†

(734)	*Caroline Hull,*[7] *m William Murphy.*†
(735)	*William Hull.*[7]†
(736)	*James Hull.*[7]†

396.	**Sarah Louise Bache,**[6] *b* 9 April, 1826; *d* 19 October, 1893; *m* 27 November, 1848, *Frederick Hayward Manby Newcombe, b* 28 February, 1819; *d* 13 March, 1890.

(737)	*George Frederick Newcombe.*[7]
(738)	*Jane Caroline Newcombe.*[7]
(739)	*Frederick Hayward Newcombe.*[7]
(740)	*Andrew Bache Newcombe.*[7]
(741)	*Charles Manby Newcombe.*[7]

397. **Andrew James Bache,**[6] *b* 9 September, 1829; *d* 29 June, 1899; *m* (1) January, 1850, *Kate Pugh, b* 18 April, 1834; *d* 14 May, 1867; *m* (2) 19 November, 1868, *Mary de Peyster Lincoln, b* 19 April, 1849; *d* 10 October, 1891.

   (742) *Kate Pugh Bache.*[7]

   (743) *Andrew James Bache,*[7] *b* 19 October, 1857; (living 1903), *unm.*

   (744) *Caroline Armande Bache.*[7]

   (745) *Archibald Gracie Bache,*[7] *b* 16 January, 1870; (living 1903), *unm.*

   (746) *Mary dePeyster Lincoln Bache.*[7]

   (747) *Katharine Rutgers Bache.*[7]

400. **George Frederick Bache,**[6] *b* 10 September, 1835; *d* 28 December, 1883; *m* 18 October, 1865, *Emeline Kirby, b* 9 January, 1845; (living 1903).

   (748) *Eloise Kirby Bache.*[7]

   (749) *Maude Emeline Bache.*[7]

   (750) *Marion B. Bache.*[7]

   (751) *George Frederick Bache.*[7]

   (752) *Claude Leon Bache,*[7] *b* 12 June, 1877; (living 1903), *unm.*

   (753) *Mabel Hall Bache.*[7]

   (754) *Alyne Bache,*[7] *b* 29 October, 1882; (living 1903).

401. **Julia Lynch Bache,**[6] *b* 15 March, 1837; *d* 15 January, 1899; *m* 28 September, 1874, *Francis A. F. Pickell, b* 13 March, 1853; (living 1903).

   (755) *Julia Frances Pickell,*[7] *b* 13 March, 1879; (living 1903).

   (756) *Caroline Bache Pickell.*[7]

404. **Charlotte A. Bache,**[6] *b* 16 January, 1848; *d* 15 August, 1865; *m* 17 January, 1865, *Charles Andrew Dückwitz*[6] (No. 421 above), *b* 29 March, 1841; *d* 21 January, 1884. O. S. P.

405. **Charlotte Barclay Bache,**[6] *b* 6 November, 1833; *d* 3 November, 1884; *m* 16 June, 1863, *William Henry Crossman, b* 20 December, 1831; *d* 19 June, 1894.

(757) *William Henry Crossman.*[7]

(758) *Florence Crossman.*[7]

(759) *Charlotte Grace Crossman.*[7]

(760) *Blanche Eva Crossman,*[7] *b* 11 December, 1872; *d* 29 January, 1875.

406. **John Henry Bache,**[6] *b* 17 August, 1836; *d* 1 March, 1893; *m* 18 May, 1858, *Frances Roe Haswell, b* 18 September, 1837; (living 1903).

    (761) *James Henry Bache,*[7] *b* 12 August, 1861; *d* 18 November, 1861.

    (762) *Marion Bache,*[7] (living 1903).

411. **William Frederick Bache,**[6] *b* 1 March, 1848; (living 1903); *m* 16 October, 1868, *Emma Adriance, b* 25 February, 1849; (living 1903).

    (763) *Rosabella Bache,*[7] *b* 17 July, 1869; *d* 10 June, 1870.

    (764) *James Theophylact Bache.*[7]

    (765) *Phillips William Bache,*[7] *b* 12 February, 1873; *d* 17 March, 1890.

    (766) *Charles Frederick Bache.*[7]

417. **John Owen Bache,**[6] *b* 22 September, 1844; disappeared May, 1895; *m* 18 September, 1873, *Mary Bleecker, b* 4 May, 1847; *d* 26 January, 1901.

    (767) *Mary Bleecker Bache,*[7] *b* 1 July, 1874; *d* 8 January, 1878.

    (768) *Grace Bache.*[7]

418. **Charlotte Gezina Duckwitz,**[6] *b* 18 October, 1834; (living 1903); *m* 24 September, 1861, *William Henry Dudley,* M.D., *b* (Mount Dudley, Roscrea, Ireland) 7 October, 1811; *d* 9 October, 1886.

    (769) *William Frederick Dudley.*[7]

    (770) *Charlotte Elizabeth Dudley,*[7] *b* 9 October, 1863; (living 1903).

    (771) *Percy Sheldon Dudley,*[7] *b* 20 August, 1867; (living 1903), *unm.*

421. **Charles Andrew Duckwitz,**[6] *b* 29 March, 1841; *d* 21 January, 1884; *m* (1) 17 January, 1865, *Charlotte A. Bache*[6] (No. 404 above), *b* 16 January, 1848; *d* 15 August, 1865; *m* (2) *Anais Monier,* (living 1903).

> (772) *Charles F. Dückwitz.*[7]†
> (773) *Theodore S. Dückwitz.*[7]†
> (774) *Florence A. Dückwitz.*[7]†
> (775) *Herbert H. Dückwitz.*[7]†

423. **Sarah Duckwitz,**[6] *b* 8 March, 1845; (living 1903); *m* 21 September, 1865, *Charles Henry Raberg, b* 3 November, 1838; (living 1903). S. P.

424. **Mary Louise Duckwitz,**[6] *b* 4 December, 1846; (living 1903); *m* 30 January, 1872, *Hubert VanWagenen Tucker, b* 13 January, 1844; *d* 16 December, 1884.

> (776) *Hubert VanWagenen Tucker,*[7] *b* 25 April, 1873; *d* 2 September, 1873.
> (777) *Frederic Randolph Tucker,*[7] *b* 5 October, 1874; *d* 28 July, 1875.

425. **Emilie Meta Duckwitz,**[6] *b* 13 November, 1848; (living 1903); *m* 13 January, 1875, *Frederick Eldredge Mason, b* 9 November, 1845; (living 1903).

> (778) *Clotilde Dückwitz Mason,*[7] *b* 21 February, 1876; (living 1903).
> (779) *Emilie Duryea Mason.*[7]

426. **William Henry Duckwitz,**[6] *b* 18 March, 1850; *d* 25 October, 1901; *m* 16 October, 1873, *Louise Crommelin, b* 26 June, 1850; (living 1903).

> (780) *Helen Louise Dückwitz,*[7] *b* 14 November, 1874; (living 1903).
> (781) *Lillian Ryder Dückwitz,*[7] *b* 29 May, 1886; *d* 9 May, 1894.

427. **Frances Adele Duckwitz,**[6] *b* 18 July, 1851; (living 1903); *m* 18 April, 1877, *John Francis Praeger, b* (Holland) 30 October, 1838; (living 1903). S. P.

428.   Kate Isabel Duckwitz,[6] *b* 14 October, 1853; (living
1903); *m* 8 April, 1891, Rev. *Albert Francis Tenney,*
b 24 July, 1847; (living 1903). S. P.

430.   Helen Sophia Lispenard,[6] *b* 8 November, 1828;[69] *d* 1
January, 1904; *m* 5 March, 1851, *Samuel Hawes Cooper,*
b 2 May, 1821; *d* 21 July, 1900.
(782) *Mary Esther Cooper,*[7] *b* 23 December, 1851;
(living 1903).
(783) *Samuel Lispenard Cooper.*[7]

433.   Julia Ann Sarah Lispenard,[6] *b* 10 December, 1832;[69]
(living 1903); *m* 16 September, 1864, *Edward Kil-*
patrick, b 13 April, 1829; *d* 5 December, 1898. S. P.

434.   Esther Maria Lispenard,[6] *b* 27 September, 1834;[69] (living
1903); *m* 24 July, 1860, *Alexander Robb, b* 1 July, 1827;
(living 1903).
(784) *William Lispenard Robb.*[7]
(785) *Julia L. Robb,*[7] *b* 3 February, 1864; (living
1903).
(786) *Louis Robb,*[7] *b* 9 May, 1866; (living 1903),
unm.
(787) *George Cooper Robb,*[7] *b* 10 July, 1868; (living
1903), *unm.*

435.   Somerville Nicholson[6] (U.S.N.), *b* 1 January, 1822;
(living 1903); *m* 2 September, 1851, *Hannah Maria*
Jones, b 16 July, 1828; *d* 6 June, 1897.
(788) *Reginald Fairfax Nicholson.*[7]
(789) *William Jones Nicholson.*[7]
(790) *Helen Maria Nicholson.*[7]
(791) *Augustus Somerville Nicholson.*[7]
(792) *Henry William Ducachet Nicholson.*[7]
(793) *Mary Blake Nicholson.*[7]
(794) *Reynolds Lispenard Nicholson.*[7]

436.   Helen Lispenard Nicholson,[6] *b* 20 December, 1823; *d* 3
June, 1899; *m* 14 December, 1854, Rev. *Edmund*
Roberts, b 14 December, 1824; *d* 10 March, 1893.

(795) *Helen Nicholson Roberts.*[7]

(796) *Annie Sutherland Roberts,*[7] *b* 28 November, 1857; (living 1903).

(797) *Elizabeth Booth Roberts,*[7] *b* 28 November, 1857; (living 1903).

437. **Annie Ducachet Nicholson,**[6] *b* 28 June, 1828; (living 1903); *m* (1) 29 July, 1850, *Daniel James Sutherland* (U.S.M.C.), *b* 16 March, 1823; *d* 15 November, 1861; *m* (2) 9 February, 1869, Dr. *Howard M. Rundlett* (U.S.N.), *b* 20 February, 1836; *d* 25 May, 1873.

> (798) *Annie Ducachet Sutherland,*[7] *b* 20 June, 1851; *d* 5 March, 1853.
>
> (799) *Mary Sutherland,*[7] *b* 15 April, 1853; *d* 12 July, 1855.
>
> (800) *Helena Bache Sutherland,*[7] *b* 15 October, 1854; *d* 13 July, 1855.
>
> (801) *Julia Florence Sutherland.*[7]
>
> (802) *Caroline Sutherland,*[7] *b* 15 November, 1858; (living 1903).
>
> (803) *Augusta Nicholson Sutherland.*[7]
>
> (804) *Anne Howard Rundlett.*[7]

438. **Augustus Satterthwaite Nicholson**[6] (U.S.M.C.), *b* 5 November, 1830; (living 1903); *m* 3 February, 1852, *Jane Findlay Jesup* (living 1903).

> (805) *Augustus Jesup Nicholson.*[7]

441. **Mary Cornelia Nicholson,**[6] *b* 14 March, 1836; (living 1903); *m* 30 July, 1860, *William C. Johnson, b* 16 July, 1823; *d* 23 January, 1893.

> (806) *Abigail Adams Johnson.*[7]
>
> (807) *Elizabeth Lispenard Johnson.*[7]

442. **Henry William Ducachet Nicholson,**[6] *b* 2 April, 1838; (living 1903); *m* 18 July, 1862, *Mary A. Janvier, b* 16 June, 1839; (living 1903).

> (808) *Somervillle Lispenard Nicholson,*[7] *b* 18 March, 1863; *d* 4 July, 1902, *unm.*
>
> (809) *Helen Bache Nicholson.*[7]

(810) *Margaret Janvier Nicholson,*[7] *b* 18 March, 1867; *d* 26 February, 1897, *unm.*

(811) *Benjamin Archer Nicholson,*[7] *b* 7 September, 1869; *d* 26 July, 1894, *unm.*

(812) *Henry Augustus Nicholson,*[7] *b* 24 December, 1871; *d* 13 March, 1886.

(813) *Atala Beale Nicholson.*[7]

(814) *Ellie Beale Nicholson,*[7] *b* 27 February, 1886; (living 1903).

444. **Leonard Lispenard Nicholson,**[6] *b* 1 October, 1842; (living 1903); *m* 19 February, 1868, *Susie C. Brawner, b* 10 October, 1844; (living 1903).

(815) *James Brawner Nicholson,*[7] *b* 10 February, 1869; (living 1903), *unm.*

(816) *Annie Ducachet Nicholson,*[7] *b* 1 September, 1870; *d* 6 February, 1876.

(817) *Leonard Lispenard Nicholson,*[7] *b* 27 September, 1873; (living 1903), *unm.*

(818) *Julia Blanche Nicholson,*[7] *b* 31 January, 1876; (living 1903).

(819) *John McGowan Nicholson,*[7] *b* 27 March, 1878; *d* 27 November, 1878.

446. **Helena E. Schmidt,**[6] *b* 2 May, 1827; (living 1903); *m* 14 December, 1852, *Alfred Ludlow Seton, b* 15 October, 1825; *d* 6 December, 1902.

(820) *Alfred Seton.*[7]

(821) *Laura Seton.*[7]

447. **Laura Schmidt,**[6] *b* 24 June, 1828; *d* 5 May, 1899; *m* 30 May, 1849, *Charles deRham, b* 20 October, 1822; (living 1903).

(822) *Elise deRham.*[7]

(823) *Henry Casimir deRham,*[7] *b* 29 July, 1852; *d* 10 July, 1853.

(824) *Charles deRham.*[7]

(825) *Henry Casimir deRham.*[7]

(826) *William deRham,*[7] *b* 3 April, 1857; *d* 29 January, 1881, *unm.*

449. **Alice Rosalie Schmidt,**[6] *b* 22 November, 1831; *d* 26 June, 1898; *m* (New York) 18 January, 1855, Baron *Edward von der Heydt, b* 30 May, 1828; *d* 4 July, 1890.

> (827) *Edward August von der Heydt,*[7] *b* 4 August, 1858; *d* 20 March, 1862.
> (828) *Julia Alice von der Heydt,*[7] *b* 1 November, 1861; *d* 8 May, 1864.

450. **F. Leopold Schmidt,**[6] *b* 28 September, 1833; (living 1903); *m* 8 December, 1858, *Melenda P. Pollen, b* 18 December, 1838; (living 1903).

> (829) *John W. Schmidt.*[7]
> (830) *Elise Melenda Schmidt.*[7]
> (831) *George Parbury Pollen Schmidt,*[7] *b* 7 March, 1863; *d* 30 November, 1880.
> (832) *Fritz Leopold Schmidt.*[7]
> (833) *Bache McEvers Schmidt,*[7] *b* 12 March, 1868; *d* 28 November, 1903, *unm.*

451. **Oscar Egerton Schmidt,**[6] *b* 24 September, 1838; (living 1903); *m* 23 February, 1865, *Charlotte Lloyd Higbee, b* 2 May, 1841; (living 1903). S. P.

452. **Pauline Schmidt,**[6] *b* 1 November, 1839; (living 1903); *m* (Berlin) 11 February, 1868, General *Hugo von Winterfeld, b* 8 October, 1836; *d* September, 1898.

> (834) *Hans Karl von Winterfeld,*[7] *b* 27 April, 1872; (living 1903), *unm.*
> (835) *Ilse Lotta von Winterfeld.*[7]

453. **Ida M. Schmidt,**[6] *b* 12 November, 1841; (living 1903); *m* (1) 11 September, 1867, Major *Leonhardt von Reuthe-Finck, b* 4 August, 1837; *d* 30 October, 1870; *m* (2) 8 April, 1874, Captain *Georg von Ciesielski, b* 8 January, 1845; *d* 8 March, 1880; *m* (3) 24 October, 1892, Colonel *Gotthardt von Hagen, b* 18 February, 1822; *d* 18 November, 1903.

> (836) *Wilhelm von Reuthe-Finck.*[7]

458. **Cornelius Roosevelt Duffie**[6] (Rev.), *b* 6 August, 1821; *d* 8 July, 1900; *m* (1) 23 June, 1863, *Sarah Brush Clark*, *b* 20 October, 1833; *d* 4 March, 1880; *m* (2) 5 May, 1891, *Lillian Agnes Pelton*, *b* 15 September, 1861; (living 1903).

    (837) *Cornelia Roosevelt Duffie*,[7] *b* 26 April, 1864; *d* 25 September, 1878, *unm.*

    (838) *Cornelius Roosevelt Duffie.*[7]

    (839) *Jane Antoinette Duffie.*[7]

    (840) *Archibald Bleecker Duffie.*[7]

460. **John Van Benthuysen Bleecker**[6] (U.S.N.), *b* 31 July, 1825; *d* 8 November, 1864; *m* 18 November, 1846, *Sarah Rosalie Lynch*, *b* 9 August, 1831; (living 1903).

    (841) *John Van Benthuysen Bleecker.*[7]

    (842) *Cornelia Bleecker.*[7]

    (843) *Mary Norton Bleecker*,[7] *b* 29 November, 1857; (living 1903).

    (844) *Rosalie Lynch Bleecker.*[7]

    (845) *Florence Coralie Bleecker.*[7]

461. **Sarah Bache Bleecker**,[6] *b* 10 July, 1827; *d* 28 October, 1866; *m* 11 January, 1849, *Anthony Lispenard Bleecker*, *b* 17 February, 1821; *d* 14 September, 1875.

    (846) *Cornelia Bleecker.*[7]

    (847) *Sarah Elizabeth Bleecker*,[7] *b* 20 May, 1853; (living 1903).

    (848) *Antonia J. Bleecker*,[7] *b* 2 January, 1856; *d* 12 September, 1869.

463. **James Bleecker**,[6] *b* 9 August, 1834; (living 1903); *m* 8 March, 1856, *Jane Clarkson Hill*, *b* 2 January, 1837; (living 1903).

    (849) *Alethea Blanche Bleecker*,[7] *b* 15 December, 1856; (living 1903).

    (850) *Alice Stuart Bleecker*,[7] *b* 27 June, 1861; *d* 29 May, 1863.

    (851) *Anthony James Bleecker.*[7]

    (852) *William Hill Bleecker.*[7]

    (853) *Helen Stuart Bleecker,*[7] *b* 27 June, 1870; *d* 9
        August, 1873.

    (854) *Edward Nelson Bleecker,*[7] *b* 19 August, 1876;
        d 25 December, 1887.

467. **Theophylact Bache Bleecker,**[6] *b* 4 August, 1835; (living
    1903); *m* 19 November, 1868, *Caroline Loretta Moore,*
    b 3 July, 1840; (living 1903).

    (855) *Charles Moore Bleecker,*[7] *b* 19 August, 1869;
        (living 1903), *unm.*

    (856) *Theophylact Bache Bleecker,*[7] *b* 8 December,
        1870; (living 1903), *unm.*

    (857) *Frances Marie Bleecker,*[7] *b* 14 January, 1878;
        d 9 April, 1894.

469. **Lydia De Witt Bleecker,**[6] *b* 24 October, 1840; (living
    1903); *m* 13 May, 1869, *Theodore Mallaby, b* 6 June,
    1816; *d* 16 June, 1892.

    (858) *Theodora Frances Mallaby,*[7] *b* 19 September,
        1871; (living 1903).

    (859) *Benjamin DeWitt Mallaby,*[7] *b* 4 September,
        1873; *d* 24 April, 1887.

    (860) *Theophylact Bache Mallaby,*[7] *b* 20 June, 1875:
        d 21 July, 1876.

    (861) *Lydia Eve Mallaby,*[7] *b* 20 June, 1875; *d* 6 De-
        cember, 1888.

    (862) *Helena Bache Mallaby,*[7] *b* 26 January, 1877;
        d 25 June, 1879.

    (863) *Katharine Lyell Mallaby,*[7] *b* 19 November,
        1879; (living 1903).

470. **Benjamin DeWitt Bleecker,**[6] *b* 13 December, 1842; (liv-
    ing 1903); *m* 10 June, 1889, *Anna Sitgreaves Cox, b* 5
    October, 1857; (living 1903).

    (864) *Benjamin DeWitt Bleecker,*[7] *b* 24 November,
        1891; (living 1903).

    (865) *Theophylact Bache Bleecker,*[7] *b* 15 July 1893;
        (living 1903).

    (866) *Lyman Cox Bleecker,*[7] *b* 15 October, 1894;
        (living 1903).

474. **Maria Pennock Hansford,**[6] *b* 14 August, 1845; *d* 15 April, 1892; *m* 7 June, 1865, *Benjamin A. Mumford, b* 5 September, 1842; (living 1903).

(867) *William Pennock Hansford Mumford,*[7] *b* 23 March, 1866; *d* 18 February, 1886, *unm.*

(868) *John Remington Mumford,*[7] *b* 22 June, 1867; *d* 11 March, 1870.

(869) *Louis Bleecker Mumford,*[7] *b* 12 October, 1869; *d* 13 October, 1890, *unm.*

(870) *Clarence Stanbury Mumford,*[7] *b* 28 July, 1871; *d* 8 August, 1871.

(871) *Mary Mumford,*[7] *b* 31 October, 1874; (living 1903).

(872) *Charles Stillman Mumford,*[7] *b* 27 November, 1876; (living 1903), *unm.*

476. **Elizabeth Wentworth Satterthwaite,**[6] *b* 7 January, 1839; (living 1903); *m* 11 November, 1863, *John S. Conduit, b* 28 October, 1838; *d* 18 September, 1869.

(873) *Wentworth Conduit,*[7] *b* 6 June, 1865; (living 1903), *unm.*

(874) *Elizabeth Ashbridge Conduit,*[7] *b* 10 November, 1867; (living 1903).

(875) *John Paul Conduit,*[7] *b* 24 July, 1869; (living 1903), *unm.*

477. **James Sheafe Satterthwaite,**[6] *b* 1 March, 1840; *d* 6 September, 1884; *m* 6 December, 1864, *Jeanie L. Buckley, b* 5 January, 1846; *d* 30 January, 1892.

(876) *Katharine Bache Satterthwaite.*[7]

(877) *Julia Lawrence Satterthwaite.*[7]

(878) *Anne Fisher Satterthwaite.*[7]

(879) *James Sheafe Satterthwaite.*[7]

(880) *Thomas Wilkinson Sattterthwaite.*[7]

478. **Sarah F. Satterthwaite,**[6] *b* 24 August, 1841; (living 1903); *m* 10 October, 1879, Rev. *William R. Nairn, b* 22 April, 1845; *d* 19 October, 1889.

(881) *Archibald Robinson Nairn,*[7] *b* 21 July, 1880; *d* 1 February, 1887.

(882) *Louisa Fisher Nairn,*[7] *b* 29 August, 1881;
(living 1903).

(883) *Elizabeth Wentworth Nairn,*[7] *b* 18 November,
1882; (living 1903).

(884) *Walter Geoffrey Nairn,*[7] *b* 29 February, 1884;
(living 1903).

(885) *Tacie Nairn,*[7] *b* 20 May, 1888; (living 1903).

479. **Thomas E. Satterthwaite**[6] (M.D.), *b* 26 March, 1843;
(living 1903); *m* 13 November, 1884, *Isabella Banks,*
(living 1903).†

482. **Franklin Satterthwaite,**[6] *b* 17 November, 1845; *d* 15
September, 1888; *m* 29 June, 1869, *Rosalie Pennington,*
b 8 December, 1848; (living 1903).

(886) *Pennington Satterthwaite,*[7] *b* 6 October, 1870;
(living 1903), *unm.*

(887) *Ethel Satterthwaite,*[7] *b* 17 July, 1873; (living
1903).

484. **Augustus VanCortlandt Schermerhorn,**[6] *b* 4 March,
1812; *d* 16 October, 1846; *m* 10 December, 1844, *Mary
Ellen Bayard, b* 5 January, 1827; *d* 25 November, 1845.
O. S. P.

486. **Elizabeth Schermerhorn,**[6] *b* 14 March, 1816; *d* 19 August, 1875; *m* 30 August, 1838, *James I. Jones, b* 25
August, 1785; *d* 3 September, 1858.

(888) *Eleanor Colford Jones.*[7]

(889) *James H. Jones,*[7] *b* 14 February, 1846; (living
1903), *unm.*

(890) *Cordelia Schermerhorn Jones.*[7]

487. **Ann White Schermerhorn,**[6] *b* 15 February, 1818; *d* 23
November, 1886; *m* 23 October, 1849, *Charles Suydam,*
b 3 December, 1818; *d* 31 December, 1882.

(891) *Charles Schermerhorn Suydam,*[7] *b* 22 August,
1850; *d* 24 February, 1887, *unm.*

(892) *Augustus VanCortlandt Suydam,*[7] *b* 13 May,
1852; *d* 24 April, 1857.

(893) *Walter Lispenard Suydam.*[7]

(894) *Helen Suydam.*[7]

488. **Helen Schermerhorn,**[6] *b* 22 July, 1820; *d* 18 December, 1893; *m* 5 June, 1838, *John Treat Irving, b* 2 December, 1812; (living 1903).

> (895) *John Irving.*[7]
> (896) *Cortlandt Irving.*[7]
> (897) *Helen Cordelia Irving,*[7] *b* 17 March, 1846; (living 1903).
> (898) *Henry Irving.*[7]
> (899) *Frances Rogers Irving,*[7] *b* 31 July, 1849; (living 1903).
> (900) *Frederick Irving,*[7] *b* 28 July, 1852; *d* 10 August, 1852.
> (901) *Edward Irving.*[7]
> (902) *Eugene Irving,*[7] *b* 2 January, 1856; *d* 4 January, 1856.
> (903) *Walter Irving.*[7]
> (904) *Marion Harwood Irving,*[7] *b* 15 February, 1860; *d* 22 May, 1877.

490. **Catherine Schermerhorn,**[6] *b* 19 March, 1828; *d* 24 October, 1858; *m* 6 June, 1850, *Benjamin Sumner Welles, b* 27 December, 1823; (living 1903).

> (905) *Helen Schermerhorn Welles.*[7]
> (906) *Catherine Welles,*[7] *b* 6 November, 1854; (living 1903).
> (907) *Benjamin Welles.*[7]
> (908) *Harriet Katherine Welles,*[7] *b* 15 October, 1858; (living 1903).
> (909) *Elisabeth Welles,*[7] *b* 15 October, 1858; *d* 2 May, 1864.

491. **Caroline Webster Schermerhorn,**[6] *b* 22 September, 1830; (living 1903); *m* 20 September, 1853, *William Astor, b* 12 July, 1830; *d* 25 April, 1892.

> (910) *Emily Astor.*[7]
> (911) *Helen Astor.*[7]
> (912) *Charlotte Augusta Astor.*[7]
> (913) *Caroline Schermerhorn Astor.*[7]
> (914) *John Jacob Astor.*[7]

492. **Anne White Bibby,**[6] *b* 4 July, 1823; *d* 11 December,
1889; *m* 27 April, 1848, *Robert Ogden Glover, b* 1 August, 1821; *d* 5 July, 1894.
  - (915) *Robert Ogden Glover.*[7]
  - (916) *Mary Weltha Glover.*[7]
  - (917) *James Andrew Glover.*[7]
  - (918) *Edward Augustus Glover.*[7]
  - (919) *Thomas Glover,*[7] *b* 1 January, 1858; *d* 5 November, 1889, *unm.*
  - (920) *Henry Warburton Bibby Glover.*[7]
  - (921) *Frances DeLancey Glover,*[7] *b* 12 July, 1861; *d* 13 August, 1862.
  - (922) *Frederick Raymond Glover,*[7] *b* 23 January, 1863; (living 1903), *unm.*
  - (923) *Agnes Glover,*[7] *b* 16 October, 1865; *d* 8 April, 1866.
  - (924) *Louisa Thebaud Glover,*[7] *b* 8 February, 1867; (living 1903).

493. **Frances Augusta Bibby,**[6] *b* 21 December, 1824; (living 1903); *m* (1) 3 February, 1847, *Thomas James De-Lancey, b* 29 March, 1822; *d* 2 October, 1861; *m* (2) 16 December, 1863, *John White Munro, b* 28 June, 1814; *d* 31 July, 1898. S. P.

494. **Augustus (Bibby) VanCortlandt,**[6] *b* 31 July, 1826; (living 1903); *m* 2 June, 1852, *Charlotte Amelia Bayley Bunch*[5] (No. 252 above), *b* 27 May, 1826; *d* 24 January, 1890.

    (The issue of this marriage are chronicled above under: 252, CHARLOTTE AMELIA BAYLEY BUNCH.[5])

498. **Henry White Groshon,**[6] *b* 17 January, 1824; (living 1903); *m* 20 May, 1851, *Amelia Wagstaff, b* 24 October, 1823; *d* 22 January, 1883.
  - (925) *Annie Wagstaff Groshon,*[7] *b* 8 August, 1852; (living 1903).

499. **John Pierre Groshon,**[6] *b* 17 September, 1825; (living 1903); *m* 14 May, 1852, *Elizabeth F. Coddington, b* 8 April, 1824; (living 1903).

(926) *Harriet White Groshon,*[7] *b* 14 April, 1853; *d* 20 September, 1855.

(927) *George Mackness Groshon,*[7] *b* 25 August, 1854; *d* 1 September, 1855.

500. **William Francis Groshon,**[6] *b* 11 June, 1827; *d* 2 December, 1888; *m* 24 January, 1849, *Adeline Ellis Bleecker, b* 6 December, 1825; *d* 10 August, 1885.

(928) *Francena White Groshon,*[7] *b* 23 July, 1851; *d* 15 December, 1853.

(929) *William Beach Carter Groshon,*[7] *b* 1 November, 1853; *d* 24 July, 1854.

(930) *Augusta Bibby Groshon.*[7]

(931) *Isabel Gourlie Groshon.*[7]

(932) *Elizabeth Bleecker Groshon,*[7] *b* 6 November, 1863; *d* 8 March, 1865.

(933) *Edward Kemeys Groshon,*[7] *b* 16 October, 1871; *d* 3 July, 1872.

501. **Henrietta Anne Elizabeth Groshon,**[6] *b* 20 January, 1829; (living 1903); *m* 4 June, 1853, *Thomas H. Wagstaff, b* 23 December, 1825; *d* 23 December, 1894.

(934) *William Wagstaff,*[7] *b* 31 August, 1854; *d* 16 February, 1864.

(935) *Fannie White Wagstaff,*[7] *b* 19 January, 1856; (living 1903).

(936) *Thomas H. Wagstaff.*[7]

(937) *J. Alexander Wagstaff,*[7] *b* 30 August, 1861; *d* 8 February, 1873.

(938) *Alice Wagstaff.*[7]

(939) *Amelia Wagstaff,*[7] *b* 18 January, 1864; *d* 9 December, 1865.

(940) *Frederick M. Wagstaff,*[7] *b* 14 January, 1869; *d* 5 May, 1875.

502. **Francena Meyer,**[6] *b* 16 December, 1833; (living 1903); *m* 24 May 1862, *Charles Louis Roulet, b* 2 July, 1833; *d* 9 August, 1862. S. P.

503. **Augustus VanCortlandt Meyer,**[6] *b* 26 April, 1835; *d* 9
July, 1901; *m* 1 May, 1861, *Josephine D. Dow, b* 10
May, 1842; (living 1903).

> (941) *Henry VanCortlandt Meyer.*[7]
> (942) *Josephine Gillson Meyer,*[7] *b* 9 November,
> 1864; *d* 4 March, 1864.

507. **Peter Jay Munro VanCortlandt,**[6] *b* 28 September, 1828;
d 8 August, 1897; *m* 27 November, 1860, *Ann Munro
Hunter, b* 23 November, 1839; *d* 23 April, 1863.

> (943) *Jessie VanCortlandt,*[7] *b* 21 April, 1863; *d* 5
> July, 1863.

511. **Alexa Charlotte Stevens,**[6] *b* 17 November, 1837; (living
1903) ; *m* 2 February, 1859, Rev. *James J. Bowden, b*
13 April, 1821; *d* 2 October, 1861.

> (944) *Richard Morris Bowden,*[7] *b* 14 November,
> 1859; *d* 24 January, 1867.
> (945) *Constance Lloyd Bowden.*[7]

514. **Anna Elliot Morris,**[6] *b* 1829; *d* 9 January, 1885; *m* 8
June, 1876, *Gouverneur Morris, b* 9 February, 1813;
d 20 August, 1888. O. S. P.

516. **Charlotte Sophia Percy Morris,**[6] *b* 20 July, 1833; *d* 19
October, 1901; *m* 13 October, 1859, *Charles Drayton
Burrill, b* 15 April, 1831; *d* 26 October, 1902.

> (946) *Drayton Burrill.*[7]
> (947) *Mary Middleton Burrill.*[7]
> (948) *Percy M. Burrill.*[7]

517. **James Morris,**[6] *b* 2 October, 1832; (living 1903) ; *m* 14
November, 1866, *Elizabeth W. Gray, b* 19 July, 1834;
d 15 October, 1899.

> (949) *Marion Gray Morris,*[7] *b* 31 January, 1868; *d*
> 26 December, 1878.

518. **Elizabeth Stuyvesant Fish Morris,**[6] *b* 25 August, 1834;
d (at Grand Gulf, Miss.,) 27 August, 1868; *m* 23 June,
1859, *William St. John Elliott Marshall* (of Natchez,
Miss.), *b* 23 June, 1837; *d* 17 October, 1876.

(950) *William St. John Elliot Marshall.*[7]
(951) *Elizabeth Morris Marshall,*[7] *b* 2 August, 1862;
(living 1903).
(952) *Sarah Elliott Marshall.*[7]

521. **Richard Lewis Morris**[6] (U.S.A.), *b* 12 December, 1840;
d 6 May, 1882; *m* 6 October, 1874, *Lillian M. Monson,*
b 24 May, 1849; *d* 20 October, 1884.
(953) *Monson Morris,*[7] *b* 1 August, 1875; (living
1903), *unm.*
(954) *Richard Lewis Morris,*[7] *b* 12 October, 1877;
d 18 October, 1877.
(955) *Helen VanCortlandt Morris,*[7] *b* 9 August,
1879; (living 1903).

522. **Stuyvesant Fish Morris**[6] (M.D.), *b* 3 August, 1843;
(living 1903); *m* 10 December, 1868, *Ellen James Van
Buren, b* 10 June, 1844; (living 1903).
(956) *Elizabeth Morris,*[7] *b* 4 October, 1869; (living
1903).
(957) *Van Buren Morris,*[7] *b* 2 July, 1871; *d* 21
March, 1872.
(958) *Ellen Van Buren Morris.*[7]
(959) *Richard Lewis Morris,*[7] *b* 26 November, 1875;
(living 1903), *unm.*
(960) *Stuyvesant Fish Morris.*[7]

523. **Helen VanCortlandt Morris,**[6] *b* 1 October, 1845; *d* 27
September, 1871; *m* 26 January, 1870, *David King, b*
29 December, 1839; *d* 8 March, 1894. (He subsequently married *Ella Louise Rives,*[6] No. 276 above).
O. S. P.

524. **Charlotte Louisa Morris,**[6] *b* 3 June, 1848; (living 1903);
m 29 November, 1882, *Martin Gilbert Wilkins, b* 7 October, 1845; *d* 10 July, 1903. S. P.

525. **Margaret Livingston Morris,**[6] *b* 22 February, 1852; *d*
29 April, 1895; *m* 9 October, 1879, *Bayard Urquhart
Livingston, b* 24 February, 1858; (living 1903).

(961) *Bayard Urquhart Livingston*,[7] *b* 26 August, 1881; (living 1903), *unm.*

(962) *Louisa Morris Livingston*,[7] *b* 31 December, 1893; (living 1903).

526. **Katharine Augusta Morris**,[6] *b* 1836; (living 1903); *m* 6 October, 1857, *Henry Delafield Phelps, b* 15 October, 1835; (living 1903).

    (963) *Robert Morris Phelps*,[7] *b* 1 August, 1858; *d* 20 February, 1894, *unm.*

    (964) *Helena VanCortlandt Phelps.*[7]

    (965) *Edgar Morris Phelps.*[7]

    (966) *Gouverneur Morris Phelps*,[7] *b* 16 November, 1878; (living 1903), *unm.*

529. **Helen Louisa Morris**,[6] *b* 9 November, 1844; *d* 16 July, 1867; *m* 24 December, 1866, Dr. *George McCulloch McGill* (U.S.A.), *b* 20 April, 1838; *d* 20 July, 1867. O. S. P.

530. **Helen VanCortlandt LeRoy**,[6] *b* 8 January, 1830; *d* 23 May, 1890; *m* 3 April, 1851, *William Pinckney Stewart, b* 21 August, 1822; *d* 5 May, 1870.

    (967) *Louisa Morris Stewart.*[7]

    (968) *Helen VanCortlandt Stewart.*[7]

    (969) *Charlotte Pinckney Stewart*,[7] *b* 24 December, 1859; *d* 3 November, 1864.

    (970) *Edward LeRoy Stewart.*[7]

533. **Augustus Newbold Morris**,[6] *b* 3 June, 1838; (living 1903); *m* 10 December, 1862, *Eleanor Colford Jones* (No. 888 above), *b* 11 May, 1841; (living 1903).

    (971) *Eleanor Colford Morris*,[7] *b* 10 November, 1863; *d* 22 November, 1863.

    (972) *Newbold Morris.*[7]

    (973) *Eva VanCortlandt Morris*,[7] *b* 10 April, 1869; (living 1903).

    (974) *William Henry Morris*,[7] *b* 8 February, 1871; *d* 17 June, 1871.

    (975) *Lewis Morris*,[7] *b* 19 June, 1873; *d* 30 March, 1875.

535. **Augusta McEvers Morris,**[6] *b* 6 October, 1851; (living 1903); *m* 10 October, 1871, *Frederic J. dePeyster, b* 5 February, 1839; (living 1903).

>(976) *Helen VanCortlandt dePeyster,*[7] *b* 12 September, 1872; (living 1903).
>
>(977) *Frederic Ashton dePeyster,*[7] *b* 29 October, 1874; (living 1903), *unm.*
>
>(978) *Frances Goodhue dePeyster,*[7] *b* 6 June, 1876; (living 1903).
>
>(979) *Augusta Morris dePeyster,*[7] *b* 25 June, 1877; (living 1903).
>
>(980) *Ella Morris dePeyster,*[7] *b* 7 July, 1881; (living 1903).

536. **Juliet Birckhead Morris,**[6] *b* 28 March, 1853; (living 1903); *m* 16 April, 1890, *Phililp Livingston, b* 9 November, 1861; (living 1903). S. P.

538. **Robert Stewart Webb,**[6] *b* 12 August, 1824; *d* 24 August, 1899; *m* (1) 18 April, 1849, *Mary Van Horne Clarkson, b* 29 March, 1822; *d* 30 October, 1880; *m* (2) 19 November, 1886, *Frances Webb Starkweather* (née *Morgan*), *b* 24 December, 1835; (living 1903).

>(981) *Robert Stewart Webb,*[7] *b* 23 August, 1850; *d* 10 September, 1870, *unm.*

541. **Helen Matilda Webb,**[6] *b* 30 November, 1827; *d* 3 October, 1896; *m* 18 April, 1860, *N. Denison Morgan, b* 22 October, 1818; *d* 20 September, 1895.

>(982) *Robert Webb Morgan.*[7]
>
>(983) *Helen Louisa Morgan,*[7] *b* 7 November, 1865; *d* 17 March, 1866.

542. **Catherine Louisa Webb,**[6] *b* 14 December, 1830; (living 1903); *m* 17 August, 1859, *James G. Benton* (U.S.A.), *b* 15 September, 1820; *d* 23 August, 1881.

>(984) *Mary Louisa Benton.*[7]
>
>(985) *James Watson Benton.*[7]

544. **Watson Webb,**[6] *b* 10 November, 1833; *d* 3 December, 1876; *m* 6 June, 1866, *Mary Hooker Parsons, b* 2 February, 1835; (living 1903).

   (986) *Francis Parsons Webb,*[7] *b* 26 September, 1868; (living 1903), *unm.*

   (987) *Helen Lispenard Webb.*[7]

   (988) *Elizabeth Newton Webb,*[7] *b* 19 August, 1877; *d* 8 July, 1883.

545. **Alexander Stewart Webb,**[6] *b* 15 February, 1835; (living 1903); *m* 28 November, 1855, *Anna E. Remsen, b* 19 July, 1837; (living 1903).

   (989) *Henry Remsen Webb,*[7] *b* 24 August, 1857; *d* 1 June, 1858.

   (990) *Helen Lispenard Webb.*[7]

   (991) *Elizabeth Remsen Webb.*[7]

   (992) *Anne Remsen Webb,*[7] *b* 7 April, 1866; (living 1903).

   (993) *Caroline LeRoy Webb,*[7] *b* 16 August, 1868; (living 1903).

   (994) *Alexander Stewart Webb,*[7] *b* 5 February 1870; (living 1903), *unm.*

   (995) *William Remsen Webb,*[7] *b* 18 November, 1872; *d* 9 March, 1899, *unm.*

   (996) *Louise dePeyster Webb,*[7] *b* 3 August, 1874; (living 1903).

546. **Louise Stephanie Stewart,**[6] *b* 21 May, 1836; *d* 7 September, 1867; *m* 21 May, 1861, *John B. Trevor, b* 27 March, 1822; *d* 22 December, 1890.

   (997) *Helen Stewart Trevor,*[7] *b* 3 April, 1862; *d* 22 March, 1864.

   (998) *Henry Graff Trevor.*[7]

547. **Sarah Lispenard Stewart,**[6] *b* 9 April, 1837; (living 1903); *m* 20 April, 1864, *Frederick Graham Lee, b* 27 November, 1840; (living 1903).

   (999) *Graham Stewart Lee,*[7] *b* 22 February, 1865; *d* 6 March, 1869.

   (1000) *Maud Stewart Lee.*[7]

548. William Rhinelander Stewart,⁶ *b* 3 December, 1852; (living 1903); *m* 5 November, 1879, *Annie M. Armstrong,* (living 1903).

    (1001) *Muriel Stewart,*⁷ *b* 5 July, 1882; *d* 7 September, 1884.

    (1002) *Anita Stewart,*⁷ *b* 17 August, 1886; (living 1903).

    (1003) *William Rhinelander Stewart,*⁷ *b* 22 December, 1888; (living 1903).

550. Mary Rhinelander Stewart,⁶ *b* 3 March, 1859; (living 1903); *m* 25 April, 1883, *Frank Spencer Witherbee,* (living 1903).

    (1004) *Lispenard Stewart Witherbee,*⁷ *b* 1 June, 1886; (living 1903).

    (1005) *Evelyn Spencer Witherbee,*⁷ *b* 7 July, 1889; (living 1903).

551. Lispenard Stewart,⁶ *b* 20 November, 1825; *d* 12 December, 1865; *m* 16 November, 1859, *Mary Horton,* b 11 September, 1840; (living 1903).

    (1006) *Sarah Amelia Stewart,*⁷ *b* 11 May, 1862; *d* 8 June, 1897, *unm.*

    (1007) *Robert Lispenard Stewart,*⁷ *b* 7 February, 1866; (living 1903), *unm.*

552. Sarah Lispenard Stewart,⁶ *b* 18 August, 1827; *d* 23 July, 1902; *m* 15 June, 1851, *Elihu Phinney,* b 20 June, 1823; *d* 20 September, 1892.

    (1008) *Alexander Stewart Phinney,*⁷ *b* 1 January, 1864; (living 1903), *unm.*

560. Virginia Garland Webb,⁶ *b* 19 August, 1839; (living 1903); *m* 5 October, 1865, *Robert Allan Forsyth,* b 22 December, 1831; *d* 4 September, 1898.

    (1009) *Robert Allan Forsyth.*⁷

    (1010) *Louisa Trevor Forsyth.*⁷

562. Herman Stewart LeRoy,⁶ *b* 8 April, 1856; (living 1903); *m* 17 September, 1880, *Clementina LeRoy Morgan,* b 19 January, 1856; *d* 22 April, 1903.

(1011) *Herman LeRoy,*[7] *b* 23 August, 1883; *d* 7 August, 1885.

(1012) *Robert LeRoy,*[7] *b* 7 February, 1885; (living 1903).

566.   **Margaret White Munro,**[6] *b* 30 August, 1845; *d* 22 July, 1885; *m* 1 June, 1871, Rev. *James deHart Bruen, b* 17 December, 1847; (living 1903).

(1013) *James Bayley Bruen.*[7]

(1014) *Henry Munro Bruen.*[7]

(1015) *Norman Jay Bruen,*[7] *b* 27 June, 1879; (living 1903), *unm.*

(1016) *John Munro Bruen,*[7] *b* 24 April, 1880; *d* 3 April, 1882.

568.   **Guy Carleton Bayley**[6] (M.D.), *b* 16 October, 1850; (living 1903); *m* (1) 23 May, 1875, *Angelica Crosby Wyckoff, b* 19 July, 1852; *d* 23 August, 1876; *m* (2) 22 April, 1885, *Ellen Lorraine Bulkeley, b* 9 September, 1851; (living 1903).   S. P.

569.   **Grace Walton Bayley,**[6] *b* 7 April, 1848; *d* 15 January, 1881; *m* 29 July, 1869, *Bernard Michael Shanley, b* 15 November, 1847; *d* 19 March, 1901.

(1017) *Michael Robert Seton Shanley.*[7]

(1018) *William Carleton Shanley.*[7]

(1019) *James Roosevelt Shanley.*[7]

(1020) *Bernard Michael Shanley.*[7]

(1021) *Arthur Shanley,*[7] *b* 28 December, 1874; *d* 22 February, 1875.

(1022) *George Doane Shanley,*[7] *b* 4 January, 1881; *d* 29 January, 1881.

572.   **Mary Catherine Seton Bayley,**[6] *b* 17 July, 1863; (living 1903); *m* (1) 27 April, 1886, *James Fox, b* 4 July, 1861; *d* 27 June, 1890; *m* (2) 21 February, 1901, *Walter Large, b* 22 March, 1856; (living 1903).   S. P.

578.   **Grace Bayley Jewett,**[6] *b* 17 July, 1853; (living 1903); *m* 20 December, 1876, *Alfred Chester Bunce, b* 12 February, 1851; (living 1903).

(1023) *Maria Roosevelt Bunce.*[7]

(1024) *Carleton Bayley Bunce,*[7] *b* 8 December, 1879;
(living 1903), *unm.*

(1025) *Elizabeth Chester Bunce,*[7] *b* 18 September,
1881; (living 1903).

(1026) *Grace Jewett Bunce,*[7] *b* 28 March, 1884;
(living 1903).

(1027) *Russell Bunce,*[7] *b* 13 May, 1886; (living
1903).

579. **Mary Williamson Jewett,**[6] *b* 20 June, 1856; (living
1903); *m* 17 October, 1883, *James Reynolds, b* 7 June,
1855; (living 1903).

(1028) *James Reynolds,*[7] *b* 31 July, 1886; *d* 6 August, 1897.

581. **Helen Baldock Bunch,**[6] *b* 21 January, 1855; (living
1903); *m* at Caracas, Venezuela, 17 July, 1880, *Luis
Eraso, b* 29 June, 1855; *d* 19 September, 1899. S. P.

584. **Emma Craig Blake,**[6] *b* 30 January, 1865; (living 1903);
m 5 October, 1892, *Benjamin Huger Rutledge, b* 4 September, 1861; (living 1903).

(1029) *Eleanor Middleton Rutledge,*[7] *b* 22 March,
1894; (living 1903).

(1030) *Emma Blake Rutledge,*[7] *b* 23 August, 1897;
(living 1903).

(1031) *Alice Weston Rutledge,*[7] *b* 1 January, 1899;
(living 1903).

(1032) *Benjamin Huger Rutledge,*[7] *b* 11 January,
1902; (living 1903).

585. **Helen Bayley Blake,**[6] *b* 10 November, 1867; (living
1903); *m* 5 October, 1892, *Oliver Middleton Rutledge,
b* 1 September, 1862; (living 1903).

(1033) *Helen Blake Rutledge,*[7] *b* 10 August, 1893;
(living 1903).

(1034) *Frances Blake Rutledge,*[7] *b* 6 May, 1895;
(living 1903).

(1035) *Oliver Middleton Rutledge,*[7] *b* 5 December, 1900; (living 1903).

(1036) *Elizabeth Rutledge,*[7] *b* 31 January, 1903; (living 1903).

587. **Elizabeth Craig,**[6] *b* 8 November, 1868; (living 1903) ; *m* 19 April, 1893, *Edward L. Braytin, b* 8 September, 1866; *d* 30 September, 1894.

(1037) *Amelia Elise Braytin,*[7] *b* 5 March, 1894; (living 1903).

589. **James Roosevelt Bayley Craig,**[6] *b* 16 April, 1874; (living 1903) ; *m* 28 April, 1899, *Frances Maude Baston, b* 2 November, 1877; (living 1903).

(1038) *Elinore Craig,*[7] *b* 28 August, 1900; (living 1903).

(1039) *Carolyn Louise Craig,*[7] *b* 10 November, 1902; (living 1903).

594. **Augustus VanCortlandt,**[6] *b* 29 July, 1855; (living 1903) ; *m* 26 September, 1889, *Ethel Wilson, b* 17 December, 1867; (living 1903).

(1040) *Charlotte Amelia VanCortlandt,*[7] *b* 29 November, 1891 ; (living 1903).

(1041) *Augustus VanCortlandt,*[7] *b* 15 May, 1893; (living 1903).

(1042) *Carolyn VanCortlandt,*[7] *b* 5 March, 1895; (living 1903).

612. **George Clarence Barclay Ward,**[7] *b* 19 February, 1872; (living 1903) ; *m* 16 November, 1896, *Coralie Chastant Brandegee, b* 29 December, 1876; (living 1903).

(1043) *Coralie Brandegee Ward,*[8] *b* 18 May, 1898; (living 1903).

615. **Susan Hastings Ward,**[7] *b* 14 December, 1872; (living 1903) ; *m* 19 June, 1900, *William Gray Lapham, b* 6 November, 1870; (living 1903).

(1044) *William Gray Lapham,*[8] *b* 1 December, 1901; (living 1903).

622. Helen Livingston Kountze,[7] *b* 14 August, 1881; (living 1903); *m* 12 December, 1902, *Robert Linlithgow Livingston, b* 23 February, 1876; (living 1903). S. P.

631. George Barclay Rives,[7] *b* 19 June, 1874; (living 1903); *m* 24 April, 1900, *Elizabeth Emlen Hare, b* 30 May, 1876; *d* 24 July, 1900. S. P.

634. Maud Gwendolen King,[7] *b* 2 October, 1876; (living 1903); *m* 12 September, 1901, *Edward Maitland Armstrong, b* 15 March, 1874; (living 1903). S. P.

656. Isabel Fords Betts,[7] *b* 17 February, 1864; (living 1903); *m* 26 April, 1886, *Robert Henry McPherson, b* 9 March, 1857; (living 1903).

  (1045) *Helen McPherson,*[8] *b* 20 February, 1887; (living 1903).

  (1046) *Robert Betts McPherson,*[8] *b* 15 July, 1890; (living 1903).

  (1047) *James Beverley McPherson,*[8] *b* 3 July, 1892; (living 1903).

658. Beverley Robinson,[7] *b* 30 April, 1866; (living 1903); *m* 8 June, 1898, *Marion Roberts, b* 23 September, 1868; (living 1903). S. P.

659. Maud deLancey Robinson,[7] *b* 19 September, 1875; (living 1903); *m* 6 January, 1897, *William J. Gordon, b* 9 October, 1874; (living 1903). S. P.

661. Frances Duer Robinson,[7] *b* 30 April, 1876; (living 1903); *m* 27 June, 1901, *Henry B. Montgomery, b* 2 July, 1852; (living 1903). S. P.

663. Julia Beverley Robinson,[7] *b* 5 September, 1872; (living 1903); *m* 20 June, 1895, *John E. Grote Higgens, b* 27 January, 1856; (living 1903).

  (1048) *Robert Grote Higgens,*[8] *b* 11 June, 1897; *d* 15 June, 1897.

  (1049) *Julia Grote Higgens,*[8] *b* 2 October, 1898; *d* 2 October, 1898.

  (1050) *Edward Grote Higgens,*[8] *b* 21 July, 1899; *d* 21 July, 1899.

664. Beverley William Robinson,[7] *b* 21 December, 1873;
(living 1903); *m* 9 November, 1898, *Madeline Meldrum
Wall, b* 6 December, 1876; (living 1903).
> (1051) *Frederick Philipse Robinson,*[8] *b* 9 September,
> 1899; (living 1903).

667. Ethel Winthrop Storer,[7] *b* 31 January, 1879; (living
1903); *m* 10 September, 1902, Rev. *John Addoms Linn,*
(living 1903). S. P.

672. Frances Duer Jones,[7] *b* 20 October, 1867; (living 1903);
m 4 September, 1889, *John James Key* (living 1903).
> (1052) *Jean Frances Key,*[8] *b* 12 January, 1891;
> (living 1903).
> (1053) *Eugene Key.*[8] †
> (1054) *Katharine Voorhis Key.*[8] †

674. Elizabeth Schermerhorn Potter,[7] *b* 12 September, 1869;
(living 1903); *m* 12 April, 1892, *Henry William James
Bagnell, b* 31 January, 1861; (living 1903).
> (1055) *Viva Margot Bagnell,*[8] *b* 11 February, 1893;
> (living 1903).
> (1056) *Hope Dorothy Bagnell,*[8] *b* 18 November,
> 1894; (living 1903).
> (1057) *Irene Helen Bagnell,*[8] *b* 2 November, 1898;
> (living 1903).

678. Anna Dorothea Scovil,[7] *b* 30 September, 1864; (living
1903); *m* 17 November, 1886, *Francis Manson Brown,
b* 27 November, 1863; (living 1903).
> (1058) *Frank Scovil Brown,*[8] *b* 10 August, 1887;
> *d* 10 August, 1887.
> (1059) *Ward Manson Brown,*[8] *b* 10 August, 1887;
> *d* 10 August, 1887.
> (1060) *Harold Theodore Brown,*[8] *b* 30 January,
> 1889; *d* 27 July, 1890.
> (1061) *Vera Lee Brown,*[8] *b* 22 September, 1890;
> (living 1903).
> (1062) *Carl Wetmore Brown,*[8] *b* 17 April, 1892;
> (living 1903).

(1063) *Frederic Cyril Brown*,[8] *b* 14 April, 1894; (living 1903).

(1064) *Eric Clowes Brown*,[8] *b* 16 July, 1897; (living 1903).

(1065) *Florence Hilda Brown*,[8] *b* 12 September, 1900; (living 1903).

679. **Frances Marion Scovil**,[7] *b* 13 April, 1866; (living 1903); *m* 5 June, 1888, *Gillmor Brown, b* 25 September, 1857; (living 1903).

(1066) *Keith Allan Brown*,[8] *b* 27 April, 1890; (living 1903).

(1067) *Dorothy Lee Brown*,[8] *b* 12 August, 1895; (living 1903).

680. **William Thomas Scovil**,[7] (M.D.), *b* 4 May, 1867; (living 1903); *m* (1) 5 October, 1891, *Susan Miranda Berlin, b* 16 April, 1867; *d* 6 May, 1895; *m* (2) 6 November, 1896, *Hattie Augusta Kessler, b* 23 February, 1872; (living 1903).

(1068) *William Arden Scovil*,[8] *b* 5 May, 1895; *d* 1 April, 1898.

(1069) *Aubrey Earle Scovil*,[8] *b* 3 March, 1899; (living 1903).

(1070) *Francis Kessler Scovil*,[8] *b* 29 April, 1900; (living 1903).

(1071) *Thomas Clayton Scovil*,[8] *b* 19 June, 1903; (living 1903).

719. **William Whitlock**,[7] *b* 28 November, 1850; (living 1903); *m* 4 December, 1894, *Fannie Moore Rogers Parkin, b* 23 June, 1853; (living 1903). S. P.

720. **Bache McEvers Whitlock**,[7] *b* 11 June, 1852; (living 1903); *m* 7 June, 1888, *Emily Ogden Simonds, b* 27 September, 1858; (living 1903).

(1072) *Bache McEvers Whitlock*,[8] *b* 15 April, 1889; (living 1903).

(1073) *Herman von Post Whitlock*,[8] *b* 23 November, 1890; *d* 20 March, 1891.

(1074) *Jeannette Emmet Whitlock*,[8] *b* 10 December,
1891 ; (living 1903).

(1075) *Anna Isabel Whitlock*,[8] *b* 22 April, 1893;
d 5 September, 1894.

(1076) *Frederick Simonds Whitlock*,[8] *b* 13 March,
1894 ; (living 1903).

(1077) *Katharine Simonds Whitlock*,[8] *b* 13 March,
1894; *d* 4 September, 1894.

722. Sir Bache Edward Cunard,[7] Bart, *b* 15 May, 1851 ; (living 1903) ; *m* 25 April, 1895, *Maud Alice Burke, b* 31 August, 1876; (living 1903).

(1078) *Nancy Claire Cunard*,[8] *b* 10 March, 1896; (living 1903).

723. Mary McEvers Cunard,[7] *b* 4 November, 1852; (living 1903) ; *m* 11 October, 1884, Col. *George Gosling, b* 1 November, 1842; (living 1903).

(1079) *George Edward Gosling*,[8] *b* 23 May, 1889; (living 1903).

(1080) *Vere Hobart Gosling*,[8] *b* 3 August, 1890; (living 1903).

725. Gordon Cunard,[7] *b* 22 May, 1857; (living 1903) ; *m* 30 December, 1889, *Edith Mary Howard, b* 11 June, 1865; (living 1903).

(1081) *Edward Cunard*,[8] *b* 25 November, 1890; (living 1903).

(1082) *Anthony Gordon Cunard*,[8] *b* 12 October, 1893; (living 1903).

(1083) *Victor Cunard*,[8] *b* 8 February, 1898; (living 1903).

726. Jeannette Emmet Cunard,[7] *b* 20 July, 1859; (living 1903) ; *m* (1) 28 July, 1883, *Edmund Leatham, b* 3 December, 1847; *d* 7 October, 1890; *m* (2) 18 November, 1896, *Arthur Neilson, b* 12 September, 1845; *d* 1 October, 1902.

(1084) *Gordon Cunard Leatham*,[8] *b* 25 December, 1884; (living 1903).

(1085) *Hubert Edward Leatham*,[8] *b* 20 July, 1886; (living 1903).

(1086) *Lorna Priscilla Leatham*,[8] *b* 27 November, 1887; (living 1903).

(1087) *Katharine Margaret Neilson,*[8] *b* 4 September, 1897; (living 1903).

(1088) *Mary Neilson,*[8] *b* 21 August, 1900; (living 1903).

727. **Annie Allen Cunard,**[7] *b* 21 June, 1863; (living 1903); *m* 15 October, 1885, Sir *Arthur Lawley,* K.C.M.G., *b* 12 November, 1860; (living 1903).

(1089) *Richard Edward Lawley,*[8] *b* 9 May, 1887; (living 1903).

(1090) *Ursula Mary Lawley,*[8] *b* 8 June, 1888; (living 1903).

(1091) *Margaret Cecilia Lawley,*[8] *b* 15 June, 1889; (living 1903).

728. **Caroline Margaret Cunard,**[7] *b* 25 May, 1866; (living 1903); *m* 16 January, 1890, *Athole Stanhope Hay, b* 25 March, 1860; (living 1903).

(1092) *Robert Athole Hay,*[8] *b* 12 December, 1890; (living 1903).

(1093) *Bache McEvers Athole Hay,*[8] *b* 24 September, 1892; (living 1903).

(1094) *Athole Hay,*[8] *b* 17 October, 1901; (living 1903).

731. **Charlotte Louise Hall,**[7] *b* 1 June, 1844; (living 1903); *m* 12 April, 1866, *Samuel J. Berry, b* 19 July, 1840; (living 1903).

(1095) *Samuel J. Berry.*[8]

(1096) *Clarence Berry,*[8] *b* 19 December, 1868; (living 1903), *unm.*

(1097) *Arthur Berry,*[8] *b* 19 December, 1868; *d* 30 December, 1868.

(1098) *Andrew Hall Berry.*[8]

(1099) *Herbert Hall Berry,*[8] *b* 21 December, 1870; *d* 1 February, 1873.

(1100) *Louis Pierce Berry,*[8] *b* 6 November, 1872; *d* 18 June, 1900, *unm.*

(1101) *Charlotte Louise Berry.*[8]

(1102) *Katharine Gillilan Berry,*[8] *b* 4 September, 1881; (living 1903).

733. Helen Bache Hall,[7] *b* 22 February, 1857; (living 1903);
m 18 October, 1883, *William Chalmers, b* 17 December,
1848; (living 1903).

    (1103) *William Hall Chalmers,*[8] *b* 31 May, 1885;
      (living 1903).

737. George Frederick Newcombe,[7] *b* 1 November, 1849;
(living 1903); *m* 25 October, 1881, *Mary Colfax Mason,
b* 14 January, 1854; (living 1903).

    (1104) *Jane Caroline Newcombe,*[8] *b* 13 March, 1886;
      (living 1903).

738. Jane Caroline Newcombe,[7] *b* 23 February, 1851; *d* 25
March, 1877; *m* 21 May, 1874, *Thomas Henry French,
b* 7 December, 1848; *d* 1 December, 1902.

    (1105) *Marie Louise French,*[8] *b* 23 December, 1875;
      d 18 September, 1891.

739. Frederick Hayward Newcombe,[7] *b* 17 February, 1853;
(living 1903); *m* 4 November, 1873, *Anna Evelina
Hopper, b* 17 June, 1856; (living 1903).

    (1106) *Frederick Hayward Newcombe,*[8] *b* 22 May,
      1875; *d* 7 September, 1875.

    (1107) *Maude Louise Newcombe.*[8]

    (1108) *Andrew Bache Newcombe,*[8] *b* 4 May, 1878;
      (living 1903), *unm.*

    (1109) *Hayward Manby Newcombe,*[8] *b* 24 April,
      1883; *d* 6 July, 1884.

740. Andrew Bache Newcombe,[7] *b* 5 May, 1856; (living
1903); *m* (1) 29 June, 1881, *Lavinia Bogardus, b* 17
June, 1858; *d* 17 October, 1890; *m* (2) 21 June, 1899,
Marion Howard Champlin, b 8 June, 1874; (living
1903). S. P.

741. Charles Manby Newcombe,[7] *b* 1 August, 1864; (living
1903); *m* 21 January, 1891, *Annie Elizabeth Pennell, b*
17 October, 1868; (living 1903).

    (1110) *Gertrude Manby Newcombe,*[8] *b* 6 October,
      1892; (living 1903).

    (1111) *Charles Manby Newcombe,*[8] *b* 6 November,
      1898; (living 1903).

742. **Kate Pugh Bache,**[7] *b* 22 October, 1853; (living 1903); *m* 2 July, 1874, *John Ransford, b* 22 October, 1848; (living 1903).

> (1112) *Harold Bolton Ransford,*[8] *b* 24 August, 1875; (living 1903), *unm.*
>
> (1113) *Henry Ransford.*[8]
>
> (1114) *Eugene Francis Ransford,*[8] *b* 26 August, 1880; *d* 8 August, 1881.
>
> (1115) *Melville Gifford Ransford,*[8] *b* 13 August, 1889; (living 1903).

744. **Caroline Armande Bache,**[7] *b* 10 October, 1864; (living 1903); *m* 9 June, 1886, *John Bonsall Ayers, b* 30 July, 1858; (living 1903).

> (1116) *Caroline Armande Ayers,*[8] *b* 5 February, 1887; (living 1903).
>
> (1117) *Madeline Ayers,*[8] *b* 13 August, 1888; (living 1903).
>
> (1118) *John Bache Ayers,*[8] *b* 24 January 1891; (living 1903).
>
> (1119) *Theodore Bache Ayers,*[8] *b* 9 August, 1893; (living 1903).

746. **Mary dePeyster Lincoln Bache,**[7] *b* 2 March, 1873; (living 1903); *m* 30 March, 1901, *Frederick Leonard Small, b* 10 November, 1865; (living 1903). S. P.

747. **Katharine Rutgers Bache,**[7] *b* 16 October, 1875; (living 1903); *m* 22 January, 1895, *A. Clinton Wilmerding, b* 24 September, 1859; (living 1903).

> (1120) *Pelham Clinton Wilmerding,*[8] *b* 21 December, 1895; (living 1903).
>
> (1121) *Hamilton Bache Wilmerding,*[8] *b* 19 November, 1900; (living 1903).
>
> (1122) *Madeline Rutgers Wilmerding,*[8] *b* 11 December, 1901; (living 1903).

748. **Eloise Kirby Bache,**[7] *b* 22 August, 1868; (living 1903); *m* 25 January, 1899, *Wilmer Otis Davis, b* 5 September, 1861; (living 1903). S. P.

749. Maude Emeline Bache,[7] *b* 22 February, 1870; (living
     1903); *m* 18 October, 1893, *William Charles Oxberry,*
     b 7 September, 1868; (living 1903).
         (1123) *Harry W. Oxberry,*[8] *b* 24 August, 1894; *d*
             18 July, 1897.
         (1124) *Robert Walter Oxberry,*[8] *b* 10 May, 1896;
             (living 1903).
         (1125) *Kenneth Bache Oxberry,*[8] *b* 7 September,
             1898; (living 1903).

750. Marion B. Bache,[7] *b* 15 September, 1871; (living 1903);
     m 3 August, 1893,[64] *Zachariah V. Flomerfelt, b* 1861;
     (living 1903).
         (1126) *Claude Bache Flomerfelt,*[8] *b* 15 June, 1896;
             (living 1903).

751. George Frederick Bache,[7] *b* 5 June, 1873; (living 1903);
     m 25 September, 1903, *Christina Groute, b* 1 August,
     1872; (living 1903). S. P.

753. Mabel Hall Bache,[7] *b* 9 March, 1879; (living 1903); *m*
     16 December, 1900, *Ward William Smith, b* 7 June,
     1876; (living 1903).
         (1127) *Ward William Smith,*[8] *b* 5 November, 1901;
             (living 1903).
         (1128) *Earl Clifton Smith,*[8] *b* 15 January, 1903;
             (living 1903).

756. Caroline Bache Pickell,[7] *b* 21 December, 1880; (living
     1903); *m* 20 October, 1902, *John Chase, b* 6 October,
     1875; (living 1903). S. P.

757. William Henry Crossman,[7] *b* 9 October, 1864; (living
     1903); *m* 28 March, 1894, *Effie Torbus Underhill* (living
     1903).
         (1129) *William Henry Crossman,*[8] *b* 7 August, 1896;
             (living 1903).
         (1130) *Grace Underhill Crossman,*[8] *b* 6 May, 1900;
             (living 1903).

758. **Florence Crossman,**[7] *b* 4 February, 1867; (living 1903); *m* 11 November, 1903, *Frank Otheman Roe, b* 15 July, 1864; (living 1903). S. P.

759. **Charlotte Grace Crossman,**[7] *b* 29 April, 1870; (living 1903); *m* 12 April, 1893, *Edgar Mortimer Carnrick, b* 21 February, 1869; (living 1903). S. P.

764. **James Theophylact Bache,**[7] *b* 30 April, 1871; (living 1903); *m* 16 November, 1894, *Agnes W. Taylor, b* 3 July, 1874; (living 1903).
   (1131) *Philip William Bache,*[8] *b* 13 March, 1898; (living 1903).

766. **Charles Frederick Bache,**[7] *b* 30 August, 1874; (living 1903); *m* 28 June, 1899, *Edith Litchfield, b* 17 November, 1876; (living 1903).
   (1132) *Richard Franklin Bache,*[8] *b* 29 August, 1903; (living 1903).

768. **Grace Bache,**[7] *b* 13 May, 1880; (living 1903); *m* 21 March, 1901, *Benjamin Franklin McQuay, b* 25 July, 1873; (living 1903). S. P.

769. **William Frederick Dudley**[7] (M.D.), *b* 30 June, 1862; (living 1903); *m* 19 November, 1890, *Laura Lightbourn Bee, b* 15 February, 1865; (living 1903).
   (1133) *Frances Halsted Dudley,*[8] *b* 12 February, 1895; (living 1903).
   (1134) *Laura Lightbourn Dudley,*[8] *b* 21 January, 1898; (living 1903).
   (1135) *William Henry Dudley,*[8] *b* 30 August, 1899; (living 1903).
   (1136) *Gordon Bee Dudley,*[8] *b* 9 May, 1901; (living 1903).

779. **Emilie Duryea Mason,**[7] *b* 20 March, 1879; (living 1903); *m* 15 April, 1903, *John Ralph Wilson, b* 13 April, 1878; (living 1903). S. P.

783. **Samuel Lispenard Cooper,**[7] *b* 16 January 1858; (living
     1903); *m* 6 January, 1885, *Elizabeth Underhill Goodsell,*
     b 25 May, 1866; (living 1903).

        (1137) *Samuel Goodsell Cooper,*[8] *b* 19 November,
          1885; (living 1903).

        (1138) *Helen Elizabeth Cooper,*[8] *b* 8 March, 1887;
          (living 1903).

        (1139) *Emily Lispenard Cooper,*[8] b 7 October, 1891;
          d 1 August, 1892.

784. **William Lispenard Robb,**[7] *b* 9 May, 1861; (living 1903);
     m 15 April, 1893, *Winifred Matthews, b* 4 June, 1869;
     (living 1903).

        (1140) *Winifred Lispenard Robb,*[8] *b* 14 February,
          1895; (living 1903).

788. **Reginald Fairfax Nicholson**[7] (U.S.N.), *b* 15 December,
     1852; (living 1903); *m* (1) 7 July, 1877, *Annie E.*
     Heap, b 19 June, 1855; *d* 11 February, 1889; *m* (2) 2
     June, 1900, *Elizabeth Code, b* 16 July, 1877; (living
     1903).

        (1141) *Mary Jones Nicholson,*[8] *b* 13 June, 1878;
          (living 1903).

        (1142) *Reginald Fairfax Nicholson,*[8] *b* 18 Decem-
          ber, 1879; *d* 2 July, 1890.

789. **William Jones Nicholson**[7] (U.S.A.), *b* 16 January, 1856;
     (living 1903); *m* 6 January, 1883, *Harriet Fenlon,* (liv-
     ing 1903).

        (1143) *William Corcoran Fenlon Nicholson,*[8] *b* 28
          December, 1883; (living 1903).

        (1144) *Helen Lispenard Nicholson,*[8] *b* 6 November,
          1893; (living 1903).

790. **Helen Maria Nicholson,**[7] *b* 17 November, 1860; (living
     1903); *m* 28 April, 1881, *Pitt Cooke, b* 16 June, 1857;
     (living 1903).

        (1145) *Mary Blake Cooke.*[8]

        (1146) *Helen Nicholson Cooke,*[8] *b* 11 November,
          1883; (living 1903).

791. **Augustus Somerville Nicholson,**[7] *b* 29 November, 1862; (living 1903); *m* 14 November, 1894, *Linnie Bell Wilkins, b* 25 December, 1868; (living 1903).

  (1147) *Hannah Adelaide Nicholson,*[8] *b* 27 September, 1895; *d* 18 January, 1903.

  (1148) *Somerville Nicholson,*[8] *b* 27 June, 1897; (living 1903).

792. **Henry William Ducachet Nicholson,**[7] *b* 17 February, 1864; (living 1903); *m* 25 June, 1889, *Rebecca Wood, b* 31 March, 1866; (living 1903).

  (1151) *Helen Sellman Nicholson,*[8] *b* 7 May, 1890; (living 1903).

  (1152) *Anna Wood Nicholson,*[8] *b* 9 June, 1893; (living 1903).

793. **Mary Blake Nicholson,**[7] *b* 4 October, 1866; (living 1903); *m* 12 November, 1889, *Henry Stoddert Matthews, b* 10 January, 1864; (living 1903).

  (1151) *Emily Corcoran Matthews,*[8] *b* 2 September, 1891; *d* 27 August, 1892.

  (1152) *Hannah Somerville Matthews,*[8] *b* 26 May, 1893; (living 1903).

  (1153) *Charles McIlvaine Matthews,*[8] *b* 18 February, 1895; (living 1903).

  (1154) *Henry Stoddert Matthews,*[8] *b* 30 September, 1896; (living 1903).

  (1155) *Lucy Haw Matthews,*[8] *b* 25 September, 1900; (living 1903).

794. **Reynolds Lispenard Nicholson,**[7] *b* 30 October, 1871; (living 1903); *m* 6 July, 1898, *Laura Marguerite Daggett, b* 17 December, 1879; (living 1903).

  (1156) *Dorothy Lispenard Nicholson,*[8] *b* 10 June 1900; (living 1903).

795. **Helen Nicholson Roberts,**[7] *b* 19 September, 1855; (living 1903); *m* 31 May, 1899, Rev. *Samuel Fitch Hotchkin, b* 2 April, 1833; (living 1903). S. P.

801. **Julia Florence Sutherland,**[7] *b* 29 July, 1856; (living
     1903); *m* 5 November, 1890, *Howard Sheild McCand-*
     lish, b 8 December, 1842; (living 1903).
        (1157) *Howard Sheild McCandlish,*[8] *b* 7 August,
           1891; (living 1903).
        (1158) *Dorothea Bache McCandlish,*[8] *b* 17 June,,
           1894; (living 1903).

803. **Augusta Nicholson Sutherland,**[7] *b* 6 June, 1861; (living
     1903); *m* 21 October, 1896, *George Lewis Stone, b* 9
     March, 1861; *d* 13 January, 1899.
        (1159) *Caroline Sutherland Stone,*[8] *b* 4 August,
           1897; (living 1903).

804. **Anne Howard Rundlett,**[7] *b* 2 April, 1870; (living 1903);
     m 17 April, 1895, *James Clark McGuire* (M.D.), *b* 1
     February, 1853; (living 1903).
        (1160) *James Clark McGuire,*[8] *b* 17 April, 1896;
           (living 1903).

805. **Augustus Jesup Nicholson**[7] (U.S.N.), *b* 19 November,
     1852; *d* 22 May, 1893; *m* 19 August, 1882, *Charlotte*
     Gunn, (living 1903). O. S. P.

806. **Abigail Adams Johnson,**[7] *b* 30 August, 1861; (living
     1903); *m* 24 December, 1889, *Milton Strong Thompson,*
     b 8 February, 1852; (living 1903).
        (1161) *Sarah Elizabeth Thompson,*[8] *b* 11 October,
           1890; (living 1903).
        (1162) *Gardiner Thompson,*[8] *b* 28 October, 1892;
           (living 1903).
        (1163) *Alexander Bryan Johnson Thompson,*[8] *b* 30
           April, 1896; *d* 25 February, 1900.
        (1164) *Milton Strong Thompson,*[8] *b* 26 October,
           1901; (living 1903).
        (1165) *Abigail Adams Thompson,*[8] *b* 3 November,
           1903; (living 1903).

807. **Elizabeth Lispenard Johnson,**[7] *b* 19 July, 1865; (living
     1903); *m* 16 November, 1887, *Walter Bell Phister, b* 28
     December, 1857; (living 1903).

(1166) *Mary Cornelia Phister,*8 *b* 1 November, 1888; (living 1903).

(1167) *Lispenard Bache Phister,*8 *b* 27 September, 1896; (living 1903).

809. **Helen Bache Nicholson,**7 *b* 13 September, 1864; (living 1903); *m* 4 October, 1893, *Harry Kimmell* (U.S.N.), *b* 10 April, 1860; (living 1903).

(1168) *Helen Marie Kimmell,*8 *b* 21 September, 1894; (living 1903).

(1169) *Harry Kimmell,*8 *b* 13 October, 1895; (living 1903).

(1170) *Atala Lamar Kimmell,*8 *b* 6 November, 1900; (living 1903).

813. **Atala Bache Nicholson,**7 *b* 26 March, 1875; (living 1903); *m* 30 November, 1899, *Lucius Q. C. Lamar, b* 26 January, 1854; (living 1903).

(1171) *Mirabeau Bonaparte Lamar,*8 *b* 7 April, 1901; (living 1903).

(1172) *Janvier Longstreet Lamar,*8 *b* 5 December, 1903; (living 1903).

820. **Alfred Seton,**7 *b* 20 October, 1853; (living 1903); *m* 5 December, 1889, *Mary Louise Barbey, b* 4 August, 1866; (living 1903).

(1173) *Mary Dorothy Seton,*8 *b* 22 December, 1890; (living 1903).

(1174) *Helen Seton,*8 *b* 25 February, 1893; (living 1903).

(1175) *Henry Seton,*8 *b* 4 July, 1894; (living 1903).

821. **Laura Seton,**7 *b* 11 August, 1855; *d* 20 September, 1898; *m* 29 April, 1875, Lieut.-General *Wilhelm von Kettler, b* 18 May, 1846; (living 1903).

(1176) *Gerhard von Kettler.*8

(1177) *Alice von Kettler,*8 *b* 8 August, 1878; (living 1903).

(1178) *Elise von Kettler,*8 *b* 3 November, 1880; (living 1903).

(1179) *Alfred von Kettler*,[8] *b* 14 November, 1887;
(living 1903).
(1180) *Edward von Kettler*,[8] *b* 28 January, 1891;
(living 1903).

822. Elise deRham,[7] *b* 18 July, 1850; *d* 17 October, 1879; *m*
26 April, 1876, *John Jay Pierrepont, b* 3 September,
1849; (living 1903).
(1181) *John Jay Pierrepont*,[8] *b* 19 March, 1877; *d* 6
January, 1878.

824. Charles deRham,[7] *b* 30 January, 1854; (living 1903);
m 13 April, 1880, *Emily Hone Foster, b* 6 June, 1856;
(living 1903).
(1182) *Henry Casimir deRham*,[8] *b* 2 February, 1882;
(living 1903), *unm.*
(1183) *Frederic Foster deRham*,[8] *b* 18 June, 1883;
(living 1903).
(1184) *Laura deRham*,[8] *b* 22 January, 1887; (living
1903).
(1185) *Charles deRham*,[8] *b* 28 April, 1888; (living
1903).
(1186) *Giraud Foster deRham*,[8] *b* 12 December,
1896; (living 1903).
(1187) *Emily Clarisse deRham*,[8] *b* 31 December,
1902; (living 1903).

825. Henry Casimir deRham,[7] *b* 12 August, 1855; (living
1903); *m* (1) 25 April, 1885, *Anna Taylor Warren* of
Troy, N. Y., *b* 23 October, 1863; *d* 7 November, 1893;
m (2) 23 April, 1895, *Georgiana Berryman, b* 27 June,
1866; (living 1903).
(1188) *Casimir deRham*,[8] *b* 3 August, 1896; (living
1903).
(1189) *William deRham*,[8] *b* 27 September, 1901;
(living 1903).
(1190) *Marion Elise deRham*,[8] *b* 12 February, 1903;
(living 1903).

829. **John W. Schmidt,**[7] *b* 18 December, 1859; *d* 3 July, 1898; *m* 5 November, 1896, *Marie Louise Stoutenburgh, b* 2 April, 1867; (living 1903). O. S. P. (She *m* (2) 6 December, 1899, George Albert Durand.)

830. **Elise Melenda Schmidt,**[7] *b* 27 January, 1861; (living 1903); *m* 6 December, 1883, *R. Dickinson Jewett, b* 6 July, 1859; (living 1903).

> (1191) *Elizabeth Melenda Jewett,*[8] *b* 8 February, 1886; (living 1903).
> (1192) *David Augustine Lawrence Jewett,*[8] *b* 26 March, 1888; (living 1903).
> (1193) *Gertrude Jewett,*[8] *b* 1 January, 1890; (living 1903).
> (1194) *Elise Bache Jewett,*[8] *b* 27 December, 1893; (living 1903).
> (1195) *George Parbury Pollen Jewett,*[8] *b* 8 August, 1896; (living 1903).
> (1196) *Richard Dickinson Jewett,*[8] *b* 14 May, 1899; (living 1903).
> (1197) *Robert Coleman Jewett,*[8] *b* 14 March, 1902; (living 1903).

832. **Fritz Leopold Schmidt,**[7] *b* 22 April, 1866; (living 1903); *m* 20 December, 1899, *Gertrude I. Townsend, b* 13 December, 1877; (living 1903).

> (1198) *Melenda Pollen Schmidt,*[8] *b* 14 February, 1901; (living 1903).

835. **Ilse Lotta von Winterfeld,**[7] *b* 8 November, 1876; (living 1903); *m* 19 March, 1901, Col. Baron *Richard von Süsskind,* (living 1903).

> (1199) *Max Theodor von Süsskind,*[8] *b* 2 January, 1902; (living 1903).

836. **Wilhelm von Reuthe-Finck,**[7] *b* 21 July, 1869; (living 1903); *m* 20 November, 1903, *Elizabeth von Krosigk.* †

838. **Cornelius Roosevelt Duffie,**[7] *b* 18 November, 1866; (living 1903); *m* 9 January, 1888, *Edith Normington Langdon, b* 26 October, 1867; (living 1903).

> (1200) *Dorothy Duffie,*[8] *b* 13 June, 1889; (living 1903).
>
> (1201) *Archibald Duncan Duffie,*[8] *b* 13 April, 1892; (living 1903).

839. **Jane Antoinette Duffie,**[7] *b* 12 December, 1868; (living 1903); *m* 14 June, 1887, *Edward Hamilton Cahill, b* 3 January, 1866; (living 1903).

> (1202) *Helen Cahill,*[8] *b* 4 November, 1892; (living 1903).

840. **Archibald Bleecker Duffie,**[7] *b* 16 April, 1871; (living 1903); *m* 19 June, 1894, *Antoinette Larocque Roe, b* 23 December, 1869; (living 1903).

> (1203) *Roe Clark Duffie,*[8] *b* 24 March, 1898; (living 1903).

841. **John Van Benthuysen Bleecker**[7] (U.S.N.), *b* 16 August, 1847; (living 1903); *m* 2 October, 1873, *Lizzie Frances Stearns, b* 27 February, 1848; (living 1903).

> (1204) *Elsie Lynch Bleecker.*[8]
>
> (1205) *John Stearns Bleecker,*[8] *b* 8 April, 1878; (living 1903), *unm.*

842. **Cornelia Bleecker,**[7] *b* 6 April, 1853; (living 1903); *m* 26 October, 1881, *Langdon Preble Wheeler, b* 12 November, 1849; *d* 11 October, 1886.

> (1206) *Bleecker Langdon Wheeler,*[8] *b* 29 May, 1883; (living 1903).

844. **Rosalie Lynch Bleecker,**[7] *b* 15 February, 1860; (living 1903); *m* 25 April, 1888, *George W. Salter* (living 1903). S. P.

845. **Florence Coralie Bleecker,**[7] *b* 10 April, 1861; (living (1903); *m* 26 May, 1887, *Thomas Ellis Brown, b* 3 February, 1856; (living 1903).

(1207) *Clinton Bleecker Brown,*[8] *b* 1 April, 1888; (living 1903).

(1208) *Thomas Ellis Brown,*[8] *b* 3 December, 1889; (living 1903).

(1209) *Bache Hamilton Brown,*[8] *b* 5 April, 1891; (living 1903).

(1210) *Otis deRaasloff Brown,*[8] *b* 16 October, 1898; (living 1903).

846. **Cornelia Bleecker,**[7] *b* 26 January, 1852; (living 1903); *m* 30 June, 1875, *Seaman J. Mallaby, b* 21 March, 1844; (living 1903).

(1211) *Francis Bleecker Mallaby.*[8]

(1212) *Thomas Kortright Mallaby,*[8] *b* 16 October, 1879; (living 1903).

(1213) *Cornelia Bleecker Mallaby,*[8] *b* 31 July, 1881; *d* 25 July, 1882.

851. **Anthony James Bleecker,**[7] *b* 15 September, 1864; (living 1903); *m* 8 September, 1892, *Bertha DeLaVergne Gilman, b* 8 June, 1863; (living 1903).

(1214) *Anthony Lispenard Bleecker,*[8] *b* 5 November, 1893; (living 1903).

(1215) *Winthrop Gilman Bleecker,*[8] *b* 18 October, 1897; (living 1903).

(1216) *Helena Roosevelt Bleecker,*[8] *b* 30 January, 1899; (living 1903).

852. **William Hill Bleecker,**[7] *b* 15 May, 1867; (living 1903); *m* 2 April, 1891, *Emma White Fish, b* 12 November, 1866; (living 1903).

(1217) *William Hill Bleecker,*[8] *b* 4 January, 1891; (living 1903).

(1218) *James Barclay Bleecker,*[8] *b* 2 May, 1893; (living 1903).

(1219) *Laura Frances Bleecker,*[8] *b* 11 October, 1895; (living 1903).

(1220) *Kenneth Bayard Bleecker,*[8] *b* 13 October, 1900; (living 1903).

876. **Katharine Bache Satterthwaite,**[7] *b* 6 November, 1866; (living 1903); *m* 2 September, 1891, *Adrian H. Larkin, b* 6 June, 1865; (living 1903).

    (1221) *James Satterthwaite Larkin,*[8] *b* 29 May, 1893; (living 1903).

    (1222) *Sarah Elizabeth Larkin,*[8] *b* 9 December, 1896; (living 1903).

    (1223) *Lawrence Larkin,*[8] *b* 21 May, 1903; (living 1903).

877. **Julia Lawrence Satterthwaite,**[7] *b* 1 July, 1868; (living 1903); *m* 25 June, 1890, *Ernest Rollin Tilton, b* 3 September, 1866; (living 1903).

    (1224) *Ernest Rollin Tilton,*[8] *b* 28 September, 1893; (living 1903).

878. **Annie Fisher Satterthwaite,**[7] *b* 6 June, 1870; (living 1903); *m* 9 December, 1891, *P. William Ström, b* 24 January, 1862; (living 1903).

    (1225) *Jeanie Satterthwaite Ström,*[8] *b* 17 January, 1895; *d* 14 July, 1896.

    (1226) *P. William L. Ström,*[8] *b* 25 June, 1898; (living 1903).

879. **James Sheafe Satterthwaite,**[7] *b* 8 January, 1872; (living 1903); *m* 6 April, 1896, *Lillie Marden, b* 18 April, 1872; (living 1903).

    (1227) *Lillie Lawrence Satterthwaite,*[8] *b* 4 April, 1898; *d* 13 December, 1898.

    (1228) *Hope Satterthwaite,*[8] *b* 12 August, 1899; (living 1903).

880. **Thomas Wilkinson Satterthwaite,**[7] *b* 25 December, 1876; (living 1903); *m* 6 March, 1902, *Lucile Carnes Weeks, b* 27 July, 1881; (living 1903).   S. P.

888. **Eleanor Colford Jones,**[7] *b* 11 May, 1841; (living 1903); *m* 10 December, 1862, *Augustus Newbold Morris*[6] (No. 533 above), *b* 3 June, 1838; (living 1903).

    (The issue of this marriage are chronicled above under: 533, AUGUSTUS NEWBOLD MORRIS.[6])

890. **Cordelia Schermerhorn Jones,**[7] *b* 23 June, 1849;[80] (living 1903); *m* 13 April, 1871, *John Steward, b* 17 July, 1847; (living 1903). S. P.

893. **Walter Lispenard Suydam,**[7] *b* 20 May, 1854; (living 1903); *m* 29 April, 1875, *Jane Mesier Suydam, b* 2 May, 1855; (living 1903).

    (1229) *Walter Lispenard Suydam.*[8]

894. **Helen Suydam,**[7] *b* 18 March, 1858; (living 1903); *m* 25 January, 1883, *Robert Fulton Cutting, b* 27 June, 1852; (living 1903).

    (1230) *Helen Cutting,*[8] *b* 16 December, 1883; (living 1903).

    (1231) *Elizabeth McEvers Cutting,*[8] *b* 4 July, 1885; (living 1903).

    (1232) *Fulton Cutting,*[8] *b* 27 December, 1886; (living 1903).

    (1233) *Charles Suydam Cutting,*[8] *b* 27 January, 1888; (living 1903).

    (1234) *Ruth Hunter Cutting,*[8] *b* 7 September, 1895; (living 1903).

    (1235) *Schermerhorn Cutting,*[8] *b* 6 February, 1897; *d* 15 March, 1897.

895. **John Irving,**[7] *b* 25 December, 1841; (living 1903); *m* 1 December, 1868, *Josephine Eichelle Peacock, b* 15 February, 1838; (living 1903).

    (1236) *Percival Ralph Irving.*[8]

    (1237) *Josephine VanCortlandt Irving,*[8] *b* 21 February, 1871; *d* 1 May, 1879.

896. **Cortlandt Irving,**[7] *b* 8 October, 1843; (living 1903); *m* 15 December, 1881, *Theresa Romeyn Beck, b* 31 January, 1848; (living 1903). S. P.

898. **Henry Irving,**[7] *b* 25 December, 1847; (living 1903); *m* 11 May, 1870, *Ella Virginia Woodburn,* (living 1903).

    (1238) *Samuel Alexander Irving,*[8] *b* 6 July, 1871; *d* 25 August, 1871.

901. **Edward Irving,**[7] *b* 1 December, 1853; *d* 21 April, 1880; *m* 12 October, 1878, *Julia Justine Aitkins, b* October, 1859; (living 1903).

> (1239) *Charles Edward Irving,*[8] *b* 27 November, 1879; (living 1903), *unm.*

903. **Walter Irving,**[7] *b* 11 February, 1857; (living 1903); *m* 12 November, 1890, *Bessie Louise VonSickler, b* 21 December, 1871; (living 1903).

> (1240) *Walter VanCortlandt Irving,*[8] *b* 13 July, 1901; (living 1903).

905. **Helen Schermerhorn Welles,**[7] *b* 22 May, 1851; (living 1903); *m* 5 January, 1875, *George Lovett Kingsland, b* 4 September, 1834; *d* 14 July, 1892.

> (1241) *Helen Schermerhorn Kingsland.*[8]
>
> (1242) *George Lovett Kingsland,*[8] *b* 12 March, 1884; (living 1903).
>
> (1243) *Ethel Welles Kingsland,*[8] *b* 21 April, 1886; (living 1903).

907. **Benjamin Welles,**[7] *b* 11 January, 1857; (living 1903); *m* 27 October, 1886, *Frances W. Swan, b* 26 November, 1863; (living 1903).

> (1244) *Emily Frances Welles,*[8] *b* 22 October, 1887; (living 1903).
>
> (1245) *Benjamin Sumner Welles,*[8] *b* 14 October, 1892; (living 1903).

910. **Emily Astor,**[7] *b* 16 June, 1854; *d* 21 November, 1881; *m* 14 March, 1876, *James J. VanAlen, b* 20 March, 1846; (living 1903).

> (1246) *Mary VanAlen,*[8] *b* 29 November, 1876; (living 1903).
>
> (1247) *James Laurens VanAlen.*[8]
>
> (1248) *Sarah Steward VanAlen.*[8]

911. **Helen Astor,**[7] *b* 27 November, 1855; *d* 12 November, 1893; *m* 18 November, 1878, *James Roosevelt Roosevelt, b* 27 March, 1854; (living 1903.)

(1249) *James Roosevelt Roosevelt,*[8] *b* 21 August, 1879; (living 1903).†

(1250) *Helen Rebecca Roosevelt,*[8] *b* 26 September, 1881; (living 1903).

912. **Charlotte Augusta Astor,**[7] *b* 29 March, 1858; (living 1903); *m* (1) 20 October, 1879, *J. Coleman Drayton, b* 4 June, 1852; (living 1903); *m* (2) 17 December, 1896, *George Ogilvy Haig* (living 1903).

(1251) *Caroline Astor Drayton,*[8] *b* 26 October, 1880; (living 1903).

(1252) *Henry Coleman Drayton,*[8] *b* 27 January, 1883; (living 1903).

(1253) *William Astor Drayton,*[8] *b* 28 November, 1888; (living 1903).

(1254) *Alida Livingston Drayton,*[8] *b* 24 November, 1890; *d* 11 August, 1898.

913. **Caroline Schermerhorn Astor,**[7] *b* 10 October, 1861; (living 1903); *m* 18 November, 1884, *Marshall Orme Wilson, b* 20 June, 1861; (living 1903).

(1255) *Marshall Orme Wilson,*[8] *b* 13 November, 1885; (living 1903).

(1256) *Richard Thornton Wilson,*[8] *b* 5 December, 1886; (living 1903).

914. **John Jacob Astor,**[7] *b* 13 July, 1865; (living 1903); *m* 17 February, 1891, *Ava Lowle Willing, b* 13 September, 1869; (living 1903).

(1257) *William Vincent Astor,*[8] *b* 15 November, 1891; (living 1903).

(1258) *Ava Alice Muriel Astor,*[8] *b* 7 July, 1902; (living 1903).

915. **Robert Ogden Glover,**[7] *b* 10 February, 1849; *d* 16 July, 1892; *m* 10 September, 1885, *Harriet D. Darrow, b* 27 January, 1861; (living 1903). O. S. P.

916. **Mary Weltha Glover,**[7] *b* 1 July, 1850; (living 1903); *m* 20 June, 1881, *Albert J. Reynaud, b* 5 May, 1853; (living 1903).

(1259) *Marguerite Marie Reynaud*,[8] *b* 12 October, 1882; (living 1903).

(1260) *Albert J. Reynaud*,[8] *b* 11 June, 1884; (living 1903).

(1261) *Henri Reynaud*,[8] *b* 8 June, 1885; (living 1903).

(1262) *Madeleine Laura Ward Reynaud*,[8] *b* 28 March, 1887; (living 1903).

(1263) *Marie Gabrielle Reynaud*,[8] *b* 23 August, 1888; (living 1903).

(1264) *George Pierre Reynaud*,[8] *b* 30 March, 1890; (living 1903).

(1265) *Louis Augustin Reynaud*,[8] *b* 23 June, 1893; (living 1903).

(1266) *Gustave Reynaud*,[8] *b* 25 July, 1895; (living 1903).

917. **James Andrew Glover,**[7] *b* 10 May, 1854; (living 1903); *m* 18 April, 1888, *Frances Livingston, b* 4 March, 1848; (living 1903).

(1267) *Susanna Livingston Glover*,[8] *b* 7 November, 1889; (living 1903).

(1268) *Anne White Livingston Glover*,[8] *b* 22 February, 1893; (living 1903).

(1269) *Ernestine Frances Livingston Glover*,[8] *b* 18 November, 1895; (living 1903).

918. **Edward Augustus Glover,**[7] *b* 29 March, 1856; (living 1903); *m* 22 June, 1885, *Nancy Helene Reynaud, b* 25 August, 1865; (living 1903).

(1270) *Edward Augustus VanCortlandt Glover*,[8] *b* 21 May, 1886; (living 1903).

(1271) *Nathalie Florence Glover*,[8] *b* 21 November, 1888; *d* 13 July, 1889.

(1272) *Thomas James Glover*,[8] *b* 25 May, 1890; (living 1903).

(1273) *Joseph Ogden Glover*,[8] *b* 8 October, 1892; (living 1903).

(1274) *Robert Ogden Glover*,[8] *b* 4 August, 1894; (living 1903).

920. **Henry Warburton Bibby Glover,**[7] *b* 1 November, 1859;
(living 1903) ; *m* 27 November, 1889, *Edith Hervé Cle-*
borne, b 16 February, 1867; (living 1903).

> (1275) *Claiborne VanCortlandt Glover,*[8] *b* 10 No-
> vember, 1890; (living 1903).
>
> (1276) *Robert Ogden Glover,*[8] *b* 3 July, 1894; (liv-
> ing 1903).
>
> (1277) *Gladys Gouverneur Glover,*[8] *b* 5 February,
> 1896; (living 1903).
>
> (1278) *John Morgan Glover,*[8] *b* 10 November, 1901 ;
> (living 1903).

930. **Augusta Bibby Groshon,**[7] *b* 10 May, 1857; (living 1903) ;
m 6 August, 1885, *M. Hoffman Wilson, b* 6 November,
1856; (living 1903).

> (1279) *Marjorie Bleecker Wilson,*[8] *b* 1 March, 1887;
> *d* 4 June, 1887.
>
> (1280) *Leonard Bleecker Wilson,*[8] *b* 3 December,
> 1888; (living 1903).
>
> (1281) *Groshon Wilson,*[8] *b* 28 February, 1890; *d* 17
> October, 1890.
>
> (1282) *Natalie deForest Wilson,*[8] *b* 16 December,
> 1891; (living 1903).

931. **Isabel Gourlie Groshon,**[7] *b* 4 March, 1862; (living 1903) ;
m 2 April, 1889, *George LeBoutillier, b* 30 September,
1850; (living 1903). S. P.

936. **Thomas H. Wagstaff,**[7] *b* 19 May, 1858; (living 1903) ;
m 4 December, 1901, *Florence Lamberti, b* 10 April,
1861; (living 1903). S. P.

938. **Alice Wagstaff,**[7] *b* 18 January, 1864; (living 1903) ; *m*
5 November, 1885, *William Hamilton Myers, b* 20 December, 1841; (living 1903).

> (1283) *Pierre Hamilton Myers,*[8] *b* 19 December,
> 1886; (living 1903).
>
> (1284) *Margaret VanCortlandt Myers,*[8] *b* 2 Sep-
> tember, 1888; (living 1093).
>
> (1285) *Carleton Wagstaff Myers,*[8] *b* 12 December,
> 1889; *d* 28 May, 1890.

(1286) *Alfred Roulet Myers,*[8] *b* 22 January, 1892;
    d 12 June, 1894.

(1287) *Alice Francena White Myers,*[8] *b* 11 June,
    1896; (living 1903).

(1288) *Elizabeth Penfold VanSchoonhoven Myers,*[8]
    b 24 December, 1898; *d* 17 September, 1903.

941. **Henry VanCortlandt Meyer,**[7] *b* 9 February, 1862; (living 1903); *m* 24 October, 1894, *Mary Raymond, b* 7 July, 1865; (living 1903).

(1289) *Raymond VanCortlandt Meyer,*[8] *b* 6 May,
    1897; *d* 22 July, 1898.

(1290) *Francena Roulet Meyer,*[8] *b* 4 December, 1898;
    (living 1903).

(1291) *Augusta VanCortlandt Meyer,*[8] *b* 23 September, 1900; *d* 7 October, 1900.

(1292) *Isabel VanCortlandt Meyer,*[8] *b* 12 October,
    1902; (living 1903).

945. **Constance Lloyd Bowden,**[7] *b* 4 June, 1861; (living 1903); *m* 14 November, 1885, *William Herbert Washington, b* 2 August, 1853; *d* 14 July, 1900.

(1293) *Bowden Washington,*[8] *b* 17 July, 1892; (living 1903).

946. **Drayton Burrill,**[7] *b* 12 May, 1861; (living 1903); *m* 2 March, 1889, *Elizabeth Steward, b* 1 April, 1864; (living 1903).

(1294) *Drayton Burrill,*[8] *b* 23 August, 1891; (living
    1903).

(1295) *Elizabeth Steward Morris Burrill,*[8] *b* 18 October, 1895; (living 1903).

947. **Mary Middleton Burrill,**[7] *b* 7 November, 1866; (living 1903); *m* 25 October, 1899, *Richard Law Kemble, b* 24 November, 1865; (living 1903).

(1296) *William Kemble,*[8] *b* 21 November, 1903;
    (living 1903).

948. Percy M. Burrill,[7] *b* 6 October, 1872; (living 1903); *m* 13 March, 1900, *Mary M. Warfield, d* 4 June, 1903. S. P.

950. William St. John Elliot Marshall,[7] *b* 28 April, 1860; (living 1903); *m* 22 October, 1885, *Constance Blessing Runcie, b* 23 August, 1862; (living 1903).

    (1297) *Jean Dale Marshall,*[8] *b* 3 March, 1893; (living 1903).

    (1298) *William St. John Elliot Marshall,*[8] *b* 30 January, 1896; (living 1903).

952. Sarah Elliot Marshall,[7] *b* 17 September, 1866; (living 1903); *m* 11 December, 1889, *Francis Lionel Mordaunt, b* 8 May, 1847; (living 1903).

    (1299) *Elizabeth Morris Mordaunt,*[8] *b* 5 February, 1891; (living 1903).

    (1300) *Mildred Cumberlye Mordaunt,*[8] *b* 31 October, 1893; (living 1903).

958. Ellen VanBuren Morris,[7] *b* 10 June, 1873; (living 1903); *m* 9 October, 1899, *Francis Livingston Pell, b* 23 September, 1873; (living 1903).

    (1301) *Walden Pell,*[8] *b* 3 July, 1902; (living 1903).

960. Stuyvesant Fish Morris,[7] *b* 22 May, 1877; (living 1903); *m* 27 December, 1900, *Elizabeth Hillis Wynkoop, b* 11 March, 1878; (living 1903).

    (1302) *Stuyvesant Fish Morris,*[8] *b* 19 February, 1902; (living 1903).

964. Helena VanCortlandt Phelps,[7] *b* 24 July, 1860; (living 1903); *m* 11 October, 1883, *Robert Temple Emmet, b* 13 December, 1854; (living 1903).

    (1303) *Robert Rutherfurd Morris Emmet,*[8] *b* 27 January, 1888; (living 1903).

    (1304) *Herman Rutgers LeRoy Emmet,*[8] *b* 25 September, 1889; (living 1903).

    (1305) *Anna Helena Emmet,*[8] *b* 23 April, 1893; (living 1903).

965. **Edgar Morris Phelps,**[7] *b* 4 September, 1876; (living 1903); *m* 21 April, 1900, *Carolyn Hunter Kane, b* 10 March, 1880; (living 1903).

   (1306) *Walter Kane Phelps,*[8] *b* 29 March, 1901; (living 1903).

   (1307) *Henry Delafield Phelps,*[8] *b* 8 October, 1902; (living 1903).

967. **Louisa Morris Stewart,**[7] *b* 18 June, 1853; (living 1903); *m* 3 June, 1875, *James Kent, b* 2 April, 1854; *d* 20 January, 1901.

   (1308) *James Kent.*[8]

   (1309) *William Pinckney Kent,*[8] *b* 27 February, 1877; *d* 17 January, 1892.

   (1310) *Helen VanCortlandt LeRoy Kent,*[8] *b* 21 September, 1879; (living 1903).

968. **Helen VanCortlandt Stewart,**[7] *b* 9 April, 1857; (living 1903); *m* 10 December, 1884, *W. Irving Kent, b* 8 January, 1861; (living 1903).

   (1311) *W. Irving Kent,*[8] *b* 4 December, 1888; (living 1903).

   (1312) *LeRoy Kent,*[8] *b* 1 December, 1889; (living 1903).

   (1313) *Stewart Kent,*[8] *b* 28 August, 1896; (living 1903).

970. **Edward LeRoy Stewart,**[7] *b* 21 June, 1866; (living 1903); *m* 24 December, 1896, *Emily B. Davis, b* 11 October, 1869; (living 1903). S. P.

972. **Newbold Morris,**[7] *b* 12 January, 1868; (living 1903); *m* 9 April, 1896, *Helen Schermerhorn Kingsland,*[8] (No. 1241 above), *b* 9 March, 1876; (living 1903).

   (1314) *Augustus Newbold Morris,*[8] *b* 2 February, 1902; (living 1903).

982. **Robert Webb Morgan,**[7] *b* 4 December, 1863; (living 1903); *m* 4 June, 1902, *Emily G. Wilson, b* 9 January, 1875; (living 1903). S. P.

984. **Mary Louisa Benton,**[7] *b* 4 June, 1860; (living 1903); *m* 4 September, 1890, *William Norwood Suter, b* 11 October, 1861; (living 1903).

> (1315) *Louis Benton Suter,*[8] *b* 13 August, 1891; (living 1903).
>
> (1316) *Helen Lispenard Suter,*[8] *b* 1 June, 1893; (living 1903).

985. **James Watson Benton,**[7] *b* 24 January, 1864; *d* 2 September, 1896; *m* 2 October, 1890, *Sarah Wharton Henry, b* 9 November, 1867; (living 1903).

> (1317) *James Webb Benton,*[8] *b* 9 July, 1892; (living 1903).

987. **Helen Lispenard Webb,**[7] *b* 25 September, 1870; *d* 12 May, 1896; *m* 18 June, 1895, *Lawson Averell Carter, b* 11 June, 1869; (living 1903).

> (1318) *Lawson Averell Lispenard Carter,*[8] *b* 11 May, 1896; *d* 12 May, 1896.

990. **Helen Lispenard Webb,**[7] *b* 27 September, 1859; (living 1903); *m* 11 May, 1887, *John E. Alexandre, b* 1 April, 1840; (living 1903).

> (1319) *Helen Lispenard Alexandre,*[8] *b* 20 June, 1889; (living 1903).
>
> (1320) *Marie Civilise Alexandre,*[8] *b* 22 November, 1891; (living 1903).
>
> (1321) *Anna Remsen Alexandre,*[8] *b* 20 November, 1895; (living 1903).

991. **Elizabeth Remsen Webb,**[7] *b* 6 July, 1861; (living 1903); *m* 14 November, 1891, *George Burrington Parsons*[6] (No. 274 above), *b* 4 March, 1863; (living 1903). S. P.

998. **Henry Graff Trevor,**[7] *b* 25 April, 1865; (living 1903); *m* 10 December, 1890, *Margaret H. Schieffelin, b* 16 December, 1870; (living 1903).

(1322) *Henry Stewart Trevor,*[8] *b* 5 September, 1891;
  d 19 November, 1891.
(1323) *George Schieffelin Trevor,*[8] *b* 13 July, 1892;
  (living 1903).
(1324) *Margaret Estelle Trevor,*[8] *b* 27 July, 1893;
  (living 1903).
(1325) *Louise Stephanie Stewart Trevor,*[8] *b* 16 July,
  1895; (living 1903).
(1326) *Henry Graff Trevor,*[8] *b* 12 September, 1898;
  (living 1903).
(1327) *Helen Lispenard Stewart Trevor,*[8] *b* 15 December, 1901; (living 1903).

1000. **Maud Stewart Lee,**[7] *b* 1 September, 1870; (living
  1903); *m* 9 November, 1893, *William J. Albert McKim, b* 3 September, 1870; (living 1903).
    (1328) *William Lee McKim,*[8] *b* 19 October, 1894;
      (living 1903).
    (1329) *Anthony Lispenard McKim,*[8] *b* 20 April,
      1896; (living 1903).
    (1330) *Cecily Albert McKim,*[8] *b* 20 February, 1898;
      (living 1903).
    (1331) *Robert Vanderburg McKim,*[8] *b* 1 December, 1901; (living 1903).

1009. **Robert Allan Forsyth,**[7] *b* 25 December, 1867; (living
  1903); *m* 8 June, 1892, *May Keokee White, b* 6 September, 1867; (living 1903).
    (1332) *Webb Monroe Forsyth,*[8] *b* 16 May, 1895;
      (living 1903).
    (1333) *William Dabney Forsyth,*[8] *b* 24 November,
      1899; (living 1903).

1010. **Louisa Trevor Forsyth,**[7] *b* 4 September, 1870; (living
  1903); *m* 3 July, 1889, *Henry Russell Drowne, b* 31
  August, 1860; (living 1903).
    (1334) *Henry Russell Drowne,*[8] *b* 3 July, 1897;
      (living 1903).

1013. **James Bayley Bruen,**[7] *b* 26 March, 1873; (living 1903); *m* 1 February, 1898, *Augusta Prescott Allison, b* 15 August, 1874; (living 1903).

> (1335) *Margaret Munro Bruen,*[8] *b* 30 December, 1899; (living 1903).
>
> (1336) *James Allison Bruen,*[8] *b* 15 November, 1901; (living 1903).

1014. **Henry Munro Bruen,**[7] (Rev.), *b* 26 October, 1874; (living 1903); *m* 14 February, 1902, *Martha Scott, b* 10 April, 1875; (living 1903). S. P.

1017. **Michael Robert Seton Shanley,**[7] *b* 25 May, 1870; *d* 29 January, 1896; *m* 19 April, 1893, *Mary Sanford.* †

> (1337) *Joseph Sanford Shanley,*[8] *b* 23 March, 1895; (living 1903).

1018. **William Carleton Shanley,**[7] *b* 13 July, 1871; (living 1903); *m* 2 April, 1894, *Mary Ledwith* (living 1903).

> (1338) *William Carleton Bayley Shanley,*[8] *b* March, 1896; (living 1903).
>
> (1339) *Bernard Shanley,*[8] *b* June, 1897; (living 1903).
>
> (1340) *Grace Shanley,*[8] *b* January, 1899; (living 1903).

1019. **James Roosevelt Shanley,**[7] *b* 1 July, 1872; (living 1903); *m* 18 June, 1897, *Adele Grace Amer, b* 5 August, 1876; (living 1903).

> (1341) *James Roosevelt Shanley,*[8] *b* 16 March, 1898; (living 1903).
>
> (1342) *Julia Dolores Shanley,*[8] *b* 6 February, 1900; (living 1903).

1020. **Bernard Michael Shanley,**[7] *b* 13 August, 1873; (living 1903); *m* 22 June, 1899, *Catherine Regina Ryan.* †

> (1343) *Mary Sanford Shanley,*[8] *b* 5 May, 1900; (living 1903).
>
> (1344) *Adele Shanley,*[8] *b* 26 July, 1901; (living 1903).

1023. **Maria Roosevelt Bunce,**[7] *b* 21 February, 1878; (living 1903) ; *m* 14 June, 1900, *Guy Carleton, b* 4 November, 1875; (living 1903).

> (1345) *Edward Jewett Carleton,*[8] *b* 9 August, 1901 ; (living 1903).

1095. **Samuel J. Berry,**[8] *b* 16 July, 1867; (living 1903) ; *m* 7 April, 1891, *Mary C. Cissel, b* 25 March, 1869; (living 1903).

> (1346) *Helen Hall Berry,*[9] *b* 11 June, 1895; (living 1903).
> (1347) *Richard Cissel Berry,*[9] *b* 18 February, 1898; (living 1903).
> (1348) *Dorothy Barnard Berry,*[9] *b* 25 April, 1903; (living 1903).

1098. **Andrew Hall Berry,**[8] *b* 21 December, 1870; (living 1903) ; *m* 4 October, 1897, *Antoinette Dorothea Droste, b* 10 February, 1876; (living 1903).

> (1349) *Doris Berry,*[9] *b* 14 April, 1899; (living 1903).
> (1350) *Ruth Berry,*[9] *b* 31 October, 1901; (living 1903).

1101. **Charlotte Louise Berry,**[8] *b* 6 November, 1872; (living 1903) ; *m* 21 January, 1896, *Richard Thurston Greene, b* 29 June, 1867; (living 1903).

> (1351) *Charlotte Louise Greene,*[9] *b* 17 January, 1897; (living 1903).
> (1352) *Helen Greene,*[9] *b* 31 January, 1900; (living 1903).

1107. **Maude Louise Newcombe,**[8] *b* 15 August, 1876; (living 1903) ; *m* 3 June, 1897, *Frank Grauer,* M.D., *b* 25 February, 1864; (living 1903).

> (1353) *Evelyn Newcombe Grauer,*[9] *b* 3 April, 1898; (living 1903).
> (1354) *Franklin Hayward Grauer,*[9] *b* 11 August, 1902; (living 1903).

1113. Henry Ransford,[8] *b* 18 June, 1877; (living 1903); *m* 16
       June, 1903, *Grace Josephine Ponton*, (living 1903).
       S. P.

1145. Mary Blake Cooke,[8] *b* 3 February, 1882; (living 1903);
       m 13 February, 1903, *William Britt, b* 10 October,
       1876; (living 1903). S. P.

1176. Gerhard vonKettler,[8] *b* 7 January, 1876; (living 1903);
       m 12 October, 1899, *Maria Wintgens, b* 12 February,
       1878; (living 1903).

         (1355) *Laura Elisabeth vonKettler,*[9] *b* 28 Septem-
                 ber, 1900; (living 1903).

1204. Elsie Lynch Bleecker,[8] *b* 23 December, 1875; (living
       1903); *m* 29 July, 1902, *Ernest G. Waymouth*, R. A.,
       b 1 August, 1869; (living 1903). S. P.

1211. Francis Bleecker Mallaby,[8] *b* 13 December, 1876; (liv-
       ing 1903); *m* 21 March, 1901, *Edith Van Dyke Fryatt,*
       b 10 May, 1876; (living 1903).

         (1356) *Edith Noel Mallaby,*[9] *b* 24 December, 1901;
                 (living 1903).

1229. Walter Lispenard Suydam,[8] *b* 3 August, 1884; (living
       1903); *m* 10 June, 1903, *Louise Lawrance White, b*
       12 September, 1886; (living 1903). S. P.

1236. Percival Ralph Irving,[8] *b* 14 December, 1869; (living
       1903); *m* 8 March, 1894, *Edith L. Keeler, b* 1869;
       (living 1903). S. P.

1241. Helen Schermerhorn Kingsland,[8] *b* 9 March, 1876;
       (living 1903); *m* 9 April, 1896, *Newbold Morris,*[7] (No.
       972 above), *b* 12 January, 1868; (living 1903).
         (The issue of this marriage is chronicled above
       under: 973, NEWBOLD MORRIS.[7])

1247. **James Laurens VanAlen,**[8] b 15 August, 1878; (living 1903); m 10 December, 1900, *Margaret Louise Post, b* 15 July, 1876; (living 1903).

    (1357) *James Henry VanAlen,*[9] b 19 September, 1902; (living 1903).

1248. **Sarah Steward VanAlen,**[8] *b* 5 July, 1881; living 1903); *m* 26 July, 1902, *Robert J. F. Collier, b* 17 June, 1876; (living 1903). S. P.

1308. **James Kent,**[8] *b* 1 March, 1876; (living 1903); *m* 24 October, 1903, *Mary Brinckerhoff Verplank, b* 28 September, 1881; (living 1903). S. P.

PART VIII.

During, or shortly prior to, 1794, the names of many of the streets in New York were changed. The earlier names, as they appear in a map of the city published with the 1798 directory, and the present locations of some of the principal streets, are as follows:

KING STREET is now *Pine Street.*
QUEEN STREET " " *Pearl Street,* from Wall Street to Park Row.
LITTLE QUEEN STREET " " *Cedar Street,* from William Street to the Hudson River.
CROWN STREET " " *Liberty Street.*
HANOVER SQUARE " " *Pearl Street,* between Old Slip and Wall Street.
PRINCESS STREET " " *Beaver Street,* between Broad Street and William.
SMITH STREET " " *William Street,* south of Wall Street and included all of Old Slip.
LITTLE DOCK STREET " " *Water Street,* between Whitehall Street and Old Slip.
FAIR STREET " " *Fulton Street,* east of Broadway.
PARTITION STREET " " *Fulton Street,* west of Broadway.
ROBINSON STREET " " *Park Place,* between Broadway and Church Street.
CHAPEL STREET " " *West Broadway,* between Barclay Street and Duane.
GREENWICH ROAD " " *Greenwich Street* to a point beyond its crossing of Chambers Street.

The following names and addresses have been taken from the directories of the years respectively indicated. No directory was published for the year 1788:

BARCLAY, *James,* merchant, 14 Hanover Sq., 1786; 1787; 1789 (described as "vendue master"); 1790 (address, Hanover Square and Old Slip).
" *David,* sergeant-at-arms to Court of Chancery, William Street, 1789; 1790 (address, 36 William St.)
" *Elizabeth,* shopkeeper, Chapel St., 1791; 1798 (address, 306 Broadway).
" *Mrs.,* shopkeeper, cor. Chapel & Warren Sts., 1793.
" *Andrew,* merchant, 45 Hanover Sq., 1791; 1796 (address, 136 Pearl St.,—doubtless the same house under new street name and number).

BARCLAY, *Andrew D.,* merchant, 127 Water St., 1797; 1798; 1799 (address, 31 Cortlandt St.) ; 1800 (residence, 127 Water St.).
"   *Daniel,* laborer, 2 Vandewater St., 1792.
"   *Daniel,* ship carpenter, Skinner St., 1793; 1794 (address, 7 Hague St.).
"   *Thomas,* ship master, 87 Fair St., 1794.
"   *Thomas,* British Consul, 142 Greenwich St., 1800; 1801; 1803 (address, 25 Robinson St.).
"   *Thomas,* Jay Street, 1802.
"   *Richard,* grocer, Mulberry St., 1796.
"   *John,* house carpenter, Mulberry St., 1794; 1795.
"   *Lewis,* shoemaker, Mulberry St., 1796; 1797.
"   *Lewis,* cordwainer, 33 East George St., 1803.
"   *Widow Mary,* 390 Pearl St., 1795.
"   *William,* carpenter, Harman St., 1796; 1797.
"   *George,* mariner, 40 Harman St., 1800.
"   *Henry,* boatman, Mott St., 1796; 1797.

BACHE, *Theophylact,* 38 Hanover Sq., 1787; 1789 (described as "merchant") ; 1790 (same); 1791 (same); 1792 (same); 1793 (same) ; 1794 (same, except that adddess is 122 Pearl St.,—doubtless the same house under a new street name and number) ; 1795 (same) ; 1796 (same); 1797 (same) ; 1798 (same) ; 1799 (same) ; 1800 (same); 1801 (same) ; 1802 (same, except that address is 87 Water St.).
"   *Theophylact & Andrew,* merchants, 87 Water St., 1803.
"   *Paul & Andrew,* merchants, 7 Water St., 1793; 1794 (address 86 Water St.,—doubtless the same house under new street number) ; 1795 (same) ; 1796 (same,—with this added: "and store, Slote Lane") ; 1797 (same) ; 1798 (same) ; 1800 (same).
"   *William,* attorney at law, 136 Pearl St., 1796; 1797 (address 118 Pearl St.,) ; 1798 (address 91 Front St.) ; 1799 (same) ; 1801 (address, 111 Water St.) ; 1802 (*house,* 120 Water St.) ; 1803 (described as "attorney at law and notary public;" address, 86 Water St.)

BAYLEY, *Richard, Mr.,* lecturer on anatomy & surgery, 15 Smith St., 1787.
"   *Richard,* surgeon, 49 Smith St., 1791; 1792 (described as "physician 49, and shop 33 Smith St.") ; 1793 (same as 1791) ; 1794 (address 46 Broadway) ; 1796 (described as "health officer," 46 Broadway) ; 1797 (same) ; 1798 (same as 1796, except address 5 State St.) ; 1800 (same, except address, 37 Greenwich St.) ; 1801 (same).
"   *widow of Richard,* Jay Street, 1802.

LISPENARD, *Leonard,* ale & porter brewer, Greenwich road, 1787; 1794 (brewer, 158 Broadway) ; 1795 (same) ; 1796 (same); 1797 (same, except address, 26 Cortlandt St.) ; 1798 (same) ; 1799 (same); 1800 (same); 1801 (same); 1802 (same) ; 1803 (address, Greenwich Road).
"   *Anthony,* brewer, Greenwich road, 1790; 1791 (same, except address, 15 King St.) ; 1793 (brewer, 15 King St., and brewery, Greenwich road) ; 1794 (brewer, Greenwich road) ; 1795 (same) ; 1796 (same) ; 1797 (same) ; 1798 (same) ; 1799 (same) ; 1800 (same) ; 1801 (same); 1802 (same) ; 1803 (same).

McEvers, *Charles, Jun.,* commission broker, 13 Water St., 1787; 1790 (described as insurance broker, 194 Water St.); 1791 (same); 1792 (same); 1793 (same); 1794 (described as merchant, 127 Water St.); 1795 (insurance broker, same address); 1796 (same); 1797 (same); 1801 (described as merchant, address, 34 Wall St.); 1802 (same); 1803 (same).

McEvers & Barclay, vendue store, 22 Hanover Sq., 1791; 1792 (vendue and commission store, same address); 1793 (same); 1794 (same); 1795 (auctioneers, same address); 1796 (same); 1797 (same); 1798 (same); 1799 (same); 1800 (same); 1801 (same).

McEvers, C. & G., auctioneers, 127 Water St., 1802; 1803.

Roosevelt, *James, Esq.,* 73 Queen St., 1787; 1789 (described as merchant, same address); 1790 (same); 1792 (same); 1793 (address, 157 Queen St.); 1794 (address, 333 Pearl St.,— doubtless same house under different street name and number); 1795 (same); 1796 (same); 1797 (same); 1798 (same); 1799 (same); 1800 (same); 1801 (same); 1802 (same); 1803 (same).

White, *Henry,* 8 Broadway, 1789; 1790; 1791 (merchant, 9 Broadway); 1792 (same); 1793 (address 9 Broad Street); 1794 (address, 19 Broadway); 1795 (same); 1796 (address, 21 Broadway); 1797 (same); 1798 (same); 1799 (same); 1800 (same); 1801 (same); 1802 (same); 1803 (same).

PART IX.

A Partial Table of Descent of the Barclays of Ury.

(For the greater portion of the names and dates set forth in this table, the writer is indebted to Robert Barclay Allardice, Esq., M.A., F.S.A. (Scot), of Lostwithiel, Cornwall, Eng.)

Col. David Barclay,[1] *b* 1610; *d* 12 October, 1686; *m* (date of contract 24 December, 1647), 26 January, 1648, Lady *Katharine Gordon, b* 11 January, 1621; *d* March, 1663.

    (1) *Robert Barclay*[2] (the apologist).

    (2) *Jean Barclay,*[2] *m* 2 January, 1685, *Sir Ewen Cameron.* †

    (3) *Lucy Barclay,*[2] *b* 1653; *d* December, 1686, *unm.*

    (4) *John Barclay*[2] (who migrated to East New Jersey. See Part IV above).

    (5) *David Barclay,*[2] *d* at sea 1684, *unm.*

   1. **Robert Barclay**[2] (the apologist), *b* 23 December, 1648; *d* 3 October, 1690; *m* 16 February, 1669, *Christian Mollison, d* 14 February, 1725.

    (6) *David Barclay,*[3] *b* 8 September, 1670; *d* 1671.

    (7) *Robert Barclay.*[3]

    (8) *Margaret Barclay,*[3] *b* 4 October, 1673; *d* 1685.

    (9) *Patience Barclay,*[3] *b* 25 November, 1675/6; *d* 22 June, 1757; *m* 8 April, 1707, *Timothy Forbes, d* 1743. †

    (10) *Katharine Barclay,*[3] *b* 26 June, 1678; *d* 9 November, 1758; *m* 17 June, 1703, *James Forbes,* d 1734. †

    (11) *Christian Barclay,*[3] *b* 15 May, 1680; *d* 1751; *m* (contract dated) 10 April, 1700, *Alexander Jaffray.* †

(12) *David Barclay,*[3] *b* 17 September, 1682; *d* 18 May, 1769; *m* (1) 12 June, 1707, *Anne Taylor, d* 3 December, 1720; *m* (2) 8 August, 1723, *Priscilla Freame, d* 9 October, 1769. (Left issue.)

(13) *Jean Barclay,*[3] *b* 27 December, 1683; *m* 12 April, 1707, *Alexander Forbes, d* 1740.†

(14) *John Barclay*[3] (who migrated to Dublin. See Part V above).

7. **Robert Barclay,**[3] *b* 25 March, 1672; *d* 27 March, 1747; *m* 6 June, 1696, *Elizabeth Brain.*†

(15) *Margaret Barclay,*[4] *b* 23 March, 1697; *d* 13 May, 1707.

(16) *Robert Barclay.*[4]

(17) *John Barclay,*[4] *b* 19 July, 1701; *d* 16 July, 1714.

(18) *Mollison Barclay,*[4] *b* 21 November, 1703; *m John Doubleday.*†

(19) *Elizabeth Barclay*[4] (known as "Bonnie Betty Barclay"), *b* 11 May, 1708; *m* Sir *William Ogilvie,* Bart., of Barras.†

(20) *David Barclay,*[4] *b* 29 April, 1710; *d* 10 October, 1783; *m* 10 January, 1737, *Mary Pardoe, b* 1712; *d* 13 December, 1772. (Left issue.)

(21) *Katharine Barclay,*[4] *b* 1 April, 1713.†

(22) *Jean Barclay,*[4] *b* 23 April, 1719; *d* 12 June, 1720.

16. **Robert Barclay,**[4] *b* 20 May, 1699; *d* 10 October, 1760; *m* 10 June, 1725, *Une Cameron.*†

(23) *Jean Barclay,*[5] *b* 22 March, 1726; *d* July, 1750, *unm.*

(24) *Robert Barclay.*[5]

(25) *David Barclay,*[5] *b* 24 September, 1737.†

(26) *Ewen Barclay,*[5] *b* 1 October, 1738; *d* 23 August, 1805, *unm.*

24. **Robert Barclay**[5] (M.P.), *b* 27 November, 1731/2; *d* 8 April, 1797; *m* (1) 3 June, 1753, his cousin, *Lucy Barclay* (daughter of David Barclay,—No. 20 above,—and

Mary Pardoe), *d* 23 March, 1757; *m* (2) 2 December, 1776, *Sarah Ann Allardice*,[1] *b* 13 July, 1757; *d* 7 July, 1833.

    (27) *Lucy Barclay*,[6] *b* 22 March, 1757; *m* 1777, *Samuel Galton*, *b* 18 June, 1753; *d* 23 October, 1844.†

    (28) *Anne Barclay*,[6] *b* 13 September, 1777; *d* 29 October, 1782.

    (29) *Une Cameron Barclay*,[6] *b* 13 September, 1778; *d* 26 September, 1809; *m* 25 July, 1800, *John Innes*, *b* 1770; *d* April, 1832.

    (30) *Robert Barclay*[6] (who added the name "Allardice").

    (31) *Margaret Barclay*,[6] *b* 4 October, 1780; *d* 16 December, 1855; *m* 27 September, 1809, *Hudson Gurney*, *b* 19 January, 1775; *d* 9 November, 1864.

    (32) *Mary Barclay*,[6] *b* 4 October, 1780; *d* June, 1799, *unm.*

    (33) *Rodney Barclay*[6] (a daughter), *b* 29 April, 1782; *d* 1853, *unm.*

    (34) *James Allardice Barclay*,[6] *b* 3 July, 1784; *d* 3 March, 1804, *unm.*

    (35) *David Stuart Barclay*,[6] *b* 3 March, 1787; *d* 1826, *unm.*

---

[1]The ALLARDICES, of Allardice, held the lands from which they took their name from the time of King William the Lion. The estate of Allardice lies in the parish of Arbuthnott, Kincardine, Scotland, and the burial aisle of the family is in the very ancient, but recently restored, church of Arbuthnott where a brass tablet inserted in the wall indicates the position of the Allardice aisle. Allardice Castle, the old family seat, dates back to 1540 or earlier. It is one of the most notable of the castles of Kincardineshire. It is still habitable, and stands on high ground overlooking the Bervie water, about two miles from the sea, where doubtless the older keep of the Allardices of that ilk had stood for centuries. When the Allardice estate was sold in 1872,—some eighteen years after the death of Capt. Robert Barclay-Allardice (No. 30 below),—it was acquired by Lord Arbuthnott and now forms part of the Arbuthnott estate.

SARAH ANN ALLARDICE was the undoubted representative of Prince David, Earl of Strathearn, son of King Robert II of Scotland, having been served and "retoured" (that is, entered in the chancery records) heir-general to his descendant, William Graham, 8th Earl of Monteith and 2nd Earl of Airth. Her son, Capt. Robert Barclay-Allardice (No. 30 below) laid claim to these titles under the Letters Patent of 21 March 1633 (and was sometimes, therefore, known as "The Claimant"), which claim was revived by his daughter Margaret Barclay-Allardice (No. 36 below), and has again been revived by her oldest son Robert Barclay-Allardice (No. 38 below).

30. **Robert Barclay=Allardice,**[6] *b* 25 August, 1779; *d* 1 May,
1854; *m* September, 1815, *Mary Dalgarno, b* 1797; *d*
30 August, 1820.

> (36) *Margaret Barclay-Allardice.*[7]
> (37) *Mary Barclay-Allardice,*[7] *b* 29 July, 1819; *d*
> 14 October, 1823, *unm.*

(The male line failing with the death, on May 1, 1854, of
Capt. Robert Barclay-Allardice,—No. 30 above,—representation
of the Barclays of Mather and Urie thereupon passed to the
oldest living male descendant of the apologist's second son (David
Barclay,—No. 12 above), who in 1854 was Charles Barclay of
Bury Hill. The present (1903) head of the family is said Charles
Barclay's grandson, Robert Barclay, Esq., of Bury Hill.)

36. **Margaret Barclay=Allardice,**[7][2] *b* 4 July, 1816; *d* 7 August, 1903; *m* (1) 2 April, 1840, *Samuel Ritchie, b* 13
August, 1813; *d* 17 September, 1845; *m* (2) 30 July,
1854, *James Tanner, b* 17 June, 1820; *d* 21 January,
1866.

> (38) *Robert Barclay-Allardice,*[8] M.A., F.S.A. (Scot),
> Mayor of Lostwithiel, Cornwall, 1899-1901,
> *b* 19 May, 1841; (living 1903), *unm.*
> (39) *Samuel Frederick Ritchie,*[8] *b* 15 October, 1843;
> *d* 14 April, 1862, *unm.*
> (40) *David Stuart Barclay-Allardice.*[8]
> (41) *Mary Hay Ritchie,*[8] *b* 7 September, 1842; *d* 30
> September, 1849.
> (42) *Augusta Graham Tanner, b* 12 August, 1859;
> *d* 21 December, 1874.

40. **David Stuart Barclay=Allardice,**[8] *b* 21 November, 1845;
(living 1903 at Providence, R. I.); *m* 15 October, 1868,
Fannie Foster Elliot, b 26 February, 1852; (living 1903).

> (43) *Robert Barclay Allardice.*[9]
> (44) *Margaret Anna Barclay-Allardice.*[9]

---

[2]License to No. 36 above to retain maiden surname for herself and her descendants, was duly registered in the books of the Lyon King of Arms at Edinburgh, on
July 2nd, 1883.

  (45) *Elliot Ritchie Barclay-Allardice.*[9]

  (46) *David Graham Barclay-Allardice.*[9]

  (47) *Clinton Barclay-Allardice,*[9] *b* 1 August, 1882; (living 1903), *unm.*

  (48) *Augusta Standish Barclay-Allardice,*[9] *b* 18 August, 1886; *d* 24 September, 1890.

  (49) *Amelia Barclay-Allardice,*[9] *b* 3 October, 1889; (living 1903).

43, **Robert Barclay-Allardice,** *b* 18 October, 1869; (living 1903); *m* 30 November, 1899, *Jessie Darling Drown,* *b* 30 March, 1871; (living 1903). S. P.

44, **Margaret Anna Barclay-Allardice,**[9] *b* 21 December, 1871; (living 1903 at Tarpon Springs, Florida); *m* (1) 14 June, 1893, *William Howard Bigelow,* *b* 22 July, 1861; *d* 19 December, 1900; *m* (2) 8 June, 1902, *John Townsend Hill,* *b* 1872; (living 1903).

  (50) *Helen Janette Bigelow,*[10] *b* 14 March, 1894; (living 1903).

  (51) *John Bigelow,*[10] *b* 10 September, 1896; (living 1903).

  (52) *Elliot Allardice Bigelow,*[10] *b* 13 October, 1897; (living 1903).

45, **Elliot Ritchie Barclay-Allardice,**[9] *b* 10 October, 1873; (living 1903); *m* 1 June, 1899, *Nettie Frances Harrington,* *b* 26 October, 1873; (living 1903).

  (53) *Carleton Barclay-Allardice,*[10] *b* 1 October, 1901; (living 1903).

46, **David Graham Barclay-Allardice,**[9] *b* 11 December, 1877; (living 1903); *m* 15 October, 1900, *Annie Firth,* *b* 13 July, 1878; (living 1903).

  (54) *Graham Stuart Barclay-Allardice,*[10] *b* 6 October, 1902; (living 1903).

PART X.

Sundry Lines of Descent of American Barclays (and Barkleys).

1. **John Barclay**[1] (Mayor of Philadelphia), *d* 8 August, 1816; *m* (1)—bond dated 24 June, 1777—*Eleanor Porter; m* (2) 11 December, 1781,[1] *Mary Searle, d* February, 1797.

> (2) *Eleanor Porter Barclay.*[2]
>
> (3) *William Searle Barclay,*[2] *b* 17 September, 1783; *d* 17 September, 1784.
>
> (4) *Mary Barclay.*[2]
>
> (5) *John Mortimer Barclay.*[2]
>
> (6) *Harriette Barclay,*[2] *b* 29 April, 1788; *d* 14 May, 1844, *unm.*
>
> (7) *Jane Barclay,*[2] *b* 31 July, 1789; *d* 23 August, 1789.
>
> (8) *Sophia Barclay,*[2] *b* 29 August, 1790; *d* 28 September, 1803.
>
> (9) *James Joseph Barclay,*[2] *b* 15 January, 1794; *d* 16 August, 1885, *unm.*
>
> (10) *Charlotte Elizabeth Barclay,*[2] *b* 18 February, 1796; *d* 9 May, 1873, *unm.*

2. **Eleanor Porter Barclay,**[2] *m* 14 July, 1798,[2] *James Cochrane.*

> (11) *Gertrude Cochrane,*[3] *b* 18 March, 1799; *d* 20 February, 1828, *unm.*

---

[1]Records of CHRIST CHURCH, Philadelphia.

[2]From NEW YORK WEEKLY MUSEUM of Saturday, 28 July, 1798:
"*Married:* On Saturday the 14th inst., at Wilmington, Delaware, by the Rev. Mr. Clarkson, JAMES COCHRANE, Esq., Member of Congress from this State, to Miss ELEANOR P. BARCLAY, daughter of John Barclay, Esq., of Chestnut Hill, near Christiana Bridge."

4. **Mary Barclay,**[2] *b* 24 January, 1785; *d* 9 October, 1872; *m* 10 March, 1814, *Clement Cornell Biddle, b* 24 October, 1784; *d* 21 August, 1855.

    (12) *John Barclay Biddle.*[3]
    (13) *George W. Biddle.*[3]
    (14) *Chapman Biddle.*[3]

5. **John Mortimer Barclay,**[2] *b* 17 January, 1787; *d* 28 October, 1855; *m* 4 October, 1814, *Margaret O'Connor, b* 30 December, 1787; *d* 29 August, 1856.

    (15) *John O'Connor Barclay.*[3]
    (16) *Clement Biddle Barclay.*[3]
    (17) *James Barclay.*[3]
    (18) *Ann O'Connor Barclay.*[3]
    (19) *Mary Barclay.*[3]
    (20) *Charles Francis Barclay,*[3] *b* 17 February, 1828; (living 1903), *unm.*

12. **John Barclay Biddle,**[3] *b* 3 January, 1815; *d* 19 January 1879; *m* 7 November, 1850, *Caroline Phillips, b* 21 January, 1821; (living 1903).

    (21) *Anna C. Biddle.*[4]
    (22) *Harriet Biddle.*[4]
    (23) *William P. Biddle*[4] (U.S.M.C.), *b* 17 December, 1853; (living 1903), *unm.*
    (24) *Clement Biddle*[4] (Surgeon U. S. N.), *b* 11 December, 1854; (living 1903).
    (25) *Elizabeth R. Biddle.*[4]
    (26) *Caroline Biddle,*[4] *b* 16 March, 1861; (living 1903).

13. **George W. Biddle,**[3] *b* 11 January, 1818; *d* 29 April, 1897; *m* 1842, *Maria McMurtrie, b* 1817; *d* 13 December, 1901.

    (27) *George Biddle.*[4]
    (28) *Algernon Sydney Biddle.*[4]
    (29) *Arthur Biddle.*[4]

14. **Chapman Biddle,**[3] *b* 22 January, 1822; *d* 9 December, 1880; *m* 14 August, 1849, *Mary Livingston Cochrane, b* 30 June, 1822; *d* 4 April, 1894.

(30) *Mary C. Biddle*,[4] *b* 16 June, 1850; (living 1903), *unm.*

(31) *Chapman Cornell Biddle*,[4] *b* 5 September, 1851; *d* April, 1873, *unm.*

(32) *Walter Livingston Cochrane Biddle*.[4]

15. **John O'Connor Barclay**,[3] *b* 10 September, 1815; *d* 7 December, 1865; *m* 6 June, 1843, *Ann Wilks Collet, b* 12 February, 1820; *d* 11 April, 1874.

(33) *Mark Wilks Collet Barclay*,[4] *b* 22 July, 1844; *d* 13 December, 1862, *unm.*

(34) *John Mortimer Barclay*.[4]

(35) *Laura Christine Barclay*.[4]

16. **Clement Biddle Barclay**,[3] *b* 8 February, 1817; *d* 10 August, 1896; *m* 24 April, 1845, *Catherine Ann Holsman, b* 11 August, 1826; *d* 29 August, 1855.

(36) *Harrison Smith Barclay*,[4] *b* 31 July, 1848; *d* 28 January, 1880, *unm.*

(37) *Daniel Holsman Barclay*,[4] *b* 25 October, 1850; *d* 24 November, 1880, *unm.*

(38) *Reginald Seyton Barclay*,[4] *b* 16 February, 1854; *d* 23 September, 1884, *unm.*

17. **James Barclay**,[3] *b* 25 March, 1821; *d* 6 January, 1892; *m* 1 October, 1845, *Margretta Lorillard Holsman, b* 28 September, 1828; *d* 10 June, 1860.

(39) *James Searle Barclay*.[4]

(40) *Julian Holsman Barclay*,[4] *b* 8 September, 1857; (living 1903), *unm.*

18. **Ann O'Connor Barclay**,[3] *b* 17 February, 1819; *d* 28 August, 1878; *m* 1 December, 1848, *Stephen Decatur Trenchard* (U.S.N.), *b* 10 July, 1818; *d* 15 November, 1883.

(41) *Edward Trenchard*.[4]

19. **Mary Barclay**,[3] *b* 24 May, 1824; *d* 19 May, 1903; *m* 12 June, 1867, Rev. *Dudley D. Smith, b* 7 September, 1831; *d* 7 November, 1902. O. S. P.

21. **Anna C. Biddle,**[4] *b* 17 September, 1851; (living 1903); *m* 15 November, 1881, *Clement Stocker Phillips, b* January, 1847; (living 1903).

> (42) *Phoebe Caroline Phillips,*[5] *b* 22 March, 1883; (living 1903).
>
> (43) *John Biddle Phillips,*[5] *b* 24 February, 1885; *d* 18 June, 1886.
>
> (44) *Mary Clifford Phillips,*[5] *b* 28 March, 1888; *d* 31 March, 1888.
>
> (45) *Clifford Brinton Phillips,*[5] *b* 9 January, 1890; *d* 31 January, 1899.

22. **Harriet Biddle,**[4] *b* 8 August, 1852; (living 1903); *m* 11 October, 1876, *DeGrasse Fox, b* 23 August, 1838; (living 1903).

> (46) *Sylvia DeGrasse Fox,*[5] *b* 29 September, 1879; (living 1903).
>
> (47) *Alice Maude Fox,*[5] *b* 19 February, 1883; *d* 26 July, 1894.

25. **Elizabeth R. Biddle,**[4] *b* 9 December, 1856; *d* 22 February, 1891; *m* 9 December, 1877, *Samuel W. Miller, b* 27 August, 1854; (living 1903).

> (48) *Charlotte Barclay Miller,*[5] *b* 3 September, 1878; *d* 10 March, 1890.
>
> (49) *Marion Spencer Miller,*[5] *b* 12 September, 1880; *d* 28 February, 1881.
>
> (50) *John Biddle Miller,*[5] *b* February, 1882; *d* 3 April, 1882.
>
> (51) *Virginia Breckenridge Miller,*[5] *b* 5 July, 1883; (living 1903).
>
> (52) *Spencer Miller,*[5] *b* 30 July, 1884; (living 1903).

27. **George Biddle,**[4] *b* 21 August, 1843; *d* 4 April, 1886; *m* 8 November, 1876, *Mary Hosack Rodgers, b* 13 December, 1847; (living 1903).

> (53) *Dorothy Pendleton Biddle,*[5] *b* 29 June, 1878; *d* 29 July, 1878.

(54) *Eleanor Kearny Biddle,*[5] *b* 2 May, 1879; (living 1903).

(55) *Constance Elizabeth Biddle,*[5] *b* 4 September, 1882; (living 1903).

(56) *Alice McMurtrie Biddle,*[5] *b* 14 February, 1884; (living 1903).

(57) *Maria Georgina Biddle,*[5] *b* 18 November, 1886; (living 1903).

28. **Algernon Sydney Biddle,**[4] *b* 11 October, 1847; *d* 8 April, 1891; *m* 28 June, 1879, *Frances Robinson, b* 7 March, 1858; (living 1903).

(58) *Moncure Biddle,*[5] *b* 7 October, 1882; (living 1903).

(59) *George Washington Biddle,*[5] *b* 24 January, 1885; (living 1903).

(60) *Francis Beverley Biddle,*[5] *b* 9 May, 1886; (living 1903).

(61) *Sydney Geoffrey Biddle,*[5] *b* 16 June, 1889; (living 1903).

29. **Arthur Biddle,**[4] *b* 23 September, 1852; *d* 8 March, 1897; *m* 18 November, 1880, *Julia Biddle, b* 16 May, 1858; (living 1903).

(62) *Edith Francis Biddle,*[5] *b* 8 October, 1881; (living 1903).

(63) *Julia Cox Biddle,*[5] *b* 16 December, 1882; *d* 16 December, 1882.

(64) *Alfred Alexander Biddle,*[5] *b* 19 December, 1885; (living 1903).

(65) *Julian Cornell Biddle,*[5] *b* 23 April, 1890; (living 1903).

32. **Walter Livingston Cochrane Biddle,**[4] *b* 21 August, 1853; *d* 2 October, 1888; *m* 1 June, 1881, *Pauline Davis Carter, b* 25 November, 1861; (living 1903). O. S. P.

34. **John Mortimer Barclay,**[4] *b* 10 February, 1848; *d* 28 January, 1896; *m* 12 December, 1878, *Mary Warner, b* 26 January, 1852; (living 1903).

 (66) *Laura Christine Barclay,*[5] *b* 11 February, 1884; (living 1903).

35. **Laura Christine Barclay,**[4] *b* 10 November, 1851; *d* 13 November, 1874; *m* 15 June, 1871, *Shippen Wallace, b* 26 February, 1850; (living 1903).

 (67) *Violet Lee Wallace.*[5]

39. **James Searle Barclay,**[4] *b* 2 July, 1851; (living 1903); *m* 8 April, 1875, *Eliza Oldfield, b* 13 November, 1855; (living 1903).

 (68) *James Searle Barclay,*[5] *b* 7 May, 1876; (living 1903), *unm.*

 (69) *Granville Oldfield Barclay,*[5] *b* 19 August, 1878; *d* 30 October, 1883.

41. **Edward Trenchard,**[4] *b* 17 August, 1850; (living 1903); *m* 11 July, 1878, *Mary Cornelia Stafford.*†

67. **Violet Lee Wallace,**[5] *b* 11 July, 1872; (living 1903); *m* 8 February, 1899, *Warren Seabury Crane, b* 10 June, 1866; (living 1903).

 (70) *Christine Wallace Crane,*[6] *b* 17 April, 1900; (living 1903).

David Hutchinson Barclay, *b* at Desertmartin, Londonderry, Ireland, 10 April, 1801; *d* at Newburgh, N. Y., 30 March, 1879; *m* (1) 9 May, 1833, *Ann Maria Speir, b* 8 December, 1807; *d* March 13, 1837; *m* (2) 25 January, 1842, *Christina Eliza Baird, b* at Warwick, N. Y., 17 March, 1809; *d* at Newburgh, N. Y., 7 October, 1896.

 (1) *Anna Jane Barclay,*[2] *b* 3 February, 1844; *d* 27 August, 1893, *unm.*

 (2) *Robert Barclay,*[2] *b* 16 March, 1846; *d* 24 August, 1847.

 (3) *David Barclay,*[2] *b* 29 December, 1848; living (1903) at Newburgh, N. Y., *unm.*

1. **George Carey Barclay,**[1] *b* Glasgow, Scotland, 21 September, 1828; *d* Brooklyn, New York, 23 November, 1897; *m* 16 September, 1852, *Mary A. Orr, b* 16 December, 1832; *d* 1 August, 1899.

    (2) *Elizabeth Barclay,*[2] *b* 4 July, 1853; (living 1903).

    (3) *William Orr Barclay.*[2]

    (4) *Reginald Barclay.*[2]

    (5) *Mary Barclay,*[2] *b* 18 March, 1862; *d* 24 July, 1896, *unm.*

    (6) *Blanche Barclay,*[2] *b* 9 July, 1868; (living 1903).

    (7) *Harold Barclay,*[2] *b* 21 May, 1877; *d* 9 November, 1877.

3. **William Orr Barclay,**[2] *b* 17 January, 1857; *d* 19 October, 1901; *m* 20 November, 1883, *Clara S. Kepner, b* 24 May, 1858; (living 1903).

    (8) *Sylvia Hortense Barclay,*[3] *b* 23 April, 1885; (living 1903).

    (9) *Beatrice Barclay,*[3] *b* 17 January, 1888; (living 1903).

4. **Reginald Barclay,**[2] *b* 14 June, 1859; (living 1903); *m* 17 May, 1897, *Bertha A. Fahys, b* 1 October, 1869; (living 1903).

    (10) *George Carey Barclay,*[3] *b* 11 April, 1898; (living 1903).

    (11) *Bertha Fahys Barclay,*[3] *b* 21 April, 1901; (living 1903).

SUNDRY LINES OF DESCENT,

compiled by

ALEXANDER BARCLAY, of St. Paul, Minnesota.

(Pages 234–299.)

---

1. **Thomas Barclay,** *b* 1728, Strabane, Ireland; *d* 20 January, 1793,[1] in Lisbon, Portugal. Was the first Consul of the U. S. to France, and was subsequently sent to Morocco in 1786 to negotiate the treaty between the United States and the Sultan of Morocco. In 1791 was sent as Consul to Morocco. His commission signed by Washington and Jefferson is now (1903) in the possession of Mrs. John Judson Barclay of Bethany, West Virginia. *m Mary Hoops,* of Philadelphia, Pa.

   (2) *Elizabeth Mease Barclay.*

   (3) *Ann L. Barclay, b* Philadelphia, 17 December, 1775; *d* Buckingham Co., Va., February, 1808.

   (4) *Robert Barclay.*

   (5) *Maria Isabella Barclay.*

2. **Elizabeth Mease Barclay,** *b* 5 October, 1773, Philadelphia, Pa.; *d* 1832 in Logan Co., Ky.; *m* 1 January, 1795, *Peyton Randolph Harrison.*

   (6) *Thomas Barclay Harrison, b* 2 November, 1795.

   (7) *Eleanor Susanna Harrison, b* 5 February, 1797; *m Benjamin Franklin Edwards.*

   (8) *Carter Henry Harrison, b* 20 September, 1798.

   (9) *Robert Carter Harrison, b* 30 April, 1800; *d* 2 October, 1803.

   (10) *Peyton Randolph Harrison, b* 30 May, 1803; *d* 21 October, 1804.

   (11) *Louisa Ann Harrison, b* 24 October, 1805; *m* ———— *Caldwell* of Russellville, Ky.

   (12) *Robert Peyton Harrison, b* 9 May, 1807.

---

[1]From NEW YORK JOURNAL AND PATRIOTIC REGISTER of Saturday, May 11, 1793: *"Died:* At Lisbon, the 20th January last, THOMAS BARCLAY, Esq., formerly a Consul of the United States."

4. **Robert Barclay,** *b* 22 May, 1779; *d* King & Queen Co., Va., 16 April, 1809; *m* 1 January, 1800, *Sarah Coleman Turner* of King & Queen Co., Va.

> (13) *Mary Elizabeth Barclay.*
> (14) *Thomas Jefferson Barclay, b* 30 September, 1805, King & Queen Co., Va.; *d unm.*
> (15) *Oriana Maria Moylen Barclay.*
> (16) *James Turner Barclay.*

5. **Maria Isabella Barclay,** *b* 17 March, 1784, Aut-il, France; *d* 4 May, 1860, Staunton, Va.; *m* 21 May, 1809, *Thomas S. Coulter.*

> (17) *Mary Jane Coulter, b* 29 March, 1810, Staunton, Va.; *d* 1 March, 1875, Staunton, Va.; *m William B. Crawford,* 17 May, 1849.

13. **Mary Elizabeth Barclay,** *b* 2 April, 1803, Hanover Co., Va.; *d* Albermarle Co., Va.; *m John Moon.*

> (18) *Barclay Moon, m Mary Massey.*
> (19) *John Schuyler Moon, m Lizzie Tompkins.*
> (20) *Frank Moon, m Marietta Appleton.*
> (21) *Lucy Reed Moon.*
> (22) *Sallie Thomasia Moon.*
> (23) *James Nelson Moon, m Casey Coleman.*
> (24) *Luther Moon, m —— Martin.*
> (25) *Anna Moon.*
> (26) *Mary Barclay Moon,* (living 1903).

15. **Oriana Maria Moylen Barclay,** *b* 11 July, 1809, King & Queen Co., Va.; *d* "Viewmont," Albermarle Co., Va.; *m Edward Moon.*

> (27) *Isaac Moon.*
> (28) *Thomas Moon.*
> (29) *Oriana Moon, m Dr. Andrews.*
> (30) *Sallie Coleman Moon.*
> (31) *Charlotte Moon,* (living 1903).
> (32) *Mary Moon, m Dr. Shepard* of Norfolk, Va.
> (33) *Edmonia Moon,* (living 1903).

16. James Turner Barclay, *b* 22 May, 1807, Hanover C. H., Va.; *d* 28 October, 1874, Hillsboro, Ala.; *m* 10 June, 1830, *Julia Ann Sowers* of Staunton, Va., *b* 30 June, 1813; (living 1903).

 (34) *Robert Gutzloff Barclay.*
 (35) *Sarah Margaret Barclay.*
 (36) *John Judson Barclay.*
 (37) *Thomas Barclay, d* in infancy.

34. Robert Gutzloff Barclay, *b* 15 July, 1832, near Charlotteville, Va.; *d* near Hillsboro, Ala., 18 November, 1876; *m* (1) *Louise Caroline Hampton,* 21st October, 1859, at Beirût, Syria; *m* (2) *Emma C. Bakenall,* 7 March, 1867, at Bethany, W. Va.

 (38) *Julia Margaret Barclay.*
 (39) *Louise Hampton Barclay, b* 6 January, 1863, Beirût, Syria; living 1903, Birmingham, Ala.; *m* 1892, *Reuben K. Edwards.*
 (40) *James Turner Barclay, b* Philadelphia, 6 January, 1868.
 (41) *Robert G. Barclay, b* Hillsboro, Ala., July, 1869.
 (42) *Selina Barclay, b* Hillsboro, Ala., 1872.

35. Sarah Margaret Barclay, *b* 23 May, 1837, Albermarle Co., Va.; *d* 21 April, 1885, at Greenwich, Conn.; *m* June, 1857, *J. Augustus Johnson.*

 (43) *Maggie Holt Johnson, b* Philadelphia; *d* Beirût, Syria.
 (44) *Julia Barclay Johnson, b* and *d* at Jaffa, Syria.
 (45) *Barclay Johnson, b* Beirût, Syria; *d* Greenwich, Conn.
 (46) *Minnie Johnson, b* Beirût, Syria; *d* Mt. Lebanon.
 (47) *Nellie Johnson, b* Beirût, Syria; *d* Greenwich, Conn.
 (48) *Julia Johnson, b* Beirût, Syria; *d* New York City.
 (49) *Tristam Burgess Johnson, b* 1881, Rutland, Vt.; living 1903, New York City.

36. **John Judson Barclay,** *b* 12 November, 1834, near Charlottesville, Va. Was Vice-Consul of the United States
at Beirût, Syria, in 1858. Was Consul at Cyprus from
1859 to 1865. Was Consul-General at Morocco from
1893 to 1896. *m Decima H. Campbell,* 7 April, 1863, in
Bethany, W. Va., *b* 12 October, 1840. Both living 1903.

> (50) *Virginia Huntington Barclay, b* Larnaca, Island
> of Cyprus, 25 March, 1864; *d* Bethany, W.
> Va., 14 September, 1882.
>
> (51) *Alexander Campbell Barclay.*
>
> (52) *John Judson Barclay, b* Wheeler, Ala., 16 Sep-
> tember, 1870.
>
> (53) *Julian Thomas Barclay, b* Wheeler, Ala., 12
> November, 1875.

38. **Julia Margaret Barclay,** *b* 6 July, 1860, Beirût, Syria;
d May, 1899, Berkeley, Cal.; *m* 1888, Rev. *S. M. Jefferson,* Louisville, Ky.

> (54) *Mary Elizabeth Jefferson, b* Walnut Hills, Cin-
> cinnati.
>
> (55) *Robert Barclay Jefferson, b* and *d* at Augusta,
> Ga.
>
> (56) *Louise Jefferson, b* Augusta, Ga.
>
> (57) *Ruth Jefferson, b* Bethany, W. Va.

51. **Alexander Campbell Barclay,** *b* June, 1866, Bethany, W.
Va.; *m* 7 October, 1893, *Nida C. Ferguson* of Rose-
burgh, Oregon, *b* 19 November, 1869, Batesville, Miss.
Both living 1903.

> (58) *Kenneth Lorraine Barclay, b* Portland, Oregon,
> 24 January, 1895.
>
> (59) *Virginia Huntington Ethel Barclay, b* Portland,
> Oregon, 15 November, 1902.

1. **William Barclay,** *b* 1669, Scotland or Ireland; *d* 1732,
Lancaster Co., Pa.; *bur* Middle Octoraro Presbyterian
Church Yard, Lancaster Co., Pa.; *m Mary* ———, *b*
1669; *d* 1757.

> (2) *John Barclay, b* 1699; *d* 1765.

(3) *Hugh Barclay.*

(4) *William Barclay.*

3. **Hugh Barclay,** *d* 1764.

(5) *Hugh Barclay.*

4. **William Barclay,** *b* 1709; *d* 1757.

(6) *John Barclay.*

(7) *Hugh Barclay.*

(8) *Hester Barclay, b* 2 August, 1756; *d* 28 February, 1796, *unm.*

5. **Hugh Barclay,** *b* 1729; *d* 1806. Lived in Rockbridge Co., Va.; *m* (1) *Mary Culbertson; m* (2) *Martha Smith.* No issue by second wife.

(9) *Hugh Barclay.*

(10) *John Barclay,* soldier in Revolutionary War; *d* cir. 1808, probably Natchez, Minn.

(11) *David Barclay,* soldier in Revolutionary War.

(12) *Elihu Barclay.*

7. **Hugh Barclay,** *b* 13 July, 1747; *d* 24 November, 1807. Came from Lancaster Co., Pa., to Bedford Co., Pa., where he died. Was a merchant and farmer. His commission as Lieut.-Col. in Revolutionary army under Washington is now (1903) in the possession of his descendant, *Richard DeC. Barclay* (No. 36 below). *m Hetty Fulton, b* 2 February, 1765; *d* 5 February, 1819.

(13) *William H. Barclay, b* 15 June, 1794; *d* March, 1824, *unm.*

(14) *Hugh F. Barclay, b* 29 September, 1795; *d* 12 July, 1796.

(15) *Francis Baily Barclay.*

(16) *Josiah Espy Barclay, b* 29 March, 1797; *d* 1825.

(17) *John Young Barclay.*

(18) *Hester S. Barclay, b* 2 January, 1801; *d* 14 February, 1881, *unm.*

(19) *Samuel Moore Barclay, b* 17 October, 1802; *d* 3 January, 1852.

(20) *George W. Barclay, b* 20 July, 1805; *d* 5 January, 1820.

9. **Hugh Barclay,** *b* 1751; *d* 1834, Bowling Green, Ky.

    (21) *Samuel Barclay.*

    (22) *John Barclay, d* in infancy.

    (23) *Mary Barclay, b* 1781; *d* 1853; *m Alexander Culbertson.*

    (24) *Hugh Barclay, b* 1784; *d* 1805; *bur* Bowling Green, Ky.

    (25) *Eli Barclay, b* 1786; *d* 1848.

    (26) *Sarah Barclay, b* 1790; *d* 1863; *m* (1) *Charles Donaldson; m* (2) *David Campbell.*

12. **Elihu Barclay,** *b* 1773; *d* cir. 1805; *m Sallie Tedford, b* 1776, dau. of Capt. Alexander Tedford, killed in battle of Guilford Court House.

    (27) *Alexander Tedford Barclay.*

    (28) *Hugh Barclay.*

    (29) *Elihu Barclay.*

15. **Francis Baily Barclay** (M.D.), *b* 29 March, 1797; *d* 12 July, 1851; *m* 30 September, 1823, *Camilla B. Bonnett, b* 14 October, 1800; *d* 1 October, 1872.

    (30) *Anna B. Barclay, b* 8 August, 1824; *d* 30 November, 1825.

    (31) *Josiah E. Barclay.*

    (32) *Hester A. Barclay, b* 29 August, 1827; *d* 25 March, 1878, *unm.*

    (33) *William W. Barclay, b* 21 April, 1829; *unm.*

    (34) *Samuel M. Barclay, b* 11 March, 1831; *d* 20 August, 1880, *unm.*

    (35) *John Jacob Barclay.*

    (36) *Richard DeC. Barclay.*

    (37) *Emma F. Barclay, b* 10 November, 1837; *unm.*

    (38) *Mary F. Barclay, b* 12 January, 1841; *unm.*

17. **John Young Barclay,** *b* 29 October, 1798; *d* 18 February, 1841. Lived in Greensburg, Pa. *m* 3 February, 1825, *Isabella Johnson, b* 10 August, 1800.

    (39) *Thomas J. Barclay.*

(40) *Hetty F. Barclay, b* 4 November, 1827; *d* 22 July, 1901.

(41) *Alexander Barclay.*

(42) *Elizabeth F. Barclay, b* 1 September, 1832.

(43) *Sarah S. Barclay, b* 5 March, 1834; *d* 13 March, 1884.

(44) *John Y. Barclay, b* 1 November, 1836; *d* 6 October, 1889, in Iowa, *unm.*

(45) *Frank Barclay, b* 1 May, 1839; living 1903, Superior, Neb. Has issue.

(46) *Isabella Barclay, b* 1 May, 1839; died young.

21. **Samuel Barclay,** *b* 17 July, 1773; *d* 24 September, 1845; *m Jane Walker* of Rockbridge Co., Va., *b* 1773; *d* 1845.

(47) *Sarah C. Barclay, b* 1796; *d* 27 September, 1823.

(48) *Philander W. Barclay, b* 16 July, 1798; *d* 7 July, 1838; *m Elizabeth Garnett;* had issue.

(49) *Joseph W. Barclay, b* 24 December, 1802; *d* 8 October, 1830; *m Mary A. Lapsley.*

(50) *Hugh Barclay.*

(51) *Jane M. Barclay, b* 14 February, 1805; *m* Rev. *Hugh Patton,* Princeton, Ind.; had issue.

(52) *Mary Barclay, b* 6 June, 1807; *d* December, 1892; *m Samuel Stubbins,* Bowling Green, Ky. Had issue.

(53) *Virginia Barclay, b* 21 October, 1809; *m Robert G. Garnett.* Lived in Clark Co., Mo.; had issue.

(54) *Samuel A. Barclay, b* 4 June, 1815; *d* 20 January, 1877, Bowling Green, Ky.; *m* (1) *Sarah Pollard; m* (2) *Louisa Douglas; m* (3) *Mary Gillis.* Had issue by each wife.

(55) *Margaret Barclay, b* 3 July, 1812; *d* 1856; *m Albert Mitchell,* Bowling Green, Ky.; had issue.

(56) *Martha D. Barclay, b* 27 February, 1819; *d* January, 1892; *m John W. McElwain* of Todd County, Ky. Had issue.

27. **Alexander Tedford Barclay,** *b* 1797; *d* 1848; *m Agnes McClung Pongue.*

 (57) *James Moore Barclay, b* 1820; *d* 1865; *m* (1) *Amelia Offut; m* (2) *Mary S. Moffett;* no issue; *m* (3) *Mary Eleanor Paxton, b* 1810; *d* 1883. Lived in Fayette County, Ky.

 (58) *Agnes Mary Barclay, b* 1834; *d* 1879; *m* Judge *James T. Patton.*

 (59) *Sarah Ellen Barclay, b* 1835; *d* 1894; *m Mettellus Woods.* No issue.

 (60) *Hannah Moore Barclay, b* 1839; living 1903 Lexington, Va.; *m* Judge *William P. Houston.*

 (61) *Archibald Hays Barclay, b* 1842; *d* 1859.

 (62) *Alexander Tedford Barclay, b* 1844; living 1903 Lexington, Va.; *m Virginia B. Moore.* Had issue.

 (63) *Elihu Barclay, b* 1846; living 1903, Lexington, Va.; *m Margaret S. Rowan.*

 (64) *J. Paxton Barclay* (M.D.), *b* 1848; living 1903, Eutaw, Ala.; *m Emeline C. Payne.*

28. **Hugh Barclay,** *b* 1799; *d* 1870; lived at Lexington, Va.; *m Mary Woods.*

 (65) *John Woods Barclay, b* 1823; living 1903, Lexington, Va.; *m Elizabeth Williams* of Kentucky.

 (66) *Michael Woods Barclay, b* 1824; *d* 1858 in Kentucky; *m Susan Miller.*

 (67) *Jane Ann Barclay, b* 1828; *d* 1847.

 (68) *Lucien Tedford Barclay, b* 1832; *d* 1895; *m Elvira D. Mather.* Lived in Chicago. Had issue.

 (69) *William Henry Barclay, b* 1833; *m Julia Crawford.* Had issue.

29. **Elihu Barclay,** *b* 1801; lived at Darien, Ga.; *m Eliza Paxton.*

 (70) *Adaliza Barclay; m Dr. Young.*

(71) *William Barclay.* Killed in battle of Gettysburg.

(72) *Elihu Alexander Barclay.*

(73) *Zenobia Barclay.*

(74) *Julius Barclay.* Confederate soldier; killed in battle.

(75) *Hugh Washington Barclay.* Living in Texas 1903.

31. **Josiah E. Barclay,** *b* 13 November, 1825; *d* 24 November, 1852; *m S. Jane Smith.*

> (76) *Samuel J. Barclay, m ——— Miller.* Had issue.
>
> (77) *Camilla Barclay, m Dr. Otto Wuth.* Had issue.

35. **John Jacob Barclay,** *b* 16 December, 1832; living 1903, Bedford, Pa.; *m* 7 October, 1873, *Laura Watson Baily; b* 5 May, 1844; *d* 11 April, 1889.

> (78) *Jessie B. Barclay, b* 5 August, 1874.
>
> (79) *William F. Barclay, b* 14 July, 1876.
>
> (80) *Hugh B. Barclay* (M.D.), *b* 26 November, 1878.
>
> (81) *Joseph J. Barclay, b* 13 December, 1880.
>
> (82) *Hetty Barclay, b* 23 January, 1886.

36. **Richard DeC. Barclay,** *b* 3 March, 1836; living 1903; *m Mary DeCharms.*

> (83) *Mary Barclay, m William Scull.*

39. **Thomas J. Barclay,** *b* 23 January, 1826; *d* 24 August, 1881. Served in Mexican War. *m* September, 1855, *Rebecca Kuhns, b* 10 May, 1832; *d* 26 February, 1901.

> (84) *Margaret A. Barclay, b* 10 June, 1857.
>
> (85) *Isabella J. Barclay, b* 8 May, 1859; *m* Dr. *John S. Crawford.*
>
> (86) *Mary M. Barclay, b* 21 July, 1860; *d* in infancy.
>
> (87) *John Barclay.*
>
> (88) *Joseph K. Barclay, b* 15 September, 1863; *m Malosing Bremat.*
>
> (89) *Rebecca Barclay, b* 5 June, 1865; *m Charles W. Fogg.* Had issue.
>
> (90) *Hetty Barclay, b* 8 September, 1867; *m John M. Jamison.* Had issue.

(91) *Sallie B. Barclay, b* 1 August, 1869; *m* Dr. *H. D. Jamison.*

(92) *Thomas Barclay, b* 30 June, 1871.

(93) *Morrison Barclay, b* 27 May, 1873; *m Helen Cashman.* Had issue.

41. **Alexander Barclay,** *b* 10 February, 1830; living 1903, Westmoreland Co., Pa.; *m Sarah Sceptre.*

(94) *Alexander Johnston Barclay, m* 27 January, 1897, *Myrtle M. Huey.*

(95) *Isabella Johnston Barclay, m* April, 1889, *Henry M. Cairns.*

(96) *Mary Barclay, m* 1897, *William Ray.*

(97) *Wilson B. Barclay, d* 6 October, 1889.

(98) *Hetty F. Barclay, d* 23 January, 1898, *m* ——— *Ulery.*

50. **Hugh Barclay,** *b* 24 December, 1802; *d* 4 September, 1878; *m Luan L. Hall, b* 1810; *d* 1869. Lived and died in Russelville, Ky.

(99) *James Samuel Barclay.*

(100) *Philander Walker Barclay.*

(101) *Joseph Crews Barclay.*

(102) *Sarah J. Barclay, b* 22 January, 1840; living Russellville, Ky., 1903; *m* Col. *John W. Caldwell* (M.C.).

(103) *John Fletcher Barclay, b* 24 May, 1842; living 1903, Atlanta, Ga.; *m Lucy Allison.*

(104) *Hugh Barclay.*

(105) *Prudence S. Barclay, b* 25 August, 1848; living 1903; *m* Judge *Walter G. Hines,* Trinidad, Col.

(106) *Virginia Garnett Barclay, b* 17 September, 1850; d October, 1892; *m* Dr. *A. C. Wright,* Bowling Green, Ky. Her son, Hugh B. Wright, was Color Sergeant with Roosevelt's "Rough Riders" in Cuban campaign of Spanish War.

(107) *Wilbur Fisk Barclay.*

87. **John Barclay,** *b* 18 February, 1862; living 1903, Greensburg, Pa.; *m Rebecca Coulter.*
> (108) *John Barclay.*

99. **James Samuel Barclay,** *b* Russellville, Ky., 17 January, 1831; *d* Oak Park, Ill., 23 January, 1902; *m Mary Elizabeth Taylor* of Springfield, Ill., 25 June, 1874; *b* Petersburg, Ill., 14 June, 1839; *d* 13 February, 1902, Oak Park, Ill.
> (109) *Luan Eliza Barclay, b* 14 May, 1875, Cairo, Ill.; living 1903, Oak Park, Ill.
> (110) *James Taylor Barclay, b* Cairo, Ill., 14 December, 1876; living 1903, Oak Park, Ill.
> (111) *Philander Walker Barclay, b* Anna, Ill., 16 September, 1878; living 1903, Oak Park, Ill.

100. **Philander Walker Barclay,** *b* 30 December, 1832; living 1903, Cairo, Ill.; *m Mary Crews.*
> (112) *Philander C. Barclay, b* 1857; living 1903.
> (113) *Frances Barclay, b* 1859; living 1903, Guaymas, Mexico; *m J. N. Naigle.*
> (114) *Hugh Barclay, b* 1867; *d* April, 1903.

101. **Joseph Crews Barclay,** *b* 16 July, 1838; living 1903, Jefferson Co., Ky.; *m* (1) *Ann Dulaney; m* (2) *Mary Ronald.*
> (115) *Florence Barclay.*

104. **Hugh Barclay,** *b* 5 March, 1846; living 1903, Louisville, Ky.; *m Kate Rizer.*
> (116) *Hugh Barclay, b* 26 December, 1872.
> (117) *Edwin R. Barclay, b* 17 November, 1875.
> (118) *Marmaduke Morton Barclay.*

107. **Wilbur Fisk Barclay,** *b* 15 April, 1853; living 1903, Louisville, Ky.; *m Alice Hargrove, b* 1853, dau. Bishop R. K. Hargrove.
> (119) *Wilbur H. Barclay, b* 18 May, 1881; *d May* 14, 1903.
> (120) *Robert H. Barclay, b* 4 January, 1883; living 1903.

118. **Marmaduke Morton Barclay,** *b* 24 August, 1879; living
Russellville, Ky., 1903; *m Frances Kington.*
(121) *Katherine Barclay.*

---

1. **James Barclay,** of County Antrim, Ireland; *b* 1730-33;
m Jean Lowery.
- (2) *Robert Barclay, b* 1757 (abt.).
- (3) *Alexander Barclay.*
- (4) *Nancy Barclay, m Samuel Robinson* in Ireland;
settled and *d* in Shippensburg, Pa. Had issue.
- (5) *John Barclay,* remained in Ireland.
- (6) *Jean Barclay.*
- (7) *James Barclay.*
- (8) *Lowery Barclay.*

3. **Alexander Barclay,** *b* 1759, County Antrim, Ireland.
Came to America about 1790; *d* 1824; lived in Hannas
Town, Westmoreland Co., Pa. In 1803 moved to Indiana Co., Pa., near Lewisville, and the farm on which
he settled has been continuously in ownership and oc-
cupancy of his descendants. *m Mary Ann Martin,* 1795,
Philadelphia; *b* in County Antrim 1766; came to
America abt. 1795.
- (9) *Jane Barclay, b* 12 May, 1797, Hannas Town,
Pa.; *d* 17 September, 1868; *m* (1) *James
Wilson,* 1816, by whom she had 1 son, *James
Wilson; m* (2) *Thomas Dixon* 1821, by whom
she had 5 dau. and 2 sons.
- (10) *John Barclay.*
- (11) *Alexander C. Barclay.*
- (12) *Nancy Barclay, b* 12 August, 1809; *d* 1888; *m
John MacFarland;* had 3 sons and 3 daughters.
- (13) *James M. Barclay.*

7. **James Barclay,** remained in Ireland ; *m* ————

> (14) *James Barclay,* came to Indiana Co., Pa., abt. 1848.
>
> (15) *Robert Barclay,* came to Indiana Co., Pa., abt. 1848.
>
> (16) *Mary Barclay,* came to Indiana Co., Pa., abt. 1848 ; *m John Barclay.*

8. **Lowery Barclay,** *b* 1779, County Antrim, Ireland. Came to America 1815. Settled in Indiana Co., Pa. ; *d* there 5 January, 1864 ; *m Martha Ann Agnew, b* abt. 1780, County Antrim, Ireland ; *d* 15 January, 1864, Indiana Co., Pa.

> (17) *Jane Barclay, b* 11 August, 1810, County Antrim, Ireland ; *d* 13 April, 1879, Du Bois, Pa. ; *m Adam Johnston,* by whom she had 3 sons and 1 daughter.
>
> (18) *James Barclay.*
>
> (19) *John Agnew Barclay.*
>
> (20) *Nancy Barclay, b* 11 July, 1817.
>
> (21) *Alexander R. Barclay, b* 9 October, 1820 ; *d* Sacramento, Cal.
>
> (22) *Matilda Barclay, b* 16 January, 1827 ; *d* 16 February, 1864.

10. **John Barclay,** *b* 12 June, 1802, Hannas Town, Pa. ; *d* 1880 ; *m* (1) ———— *Rankin,* by whom he had 3 sons and 4 daughters ; *m* (2) Mrs. *Ann (Clark) Cameron,* by whom he had 2 sons.

> (23) *Martha Barclay, m William Ehrhart;* living Blairsville, Pa., 1903. Had 1 son and 1 daughter.
>
> (24) *Mary Ann Barclay, m William Bracken.* Had 3 children.
>
> (25) *Elizabeth Barclay,* living Wilkinsburg, Pa., 1903 ; *m John McIntosh;* had 2 sons and 2 daughters.
>
> (26) *Alexander Barclay, m Elizabeth Collasier.* Had issue.

(27) *James M. Barclay,* living 1903 near Lewisville,
Pa.

(28) *Caroline Barclay,* living Jefferson Co., Pa.,
1903; *m* ———— *Lang.*

(29) *William Barclay,* lived at Turtle Creek, Pa.
Had issue.

(30) *John C. Barclay,* lived at Wheeling, Va. Had
issue.

(31) *Thomas Benton Barclay,* living Indiana 1903;
m ———— *Sutton.*

11. Alexander C. Barclay, *b* 1 March, 1806, near Lewisville,
Pa.; *d* 3 April, 1873; *m* 2 December, 1830, *Nancy Gal-
lagher* of Livermore, Pa.

(32) *John Wallace Barclay.*

(33) *William Porter Barclay,* *b* 9 April, 1834; *d* 1
January, 1872, Philadelphia.

(34) *Nelson Clark Barclay.*

(35) *Cyrus N. Barclay.*

(36) *Artemas C. Barclay,* *b* 4 August, 1848. Married. Living Philadelphia, 1903.

(37) *Nancy G. Barclay,* *b* 25 October, 1850; living
Pittsburg, Pa., 1903.

13. James M. Barclay, *b* 15 October, 1813, near Lewisville,
Pa.; *d* 1865; *m* 1836, *Jane Ferguson,* *b* 1813; *d* 1887.

(38) *David Douglas Barclay.*

(39) *Mary Jane Barclay,* *b* 15 December, 1844; *m*
Joel Andrew. Had issue.

(40) *Alexander Ralston Barclay,* *b* 30 April, 1848.
Had issue.

18. James Barclay, *b* 19 February, 1813, County Antrim, Ireland; *d* 3 July, 1864, Indiana Co., Pa.; *m* *Phoebe Har-
rold.*

(41) *Elizabeth Barclay.*

(42) *Margaret Barclay.*

(43) *Matilda Barclay.*

(44) *Phoebe Barclay.*

(45) *William Barclay.*

19. **John Agnew Barclay,** *b* 13 August, 1815, Indiana Co.,
     Pa.; *d* 17 June, 1885, Indiana Co., Pa.; *m* 1 May, 1841,
     Margaret Medlar Lomison, b 1820, Northumberland Co.,
     Pa.; *d* 10 March, 1883, Indiana Co., Pa.

> (46) *William Franklin Barclay.*
>
> (47) *Watson Lowery Barclay, b* 13 August, 1844,
>   Indiana Co., Pa.; *d* 7 June, 1864.
>
> (48) *John Foster Barclay, b* 27 December, 1846;
>   living 1903 Vandergrift, Pa.
>
> (49) *Martha Ann Barclay, b* 8 June, 1849; *d* 28
>   August, 1895.
>
> (50) *Mary Catherine Barclay, b* 27 March, 1852;
>   *d* 27 June, 1886.
>
> (51) *Sarah Margaret Barclay, b* 8 November, 1855;
>   *d* 20 May, 1892.
>
> (52) *Virginia Bell Barclay, b* 27 April, 1859; living
>   1903 Homer City, Pa.

32. **John Wallace Barclay,** *b* 16 April, 1832; *d* 26 December,
     1901, in Florida; *m Mary P. Elgin.*

> (53) *James Barclay,* living Allegheny City, Pa., 1903.
>
> (54) *Frank Barclay,* living Jacksonville, Fla., 1903.

34. **Nelson Clark Barclay,** *b* 17 February, 1836; living 1903
     Altoona, Pa.; *m* 12 September, 1867, *Sarepta Russell,
     b* 17 May, 1838, of West Bridgewater, Pa.

> (55) *Walter C. Barclay, b* 8 June, 1868; living 1903
>   N. Y. City; *m Lola McComas.*
>
> (56) *Frank R. Barclay, b* 28 May, 1870; living 1903
>   Altoona, Pa.; *m Rebekah Brighal.* Issue:
>   *Clara Barclay.*

35. **Cyrus N. Barclay,** *b* 31 March, 1844; living 1903, Altoona,
     Pa.; *m Christie Milsse* of Pottsville, Pa.

> (57) *Helen T. Barclay, b* 10 September, 1869.
>
> (58) *Bertha M. Barclay, b* March, 1872; *m W. B.
>   McCrea.*

38. David Douglas Barclay, *b* 13 April, 1837; living 1903 Pittsburg, Pa.; *m*, 1862, *Elizabeth Rainbow.*

> (59) *Laura Barclay, m Geo. Kerbey.* Had issue.
> (60) *Edgar M. Barclay.* Had issue.
> (61) *James B. Barclay.*
> (62) *Hattie M. Barclay.*

46. William Franklin Barclay (M.D.), *b* 13 February, 1842, Indiana Co., Pa.; living 1903 Pittsburg, Pa.; *m* (1) *Emma Sarah Broun,* by whom he had 3 sons; *m* (2) 25 March, 1886, *Annie Negley Wills, b* 6 June, 1864, Pittsburg, Pa., by whom he had a daughter.

> (63) *Albert Hampton Barclay.*
> (64) *Paul Lowery Barclay, b* 17 October, 1872; *d* 14 December, 1876.
> (65) *Henry Carlton Barclay, b* 17 June, 1875, Saltsburg, Pa.; living 1903 Boston, Mass.
> (66) *Athalie Griffiths Barclay, b* 30 December, 1889, Pittsburg, Pa.; living 1903.

63. Albert Hampton Barclay, *b* 31 July, 1869, Saltsburg, Pa.; living 1903 New Haven, Conn.; *m Laura W. Williams* in Rochester, N. Y., 7 December, 1898, *b* 20 September, 1873.

> (67) *Lois W. Barclay, b* 21 April, 1901, New Haven, Conn.

---

1. John Barclay, *d* abt. 1800; lived near Belair, Harford Co., Md.; *m Elizabeth Gill.*

> (2) *John Gill Barclay,* lived in Kentucky.
> (3) *Joshua Gill Barclay.*
> (4) *James Barclay.*
> (5) *Robert Barclay,* lived 1820 in Lancaster Co., Pa.
> (6) *William Pinckney Barclay.*
> (7) *George Washington Barclay.*

3. **Joshua Gill Barclay,** *b* 26 June, 1784, Harford Co., Md.;
   settled in 1808 in Louisville, Ky.; *d* 5 April, 1851; *m*
   (1) *Julia Berthond,* dau. Nicholas Berthond; *m* (2)
   January, 1820, *Sarah Wheeler, b* 16 January, 1797; *d*
   11 January, 1862.

   > (8) *Julia Barclay, b* 20 September, 1817, Louisville,
   >   Ky.; *d* 14 January, 1883; *m Napoleon B.
   >   Barclay* (No. 18 below).
   > (9) *John Rowan Barclay.*
   > (10) *Sarah Hillery Barclay, b* 17 May, 1824; *d* 6
   >   July, 1825.
   > (11) *Mary Deborah Barclay.*
   > (12) *William Chapline Barclay, b* 8 September, 1827,
   >   Louisville, Ky.; *d* 31 October, 1901, in Wells-
   >   burg, W. Va. Had issue. *m* (1) *E. W.
   >   Kuhn,* 2 December, 1852; *m* (2) *M. R. Merry-
   >   man,* 3 July, 1855.
   > (13) *Virginia Priscilla Barclay.*
   > (14) *Sophia Caroline Barclay, b* 15 April, 1831; *d*
   >   13 September, 1851.
   > (15) *Emily Wilson Barclay.*
   > (16) *Hanson Wheeler Barclay.*
   > (17) *Sallie Henrietta Barclay, b* 17 May, 1840,
   >   Trimble Co., Ky.; *d* 17 May, 1860.

6. **William Pinckney Barclay,** *b* Harford Co., Md.; *d* Kentucky; *m Rachel* ———.

   > (18) *Napoleon Bonaparte Barclay.*
   > (19) *Louisa Anna Barclay.*

7. **George Washington Barclay,** *b* 5 March, 1794, Harford
   Co., Md.; *d* April, 1865; *m* (1) *Matilda Wheeler; m*
   (2) April 15, 1823, *Catherine Griffith, d* 30 April, 1880.

   > (20) *Mary Eliza Barclay, b* 31 May, 1825; *d* 5 Sep-
   >   tember, 1832.
   > (21) *Georgiana Barclay.*
   > (22) *Catherine Barclay, b* 23 July, 1830; *d* 28 June,
   >   1836.

(23) *Robert G. Barclay, b* 10 December, 1832; *d* 1870, New Orleans.

(24) *John N. Barclay, b* 22 November, 1835; *d* 10 August, 1841.

(25) *Charles R. Barclay, b* 17 December, 1838; *d* 17 April, 1863, Washington, D. C.

9. **John Rowan Barclay,** *b* 26 January, 1822; living 1903, Milton, Ky.; *m* (1) *Mary H. Rose* of Wellsburg, W. Va., December, 1843, *b* 23 February, 1823; *m* (2) 8 September, 1859, (?) No issue.

(26) *Mahala R. Barclay, m* 1890, Judge *J. H. Gossam* of Milton, Ky.

(27) *Sallie Barclay, d* 3 November, 1886; *m* ——— *Strother.*

(28) *Mary H. Barclay, m* 1870, *William C. Pryor.* Had issue.

11. **Mary Deborah Barclay,** *b* 26 October, 1825, Louisville, Ky.; *d* 12 January, 1852; *m* 31 May, 1843, *Henry Lawrence.*

(29) *Alice Lawrence.*

(30) *Barclay Lawrence.*

(31) *Joseph Lawrence.*

13. **Virginia Priscilla Barclay,** *b* 21 June, 1829, Louisville, Ky.; *m* 1 May, 1851, *John Hanson Wheeler, b* 8 March, 1826.

(32) *Russell Barclay Wheeler.*

15. **Emily Wilson Barclay,** *b* 14 April, 1833, Trimble Co., Ky.; living 1903; *m* at "Fancy Farm," Trimble Co., Ky., 14 June, 1853, *Robert Taliaferro, b* 16 May, 1805, Caroline Co., Va.

(33) *Augustus Taliaferro, b* 14 April, 1854, La Grange, Oldham Co., Ky.; *m* 26 June, 1895, *Virginia Ranson Kerr.*

(34) *Rowan Barclay Taliaferro, b* 11 October, 1855, La Grange, Oldham Co., Ky; *m* 26 October, 1879, *Alice Ramsey.*

(35) *Emma Taliaferro,* *b* 22 January, 1859, La Grange, Oldham Co., Ky.; *m* 30 September, 1896, *John M. Bellamy.*

(36) *Elizabeth Ward Taliaferro,* *b* 14 September, 1864, Louisville, Ky.; *m* 19 February, 1884, *James K. Broughton.*

(37) *Virgie Taliaferro,* *b* 20 December, 1866, Bullett Co., Ky.; *m* 4 March, 1902, *Charles Wesley Forman.*

16. Hanson Wheeler Barclay, *b* 28 December, 1834, Trimble Co., Ky.; *d* 7 February, 1902, at Louisville, Ky.; *m* (1) *Pattie O. Stewart,* 26 October, 1858, at Cincinnati, O.; *m* (2) 18 June, 1863, in Jefferson Co., Ky., *Susan Mary Lewis,* *b* 23 November, 1837.

(38) *Warner Lewis Barclay,* *b* 18 June, 1864, Louisville, Ky.; living 1903.

(39) *Rowan Chapline Barclay,* *b* 12 September, 1866, Louisville, Ky; *m Hattie Henderson,* 12 October, 1892.

(40) *Mary Helen Barclay,*   ⎱Twins, *b* 22 Oc-
(41) *William Dougherty Barclay,*⎰tober, 1869, Louisville, Ky.   He *m Etta M. Boxley,* 19 December, 1895, Odessa, Mo.

(42) *Sue Virginia Barclay,* *b* 30 November, 1871, Louisville, Ky.; *m* 12 September, 1892, *James M. Vaughan.*   Had issue.

18. Napoleon Bonaparte Barclay, *b* Pennsylvania 11 October, 1812; *d* 28 February, 1853, Trimble Co., Ky.; *m* 13 November, 1836, *Julia Barclay* (No. 8 above); *b* 20 September, 1817, Louisville, Ky.; *d* 14 January, 1883, Columbus, Mo.

(43) *Sarah Elizabeth Barclay.*

(44) *Mary Julia Barclay.*

(45) *Emma Virginia Barclay.*

(46) *Lucy Rowan Barclay.*

(47) *Sophia Chapline Barclay.*

(48) *Alice Gray Barclay,* *b* 27 August, 1849, Trimble Co., Ky.; *d* 31 May, 1853.

(49) *Anna Hooper Barclay.*

21. **Georgiana Barclay,** *b* 27 September, 1827; *d* 18 October, 1864, Washington, D. C.; *m* 2 July, 1850, *Lambert A. Whitely.*

> (50) *Mary Barclay Whitely, b* 4 April, 1851; *m* 12 May, 1880, *William M. Dove* of Washington, D. C.
>
> (51) *Kate Whitely, b* 23 August, 1853; *d* 31 March, 1867.
>
> (52) *Alice Whitely, b* 29 October, 1856; *d* 1861.

32. **Russell Barclay Wheeler,** *b* 26 February, 1852, Madison, Ind.; *d* 5 January, 1891, Louisville, Ky.; *m* 7 November, 1880, *Mildred Stewart.*

> (53) *Edwin Stewart Wheeler, b* 23 June, 1881, Louisville, Ky.
>
> (54) *Isaac Miller Wheeler, b* 5 October, 1885, Louisville, Ky.

43. **Sarah Elizabeth Barclay,** *b* 9 September, 1837, Trimble Co., Ky.; *m Jesse C. Wilhorte,* 16 November, 1859, at Leavenworth, Kan.

> (55) *Minnie Belle Wilhorte, b* 10 October, 1861; *m Jesse M. West.*
>
> (56) *Julian Barclay Wilhorte, b* 21 February, 1865, Kansas City, Mo.
>
> (57) *James Ely Wilhorte, b* 7 October, 1868, Waverly, Mo.; *m Maude Blodgett.*
>
> (58) *Kate Thatcher Wilhorte, b* 14 November, 1870, Waverly, Mo.
>
> (59) *Elizabeth Evelyn Wilhorte, b* 3 September, 1872, Columbus, Mo.
>
> (60) *Frederick Shelton Wilhorte, b* 28 April, 1875, St. Louis, Mo.
>
> (61) *Edward Swartz Wilhorte, b* August, 1877, St. Louis, Mo.

44. **Mary Julia Barclay,** *b* 7 October, 1839, Madison, Ind.; *m* (1) *Alexander H. Thacher,* 11 April, 1861, at Leavenworth, Kas., *d* Arkansas, 29 September, 1870; *m* (2)

James B. Sorency, 26 March, 1872, at Holden, Mo.; *d* Odessa, Mo., 25 June, 1895.

> (62) *Kate DeM. Thacher*, *b* 30 January, 1862; *d* in infancy.
>
> (63) *George Barclay Thacher*, *b* 2 February, 1864, Springfield, Mo.; *m Annie E. Zimmerman.*
>
> (64) *Phillip Edgar Thacher*, *b* 19 June, 1866, Warrensburg, Mo.; *d* in infancy.
>
> (65) *Julia Barclay Sorency*, *b* 17 November, 1873, Columbus, Mo.; *d* 25 June, 1880.
>
> (66) *Alice Gray Sorency*, *b* 3 April, 1878; *d* in infancy.
>
> (67) *James B. Sorency*, *b* 24 April, 1875.
>
> (68) *Allan Gray Sorency*, *b* 2 April, 1880.

45. **Emma Virginia Barclay**, *b* 10 September, 1841, Madison, Ind.; *m* 28 October, 1857, *George W. Snyder*, at Milton, Ky.

> (69) *Charles Allan Snyder*, *b* 11 February, 1860; *d* 29 March, 1863.
>
> (70) *Rowan Barclay Snyder*, *b* 15 September, 1863; *m* 25 January, 1888, *Effie L. Gibbs.*
>
> (71) *Jesse Lee Snyder*, *b* 8 March, 1866; *d* 11 March, 1868.
>
> (72) *Allan Lee Snyder*, *b* 2 April, 1868; *d* 1 December, 1875.
>
> (73) *Frederick N. Snyder*, *b* 13 March, 1870; *d* 6 September, 1875.
>
> (74) *George Baker Snyder*, *b* 6 September, 1874.
>
> (75) *Julia M. Snyder*, *b* 27 February, 1877; *d* 25 July, 1887.

46. **Lucy Rowan Barclay**, *b* 2 February, 1844, Madison, Ind.; *d* 24 June, 1887; *m* (1) *William H. Ruel*, 6 May, 1860, Leavenworth, Kan., *d* June, 1871; *m* (2) *P. S. Baker*, November, 1875, in Kansas City.

> (76) *Lucy Ellen Ruel*, *b* August, 1867; *m Charles E. Ferguson*, October, 1886.

(77) *Alene Kendall Baker, b* 26 December, 1876.

(78) *Henry Carroll Baker.*

(79) *Peter Napoleon Baker.*

47. **Sophia Chapline Barclay,** *b* 8 October, 1847, Trimble Co., Ky.; *m* June, 1864, *Gilbert G. Crandall* at Kansas City, Mo.

(80) *Amos Barclay Crandall, b* July, 1867.

(81) *Henry Ruel Crandall, b* 1873.

(82) *George Parker Crandall, b* November, 1876.

(83) *Maude Crandall, b* January, 1882.

49. **Anna Hooper Barclay,** *b* 26 December, 1851, Trimble City, Ky.; *d* February, 1896; *m* 17 July, 1869, *John Meredith Bellamy* at Waverly, Mo.

(84) *Sarah Elizabeth Bellamy, b* 6 August, 1874; *m William J. Prigmore.*

(85) *William Bradford Bellamy, b* January, 1877.

(86) *Berthond Taylor Bellamy, b* September, 1879.

(87) *Delia Vaughn Bellamy, b* August, 1882.

(88) *Julia Pearl Van Dyke Bellamy, b* 1885.

(89) *Edith Simms Bellamy, b* 1887.

(90) *Frances May Bellamy, b* 1889.

(91) *Harold Meredith Bellamy, b* 1891.

---

1. **James Barclay,** *b* 1722; *d* 1792; *m Margaret Fowlan, d* 15 December, 1816. Lived in Warrington Township, Bucks Co., Pa.

(2) *James Barclay,* of Philadelphia.

(3) *John Barclay.*

(4) *Hugh Barclay.*

(5) *Sarah Barclay, m* ——— *Huffty.*

(6) *Mary B. Barclay, m* ——— *Barr.*

(7) *Richard Barclay.*

3. **John Barclay,** *b* 1749; *d* 15 September, 1824, Philadelphia; *bur* in Neshaminy Church graveyard, Warwick Township, Bucks Co., Pa.

His Public Services:

1776, Jan. 8.   Commissioned Ensign in 4 Batallion under Col. Anthony Wayne.

   Oct. 1.   Promoted to 2d Lieut.

1777, Jany.   Commissioned 1st Lieut. 5th Reg. Penn. line.

   June 13.   Commissioned Capt.-Lieut.

1781, Jany. 1.   Retired with brevet rank of Captain.

1782, Dec. 23.   Appointed Justice of the Peace.

1787,   A delegate to State Convention to ratify Federal Constitution.

1788, Aug. 14.   Appointed Justice of Court of Quarter Sessions.

1789-90.   A member of State Constitutional Convention.

1790, Feb. 27.   Appointed Presiding Justice, Court of Common Pleas.

1791, Aug. 17,⎱ An associate Judge of the Courts of
to 1803, Jany. 2.⎰   Bucks Co.

1804,   A member of the State Senate.

Was President of the Bank of the Northern Liberties of Philadelphia.

Was a member of the Pennsylvania Society of the Cincinnati.

   (8) *John Louis Barclay.*

   (9) *James M. Barclay.*

8. **John Louis Barclay,** *m Lucy Bowmar.*

   (10) *Herrmon Bowmar Barclay.*

   (11) *James C. Barclay.*

   (12) *Fannie Barclay, d* young.

9. **James M. Barclay,** *b* 1813; *d* 1863; *m* 24 May, 1849, *Hetty Mary Bowmar, b* 30 October, 1831; *d* 20 December, 1858. (Only child of Robert H. and Martha Hoggin Bowmar.)

   (13) *Pattie Barclay, b* 1851, Versailles, Ky.; *m* 15 July, 1876, *William H. Lex* of Philadelphia, by whom she had 1 son, *Barclay Lex, b* 1889.

(14) *John Barclay, b* 1852; *d* 1898, *unm.*

(15) *Nannie L. Barclay, b* 1854, Versailles, Ky.; *m* April, 1874, *Samuel Nevins* of Philadelphia, by whom she had 3 daughters.

10. **Herrmon Bowmar Barclay,** *m Annie Brond* of Lexington, Ky.

(16) *Alexander Barclay, d* at the age of 21, *unm.*

11. **James C. Barclay,** *m W. Burbridge,* Lexington, Ky.

(17) *James C. Barclay,* Jr.

---

1. **William Barclay,** lived in County Tyrone, Ireland.

(2) *James Barclay.*

2. **James Barclay,** lived in County Tyrone, Ireland; *m Catherine Edmonds.*

(3) *Samuel Barclay.*

3. **Samuel Barclay,** *b* 29 December, 1802, Poplar Hill, Tullyhogue, County Tyrone, Ireland. Came to America in 1844; *d* 31 October, 1879, in New York City; *m* 16 December, 1828, *Sarah Hunter* at Stuartstown, County Tyrone, Ireland; *b* County Tyrone 5 October, 1805; *d* N. Y. City 7 December, 1848.

(4) *James H. Barclay.*

(5) *Henry Barclay.*

(6) *Thomas Barclay, b* 22 February, 1834; *d* 19 January, 1894. Had issue living 1903 in California.

(7) *Eliza Barclay.*

(8) *Mary Barclay, b* 27 June, 1839; *d* 17 September, 1876; *m Thomas Kerr.*

(9) *Catherine Barclay, b* 17 August, 1842; *m* (1) *George G. Mitchell; m* (2) 25 October, 1886, Dr. *Z. Swift Webb.*

(10) *Sarah Barclay, b* 30 May, 1846, New York City; living 1903 Jefferson, Iowa; *m John Stevenson.* Have 10 children living 1903.

4. **James H. Barclay,** *b* 16 December, 1829, County Tyrone, Ireland; *d* 6 December, 1886; *m* 22 February, 1858, *Hannah Viola Flint* of Reading, Mass., *b* 25 November, 1839; *d* 10 September, 1879, at Mt. Vernon, N. Y.

> (11) *James F. Barclay, b* 19 June, 1859; *m* 12 December, 1900, *Lee A. Hernboldt.*
>
> (12) *Viola H. Barclay, b* 23 May, 1863; *m* 3 March, 1891, *John Mintjen.*
>
> (13) *Grace F. Barclay, b* 27 April, 1865; *m* 18 October, 1890, *Elmo P. Hernboldt.*
>
> (14) *Nellie Barclay, b* 2 December, 1866; *m Rufus K. Mulford,* 5 December, 1893.
>
> (15) *Robert Hall Barclay, b* 27 June, 1870; *m* 27 June, 1897, *Marion Hobley.*
>
> (16) *Nathan Straus Barclay, b* 23 September, 1878.

5. **Henry Barclay,** *b* 8 April, 1832, "Templereagh," County Tyrone, Ireland. Served in American Civil War as Captain of Co. K, 12th Regt., N. G. S. N. Y., and in 25th Regt. of N. Y. Volunteer Cavalry. Living 1903 Brooklyn, N. Y. *m* (1) 27 October, 1851, *Margaret Nightingale* (by whom he had 9 children), *b* 12 April, 1832, N. Y. City; *d* 9 August, 1874; *m* (2) 4 September, 1876, *C. Cecilia Corell, b* 4 October, 1846; dau. John & Louisa A. Corell.

> (17) *John N. Barclay, b* 7 December, 1853; *d* 8 February, 1859.
>
> (18) *James H. Barclay, b* 23 April, 1855; *d* 13 February, 1857.
>
> (19) *Margaret E. Barclay, b* 12 October, 1857; *m* 25 November, 1880, *Lewis H. Miller* at Katonah, N. Y.
>
> (20) *Henry L. Barclay, b* 26 February, 1859.
>
> (21) *Sarah H. Barclay, b* 4 March, 1861; *m* October, 1882, *George Rudischhauser.*
>
> (22) *William N. Barclay, b* 3 October, 1862.
>
> (23) *Anna J. A. Barclay, b* 6 July, 1864; *d* 15 January, 1902; *m* 15 June, 1886, *Leemon Brundage.*

    (24) *Samuel Corbet Custer Barclay, b* 7 May, 1867;
        d 3 February, 1870.

    (25) *Mary L. Barclay, b* 3 March, 1871; *m* 7 August,
        1901, *Robert F. Stockton.*

    (26) *Cecil Dykers Barclay, b* 31 August, 1878.
        Served in Spanish-American War. Living
        1903.

7. **Eliza Barclay,** *b* 31 October, 1836, County Tyrone, Ireland; *d* 1 June, 1870; *m* 19 November, 1858, *George G.
Mitchell.*

    (27) *Florence Elizabeth Mitchell, b* 8 July, 1860.
    (28) *Maud Mary Mitchell.*

28. **Maud Mary Mitchell,** *b* 20 September, 1868; *m* 16 June,
1892, *Albert T. Strauch.*

    (29) *Albert T. Strauch, Jr., b* 10 May, 1893.
    (30) *Marion Webb Strauch, b* 18 August, 1895.
    (31) *Edmond Mitchell Strauch, b* 16 June, 1898.

---

1. **George Barclay,** *b* 3 July, 1780, Cupar, Fifeshire, Scot-
land; *d* 10 August, 1857, in Canada; *m* 24 January, 1801,
Janet Tulis, b 22 December, 1779, Cupar, Fifeshire,
Scotland; *d* 12 November, 1866, in Canada.

    (2) *George Barclay, b* 16 December, 1801, Cupar,
        Scotland.

    (3) *Jane Barclay, b* 22 August, 1803, Cupar, Scot-
        land.

    (4) *Elizabeth Barclay, b* 2 October, 1805, Cupar,
        Scotland.

    (5) *James Barclay, b* 1 October, 1807, Cupar, Scot-
        land; *d* 4 June, 1808.

    (6) *Margaret Barclay, b* 3 July, 1810, Cupar, Scot-
        land.

    (7) *Nancy Barclay, b* 20 October, 1812, Cupar, Scot-
        land.

    (8) *James Barclay.*

(9) *David Lyons Barclay, b* 15 June, 1819, Pickering, Ontario.

(10) *William Sleegh Barclay.*

(11) *Eli Gorham Barclay, b* 13 February, 1825.

8. **James Barclay,** *b* 29 October, 1815, Cupar, Fifeshire, Scotland; *d* 3 November, 1869; *m Hannah Caroline Parnham,* 17 September, 1837, *b* England, 8 November, 1818.

(12) *Almira Eveline Barclay, b* 2 August, 1838, Pickering, Ont.; *d* 22 March, 1879.

(13) *George James Barclay, b* 10 October, 1840.

(14) *Anne Jane Barclay, b* 13 September, 1842.

(15) *Eli David Barclay, b* 11 December, 1844; *d* 10 August, 1889.

(16) *William Henry Barclay.*

(17) *Albert Ernest Barclay, b* 21 February, 1850.

(18) *Walter Franklin Barclay, b* 31 March, 1853; *d* 18 September, 1872.

(19) *Lyman Theophilus Barclay, b* 14 May, 1855.

(20) *Carolina Matilda Barclay, b* 25 June, 1858; *d* 30 August, 1879.

(21) *Helena Louise Josephine Barclay, b* 8 November, 1861.

10. **William Sleegh Barclay,** *b* 25 December, 1821; *d* 10 December, 1892, in Black River Falls, Wis.; *m Jane Preston, b* 23 October, 1824, in Canada; *d* 3 July, 1870.

(22) *David Barclay.*

(23) *George Barclay, b* Canada, 1848; *d* Black River Falls, Wis., 24 July, 1870, *unm.*

(24) *A. Barclay, b* 28 April, 1851; *d unm.*

(25) *Mary A. Barclay, b* Canada 18 July, 1853; living 1903, Sechlerville, Wis.; *m William Edgar Hilts.*

(26) *James H. Barclay, b* Canada 17 August, 1855; *d* Canada 3 November, 1855.

(27) *Thamar G. Barclay, b* Canada 14 January, 1857;
living (unmarried) 1903 Black River Falls,
Wis.

(29) *Lydia M. Barclay, b* Canada 24 December, 1858;
living 1903 Black River Falls; *m* 29 February,
1884, *William B. Sinclair* at Medford, Ont.

(30) *Robert H. Barclay.*

(31) *Nancy Jane Barclay, b* Canada 22 August, 1864;
d Canada 31 October, 1879.

16. **William Henry Barclay,** *b* 27 November, 1846; *d* 19 February, 1900; *m Retta Hough*, 20 October, 1870; *b* 28
October, 1848.

(32) *Frederick L. Barclay, b* 7 June, 1871; living
1903 Elizabeth, Minn.

(33) *William Barclay, b* August, 1874; *d* in infancy.

(34) *Gertrude H. Barclay, b* 27 October, 1879.

(35) *Maude E. Barclay, b* 10 October, 1882.

(36) *Walker H. Barclay, b* 10 December, 1884.

22. **David Barclay,** *b* 14 June, 1846, Pickering, Ontario.
Came to Wisconsin in 1868; *d* 17 November, 1900, Black
River Falls, Wis.; *m* (1) 11 August, 1872, *Jennie
Roberts, d* 8 July, 1875, by whom he had 1 child, a son;
m (2) in 1878, *Alma Bjerke, b* Norway, 21 October,
1847.

(37) *Wilton Leroy Barclay.*

(38) *Bertha Barclay, b* 3 March, 1879, Black River
Falls, Wis.; living 1903.

(39) *Robert Barclay, b* 21 March, 1882, Black River
Falls, Wis.; *d* in infancy.

30. **Robert H. Barclay,** *b* 10 October, 1861, Canada; living
1903 near Black River Falls, Wis.; *m Annie Thompson.*

(40) *Gertrude Barclay, b* 9 June, 1891.

(41) *Mabel Barclay, b* 11 January, 1893.

(42) *Myrtle Barclay, b* 26 April, 1896.

(43) *Frederick Barclay, b* 1 May, 1899.

(44) *Erle Barclay, b* 1 January, 1901.

37. **Wilton Leroy Barclay,** *b* 8 February, 1875, Melrose, Wis.; living 1903 in St. Paul, Minn.; *m* 23 December, 1899, *Edith Mae Kelsey.*

    (45) *Nita Hope Barclay, b* 8 February, 1901; living St. Paul, Minn, 1903.

---

1. ——— **Barclay,** of County Tyrone, Ireland.

    (2) *John Barclay.*

    (3) *George Barclay.* Is said to have served as a soldier in the Revolutionary War. After the war, returned to Ireland.

2. **John Barclay,** *b* County Tyrone, Ireland. Came to America about 1771. Served in Revolutionary War as Private, Ensign, 2d Lieutenant, 1st Lieutenant, Captain and Adjutant in 5th Penn. Regt. of Foot under Col. Francis Johnson. After the war, settled in Franklin Co., Pa., near Shippensburg. Died in Fannettsburg, Pa. *m Ann Tate.*

    (4) *Francis Barclay.*

    (5) *Robert Barclay, m Elizabeth Desert.*

    (6) *John Barclay,* private in war 1812; moved to Iowa; *m Nancy Giffen.*

    (7) *William Barclay, m Ann McElbee.*

    (8) *George Barclay,* lived in Ohio; *m Martha Knave.*

    (9) *Andrew Barclay, b* 24 December, 1790; *d* 14 October, 1859; soldier war 1812; *m Sarah Stark.*

    (10) *James Barclay, d unm.*

    (11) *Katherine Barclay,* died young.

    (12) *David Barclay,* died young.

    (13) *Margaret Barclay, m* ——— *McCune.*

    (14) *Polly Barclay, m* ——— *Gordon.*

    (15) *Fanny Barclay, m* ——— *Harvey.*

    (16) *Jane Barclay, m* ——— *Collins.*

    (17) *Elizabeth Barclay, m* ——— *Winman.*

    (18) *Nancy Barclay, m* ——— *McDonald.*

4. **Francis Barclay,** *b* Franklin Co., Pa., 1773; *d* Poland, O., 1846; *m Elizabeth Wilson, b* Franklin Co., Pa., 1779; *d* Youngstown, O., 1850.

    (19) *John Barclay, b* Franklin Co., Pa., 1798; *d* Youngstown, O., 1825, *unm.*

    (20) *Mary Barclay, b* Franklin Co., Pa., 1800; *d* Poland, O., 1814, *unm.*

    (21) *James Barclay, b* Franklin Co., Pa., 1802; *d* 23 May, 1875; *m Elizabeth McCullough.*

    (22) *Robert Barclay, b* Franklin Co., Pa., 1803; *d* Aurora, Ill., 21 October, 1872; *m Laura Burroughs.*

    (23) *Francis Barclay, b* Poland, O., 1805; *d* Youngstown, O., 1863; *m Angeline Crandall.*

    (24) *Andrew Barclay, b* Poland, O., 1806; *d* Butler Co., Pa., 1870; *m* ——— *Johnson.*

    (25) *Ann Barclay, b* Poland, O., 1808; *d* Swanville, Iowa, 1880; *m Ira Davis.*

    (26) *George W. Barclay, b* Poland, O., 1810; *d* Portage Co., Ohio, 1891; *m* (1) ——— *Dawson; m* (2) *Mariah Greenleaf.*

    (27) *David Barclay, b* Poland, O., 1812; *d* Painsville, O., 1890; *m* ——— *Moril.*

    '(28) *William Barclay, b* 9 May, 1814; *d* Youngstown, O., 1886; *m Mary Morley.*

    (29) *Joseph Barclay.*

    (30) *Jane Barclay, b* Poland, O., 1817; *d* Poland, O., 1877; *m William Eaton.*

    (31) *Alexander Barclay, b* 1819; *d* 1 March, 1899; *m* (1) *Mary Moss; m* (2) ——— *Leggett.*

    (32) *Isaac Barclay, b* Poland, O., 1822; *d* Trumbull Co., O., 1887; *m* (1) ——— *Silliman; m* (2) *Mary Holcomb.*

    (33) *Eliza Barclay, b* 1823; *d* Butler Co., Pa., 1890; *m Reuben McMillan.*

29. **Joseph Barclay,** *b* Poland, O., 1816; *d* Youngstown, O., 1887. Was a member of House of Representatives, 62d Assembly, Ohio; *m Lovina Crandall, b* 1817; *d* 1892.

(34) *Charles D. Barclay.*

(35) *George Willson Barclay, b* 24 July, 1843; *d* 13 May, 1845.

(36) *Lucy Z. Barclay.*

34. **Charles D. Barclay,** *b* 29 April, 1839.   Served in War of Rebellion in 26th Regt., Ohio V. I.; *m Eleanor Sprague* of Cheltenham, Eng.

>   (37) *Eliza E. Barclay, b* 3 December, 1864; *m George Griffith.*
>
>   (38) *Joseph Edmund Barclay, b* 4 November, 1867; *d* 27 October, 1872.
>
>   (39) *Grace T. Barclay, b* 2 January, 1869; *m T. C. Stanford.*
>
>   (40) *Florence Barclay, b* 6 June, 1870; *d* 5 October, 1870.
>
>   (41) *Porter W. Barclay, b* 31 March, 1875.
>
>   (42) *Isaac W. Barclay.*
>
>   (43) *Charles Barclay, b* 9 May, 1880.
>
>   (44) *Blanche E. Barclay, b* 6 August, 1883; *d* 25 November, 1901.

36. **Lucy Z. Barclay,** *b* 2 July, 1848; *m Oliver Creed.*

>   (45) *I. O. Creed, b* 23 May, 1867.
>
>   (46) *Mildred M. Creed, b* 15 February, 1869.
>
>   (47) *Grace Creed, b* 26 September, 1871; *m Joseph Higley.*
>
>   (48) *Alice M. Creed, b* 28 May, 1873; *m George Higley.*
>
>   (49) *Bessie M. Creed, b* March, 1875.
>
>   (50) *Julia H. Creed, b* October, 1877; *d* 7 September, 1896.
>
>   (51) *George P. Creed, b* 15 May, 1878.
>
>   (52) *Florence R. Creed, b* 19 February, 1880.

42. **Isaac W. Barclay,** *b* 15 December, 1876; *m Lilly M. Horton.*

>   (53) *Arleigh Clide Barclay, b* 6 August, 1903.

1. **George Barclay,** *b* Ireland, 1755; came to America about 1780, from Portadown, County Armagh; *d* 1849 in Beaver County, Pa. Settled first near Mt. Pleasant, Westmoreland Co., Pa.; afterwards (1785) in Beaver County. His ancestors lived in Paisley, Scotland. *m Nancy Hamilton.*
    - (2) *Thomas Barclay.*
    - (3) *Martha Barclay, b* 11 October, 1790, Philadelphia, Pa.; *m Thomas Bradshaw.*
    - (4) *John Barclay.*
    - (5) *William Barclay.*
    - (6) *James Barclay.*
    - (7) *Jane Barclay, b* 28 May, 1799, Beaver Co., Pa.; *m Daniel Means.*
    - (8) *Nancy Barclay, b* 14 November, 1801, Beaver Co., Pa.; *m James Strain.*

2. **Thomas Barclay,** *b* 14 February, 1780, Ireland; *d* 1832, Beaver Co., Pa.; *m Jane Hunter, b* 1 August, 1789, Ireland; *d* 1860, Beaver Co., Pa.
    - (9) *George Barclay.*
    - (10) *John Barclay.*
    - (11) *Robert Hunter Barclay.*
    - (12) *Eliza Barclay, b* 10 January, 1818; *d* Beaver Co., Pa.; *m* ———— *Henderson.*
    - (13) *Nancy Barclay, b* 13 March, 1820; *m William Laird.*
    - (14) *James Barclay.*
    - (15) *William Barclay, b* 19 December, 1823; *d* early in life.
    - (16) *Mary Barclay.*
    - (17) *Jane Barclay, b* 10 March, 1830; living 1903, Beaver, Pa.; *m William S. Barclay* (No. 18), *b* 31 March, 1830; *d* 1902.

4. **John Barclay,** *b* 7 May, 1793, Pa.; *d* 1869, Beaver Co., Pa.; *m Elizabeth Shannon.*
    - (18) *William S. Barclay.*
    - (19) *Agnes Barclay.*
    - (20) *Sarah Barclay, m* ———— *Allison.*

5. **William Barclay,** *b* 12 November, 1795, Pa.; *d* 1885, Beaver Co., Pa.; *m* (1) ——— *McCullough,* by whom he had 2 sons and 1 daughter; *m* (2) *Isabel Scott,* by whom he had 1 son and 2 daughters.

    (21) *George W. Barclay.*

    (22) *Josephus Barclay, d* 1863 in the Civil War.

    (23) *Rebecca Jane Barclay, m Samuel Harbison.*

    (24) *Frazier Barclay,* living 1903 New Brighton, Pa.; *m Elizabeth Wilson.*

    (25) *Martha Barclay.*

    (26) *Maria Barclay, m* ——— *Newkirk.*

6. **James Barclay,** *b* 4 February, 1797, Pa.; *d* 1870; *m Ellen Porter.*

    (27) *Dr. George J. Barclay, b* 1826; *d* 1879, N. Y. City.

    (28) *John P. Barclay,* living 1903; *m* (1) ——— *Newkirk; m* (2) *Nancy Rail.*

    (29) *Dr. J. Thomas Barclay.*

    (30) *Dr. B. Frank Barclay, b* 1838; living 1903, Paris, France, *unm.*

9. **George Barclay,** *b* 17 May, 1812; *d* 1886, Beaver Co., Pa.; *m Elizabeth Hunter.*

    (31) *Caroline Virginia Barclay.*

    (32) *Thomas Barclay, d* 1864, battle Fair Oaks.

    (33) *Robert Hunter Barclay.*

    (34) *Arthur Stanley Barclay.*

    (35) *Nancy Amelia Barclay, b* 1814; living 1903, Beaver Co., Pa.

    (36) *Eliza Jane Barclay.*

    (37) *Mary Jane Barclay.*

    (38) *Euphemia Barclay.*

    (39) *Almira Barclay.*

    (40) *George Jennings Barclay.*

10. **John Barclay,** *b* 13 February, 1814; *d* Beaver Co., Pa.; *m Maria Gailey, b* 13 July, 1816.

    (41) *Sarah Jane Barclay, b* 15 April, 1843.

> (42) *Mary Anne Barclay, b* 16 March, 1845; *m James McLaughlin.*
>
> (43) *James Gailey Barclay.*
>
> (44) *Virginia Alice Barclay.*
>
> (45) *Agnes Barclay, b* 20 October, 1853.
>
> (46) *John Thomas Barclay.*

11. **Robert Hunter Barclay,** *b* 10 January, 1816; *d* 1902, Beaver, Pa.; *m* 25 June, 1844, *Mary Johnston, b* 8 January, 1823; living 1903, Beaver Co., Pa.

> (47) *Francis Johnston Barclay.*
>
> (48) *Sarah Jane Barclay.*
>
> (49) *William Hunter Barclay.*
>
> (50) *Mary Adaline Barclay.*
>
> (51) *Elizabeth C. Barclay.*
>
> (52) *Thomas Howard Barclay.*
>
> (53) *Margaret Malinda Barclay.*
>
> (54) *George Stanley Barclay.*
>
> (55) *Harry Mitchell Barclay, b* 7 November, 1865; *m Matilda McClay.*
>
> (56) *Ettie Olga Barclay.*

14. **James Barclay,** *b* 27 February, 1822, Pa.; settled in Black Hawk Co., Iowa, 1853; *d* 13 July, 1893; *m* 6 January, 1845, *Lucinda Glass, b* 9 March, 1823; *d* 1 October, 1899.

> (57) *Erskine B. Barclay.*
>
> (58) *Boston F. Barclay, b* 4 October, 1850; *d* 13 July, 1888.
>
> (59) *Jennie K. Barclay, b* 8 June, 1856.
>
> (60) *Mary Ann Barclay, b* 3 September, 1858; *d* 14 February, 1868.
>
> (61) *John A. Barclay, b* 20 February, 1864.

16. **Mary Barclay,** *b* 16 March, 1826; *m William Anderson.*

> (62) *James Y. Anderson, m Rose Kinsey.*
>
> (63) *Araminta Anderson, m Edward Dash.*

18. **William S. Barclay,** *b* 31 March, 1830; *d* 1902; *m Jane Barclay* (No. 17), *b* 10 March, 1830; living 1903, Beaver, Pa.

    (64) *Ida Barclay.*

    (65) *Stella Barclay, b* 29 January, 1856; living 1903, Philadelphia, Pa.

    (66) *Harry Barclay, b* 1860; living 1903, Beaver, Pa.

    (67) *Robert Barclay, b* 1862; living 1903, Beaver, Pa.

    (68) *Frank Barclay, b* 1864; *d* 1898.

    (69) *Joseph Barclay, b* 1866; *m Lizzie Day.*

    (70) *Wilson Barclay, b* 1870; *d* 1873.

19. **Agnes Barclay,** living 1903, Beaver, Pa.; *m Matthew S. Quay* (U. S. Senator from Pennsylvania).

    (71) *John Barclay Quay, b* 20 June, 1856; *d* 24 November, 1856.

    (72) *Stanley Anderson Quay, b* 27 January, 1858; *d* 27 April, 1859.

    (73) *Elizabeth Shannon Quay, b* 26 January, 1860; *d* 1 March, 1863.

    (74) *Sarah Quay, b* 27 January, 1862; *d* 16 November, 1862.

    (75) *Richard Roberts Quay.*

    (76) *Andrew Gregg Curtin Quay.*

    (77) *Mary Agnew Quay.*

    (78) *Coral Quay, b* 15 May, 1872.

    (79) *Jerome Anderson Quay, b* 11 December, 1874; *d* 11 August, 1875.

    (80) *Susan Willard Quay, b* 26 April, 1876.

21. **George W. Barclay,** *b* 1824; living 1903, Washington, Pa.; *m* 25 October, 1848, *Keziah Johnston.*

    (81) *William F. J. Barclay.*

    (82) *Sarah Barclay.*

25. **Martha Barclay,** living 1903, New Brighton, Pa.; *m James J. Mitchell.*

    (83) *Kirt Mitchell.*

29. **Dr. J. Thomas Barclay**, *b* 1836, Beaver, Pa.; living 1903, Cleveland, O.; *m* 1862, *Hannah P. Hisey, b* 1844; *d* 1898.

    (84) *Rose Barclay, b* 1863; living 1903; *m Levi A. Sackett, d* 12 April, 1897.

    (85) *Ella Barclay, b* 1868; living 1903.

    (86) *Ada Barclay, b* 1870; living 1903.

31. **Caroline Virginia Barclay**, *b* 1840; *d* 1900, Beaver Co., Pa.; *m* 1865, *David Scott, b* 1830; living 1903, Beaver Co., Pa.

    (87) *Marian Scott, b* 1866.

    (88) *John Wishart Scott, b* 1867.

    (89) *Jane Scott, b* 1873.

    (90) *Mary Scott,* living 1903, Alleghany, Pa.; *m* Rev. *Ira G. McCreary.*

33. **Robert Hunter Barclay**, *b* 11 February, 1847; *d* 2 March, 1894, Beaver Co., Pa.; *m* 1871, *Hannah Christy Potter, b* 7 May, 1852; living 1903.

    (91) *Elizabeth H. Barclay, b* 18 May, 1872; living 1903, Beaver Co., Pa.

    (92) *George P. Barclay, b* 8 April, 1875; living 1903, Beaver Co., Pa.

    (93) *Dr. Abram C. Barclay, b* 18 September, 1877; living 1903, Pittsburgh, Pa.

    (94) *James R. Barclay, b* 6 August, 1880; living 1903, Beaver Co., Pa.

    (95) *Amos E. A. Barclay, b* 13 October, 1890; living 1903, Beaver Co., Pa.

34. **Arthur Stanley Barclay**, *b* 1854; living 1903, Beaver Co., Pa.; *m Clara Morgan;* living 1903, Beaver Co., Pa.

    (96) *Arthur Jennings Barclay.*

    (97) *Earle Barclay.*

    (98) *Lila Barclay.*

    (99) *Gwendolen Barclay.*

43. **James Gailey Barclay**, *b* 20 March, 1849; living 1903, Beaver Co., Pa.; *m* (1) *Fannie Kair,* 17 September,

1876, by whom he had a daughter; *m* (2) *Annie White,* 18 June, 1879, by whom he had a daughter and a son.

(100) *Fannie A. Barclay, b* 10 July, 1877.

(101) *Elizabeth Barclay, b* 4 July, 1881.

(102) *Curtis C. Barclay, b* 5 August, 1883.

44. **Virginia Alice Barclay,** *b* 20 February, 1851; living 1903, New Brighton, Pa.; *m David Morgan.*

(103) *Lola V. Morgan, b* April, 1877.

(104) *Mary Edna Morgan, b* July, 1879.

46. **John Thomas Barclay,** *b* June, 1858; living 1903, Beaver Co., Pa.; *m Alice Mason.*

(105) *Nannie B. Barclay, b* 12 September, 1884.

(106) *Charles H. Barclay, b* 10 December, 1885.

(107) *Nellie M. Barclay, b* 26 September, 1887.

(108) *Ida E. Barclay, b* 27 July, 1890.

(109) *Edith O. Barclay, b* 24 March, 1892.

(110) *Ina F. Barclay, b* 10 September, 1894.

(111) *Mary J. Barclay, b* 31 July, 1896.

(112) *John M. Barclay, b* 1 August, 1898.

47. **Francis Johnston Barclay,** *b* 2 July, 1845; living 1903, Beaver Co., Pa.; *m* 10 October, 1867, *Sarah Elizabeth Johnston.*

(113) *Benoni Hunter Barclay, b* July, 1868; *d* 7 April, 1887.

(114) *Robert James Barclay, b* 8 January, 1876; *d* 4 April, 1877.

(115) *Thomas Dawson Barclay, b* 14 August, 1877; *m* 14 March, 1900, *Charlotte Spearhous.*

48. **Sarah Jane Barclay,** *b* 11 June, 1847; *m* 18 September, 1867, *Benjamin McGaffick.*

(116) *Robert McGaffick, m Margaret Spearhaus.*

(117) *Dallas McGaffick, m Della Stephenson.*

(118) *John Johnston McGaffick, m Jennie Spearhaus.*

(119) *Lulela McGaffick, m William Hunter.*

(120) *William McGaffick, m Bertha Taylor.*

(121) *Herfie McGaffick, m Maud May.*

49. **William Hunter Barclay,** *b* June, 1849; living 1903, Beaver Co., Pa.; *m* 3 July, 1877, *Jennie Graham.*

  (122) *Nancy Florence Barclay.*

50. **Mary Adaline Barclay,** *b* 15 October, 1850; living 1903, Beaver, Pa.; *m* 18 September, 1873, *Todd H. Anderson.*

  (123) *Harry Anderson, b* 11 March, 1874.
  (124) *William Anderson, b* and *d* 1876.
  (125) *Charles R. Anderson, b* 7 May, 1877.
  (126) *Clarence Anderson, b* 16 August, 1879.
  (127) *Samuel B. Anderson, b* 25 October, 1886.
  (128) *Glenn Anderson, b* 7 August, 1891.

51. **Elizabeth C. Barclay,** *b* 8 October, 1853; living 1903, Beaver Co., Pa.; *m* 18 September, 1873, *William James Johnston.*

  (129) *George Curtice Johnston.*
  (130) *Annie Mary Johnston.*

52. **Thomas Howard Barclay,** *b* 15 April, 1858; *m* 12 August, 1886, *Ellen M. Crawford.*

  (131) *Harlan C. Barclay, b* 24 March, 1887.
  (132) *Robert W. Barclay, b* 3 February, 1889.
  (133) *Fay E. Barclay,* } *b* August, 1890; *d* July,
  (134) *May Barclay,*   }   1891.

53. **Margaret Malinda Barclay,** *b* 13 April, 1860; *m* 25 June, 1885, *James A. Dawson.*

  (135) *Ettie M. Dawson, b* 22 June, 1886.
  (136) *Mary H. Dawson, b* 17 May, 1896.

54. **George Stanley Barclay,** *b* 21 November, 1862; *m* 28 October, 1886, *Rosanna Dowds.*

  (137) *Robert James Barclay, b* 1 November, 1896.
  (138) *Ines Viola Barclay, b* 19 March, 1899.

56. **Ettie Olga Barclay,** *b* 28 December, 1867; *m* 21 September, 1887, *Willington S. Moore.*

  (139) *Mary H. Moore, b* 8 August, 1888.
  (140) *Forest W. Moore, b* 22 September, 1893.

57. **Erskine B. Barclay,** *b* 9 April, 1848, Ossian, Ind.; living 1903, Littleton, Iowa; *m* 25 May, 1871, *Eliza, J. Barber, b* 2 November, 1845.

    (141) *John Erskine Barclay.*
    (142) *Charles Sumner Barclay.*
    (143) *Nellie Maud Barclay, b* 25 December, 1876.
    (144) *Daisy Lillian Barclay, b* 25 October, 1878.
    (145) *Elbert Earl Barclay, b* 5 April, 1882.
    (146) *Agnes Mabel Barclay, b* 15 April, 1889.

64. **Ida Barclay,** *b* 27 January, 1854; living 1903, Beaver Co., Pa.; *m* 1873, *Alexander Hunter.*

    (147) *Stella Hunter.*
    (148) *Ethel Hunter.*
    (149) *Howard Leland Hunter.*

75. **Richard Roberts Quay,** *b* 15 November, 1863; *m* 12 June, 1895, *Elizabeth Waters.*

    (150) *Matthew Stanley Quay, b* 4 June, 1897.
    (151) *Elizabeth Waters Quay, b* 13 September, 1899.

76. **Andrew Gregg Curtin Quay,** *b* 3 January, 1866; *m* 7 July, 1899, *Mary Dempsey.*

    (152) *Andrew Gregg Curtin Quay, b* 28 September, 1900.

77. **Mary Agnew Quay,** *b* 2 October, 1868; *m Lewis Davidson,* 29 January, 1896.

    (153) *Agnes Quay Davidson, b* 22 October, 1896.

122. **Nancy Florence Barclay,** *b* 8 April, 1878; *m* 24 January, 1901, *Andrew H. Watterson.*

    (154) *Mary Elizabeth Watterson, b* 18 February, 1902.

129. **George Curtice Johnston,** *b* 6 June, 1874; *m* 2 May, 1893, *Lillian Bell Hinewar.*

    (155) *Anna Elizabeth Johnston, b* 30 March, 1894.
    (156) *Harry Jennings Johnston, b* 1 December, 1896.

130. **Annie Mary Johnston,** *b* 5 January, 1879; *m* 10 November, 1898, *Oliver A. Reed.*

> (157) *Willard Johnston Reed, b* 19 August, 1900.

141. **John Erskine Barclay,** *b* 25 May, 1872; *m* 25 December, 1897, *Georgia E. Smith, b* 10 December, 1874.

> (158) *Berdena J. Barclay, b* 14 June, 1901.

142. **Charles Sumner Barclay,** *b* 25 December, 1874; *m* 25 December, 1899, *Minnie E. Kingsbury.*

> (159) *Esther Marie Barclay, b* 24 December, 1900.

---

1. **Robert Barclay.**

> (2) *Robert Barclay.*
> (3) *John Barclay,* lived in Philadelphia.

2. **Robert Barclay,** served in war of 1812; *d* soon afterwards; *m Ann* ———

> (4) *James Barclay.*
> (5) *Robert Barclay.*
> (6) *John Barclay, d* New Orleans 1844; *m Sarah Cook.*

4. **James Barclay,** *b* 21 September, 1810, Doylestown, Bucks Co., Pa.; *d* 29 August, 1896; *m Elizabeth Dyer.*

> (7) *John D. Barclay.*
> (8) *Ann Elizabeth D. Barclay, b* 4 September, 1837, Dyerstown, Pa.
> (9) *James Barclay.*

5. **Robert Barclay,** *d* Philadelphia, 1881; *m Mary Ann Drexel.*

> (10) *Ann Eliza Barclay, b* 31 July, 1835; *d* 22 October, 1876.
> (11) *Sarah Barclay, b* 31 May, 1841, Philadelphia.
> (12) *Robert Barclay, b* 7 June, 1843; *d* 28 October, 1877.
> (13) *Emma Barclay, b* 8 August, 1845, Philadelphia.
> (14) *William Barclay, b* 24 January, 1848, Philadelphia.

7. **John D. Barclay,** *b* 17 November, 1834, Philadelphia; *d* 1903; *m Caroline A. Thompson, d* 16 January, 1872.

> (15) *Joseph D. Barclay.*
> (16) *William F. Barclay.*
> (17) *John F. Barclay, b* 31 May, 1861, Dyerstown, Pa.
> (18) *Carrie A. Barclay, b* 23 December, 1865, Dyerstown, Pa.
> (19) *Charles T. Barclay, b* 7 March, 1867; *d* 1873.

9. **James Barclay,** *b* 20 August, 1841, Dyerstown, Pa.; *m Clara A. McClain, b* 3 October, 1848.

> (20) *Bertha E. Barclay, b* 15 April, 1881, Dyerstown, Pa.
> (21) *Lillian Barclay, b* 13 July, 1884.

15. **Joseph D. Barclay,** *b* 1 August, 1858, Philadelphia; *m Ida Ullmer.*

> (22) *Charles C. Barclay, b* 10 September, 1881, Philadelphia.
> (23) *Frank L. Barclay,* } *b* 22 August, 1883, Phila-
> (24) *Maud L. Barclay,* } delphia.
> (25) *Ethel Barclay, b* 26 June, 1886, Philadelphia.
> (26) *Joseph H. Barclay, b* 19 June, 1890, Philadelphia.

16. **William F. Barclay,** *b* 4 October, 1859, Philadelphia; *m Maggie Desmond.*

> (27) *Mary D. Barclay, b* 14 May, 1889, Philadelphia.
> (28) *Thomas Barclay, b* 12 August, 1890, Philadelphia.
> (29) *Helen Barclay, b* 25 November, 1892, Philadelphia.
> (30) *Alice Barclay, b* 30 June, 1895, Philadelphia.
> (31) *William Barclay, b* 3 January, 1901, Philadelphia.

1. **Richard Barclay,** *b* North of Scotland. Came to America abt. 1735; *m* ———— *Cragg.*

> (2) *John Barclay,* said to have served as Colonel in Revolutionary War.
>
> (3) *Hugh Barclay,* a merchant in Philadelphia.
>
> (4) *Richard Barclay.*
>
> (5) ———— *Barclay,* a daughter; *m* ———— *Barnhill* of Kentucky.

4. **Richard Barclay,** *b* 1766 Philadelphia; *d* Northumberland Co., Pa., 1846; *m Hannah Smith.*

> (6) *George Barclay.*
>
> (7) *Effie Barclay.*
>
> (8) *John Barclay.*
>
> (9) *James Barclay.*
>
> (10) *Margaret Barclay.*
>
> (11) *Ann Barclay.*
>
> (12) *Smith Barclay.*

6. **George Barclay,** *b* 12 February, 1789, Montgomery Co., Pa.; *d* July, 1828, Northumberland Co., Pa.; *m Hetty Murray.*

> (13) *James M. Barclay.*
>
> (14) *Effie C. Barclay, b* 1818; *d* 30 June, 1895.
>
> (15) *Richard Barclay, b* 23 January, 1822.
>
> (16) *Thomas Barclay, b* 20 January, 1824.
>
> (17) *John Barclay, b* 28 December, 1826.
>
> (18) *Annabel Barclay, b* 7 December, 1828; living 1903.

13. **James M. Barclay,** *b* 17 June, 1817, Lycoming Co., Pa.; *d* 1850, Pottsgrove, Pa.; *m Mary Britton, d* 1890.

> (19) *Urana H. Barclay.*
>
> (20) *George N. Barclay.*
>
> (21) *Margaret Barclay, b* 1846; *d* 1848.
>
> (22) *Britton Barclay, m Margaret Cottoner.* Had issue.

19. **Urana H. Barclay,** *b* 1842; *m David Shoemaker* of Mill-
ville, Pa.

   (23) *George Shoemaker,* living 1902; *m* and had
   issue.

   (24) *Henry Shoemaker, m Ida Stadler;* living 1903;
   had issue.

   (25) *William Shoemaker,* living 1903, *unm.*

20. **George N. Barclay,** *b* 1844; living 1903, Milton, Pa.; *m
   Elizabeth Murdock.*

   (26) *Nellie Barclay, d* in infancy.

   (27) *Jennie Barclay, b* 16 October, 1874; living 1903,
   Columbia, Pa.; *m James Harrison.* Had issue.

   (28) *James H. Barclay, b* 3 October, 1879; living
   1903, Milton, Pa., *unm.*

1. **William Barclay,** lived in Philadelphia.

   (2) *William J. Barclay.*

   (3) *Mary Barclay.*

2. **William J. Barclay,** *b* 1 January, 1804, Philadelphia; *d* 9
   March, 1859, in Philadelphia; *m* 8 September, 1842,
   Anna Musgrave, d 1 February, 1847.

   (4) *Charles J. Barclay.*

   (5) *Anna Musgrave Barclay, b* 17 January, 1847;
   living 1897, *m.*

4. **Charles J. Barclay** (U.S.N.), *b* 8 September, 1843; *m
   Annie T. Tohey,* 17 February, 1868, in New Bedford,
   Mass.

   (6) *Edith M. Barclay, b* 10 June, 1877.

1. **Robert Charles Colquhoun Barclay,** *b* 16 July, 1822, Six
   Mile Cross, near Belfast, Ireland; *d* 25 January, 1891,
   in England; *m Annie Dobson, b* 25 October, 1846; living
   1903, England.

(2) *Isabelle Barclay, b* 25 December, 1864; living 1903, England; *m* 15 July, 1897, *David Far-ragher.*

(3) *Hamilton C. Barclay, b* 22 February, 1866, Bleasdale, Lancashire, Eng. Came to America 1880. Living 1903, Newberg, Oregon.

(4) *Charles C. Barclay.*

(5) *Mary H. Barclay, b* 3 January, 1870, Bleasdale, Lancashire, Eng; living 1903, England.

(6) *Frank A. Barclay, b* 12 December, 1873, Bleasdale, Lancashire, Eng. Came to America 1892. Living Chatfield, Minn., 1903; *m Grace Arnold,* 1899.

(7) *Alexander V. Barclay, b* 14 February, 1875, Bleasdale, Lancashire, Eng. Came to America 1893. Living Dickinson, N. D., 1903.

(8) *Annie Barclay, b* 16 February, 1877, Bleasdale, Lancashire, Eng. Living 1903, England.

(9) *Kenneth Barclay, b* 16 May, 1885, in England. Came to America 1902. Living St. Paul, Minn., 1903.

4. **Charles C. Barclay,** *b* 6 January, 1868, Bleasdale, Lancashire, Eng. Came to America 1884. Living St. Paul, Minn., 1903; *m Alice Alexander,* 15 April, 1891.

(10) *Marguerite Barclay, b* 21 January, 1892, St. Paul, Minn.; living St. Paul, Minn., 1903.

---

1. ———— **Barclay,** of Pennsylvania. It is said that he took part in the Revolutionary War, and at the close was granted a tract of land on which a part of Philadelphia now stands. After his death, his widow and her three sons and two daughters moved to Missouri.

(2) *John Barclay.*

(3) *Joseph Barclay.*

(4) ———— *Barclay.*

2. **John Barclay,** *b* abt. 1804 (probably in Pittsburgh, Pa.);
   d 1873, St. Louis, Mo.; *m Julia Pensoneau.*

> (5) *James Francis Barclay.*
> (6) *Julia Barclay, d* 1878; *m Joseph Boismenne.*
> (7) *Amelia Barclay, d* 1872; *m James Williams.*
> (8) *Elizabeth Barclay, d* 1891; *m Antoine Chouquette.*
> (9) *Mary A. Barclay,* living 1903, St. Louis, Mo., *unm.*

5. **James Francis Barclay,** *b* 1837, Cohokia, Ill.; *d* 1890,
   Kansas City, Mo.; *m Eleanor Ford,* 7 June, 1863.

> (10) *William A. Barclay, b* 1865, E. St. Louis, Mo.;
> living 1903, Kansas City, Mo.
> (11) *Catherine Barclay, b* 1869, Kansas City, Mo.;
> *d* 1872.
> (12) *May Barclay, b* 1871, Kansas City, Mo.; *d* 1880.
> (13) *Nona L. Barclay, b* 1875, Kansas City, Mo.; *m*
> 1899, *J. C. Jordan.*
> (14) *James F. Barclay, b* 1878, Kansas City, Mo.;
> *d* 1881.
> (15) *Charlotte Barclay, b* 1884, Kansas City, Mo.;
> *d* 1899.
> and 4 other children, who died less than a year old.

---

1. **William Barclay,** lived in Ireland. (Had two brothers
   and one sister.)

> (2) *James J. Barclay.*

2. **James J. Barclay,** *b* Fimaley, Ireland, 1819; *d* St. Louis,
   Mo., August, 1889. Served in Co. F, Maryland Volunteers, during Mexican War. Honorably discharged
   December, 1847. *m Margaret Kane* in Philadelphia
   (St. Joseph's Church); *b* Galway, Ireland. Had 2 sons
   and 7 daughters. Sons living in 1897.

> (3) *William E. Barclay,* living in St. Louis, Mo.,
> 1897.

1. **John Barclay,** *b* 1800, Parish of Abercorn, Linlithgow-shire, Scotland; *m Jane Angus, b* 1812.

    (2) *James Barclay.*

2. **James Barclay,** *b* Edinburgh, Scotland, 1833. Came to Cincinnati, O., in 1857. *m* in Cincinnati, 1858, *Christina Veitch* of Edinburgh, Scotland.

    (3) *John Barclay, b* Cincinnati, O., 9 March, 1859; *m* 25 October, 1886, *Elizabeth Schmidt.*

    (4) *Elizabeth Jane Barclay, b* Cincinnati, O., 16 June, 1860.

    (5) *Christina Barclay, b* Cincinnati, O., 24 September, 1862; *m* 24 October, 1886, *Arthur H. Morrow.*

    (6) *James Barclay, b* Edinburgh, Scotland, 27 September, 1864.

    (7) *Jane Barclay, b* Chicago, Ill., 29 June, 1866.

    (8) *Alexander Barclay, b* Cincinnati, O., 7 September, 1868; *m* 28 April, 1895, *Nettie Hill.*

    (9) *William C. Barclay, b* Cincinnati, O., 27 February, 1871.

---

1. **Bartholomew Barclay,** *b* 1780, Knox, Albany Co., N. Y.; *d* 6 May, 1857, Fredonia, N. Y.; *m* (circ.) 1807, *Katherine Gibbs, b* 1788; *d* 1871.

    (2) *Charles Edward Barclay.*

    (3) *James Henry Barclay.*

    (4) *George Theodore Barclay.*

    (5) *Harriet Elizabeth Barclay.*

    (6) *Sidney De Witt Barclay.*

    (7) *Egbert Wallace Barclay.*

    (8) *Sheldon Spencer Barclay, b* 1823, Pulaski, N. Y.; *d* 1896, Corry, Pa.; *m Helen Payne,* 1847, Holly, N. Y.

    (9) *Katherine Gibbs Barclay, b* 1823, Pulaski, N. Y.; *d* 1826.

    (10) *Helen Mar Barclay.*

2. **Charles Edward Barclay**, *b* 28 December, 1808, Albany,
   N. Y.; *d* 1 March, 1879, Columbus, Pa.; *m* (1) *Charlotte Cole, 1830; m* (2) *Malinda Ward* (widow), 1862.

   (11) *Maria Louise Barclay.*

   (12) *Mary Olive Barclay, b* 1838, Dunkirk, N. Y.;
   living 1903, Corry, Pa.

   (13) *Charlotte Eliza Barclay.*

   (14) *Edward M. Gibbs Barclay, b* 1842, Fredonia,
   N. Y.; *d* 1902, Sandusky, O.; *m Harriet
   Palmer.*

   (15) *Emily Stativa Barclay.*

   (16) *Florence Caroline Barclay.*

   (17) *Helen Catherine Barclay, b* 1848, Fredonia,
   N. Y.; *d* 1880.

3. **James Henry Barclay,** *b* abt. 1812, Albany, N. Y.; *d* 1885,
   Dunkirk, N. Y.; *m* (1) *Genette Langdon*, 1835, Dunkirk, N. Y., by whom he had 1 daughter and 2 sons; *m*
   (2) *Lucy Wilcox*, 1857, Dunkirk, N. Y., by whom he
   had 1 son.

   (18) *Delia Isabell Barclay, b* 1834, Dunkirk, N. Y.;
   living 1903, Hutchinson, Kan.; *m* ———
   Crosby.

   (19) *John Langdon Barclay, b* 1838, Dunkirk, N. Y.;
   living 1903, Dunkirk; *m* (1) *Sarah Christy;
   m* (2) *Kate Trestler.*

   (20) *Eugene La Droit Barclay, b* 1839, Dunkirk,
   N. Y.; *d* 1871, Dunkirk.

   (21) *William Wilcox Barclay, b* 1859, Laona, N. Y.;
   living 1903, Brooklyn, N. Y.

4. **George Theodore Barclay,** *b* 1814, Lennox, Mass.; *d* 1893,
   Red Wing, Minn.; *m Sarah Ann Hanson*, 1841, Auriesville, N. Y.

   (22) *Henrietta Barclay.*

5. **Harriet Elizabeth Barclay,** *b* 1816, Lennox, Mass.; *d*
   1868, Middlebury, N. Y.; *m Horace Crary*, 1851.

(23) *Courtenay Dennison Crary, b* 1852, Gallupville, N. Y.; living 1903, Chicago; *m Charlotte Vroman.*

(24) *Catherine Crary, b* 1858, Gallupville, N. Y.; living 1903, Wheaton, Ill.; *m Charles Daubé.*

6. **Sidney DeWitt Barclay,** *b* 1818, Pulaski, N. Y.; *d* 1861, N. Y. City; *m Elizabeth Randall,* 1847, N. Y.

(25) *Frances Coralin Barclay.*

7. **Egbert Wallace Barclay,** *b* 1819, Pulaski, N. Y.; *d* 1897, Chicago; *m Helena Walworth Matteson,* 1842, Jamestown, N. Y.

(26) *Alice Tracy Barclay, b* abt. 1845, Fredonia, N. Y.; living 1903, Chenoa, Ill.; *m Richard M. Moore.*

(27) *Cora Matteson Barclay.*

(28) *Sarah Apphia Barclay.*

(29) *Gertrude Agnes Barclay, b* 1851, Dunkirk, N. Y.; living 1903, Chicago; *m Howard Smith.*

10. **Helen Mar Barclay,** *b* 4 September, 1830, Pulaski, N. Y.; living 1903, N. Y. City; *m Smith Ely Goodrich.*

(30) *Edward Ward Goodrich, b* 1858, Fredonia, N. Y.; *d* 1860, Titusville, Pa.

(31) *Sidney Barclay Goodrich, b* 1862, Union, Pa.; living 1903, N. Y. City; *m Alide F. Braynard.*

11. **Maria Louise Barclay,** *b* 1836, Dunkirk, N. Y.; living 1903, N. Y. City; *m Carlton Hinman.*

(32) *Helen Zaidee Hinman, b* 20 October, 1856, Dunkirk, N. Y.; *d* 6 November, 1864, Louisville, Ky.

(33) *Charles Carlton Hinman, b* 19 December, 1857, Dunkirk, N. Y.; *d* 1857, Dunkirk.

(34) *Frank Barclay Hinman, b* 10 March, 1866, Louisville, Ky.

13. **Charlotte Eliza Barclay,** *b* 1840, Dunkirk, N. Y.; *d* 1885, Meadville, Pa.; *m Timothy Stillman.*

    (35) *Edward Stillman, b* Dunkirk, N. Y.

    (36) *Kate Louise Stillman, b* 1863, Columbus, Pa.

    (37) *Charlotte Stillman, b* 1865, Dunkirk, N. Y.

    (38) *Ruel Barclay Stillman, b* 1866, Dunkirk, N. Y.

    (39) *Albert Abel Stillman, b* Meadville, Pa.

    (40) *Clara Blanchard Stillman, b* Meadville, Pa.

    (41) *Charles Edward Stillman, b* 1879, Meadville, Pa.

15. **Emily Stativa Barclay,** *b* 1844, Fredonia, N. Y., *d* 1890, Chicago; *m Hiram S. Wheeler,* 1860.

    (42) *Charles Carlton Wheeler, b* Fredonia, N. Y.

    (43) *Edward Lester Wheeler, b* Chicago.

    (44) *Florence Louise Wheeler, b* Chicago.

    (45) *Mary Alice Wheeler, b* Chicago.

    (46) *Hiram Eugene Wheeler, b* Chicago.

16. **Florence Caroline Barclay,** *b* 1846, Fredonia, N. Y.; living 1903, Butler, Pa.; *m R. W. Hall.*

    (47) *Jessie Barclay Hall, b* 1870, Titusville, Pa.

22. **Henrietta Barclay,** *b* 1842, Auriesville, N. Y.; living 1903, Minneapolis, Minn.; *m James Wright,* 6 December, 1856, De Witt, Iowa.

    (48) *Nellie Wright, b* 15 July, 1858, Dunleith, Ill.; living 1903, Minneapolis, *unm.*

    (49) *Martin Vory Wright, b* 10 July, 1863, Red Wing, Minn.; *d* 1884, Red Wing, Minn., *unm.*

    (50) *Henrietta Barclay Wright.*

    (51) *Rosamond Wright.*

    (52) *Sarah Wright, b* August, 1880, Red Wing, Minn.; *d* October, 1880.

25. **Frances Coralin Barclay,** *b* 1848, N. Y. City; living 1903, N. Y. City; *m James A. Seaman.*

    (53) *Elizabeth Barclay Seaman.*

    (54) *Caroline R. Seaman, b* 1846, N. Y.; living 1903, N. Y., *unm.*

(55) *Robert R. Seaman, b* 1866; living 1903, *unm.*

(56) *Helen Frances Seaman, b* 1871; living 1903, *unm.*

27. **Cora Matteson Barclay,** *b* 1846, Fredonia, N. Y.; living 1903, Chicago; *m* (1) *James Oliver; m* (2) *Carl Matteson.*

> (57) *Mabel Matteson, b* Chicago, 1882.
>
> (58) *Beatrice Matteson, b* Chicago, 1885.

28. **Sarah Apphia Barclay,** *b* 1848, Buffalo, N. Y.; living 1903, Brooklyn, N. Y.; *m* 23 March, 1872, *William E. Roach,* St. Thomas, Canada.

> (59) *Winifred Roach, b* 18 February, 1873, Erie, Pa.; *d* 24 August, 1873.
>
> (60) *William E. Roach, b* 7 June, 1874, Chicago; *d* 24 September, 1898, Lancaster, Pa.
>
> (61) *Cora Matteson Roach.*
>
> (62) *Elizabeth Gertrude Roach, b* 10 March, 1878, Chicago.
>
> (63) *Clara Winewood Roach, b* 6 January, 1882, Chicago; *d* February, 1882.
>
> (64) *David J. Matteson Roach, b* 13 July, 1887, Erie, Pa.

50. **Henrietta Barclay Wright,** *b* 22 March, 1868, Red Wing, Minn.; living 1903, St. Paul, Minn.; *m* 28 December, 1899, *Herbert Nininger Paist, b* St. Paul, Minn., 13 October, 1861.

> (65) *Lawrence Barclay Paist, b* August, 1901, Minneapolis, Minn.

51. **Rosamond Wright,** *b* 13 January, 1878, Red Wing, Minn.; living 1903, Minneapolis, Minn.; *m Howard Reno,* 1901.

> (66) *John Christmas Reno, b* 6 March, 1902.

53. **Elizabeth Barclay Seaman,** *b* 1863, N. Y.; living 1903, N. Y.; *m John Mortimer Huiell,* 8 September, 1897.

> (67) *Barclay V. Seaman Huiell, b* 1898, Richmond Hill, N. Y.

61. **Cora Matteson Roach,** *b* 30 September, 1876, Chicago;
m 5 October, 1899, *Raymond A. Millard,* Montrose, Pa.
  (68) *Raymond Eugene Millard, b* 30 March, 1901,
  Kane, Pa.

———

1. ——— **Barclay,** of England or Scotland.   Came to America and located at Bensalem, Bucks Co., Pa.; *d* abt. four
years after coming to America.
  (2) *John Barclay,* went to Ohio.
  (3) *Thomas Barclay,* returned to England.
  (4) *William Barclay,* a sailor.
  (5) *Moses Barclay.*

5. **Moses Barclay,** came to America with his parents when 8
years old, and located at Bensalem, Bucks Co., Pa.
Afterwards settled in Burlington Co., New Jersey.
  (6) *John W. Barclay,* living 1897, Camden, N. J.
      (an old man).   No sons living in 1897.
  (7) ——— *Barclay,* an old man, living in 1897.   No
      sons living in 1897.

———

1. **Samuel Barclay,** *b* 1853; *m Mary Everett.* Lived near
Suffolk, Va.   Came from New York City.   Had a
brother who served in the Revolutionary War.
  (2) *Samuel Barclay.*
  (3) *William Barclay, d* 1857.
  (4) *John Barclay, d* 1864.
  (5) *Sarah Barclay, d* 1880.
  (6) *Nellie Barclay, d* 1889.
  (7) *Julia Barclay, d* in infancy.

2. **Samuel Barclay,** *b* 1815; *d* 5 December, 1890; *m* 4 August,
1856, *Amanda Hill.*
  (8) *Samuel Barclay, b* 30 May, 1857; *m Martha
      Sykes.*   No issue.

(9) *Julia Barclay, b* 4 August, 1859; *m Joshua Harrell.* Had issue.

(10) *Christopher C. Barclay, b* 12 January, 1864; living Norfolk, Va., 1903; *m Eugenia Cox.* Had issue.

(11) *Mary Barclay, b* 17 March, 1866; *m William Ballance.*

(12) *Sarah Barclay, b* 17 March, 1868; *m George Gray.*

(13) *Eugene Bohanous Barclay, b* 26 April, 1870; *m Sari Nunnelly.*

(14) *John Everett Barclay, b* September 9, 1872; *m Irene Lonsberry.* Had issue.

(15) *Starks Jerome Barclay, b* 23 December, 1875; unmarried 1903.

(16) *Laura Barclay, b* 1 August, 1878; unmarried 1903.

----

1. **David Barclay,** *b* Pennsylvania, 1798; *d* Lyons, N. Y., 1856. Was a soldier in War of 1812.

    (2) *George Barclay.*

    (3) *John Barclay.*

    (4) *Charles Barclay.*

    (5) *William Barclay,* living Jamestown Centre, Mich., 1903.

    (6) *Ezra Barclay.*

    (7) *Elizabeth Barclay.*

    (8) *Jane Barclay.*

    (9) *Spencer Barclay,* living 1903, Potsdam, N. Y.

2. **George Barclay.**

    (10) *George Barclay,* living 1903, St. Louis, Mo.

3. **John Barclay.**

    (11) *Charles Barclay,* living 1897, Adams Basin, N. Y.

    (12) *Lewis Barclay,* living 1903, Grand Ledge, Mich.

4. **Charles Barclay**, *b* 1 May, 1819, Lyons, N. Y.; *d* 12 February, 1884, Grand Rapids, Mich. Was a soldier in War of the Rebellion.

    (13) *Warren Y. Barclay.*

13. **Warren Y. Barclay**, *b* Otisco, Mich., 27 March, 1851; living 1903, Grand Rapids, Mich.; *m* 16 April, 1873, *Dora A. Bigelow*, at Grand Rapids.

    (14) *Jennie Myrtle Barclay, b* 18 January, 1874, Grand Rapids.

    (15) *Warren D. Barclay, b* 27 January, 1877; *d* 1881, Grand Rapids.

    (16) *Stella Belle Barclay, b* 9 September, 1881, Grand Rapids.

    (17) *Wallace Guy Barclay, b* 30 July, 1883, Grand Rapids.

---

1. **James Barkley**, came from Dublin, Ireland, with the "Clinton Party," by ship "George & Anne." Landed at Cape Cod 4 October, 1729. Went first to New York City, then to Basking Ridge, N. J. (having relatives in both places), and subsequently settled in what is now Orange Co., N. Y. *m Mary Moffat.*

    (2) *Mary Barkley, d* in infancy.

    (3) *Samuel Barkley.*

    (4) *John Barkley.*

    (5) *James Barkley.*

    (6) *William Barkley.*

    (7) *Thomas Barkley.*

    (8) *Margaret Barkley.*

3. **Samuel Barkley**, *b* 26 October, 1743; *d* 17 April, 1814; lived in Sullivan Co., N. Y.; *m* (1) *Catherine Mc-Claughry*, 28 December, 1769, by whom he had 5 children; *m* (2) *Nancy McCurdy*, 15 February, 1787, by whom he had 8 children.

    (9) *Mary Barkley.*

    (10) *Jane Barkley.*

(11) *Samuel Barkley.*

(12) *Thomas Barkley, b* 3 May, 1783; *d unm.*

(13) *Elizabeth Barkley.*

(14) *Robert M. Barkley, b* 20 January, 1788; *d unm.*

(15) *James S. Barkley, b* 23 November, 1789; *d unm.*

(16) *Catherine Barkley, b* 24 April, 1792; *d* 22 December, 1879; *m Robert S. Crawford.* No issue.

(17) *Margaret Barkley* ("Peggy"), *b* 6 December, 1794; *d unm.*

(18) *Andrew King Barkely.*

(19) *John Barkely, b* 3 April, 1800; *d* in infancy.

(20) *Marcus Barkley, b* 17 April, 1804; *d unm.*

(21) *Nancy Barkley.*

4. **John Barkley,** *b* 1745; *d* 7th September, 1786; *m Mary Crawford,* dau. James and Jean (Crawford) Crawford, *b* 6 May, 1752; *d* 4 September, 1786.

(22) *Nathan Barkley.*

(23) *William Barkley, d unm.*

(24) *Jane Barkley.*

5. **James Barkley,** *m Elizabeth Crawford,* dau. James and Jean (Crawford) Crawford, *b* 27 November, 1753.

(25) *John Barkley, d unm.*

(26) *Ellen Barkley, m Daniel Hunter.*

(27) *Betsey Barkley, d unm.*

(28) *Samuel Barkley, d unm.*

(29) *Joshua Barkley, m Agnes Millspaugh.*

(30) *Daniel Barkley.*

(31) *Moses Barkley, d unm.*

6. **William Barkley,** *m Sarah Gaston.*

(32) *Joseph Barkley.*

(33) *James Barkley.*

(34) *Hugh Barkley.*

(35) *William Barkley.*

(36) *Jane Barkley.*

(37) *Mary Barkley, d unm.*

7. **Thomas Barkley,** *d* 1821; *m* 7 December, 1779, *Sarah Crawford, b* 11 February, 1763; *d* 19 September, 1826; dau. James and Jean (Crawford) Crawford.

    (38) *James Barkley.*

    (39) *Mary Barkley.*

    (40) *David Barkley.*

    (41) *John Barkley.*

    (42) *Jonathan Barkley, b* 9 April, 1789.

    (43) *Jane Barkley, b* 19 February, 1791; *m Nathan Haines,* 27 October, 1808. Had 8 children.

    (44) *Josiah Barkley.*

    (45) *Margaret Barkley, b* 10 February, 1795; *m* (1) *Johnston Young; m* (2) *Nelson Harris.* Had 5 children.

    (46) *Thomas Barkley, b* 21 December, 1797; *m Mary Crawford.*

    (47) *William Moffat Barkley, b* 24 December, 1799; *d* 12 March, 1800.

    (48) *Elizabeth Barkley, b* 5 May, 1801; *m David Arnot.* Had 10 children.

8. **Margaret Barkley,** *m James Sears.*

    (49) *Mary Sears.*

    (50) *William Sears, m Mary Crawford.*

    (51) *James Sears.*

    (52) *John Sears, m Phoebe Conger.*

    (53) *Samuel Sears.*

    (54) *Eliza Sears.*

9. **Mary Barkley,** *b* 23 October, 1770; *m P. Millspaugh.*

    (55) *Agnes Millspaugh, m John B. Hall.*

    (56) *Mary Millspaugh, m* Dr. ———— *Stanson.*

    (57) *Susan Millspaugh, m* ———— *White.*

    (58) *Comfort Millspaugh, d unm.*

    (59) *Marcus Millspaugh.*

    (60) *Elizabeth Millspaugh, m* ———— *Parsons.*

10. **Jane Barkley,** *b* 13 September, 1778; *m Henry Christ,* 21 January, 1802.

(61) *Samuel Christ, m Catherine Hunter.*
(62) *Millspaugh Christ, m ——— Hunter.*
(63) *Blake Christ.*
(64) *John Christ.*
(65) *Henry Christ, m Miriam Hollister.*
(66) *Jane Christ, m ——— Corey.*
(67) *Mary Christ, m Stephen Wood.*
(68) *Parna Christ, d unm.*

11. **Samuel Barkley,** *b* 13 December, 1780; *m* (1) *Catherine Crawford,* by whom he had 6 children; *m* (2) *Parney Hurd,* by whom he had 2 children.

The descendants of Samuel Barkley spelled their names "Barclay."

(69) *Margaret Barclay.*
(70) *Alexander Crawford Barclay.*
(71) *Mary Ellen Barclay.*
(72) *Marcus S. Barclay.*
(73) *Rachel Barclay.*
(74) *Nancy Barclay, d unm.*
(75) *James S. Barclay.*
(76) *Catherine Barclay.*

13. **Elizabeth Barkley,** *b* 28 August, 1786; *m* 28 February, 1807, *George Pitts.*

(77) *Virgil Pitts.*
(78) *Samuel Pitts.*
(79) *Harvey Pitts, m Loretta Norris.*
(80) *Henry Pitts.*
(81) *James B. Pitts, m Elizabeth Cromell.*
(82) *Matilda Pitts, m Daniel Schaffer.*
(83) *Marcus B. Pitts, m Mary Allen.*

18. **Andrew King Barkley,** *b* 31 July, 1797; *d* 23 May, 1875; *m Patty Smith.*

(84) *William Berger Barkley, d unm.*

21. **Nancy Barkley,** *b* 9 January, 1807; *m* 23 January, 1838, *Leander Crawford.*

(85) *James Barkely, b* 2 November, 1838; *d* 24 October, 1866; *m Mary C. Carpenter.*

(86) *Anna Barkley, m Alsop Purdy.*

(87) *Ella Barkley, m Albert Bull.*

22. Nathan Barkley, *m Sally Ann Patterson.*

(88) *Ellen Jane Barkley, m Matthew Brown.*

24. Jane Barkley, *b* 12 March, 1784; *d* 6 March, 1823; *m* 29 January, 1803, *James W. Crawford,* son of William and Margaret (Buchanan) Crawford.

(89) *William B. Crawford.*

(90) *David Crawford.*

30. Daniel Barkley, *m* (1) *Sally Barclay,* dau. Capt. James and Mary Barclay, by whom he had 4 children; *m* (2) *Sarah (Dickerson) Crawford,* widow of George Crawford, son of John and Sarah Barkley Crawford.

(91) *James Barkley, m Nancy Stevenson.*

(92) *Alfred Barkley.*

(93) *Gaston Barkley, m Caroline Lease.*

(94) *Virgil Barkley.*

(95) *Robert Barkley, m* ——— *Campbell.*

(96) *Elizabeth Barkley.*

(97) *Mary Barkley.*

32. Joseph Barkley, *m Susannah Cooper.*

(98) *Sarah Barkley, m* (1) *James Comfort; m* (2) *James Scaff.*

(99) *Mary Barkley, d unm.*

(100) *William Cooper Barkley.*

(101) *Eliza Barkley, m Ira Clark.*

(102) *Barbara M. Barkley, m David Lease.*

(103) *Henry Barkley, m Catherine Lybolt.*

(104) *Jane Barkley, m Sylvester Kent.*

(105) *Sidney Barkley, d unm.*

(106) *Milton Barkley, d unm.*

(107) *Rachel Barkley, d unm.*

(108) *Susan Barkley, m Torrence Sheen.*

33. **James Barkley,** *m Mary* ———.

> (109) *James Barkley, m Cornelia VanGordon.*
> (110) *Sarah Barkley, m Daniel Barkley.*
> (111) *Lucretia Barkley, m* (1) *Alex. Millspaugh; m* (2) ——— *Harris.*

34. **Hugh Barkley,** *m Jane Thompson,* dau. Robt. A. Thompson.

> (112) *William Thompson Barkley, d unm.*
> (113) *Maria Barkley, m David C. Bull.*
> (114) *Isabella Barkley, m Robert Milligan.*
> (115) *Jane Barkley, d unm.*
> (116) *Harriet Barkley, d unm.*

35. **William Barkley,** *m Sarah Crawford,* dau. Alex. and Margaret (Miller) Crawford.

> (117) *Maria Barkley, m Cornelius Barnes.*
> (118) *Catherine Barkley, m James Barnes.*
> (119) *Caroline Barkley, m Andrew Low.*
> (120) *Ann Eliza Barkley, m Peter Westerveldt.*
> (121) *Hugh Barclay, m Phoebe Fulton.*
> (122) *John Barkley, m Michal Andrews.*
> (123) *Margaret Barkley, d unm.*
> (124) *Jane Barkley, d unm.*
> (125) *Isaiah Barkley, d unm.*
> (126) *Thomas Barkley, d unm.*

36. **Jane Barkley,** *m John Millspaugh.*

> (127) *William Millspaugh.*
> (128) *Nathaniel Millspaugh.*
> (129) *Mowbray Millspaugh, m Margaret Corkey.*

38. **James Barkley,** *b* 27 July, 1780; *m Ann Haines* (or *Harris*), 2 January, 1808.

> (130) *Hiram Barkley.*
> (131) *Fanny Barkley.*
> (132) *Alfred Barkley.*
> (133) *Sarah Barkley.*
> (134) *Jonathan Barkley.*

(135) *Parmela Barkley.*
(136) *Eliza Jane Barkley.*
(137) *Ann Barkley, m James Johnson.*
(138) *Rowanna Barkley.*
(139) *Abigail Barkley.*

39. **Mary Barkley,** *b* 18 October, 1783; *m Archibald Crawford.*
(140) *Emily Crawford, m Aaron Higby.*
(141) *Sarah Crawford, m Dr. John Hunter.*
(142) *Alfred Crawford, m Catherine Hunter.*
(143) *James McC. Crawford, m Blondina Terellager.*
(144) *David A. Crawford, m Mary VanKeuren.*
(145) *Robert Crawford, d unm.*
(146) *Eleanor Crawford, m Henry VanKeuren.*
(147) *Elizabeth Crawford, d in infancy.*
(148) *Moses A. Crawford, m Antoinette Brown.*
(149) *John Duryea Crawford, m Maria Townley.*
(150) *Mary Elizabeth Crawford, m Oliver Taylor.*

40. **David Barkley,** *b* 25 November, 1785; *m* (1) *Jane Hanmore*—6 children; *m* (2) *Charlotte Warner*—2 children.
(151) *Rachel Ann Barkley, m Jacob Schaffer.*
(152) *Sarah Jane Barkley, m Solomon Derwight.*
(153) *Thomas Barkley, m Josephine Bellman.*
(154) *Alexander Barkley, m Susan Lockwood.*
(155) *Janson Barkley.*
(156) *David Barkley.*
(157) *Job Barkley, m Nettie Smith.*
(158) *Janet Barkley, m William Henry Rogers.*

41. **John Barkley,** *b* 27 July, 1787; *m* 17 January, 1809, *Martha Haines,* dau. John Haines.
(159) *Sarah Barkley.*
(160) *Bayard Barkley.*
(161) *Mary Barkley, m Nathaniel Higby.*
(162) *Thomas Barkley.*
(163) *Permelia Barkley.*
(164) *Haines Barkley.*
(165) *Eliza Barkley.*
(166) *Margaret Jane Barkley.*

44. **Josiah Barkley,** *b* 25 January, 1793; *m* (1) *Frances Haines*—5 children; *m* (2) *Margaret Christ Potts.*
    (167) *Crawford Barkley.*
    (168) *Bayard Barkley.*
    (169) *William Moffat Barkley.*
    (170) *Henry Barkley.*
    (171) *Mary Barkley.*

69. **Margaret Barclay,** *m Clinton Marsh.*
    (172) *Katherine Marsh.*
    (173) *Elizabeth W. Marsh, m T. Leroy Case.*
    (174) *Alexander B. Marsh.*
    (175) *Barkley Marsh, m Julia Knight.*
    (176) *Alanson B. Marsh.*

70. **Alexander Crawford Barclay,** *b* Sullivan Co., N. Y., 15 April, 1811; *d* Hocking Co., Ohio, 3 December, 1886; *m* 1838, *Eliza Strawn.*
    (177) *Catherine Barclay, m Amos Funk.*
    (178) *John Barclay, unm.*
    (179) *Rebecca Barclay, m Peter Getz.* Living Sandusky, Ohio, 1903.
    (180) *Marcus Barclay, b* 30 June, 1846. Living 1903, Columbus, Ohio, *unm.* Was born in Hocking Co., Ohio; went to Washington C. H., Ohio; was Mayor of the town 8 years (4 terms).
    (181) *Adeline Barclay, m Alexander McCowen.*
    (182) *Darius Barclay,* living 1903, in Logan Co., Ohio, *unm.*
    (183) *Nancy Barclay,* living 1903, Princeton, Mo.; *m John Davis.*
    (184) *Amanda Barclay,* living 1903, Nashport, O.; *m L. C. Prior.*
    (185) *Margaret Barclay,* living 1903, Newark, O.; *m Howard Prior.*
    (186) *Annie Barclay,* dec'd.
    (187) *Charles H. Barclay,* living 1903, near Logan, O.; *m Eva Bury.*

71. **Mary Ellen Barclay,** *m Alanson Bookstaver.*

    (188) *Samuel Bookstaver.*

    (189) *Mary Catherine Bookstaver, m Joseph Clark,* son of Ira and Eliza (Barkley) Clark.

    (190) *A. Augustus Bookstaver, m Harriet Fisher.*

    (191) *Marcus B. Bookstaver, m Mary Low,* dau. Andrew and Carrie (Barkley) Low.

    (192) *Helen Bookstaver, m William Puff.*

    (193) *William Bookstaver, m Margaret Rowe.*

    (194) *Agnes Bookstaver, m William Barnes,* son of James and Catherine (Barkley) Barnes.

    (195) *Annie Bookstaver.*

    (196) *Carrie Bookstaver.*

72. **Marcus S. Barclay,** *b* Orange Co., N. Y.; *m Amy Fraer; d* November, 1901.

    (197) *Lydia P. Barclay.*

    (198) *Crawford S. Barclay.*

    (199) *James T. Barclay.*

    (200) *Preston Wade Barclay.*

    (201) *Nellie Barclay.*

    (202) *Emily Barclay, b* 1852; *d* 1859.

    (203) *Cora Barclay.*

73. **Rachel Barclay,** *m J. Crawford.*

    (204) *Alexander B. Crawford, m Sarah E. Carpenter.*

    (205) *Anna Eliza Crawford, m Samuel W. Chamberlain.*

75. **James S. Barclay,** *m Hannah Mosher.*

    (206) *Kate Barclay, m George Nichols.* Has issue living 1903.

    (207) *Marcus Barclay, b* January, 1861; living 1903, Nodaway Co., Mo.

    (208) *Winifred Barclay, b* 26 March, 1870.

76. **Catherine Barclay,** *m Alfred Hall.*

    (209) *James Hall.*

    (210) *Catherine Hall.*

    (211) *Frank Hall.*

    (212) *Elmer Hall.*

197. **Lydia P. Barclay**, *b* 1 February, 1841; *m* (1) *Gregg Sweeney,* living Basin, Wyoming, 1903; *m* (2) *R. H. Austin.*

> (213) *Grace Barclay, b* 1867; *m Samuel Smith.* Has issue living 1903.
>
> (214) *Robert Barclay, b* March, 1869; *unm* 1903.
>
> (215) *Harry Barclay, b* 16 December, 1871.

198. **Crawford S. Barclay**, *b* 23 October, 1842; living 1903, West Liberty, Iowa; *m Emma Wonsetler.*

> (216) *Wade C. Barclay.*
>
> (217) *Ralph W. Barclay, b* 29 April, 1875.
>
> (218) *Josephine Barclay, b* 3 October, 1877.
>
> (219) *Alberta Barclay, b* 6 January, 1881; *d* 7 January, 1881.
>
> (220) *Paul V. Barclay, b* 13 August, 1882.
>
> (221) *Marcus Barclay, b* 26 May, 1884.

199. **James T. Barclay**, *b* 30 January, 1845; living 1903, Des Moines, Iowa; *m Ava Givens.*

> (222) *Maude Barclay, b* 1873.
>
> (223) *Frederick Barclay.*
>
> (224) *Blanche Barclay.*
>
> (225) *Beatrice Barclay.*
>
> (226) *Aloise Barbara Barclay.*

200. **Preston Wade Barclay**, *b* February, 1847; living 1903, Chicago, Ill.; *m Anita Labbe.*

> (227) *Mion Elizabeth Barclay.*
>
> (228) *Shirley Barclay.*
>
> (229) *Donald Barclay.*

201. **Nellie Barclay**, *b* May, 1850; living 1903, Norfolk, Neb.; *m R. Harry Reynolds.*

> (230) *Blanche Reynolds, b* 19 August, 1878; *d* 10 January, 1884.
>
> (231) *Marcus Thomas Reynolds, b* 25 January, 1891.
>
> (232) *Amy Reynolds, b* 5 July, 1892.

203. **Cora Barclay,** *b* 23 April, 1862; living 1903, Ames, Iowa;
   m Alvin B. Noble.

> (233) *Nellie L. Noble, b* 2 November, 1892.
> (234) *Margaret Noble.*
> (235) *Barclay E. Noble.*

216. **Wade Crawford Barclay,** (Rev.), *b* 8 August, 1874; living
   Lisbon, Iowa, 1903; *m* 1 January, 1901, *May Hartley,* at
   Los Angeles, Cal.

> (236) *Lois Margerie Barclay, b* 23 March, 1902.

---

1. **John Barkley,** *b* Scotland.

> (2) *Iddings Barkley.*

2. **Iddings Barkley,** *b* 12 April, 1781, Churchtown, Pa.; *d*
   27 October, 1857, Bloomsburg, Pa. Lived Pottsville,
   Pa., from 1804 until 1806; moved to Hemlock Township,
   Columbia Co., Pa.; and later to Bloomsburg, Pa,; *m*
   Mary Jackson abt. 1803, a Quakeress of English descent,
   b 16 April, 1775, Berks Co., Pa.; *d* 7 March, 1854.

> (3) *Minerva Barkley.*
> (4) *John J. Barkley.*
> (5) *Sarah Barkley.*
> (6) *Mary E. Barkley, b* 1811; *d* 6 February, 1892;
>   *m Moore Furman.* No issue.
> (7) *Lewis Iddings Barkley,* ⎫ Twins.
> (8) *Joseph Evans Barkley,* ⎭
> (9) *Susan Barkley, b* July, 1816; d July, 1896; *m*
>   *John F. Funston.* Issue, 1 child, *d* in infancy.

3. **Minerva Barkley,** *b* 14 October, 1804; *d* 3 December,
   1883, Bloomsburg, Pa.; *m John R. Moyer, b* 18 September,
   1799; *d* 29 April, 1879, Bloomsburg, Pa.

> (10) *Sarah Moyer, b* 11 January, 1826; living 1903;
>   *m John G. Quick,* 14 December, 1853.
> (11) *Elizabeth McNeal Moyer, b* 7 June, 1828; *d* 18
>   March, 1830.

(12) *Iddings Barkely Moyer, b* 10 August, 1830; *d* 14 August, 1835.

(13) *Charles Augustus Moyer, b* 21 September, 1832; living 1903, Bloomsburg, Pa.; *m* (1) *Mary E. Boone,* 27 January, 1859; *m* (2) *Martha Robison.*

(14) *Albert Moyer, b* 5 February, 1835; living 1903; *m Mary Colsher,* 2 April, 1863.

(15) *Lucy A. Moyer, b* 11 August, 1837; *d* September, 1878; *m E. M. Sheldon,* 26 March, 1864.

(16) *Lucas N. Moyer, b* 30 September, 1840; living 1903; *m Hattie E. Eyer,* 16 December, 1862.

(17) *John Lewis Moyer, b* 3 March, 1843; living 1903; *m Effie Vance,* 13 October, 1874.

(18) *William Stine Moyer, b* 25 May, 1846; *d* 13 December, 1902; *m Martha Menagh,* 22 March, 1875.

4. **John J. Barkley,** *b* 23 August, 1806, Hemlock Township, Columbia Co., Pa.; *d* 5 July, 1876, Bloomsburg, Pa.; *m Rachel McBride,* 18 December, 1828; *b* 25 December, 1809; *d* 7 April, 1876.

(19) *William McBride Barkley, b* 23 October, 1829; *d* in far west, 1850-5, *unm.*

(20) *Maria Hunter Barkley, b* 11 October, 1831; living 1903, Ft. Scott, Kan.; *m* Dr. *John S. Redfield,* 13 August, 1857. Had issue.

(21) *Iddings Barkley.*

(22) *James L. Barkley.*

(23) *Charles Gillespie Barkley.*

(24) *Eli S. Barkley, b* 26 September, 1841; *d* 3 May, 1867, Bloomsburg, Pa.; *m Margaret M. Snyder,* 2 November, 1863; *d* 14 June, 1865. No issue.

5. **Sarah Barkley,** *b* 12 December, 1808; *d* 5 March, 1896, Bloomsburg, Pa.; *m* (1) *Elias Furman, d* 27 December, 1833, by whom she had 1 child—a daughter; *m* (2)

Robert Cathcart, b 31 July, 1803; *d* 4 November, 1884, by whom she had 2 children.

> (25) *Mary Cordelia Furman, b* 25 July, 1833; *d* 28 February, 1903; *m* (1) Rev. *William Cathcart; m* (2) Rev. *T. E. Hughes.*
>
> (26) *Margaret Jane Cathcart, b* 18 March, 1841; living 1903; *m Calvin Achenbach.*
>
> (27) *Andrew Barkley Cathcart, b* 22 December, 1844; living 1903, Bloomsburg, Pa.

7. **Lewis Iddings Barkley,** *b* 12 April, 1814; *d* March, 1843, Bloomsburg, Pa.; *m* 1 November, 1838, *Mahalah Quick, b* 12 April, 1819; living 1903.

> (28) *John Q. Barkley, b* 14 November, 1839; *d* 17 February, 1897, *unm.*
>
> (29) *Mary Elizabeth Barkley, b* 23 September, 1841; *d* 25 January, 1902, *unm.*

8. **Joseph Evans Barkley,** *b* 13 April, 1814; *d* 13 March, 1887, Bloomsburg, Pa.; *m Julia A. Melick.* Living 1903, Bloomsburg, Pa.

> (30) *Sarah M. Barkley.*
>
> (31) *Glovenia J. Barkley.*

21. **Iddings Barkley,** *b* 23 October, 1833; *d* 21 December, 1869, Philadelphia; *m Emma* ———. Living 1903, Philadelphia.

> (32) *Iddings Barkley.*
>
> (33) *Charles Barkley.*
>
> (34) *William Barkley,* living Philadelphia, 1903.

22. **James L. Barkley,** *b* 9 March, 1836; lived Jersey Shore, Pa.; *d* 10 November, 1902, Dexter, Mo.; *m Rilla Webb.* Living 1903, Jersey Shore, Pa.

> (35) *Edward Barkley,* living 1903, Jersey Shore, Pa., and 3 others, who died in infancy.

23. **Charles Gillespie Barkley,** *b* 30 January, 1839; *d* 10 October, 1900, Bloomsburg, Pa.; *m* 2 June, 1864, *Margery*

Ann Wilson, b 27 June, 1841, at Washingtonville, Pa.
Living 1903, Bloomsburg, Pa.

> (36) *Mary Garrison Barkley, b* 23 September, 1865;
> living 1903, Scranton, Pa.; *m* 2 April, 1901,
> *Frederick C. Williams.*
>
> (37) *Josephine Redfield Barkley.*
>
> (38) *Jennie Wilson Barkley, b* 1 June, 1872; living
> 1903, *unm.*

30. **Sarah M. Barkley,** *b* 23 February, 1844; living 1903; *m*
25 November, 1868, *Chester M. Furman.*

> (39) *Josiah H. Furman.*
>
> (40) *Julia H. Furman.*
>
> (41) *Henry F. Furman.*
>
> (42) *Boyd W. Furman, m* 30 May, 1897, *Alice M.
> Dillon.* Had issue.
>
> (43) *Clinton Furman.*
>
> (44) *Clara G. Furman.*

31. **Glovenia J. Barkley,** *b* 9 January, 1848; living 1903; *m*
5 July, 1870, *Elias R. Furman.*

> (45) *Howard C. Furman, m Mary Purcel.* Had issue.
>
> (46) *Kenneth K. Furman, m Eva Warrich.* Had
> issue.

37. **Josephine Redfield Barkley,** *b* 30 May, 1868; living 1903;
m 25 June, 1901, *Warren H. Eyer.*

> (47) *Charles Barkley Eyer, b* 14 June, 1902.

LINE OF DESCENT

FROM

JOHN BARKLEY, of County Londonderry, Ireland,

compiled by

RICHARD WARREN BARKLEY, of the New York Bar.

(Pages 300-331.)

---

1. **John Barkley,** *b* in County Londonderry, Ireland.; *d* 1785, Fayette County, Pennsylvania.

   (2) *Ann Barkley, d* 18 July, 1817, "on Brush Creek, Ohio;" *m* ——— *Pollock.*

   (3) *Jane* (or *Catherine*) *Barkley, m John* (or *Jonathan*) *Swearingen.*

   (4) *Mary Barkley, m James* (or *Joseph*) *Scott,* "in Pennsylvania."

   (5) *John Barkley.*

   (6) *James Chambers Barkley.*

5. **John Barkley,** *b* 1747; *d* 23 July, 1828, in Jessamine County, Kentucky; *m* 8 August, 1775, *Susannah Lucas, b* 1757; *d* 7 December, 1822.

   (7) *Samuel Barkley.*

   (8) *Sarah Barkley, b* 2 July, 1778.

   (9) *John Barkley, b* 27 June, 1780; *d* 9 November, 1812.

   (10) *George Barkley.*

   (11) *Susannah Barkley, b* 24 August, 1785; *d* 6 September, 1819; *m* Capt. *James Price* and left issue.

   (12) *Joseph Barkley, b* 2 December, 1787; *d* 22 December, 1814.

   (13) *Dorcas Barkley, b* 13 December, 1789; *d* 17 November, 1818; *m* ——— *Hushman.*

   (14) *William Barkley, b* 21 August, 1792; *d* 26 November, 1812.

(15) *Nancy Barkley, b* 3 February, 1794; *d* 3 May, 1819.

(16) *Polly Barkley, b* 19 December, 1796; *d* 4 February, 1817.

(17) *James Barkley, b* 4 September, 1801; *d* 1853, leaving issue.

6. **James Chambers Barkley,** *b* abt. 1750; *d* 24 August, 1826, in Lewis County, Kentucky; *m Catherine Crawford, b* 16 April, 1760, daughter of William and Elinor Crawford.

    (18) *William Crawford Barkley.*

    (19) *Mary ("Patty") Barkley.*

    (20) *James Chambers Barkley.*

7. **Samuel Barkley,** *b* 2 August, 1776; *d* 23 November, 1831; *m* 23 February, 1804, *Jane Singleton, b* 3 April, 1787; *d* 26 August, 1860, daughter of Mason Singleton, of Virginia.

    (21) *John Barkley, b* 6 November, 1805.

    (22) *Levi Barkley.*

    (23) *Isaac Barkley.*

    (24) *James Francis Barkley.*

    (25) *Susan Mary Barkley, b* 14 August, 1816; *d unm.*

    (26) *Mason Singleton Barkley.*

    (27) *Samuel Barkley, b* 26 December, 1820; *d* 27 July, 1891; *m Katherine Miller.* O. S. P.

    (28) *George Mathias Barkley.*

    (29) *Joseph Barkley, b* 1 August, 1826; *d* 13 March, 1833.

10. **George Barkley,** *b* 7 December, 1782; *d* 21 January, 1815; *m* 10 July, 1806, *Martha Ellison Higbee, b* 13 January, 1789, in Fayette County, Kentucky; *d* 31 January, 1870, daughter of John and Margaret (Ellison) Higbee, of Middlesex County, New Jersey.

    (30) *Margaret Ellison Barkley, b* 19 June, 1807; *d* March, 1883; *m* Judge *William Clark.* O. S. P.

    (31) *John Barkley.*

(32) *William Lucas Barkley.*

(33) *Mary Ann Barkley.*

18. **William Crawford Barkley,** *b* 13 July, 1786; *d* 29 December, 1874, Lewis County, Kentucky; *m* 2 January, 1812, *Mary Hendrickson, b* 2 June, 1793; *d* 4 November, 1840; daughter of Daniel Hendrickson.

(34) *John Crawford Barkley.*

(35) *James Hendrickson Barkley, d* in infancy.

(36) A child, *d* in infancy.

(37) *William George Washington Barkley, b* 19 February, 1817; *d* 9 May, 1837.

(38) *Sarah Ann Barkley.*

(39) *Mary Catherine Barkley.*

(40) *Eliza Jane Barkley, b* 6 February, 1823; *d unm.*

(41) *Rebecca Barkley.*

(42) *Daniel Lafayette Barkley.*

(43) *James Herbert Barkley.*

(44) *Henry Clay Barkley.*

(45) *Samuel Boyd Barkley.*

(46) *Thomas Jefferson Barkley.*

(47) A son, *d* in infancy, 26 January, 1836.

19. **Mary ("Patty") Barkley,** *b* 20 September, 1792; *d* 14 January, 1830; *m* 29 January, 1818, *William Boyd, b* 1 March, 1791, in Pennsylvania; *d* 27 January, 1857, son of David Boyd.

(48) *David Henderson Boyd, b* 10 January, 1820; *m* 1 November, 1839, *Jemima Fry,* and had 12 children.

(49) *Catherine Crawford Boyd.*

(50) *Amanda Melvina Boyd.*

20. **James Chambers Barkley,** *b* 12 March, 1796; *d* 30 April, 1855, at Lexington, Kentucky; *m* 7 June, 1818, *Rebecca Hart, b* 1 December, 1798, in Hopewell Township, Hunterdon County, New Jersey; *d* 6 August, 1876, daughter of Richard and Francina (Mershon) Hart.

(51) *Sallie Hart Barkley, b* and *d* 1819.

(52) *Crawford Hart Barkley.*

(53) *Benjamin Franklin Barkley.*

(54) *Francina Barkley.*

(55) *Richard Hart Barkley.*

(56) *Henry Benton Barkley.*

(57) *Mary Matilda Barkley,* b 6 April, 1830; d 12 March, 1847.

(58) *James Chambers Barkley.*

(59) *David Maple Barkley.*

(60) *John Barkley,* b 3 June, 1837; d 14 December, 1898, *unm.*

(61) *Joab Hickson Barkley,* b 5 April, 1838; d 2 February, 1869, *unm.*

(62) *Martha Emeline Barkley,* b and d in 1840.

22. **Levi Barkley,** b 6 February, 1807; d near Palmyra, Missouri, 28 February, 1883; m (1) 10 May, 1832, *Elizabeth Grimes,* b in Clark County, Kentucky, 8 March, 1812; d 22 November, 1852. No issue by second marriage.

    (63) *Jane Barkley,* b 29 March, 1833; d 27 December, 1854; m Dr. *James Ellis.* Issue: James Ellis, Jr., d in infancy.

    (64) *Mary Susan Barkley,* b 30 September, 1834; d 1842.

    (65) *Samuel Barkley.*

    (66) *Charles Grimes Barkley,* b 23 July, 1837; d 9 January, 1849.

    (67) *Levi Barkley,* b 14 April, 1840; (living 1903), *unm.*

    (68) *Elizabeth Helen Barkley,* b 29 October, 1841; d 25 February, 1862.

    (69) *Martha Bishop Barkley.*

    (70) *Sydney Frances Barkley.*

    (71) *Isaac Mason Barkley.*

    (72) *Philip Napoleon Barkley,* b 24 December, 1850; d 9 February, 1851.

    (73) *Maria Barkley,* b 22 November, 1852; (living 1903); m *Joseph L. Hatcher,* (living 1903). Issue: *Josephine Lee Hatcher,* b 1879; d 1884.

23. Isaac Barkley, *b* 14 May, 1809; *d* 2 August, 1874; *m* (1)
8 November, 1832, *Eliza T. Bryan, b* 23 December, 1814;
d 25 November, 1835, by whom he had two children;
m (2) 11 December, 1838, *Ann Eliza Custer, b* 17 July,
1818; *d* 8 July, 1863.

(74) *John Barkley.*

(75) *Mary Jane Barkley, b* 30 October, 1835; *d* 5
May, 1847.

(76) *Elizabeth Barkley.*

(77) *Margaret Jane Barkley, b* 8 March, 1841; *d*
29 January, 1863.

(78) *Anna Eliza Barkley.*

(79) *Samuel C. Barkley.*

(80) *Joseph Henry Barkley, b* 11 September, 1848;
d 19 April, 1900, *unm.*

(81) *George Levi Barkley, b* 3 May, 1851; (living
1903), *unm.*

(82) *Mary Susan Barkley.*

(83) *Alice Barkley.*

24. James Francis Barkley, *b* 12 February, 1814; *d* 23 June,
1867; *m* 13 May, 1834, *Elizabeth M. Pitts, b* 15 January,
1815; *d* 29 December, 1884, daughter of Younger and
Elizabeth (Rogers) Pitts.

(84) *Cassa Jane Barkley.*

(85) *Mary Elizabeth Barkley, b* and *d* in February,
1838.

(86) *Samuel Isaac Barkley.*

(87) *Dillard Barkley, b* 1844; *d* 1848.

(88) *George Mathias Barkley.*

(89) *Lela Frank Barkley, b* 1852; (living 1903); *m*
Joseph Austin Fisher. S. P.

26. Mason Singleton Barkley, *b* 29 January, 1818; *d* 1883;
m 23 June, 1842, *Narcissa E. Hawkins.*

(90) *Cassa Jane Barkley.*

(91) *Mary Elizabeth Barkley, b* 1846; *d* 1848.

(92) *James Francis Barkley, b* 31 January, 1848;
(living 1903); *m* 26 June, 1901, *Mary
Bronaugh.*

(93) *Susan Alice Barkley, b* 1850; *d* 1852.
(94) *William Clark Barkley, b* 17 November, 1854; *d* 29 November, 1872, *unm.*
(95) *Lily Belle Barkley, b* 24 March, 1857; (living 1903), *unm.*

28. **George Mathias Barkley,** *b* 17 February, 1824; *d* 30 July 1883; *m* 25 October, 1854, *Frances A. Scott, b* 1 October, 1831; *d* 11 September, 1879, daughter of William and Sarah (Metcalf) Scott.

(96) *William Scott Barkley, d in infancy.*
(97) *Lucy Barkley,* (living 1903); *m W. R. Sadler.* S. P.
(98) *Scott Barkley, d* September, 1898, *unm.*

31. **John Barkley,** *b* 31 December, 1809; *d* 21 January, 1853; *m* 9 August, 1838, *Salllie Reid Green, b* 19 September, 1816; *d* 16 November, 1876, daughter of Judge John Green, of Danville, Kentucky.

(99) *John Green Barkley.*
(100) *Mary Jones Barkley, b* 19 June, 1841; (living 1903); *m* 1871, Rev. *William R. Brown.* S. P.
(101) *George Barkley, b* 17 September, 1843; *d* 1875, *unm.*
(102) *Jessamine Barkley.*
(103) *Martha Bertha Barkley, b* 15 April, 1848; (living 1903); *m William L. Green.* S. P.
(104) *Sarah Addie Barkley.*
(105) *William Craig Barkley, b* 1 July, 1853; (living 1903), *unm.*

32. **William Lucas Barkley,** *b* 10 January, 1811; *d* 23 September, 1885; *m* 1843, *Adeline Stout, b* 17 December, 1825; *d* 20 February, 1901, daughter of David Stout, of Versailles, Ky.

(106) *Martha Barkley.*
(107) *Margaret Clarke Barkley.*

(108) *Mary Ann Barkley, b* 1 March, 1850; *d* 12 May, 1855.

(109) *Adeline Barkley, b* 4 April, 1854; *d* 1892; *m* Dr. *Frank O. Young.* O. S. P.

(110) *William Barkley, b* 23 November, 1856; *d* 17 March, 1858.

(111) *John S. Barkley, b* 14 April, 1859; (living 1903) ; *m Eva Cloke.* S. P.

(112) *Eugenia Barkley.*

(113) *William Lucas Barkley.*

(114) *Allen Barkley, b* 1 March, 1869; *d* 26 November, 1869.

33. **Mary Ann Barkley,** *b* January, 1813; *d* 27 March, 1871; *m* (1) 29 April, 1830, Dr. *Stephen Edward Jones, d* 11 April, 1833; *m* (2) 13 November, 1838, *John Lafon, b* 1800; *d* May, 1848.

(115) *Mary W. Jones, b* 23 May, 1831; *d* 11 April, 1840.

(116) *Stephen Edward Jones.*

(117) *Mary W. Lafon, b* 13 April, 1840; (living 1903), *unm.*

(118) *Alice Lafon, b* 10 November, 1842; *d* 24 September, 1858.

(119) *George Barkley Lafon, b* 18 April, 1846; *d* in infancy.

34. **John Crawford Barkley,** *b* 3 October, 1812; *d* 9 December, 1879; *m* 24 December, 1839, *Mary Boone Reeder, b* 13 January, 1820; *d* 2 December, 1874, dau. Benjamin and Elizabeth (Wallingford) Reeder.

(120) *William Benjamin Barkley.*

(121) *Henry Clay Barkley.*

(122) *Mary Davis Barkley, b* 18 November, 1845; (living 1903), *unm.*

(123) *Elizabeth Hayes Barkley, b* 21 April, 1847; *d* 8 April, 1876, *unm.*

(124) *Georgia Ann Barkley, b* 26 July, 1850; *d* 10 July, 1876, *unm.*

(125) *James Thomas Barkley, b* 24 October, 1852;
d 18 December, 1891, *unm.*

(126) *Frank Barkley.*

(127) *Asa Barkley, b* 8 July, 1859; (living 1903),
unm.

38. **Sarah Ann Barkley,** *b* 5 November, 1818; *d* 10 October,
1862; *m* 18 December, 1845, *William Thomson, b* 1812,
Baltimore, Md.; *d* 18 April, 1869.

(128) *Mary Agnes Thomson, b* 27 October, 1846;
(living 1903); *m* 30 November, 1887, *Henry
L. Newell.* S. P.

(129) *William Henry Thomson, b* 13 November,
1848; *d* 21 December, 1883, *unm.*

(130) *John James Thomson.*

(131) *Ann Eliza Thomson, b* 21 July, 1852; *d* 2
April, 1883; *m* 20 March, 1877, *Charles
Pollitt.* O. S. P.

(132) *Margaret Boyd Thomson.*

(133) *Edward Wallingford Thomson, b* 1 July, 1859;
(living 1903); *unm.*

(134) *Thomas Samuel Thomson.*

39. **Mary Catherine Barkley,** *b* 22 March, 1821; *d* 15 April,
1857; *m Andrew Fleming Blount, b* 20 June, 1820; *d*
15 August, 1901.

(135) *Presley Coliver Blount, b* 4 October, 1855; *d*
3 November, 1856.

(136) *John Clay Blount.*

41. **Rebecca Barkley,** *b* 4 October, 1824; *d* 4 May, 1900; *m*
23 March, 1843, *Amos Means, b* 15 September, 1811; *d*
1886.

(137) *Mary Elizabeth Means.*

(138) *George Means.*

(139) *Eliza W. Means, b* 27 January, 1850; (living
1903), *unm.*

(140) *William Henry Means, b* 15 June, 1852; (living 1903) ; *m* 1 October, 1889, *Amanda West Wall.* S. P.

(141) *Robert Means, b* 23 September, 1854; *d* 30 September, 1857.

(142) *James Barkley Means.*

(143) *Amos Nesbitt Means, b* 4 September, 1859; *d* 2 October, 1873.

(144) *Henrick Monroe Means, b* 28 January, 1873; (living 1903) ; *m* 16 April, 1903, *Ida M. Willis.*

42. **Daniel Lafayette Barkley,** *b* 4 July, 1826; *d* 24 January, 1900; *m* 5 June, 1867, *Rose Crum, b* 1 August, 1836; (living 1903), dau. Abram and Rebecca Crum.

(145) *George William Barkley, b* 11 June, 1868; (living 1903), *unm.*

(146) *Claire Barkley, b* 9 March, 1870; (living 1903), *unm.*

(147) *Tempa Barkley, b* and *d* August, 1872.

(148) *Ella Mae Barkley.*

43. **James Herbert Barkley,** *b* 3 July, 1828; *d* 4 October, 1895; *m Martha Louise Halbert, b* 16 February, 1841; (living 1903), dau. Daniel and Rachel (Thomas) Halbert.

(149) *Mintie Emma Barkley.*

(150) *Mary Belle Barkley.*

(151) *George William Barkley.*

(152) *Katherine Davis Barkley, b* 1875; (living 1903) ; *m C. F. Adams.*

(153) *Nellie Halbert Barkley, b* 1880; (living 1903).

44. **Henry Clay Barkley,** *b* 14 May, 1830; *d* 15 January, 1897; *m* 6 May, 1861, *Isabella Imogene Howell, b* 7 September, 1840; *d* 8 August, 1897, dau. Abraham Price and Mary Ann (Schute) Howell.

(154) *Charles Henry Barkley, b* 18 March, 1862; *d* 2 September, 1865.

(155) *Howell Finch Barkley, b* 14 August, 1864; *d* 23 May, 1894, *unm.*

(156) *Harry Herbert Barkley, b* 16 January, 1869; (living 1903); *m* 11 November, 1896, *Lillian E. Smoot.* S. P.

(157) *Isabella Lee Barkley.*

(158) *Frank Owens Barkley.*

(159) *Helen Gray Barkley, b* 13 December, 1877; (living 1903), *unm.*

(160) *Mary Florence Barkley, b* 17 February, 1880; (living 1903), *unm.*

45. **Samuel Boyd Barkley**, *b* 19 December, 1831; (living 1903); *m* 3 January, 1867, Mrs. *Rebecca Salena Taylor, b* abt. 1842; *d* 6 December, 1878; dau. of Joshua Carle.

(161) *Lucile May Barkley.*

(162) *Cora Belle Barkley, b* 27 August, 1869; *d* 4 January, 1896.

(163) *William Henry Barkley, b* 12 September, 1872; (living 1903), *unm.*

(164) *Franklin Carle Barkley, b* 19 May, 1875; (living 1903); *m* 25 February, 1903, *Janie Derrett.*

(165) *Anna Eliza Barkley, b* 30 August, 1878; (living 1903), *unm.*

46. **Thomas Jefferson Barkley**, *b* 26 February, 1834; (living 1903); *m Caroline Warder, b* 14 June, 1847; (living 1903).

(166) *William Thomas Barkley.*

(167) *Charles Henry Barkley, b* 28 March, 1869; (living 1903), *unm.*

(168) *Caroline Isabel Barkley, b* 6 February, 1872; (living 1903); *m John P. McCartney.* S. P.

(169) *Mary Alice Barkley.*

49. **Catherine Crawford Boyd,** *b* 29 August, 1821; *d* 2 October, 1870; *m* 7 June, 1843, *Curtis Smith Pemberton, b* 24 October, 1819; *d* 8 June, 1861.

> (170) *Mary Amanda Pemberton.*
>
> (171) *Sarah Wadsworth Pemberton, b* 6 August, 1846; *d* 10 February, 1866; *m George W. Ross.* Issue: *George Curtis Ross,* who *d* in infancy.
>
> (172) *Henrietta Wadsworth Pemberton.*
>
> (173) *William Anson Pemberton, b* 16 December, 1850; *d* 24 April, 1868.
>
> (174) *George Collings Pemberton, d* in infancy.
>
> (175) *James Murfin Pemberton, b* 9 December, 1855; (living 1903), *unm.*

50. **Amanda Melvina Boyd,** *b* 10 August, 1823; (living 1903); *m* 23 August, 1843, *William S. Bridges, b* 20 April, 1815; *d* 8 October, 1870.

> (176) *Mary Catherine Bridges, b* 19 June, 1844; *d* 7 May, 1848.
>
> (177) *John Dillon Bridges.*
>
> (178) *Elizabeth Kelley Bridges, b* 22 April, 1854; *d* 26 November, 1855.
>
> (179) *Henry Barkley Bridges.*

52. **Crawford Hart Barkley** (Rev.), *b* 19 September, 1821; *d* 12 December, 1885; *m* (1) *Elizabeth Best, b* 26 November, 1828; *d* 24 December, 1852, by whom he had three children; *m* (2) *Frances Reddish, b* 29 May, 1828; *d* 7 December, 1900.

> (180) *Robert Best Barkley, b* 13 June, 1848; (living 1903), *unm.*
>
> (181) *Mary Cornelia Barkley, b* 13 September, 1850; *d* 2 April, 1901; *m* Dr. *Marshall P. Robinson.* O. S. P.
>
> (182) *Elizabeth Crawford Barkley, b* 18 December, 1852; (living 1903), *unm.*
>
> (183) *Frances Barkley, b* 19 October, 1856; (living 1903); *m* (1) *William Peck; m* (2) *J. J. Fenn.* S. P.

(184) *John Crawford Barkley, b* 17 December, 1857;
    d 13 April, 1878.

(185) *Joseph F. Barkley, b* 19 February, 1860; *d* 4
    December, 1891, *unm.*

(186) *James Hickman Barkley.*

(187) *George Marshall Barkley, b* 22 September,
    1864; *d* 28 February, 1865.

(188) *Owen Barkley, b* 9 November, 1867; *d* 1902,
    unm.

(189) *Lamotie Barkley.*

53. **Benjamin Franklin Barkley** (M.D.), *b* 14 November,
    1822; *d* 25 December, 1882; *m Malinda E. Duncan, b* 18
    March, 1827; (living 1903); dau. Mason Duncan (1785-
    1859) of Culpepper Co., Va., and Juliet (Jackson, Win-
    chester, Va.) Duncan, 1807-1895.

(190) *Leslie Crawford Barkley, b* 18 July, 1846.

(191) *Francina Alice Barkley.*

(192) *Leonidas Marue Barkley.*

(193) *Rovena Gertrude Barkley.*

(194) *Laura Josephine Barkley.*

(195) *James Mason Barkley, b* 5 February, 1861;
    (living 1903), *unm.*

(196) *Lillian May Barkley, b* 1863; *d* 1878.

54. **Francina Barkley,** *b* 24 February, 1824; *d* 19 April, 1903;
    m (1) 1845-6, *George Neal, b* 10 August, 1892; *d* 18
    March, 1854; *m* (2) 2 October, 1855, *Stephen Pendle-
    ton Waller, b* 12 April, 1812; *d* 8 February, 1871.

(197) *Jesse Crawford Neal.*

(198) *Charles Waller.*

(199) *Laura Waller.*

(200) *John Waller, b* 28 June, 1862; (living 1903);
    m 22 June, 1887, *Jennie B. Smith, b* 17 May,
    1865; (living 1903). S. P.

(201) *Anna Mac Waller, b* 17 March, 1864; (living
    1903), *unm.*

(202) *Clarence Waller, b* 8 September, 1866; *d* No-
    vember, 1868.

55. **Richard Hart Barkley,** *b* 2 February, 1826; *d* 2 October, 1865; *m* Mrs. *Cornelia (Logan) Irvin, b* 1 June, 1836; *d* 2 April, 1862.

   (203) *Ethelbert Logan Barkley.*

56. **Henry Benton Barkley** (M.D.), *b* 2 November, 1827; *d* 21 April, 1884; *m* 7 January, 1858, *Mary Jane Gooch, b* 1838; *d* 1865.

   (204) *Francina Mildred Barkley.*

58. **James Chambers Barkley,** *b* 11 March, 1832; *d* 4 September, 1898; *m* 1858, *Melinda Catherine Warren, b* 18 October, 1840; *d* 4 February, 1868, dau. of Thomas and Melinda (Cornelison) Warren.

   (205) *Richard Warren Barkley.*
   (206) *Margaret Francina Barkley.*

59. **David Maple Barkley** (M.D.), *b* 29 January, 1834; (living 1903); *m* 25 October, 1860, *Georgia Owen, b* 11 June, 1833; (living 1903), dau. of Gwynn and Mary (Puryear) Owen.

   (207) *Margaret Alice Barkley.*
   (208) *Mary Emeline Barkley, b* and *d* 1864.
   (209) *David Owen Barkley, b* and *d* 1865.
   (210) *Edward Owen Barkley.*
   (211) *Gracie Belle Barkley, b* 1870; *d* 1876.
   (212) *Harry Oldham Barkley, b* 14 November, 1872; (living 1903); *m* Fannie Onan.* Issue: *Harry Onan Barkley, b* 5 December, 1901; *d* December, 1902.

65. **Samuel Barkley,** *b* 11 February, 1836; *d* 20 July, 1890; *m* 5 January, 1871, *Madeline Gillispie, b* 7 December, 1851; (living 1903), dau. of Alexander and Mary (Whaley) Gillispie.

   (213) *Alexander Lee Barkley* (Rev.), *b* 16 April, 1872; (living 1903), *unm.*

(214) *Mary E. Barkley, b* 16 August, 1873; *d* 6 December, 1882.

(215) *Thomas G. Barkley, b* 18 December, 1874; (living 1903), *unm.*

(216) *Harry C. Barkley.*

(217) *Dana V. Barkley, b* 15 March, 1878; *d* 6 August, 1879.

(218) *Julia Z. Barkley, b* 20 October, 1879; (living 1903), *unm.*

(219) *James P. Barkley, b* 12 April, 1881; (living 1903), *unm.*

(220) *Esther B. Barkley, b* 24 March, 1883; (living 1903), *unm.*

(221) *Grover Cleveland Barkley, b* 14 January, 1885; (living 1903).

(222) *Llewellyn F. Barkley, b* 17 March, 1887; (living 1903).

69. **Martha Bishop Barkley,** *b* 4 August, 1843; (living 1903); *m* 21 March, 1867, *Willis Baxter, b* 22 March, 1839; (living 1903).

(223) *Elizabeth Baxter, b* 16 February, 1868; (living 1903), *unm.*

(224) *Alvin Baxter, b* 2 March, 1884; (living 1903).

(225) *Nellie Baxter, b* 12 June, 1886; (living 1903).

70. **Sydney Frances Barkley,** *b* 11 April, 1845; *d* 16 December, 1872; *m Joseph L. Hatcher, b* 9 September, 1841; (living 1903).

(226) *Edwin Barkley Hatcher, b* 1 May, 1867; (living 1903), *unm.*

(227) *Samuel O. Hatcher, b* 16 October, 1869; *d* 10 December, 1885.

(228) *Anna Grimes Hatcher, b* August, 1871; *d* September, 1872.

71. **Isaac Mason Barkley,** *b* 19 February, 1848; (living 1903); *m* 1 February, 1888, *Huldah Katherine Gash,*

b 24 February, 1861; (living 1903), dau. of Moses B and Katherine (Nichols) Gash.

(229) *Catherine Barkley, b* 5 November, 1888.

(230) *Leon Talmage Barkley, b* 27 August, 1890.

(231) *Mary D. Barkley, b* 29 December, 1892.

(232) *Elizabeth Barkley, b* 13 May, 1895.

(233) *Isaac C. Barkley, b* 21 February, 1898.

(234) *Champ Clark Barkley, b* 13 December, 1900.

74. **John Barkley,** *b* 9 September, 1833; *d* 4 August, 1863; *m Elizabeth M. Miller, b* 12 January, 1834; (living 1903), dau. of Ozbert and Eveline (Custer) Miller.

(235) *Martha C. Barkley, b* 26 August, 1856; (living 1903); *m William K. Nichols, b* 7 February, 1847. S. P.

(236) *Mary A. Barkley.*

(237) *Evelyn L. Barkley.*

(238) *John O. Barkley.*

76. **Elizabeth Barkley,** *b* 25 September, 1839; (living 1903); *m* 22 November, 1860, *Hugh H. McDowell, b* 18 September, 1835; (living 1903).

(239) *Anna McDowell, b* 21 September, 1862; *d* 7 January, 1864.

(240) *Elizabeth Miller McDowell, b* 2 November, 1863; *d* 29 January, 1864.

(241) *Margaret Barkley McDowell, b* 6 March, 1865; *d* 20 March, 1873.

(242) *Mary Susan McDowell, b* 1 August, 1869; (living 1903), *unm.*

78. **Anna Eliza Barkley,** *b* 6 October, 1843; (living 1903); *m* 5 November, 1867, *William Steele, b* 8 August, 1843; (living 1903).

(243) *Elizabeth Steele, b* 4 October, 1868; (living 1903); *m* 18 October, 1894, *R. L. Walker,* (living 1903).

(244) *Sarah Steele.*

79. **Samuel C. Barkley**, *b* 14 February, 1847; (living 1903);
   m 22 October, 1885, *Elizabeth H. Byrne*, (living 1903).
   - (245) *Julia Byrne Barkley, b* 3 April, 1887.
   - (246) *Anna Custer Barkley, b* 14 November, 1888.
   - (247) *Isaac R. Barkley, b* 1 November, 1890.
   - (248) *Mary Barkley, b* 5 November, 1892.
   - (249) *Robert B. Barkley, b* 22 June, 1895.
   - (250) *Joseph H. Barkley, b* 27 February, 1903.

82. **Mary Susan Barkley**, *b* 5 July, 1857; (living 1903); *m*
   3 April, 1883, *William R. Doty, b* 22 October, 1838;
   (living 1903).
   - (251) *Jesse Barkley Doty, b* 29 December, 1883.
   - (252) *Anne Steele Doty, b* 24 July, 1885.
   - (253) *Susan Dunn Doty, b* 29 July, 1887.
   - (254) *William Royalston Doty, b* 4 November, 1889.
   - (255) *Alice Florida Doty, b* 18 October, 1892.
   - (256) *Elizabeth Custer Doty, b* 22 February, 1895.

83. **Alice Barkley**, *b* 1 January, 1860; (living 1903); *m* 15
   June, 1893, *T. B. Walker*, (living 1903).
   - (257) *George Barkley Walker, b* 18 June, 1896.
   - (258) *T. B. Walker, b* 15 July, 1901.

84. **Cassa Jane Barkley**, *b* 3 August, 1835; *d* 28 July, 1898;
   m 7 May, 1868, *William T. Hearne, b* 22 January, 1835;
   (living 1903).
   - (259) *Elizabeth Hearne, b* 13 September, 1869; *d*
     1 September, 1893.
   - (260) *Frank Barkley Hearne, b* 24 September, 1871;
     (living 1903); *m* 25 April, 1899, *Roberta
     Lee Crumbaugh*, (living 1903).

86. **Samuel Isaac Barkley**, *b* 1 September, 1840; (living
   1903; *m* May, 1866, *Catherine Maria Lydick, b* 21
   January, 1845; (living 1903), dau. of John and Anna
   Whitaker (Biddle) Lydick.
   - (261) *Lena Barkley, b* 17 February, 1867; (living
     1903), *unm.*
   - (262) *Lora Barkley, b* 27 September, 1868; *d* 2 No-
     vember, 1877.

88. **George Mathias Barkley,** *b* 18 June, 1847; (living 1903);
m (1) 1 November, 1876, *Rebecca LaRue Helm, b* 3
March, 1844; *d* 28 December, 1880, dau. Rev. Squire
LaRue Helm and Sarah Ellen (Atwill) Helm, by whom
he had one child; *m* (2) *Emma Sidney Skillman, b* 24
November, 1860; *d* 1 February, 1902, dau. of Richard
S. and Hester (Atwill) Skillman, by whom he had a
daughter.

> (263) *George LaRue Barkley, b* 8 July, 1878; (living
> 1903).
> (264) *Murray Barkley, b* 7 November, 1886; (living
> 1903).

90. **Cassa Jane Barkley,** *b* 27 May, 1844; (living 1903); *m*
Benjamin M. Arnett, (living 1903).

> (265) *James Barkley Arnett, b* 3 March, 1871;
> (living 1903), *unm.*
> (266) *Louis Wagner Arnett, b* 10 June, 1877;
> (living 1903), *unm.*

99. **John Green Barkley,** *b* 5 June, 1839; (living 1903); *m*
14 December, 1859, *Eliza Virginia Read, b* 11 November, 1839; (living 1903), dau. of Henry Adlott Read
and Ann Teresa (Smith) Read.

> (267) *James Weir Barkley, b* 26 May, 1861; (living
> 1903), *unm.*
> (268) *Sallie Read Barkley, b* 25 April, 1863; (living
> 1903), *unm.*
> (269) *John Green Barkley, b* 22 February, 1865;
> (living 1903), *unm.*
> (270) *Henry Read Barkley.*
> (271) *Mary A. Barkley, b* 14 October, 1871; (living
> 1903); *m H. C. Clark,* (living 1903). S. P.
> (272) *Susan Bell Barkley, b* 17 November, 1876;
> (living 1903), *unm.*
> (273) *Jessamine Barkley, b* 1 August, 1880; (living
> 1903), *unm.*

102. Jessamine Barkley, *b* 26 January, 1846; (living 1903);
m 22 October, 1867, *Edward W. C. Humphrey, b* 23
May, 1844; (living 1903).

(274) *Catherine Prather Humphrey.*

(275) *Sally Green Humphrey.*

(276) *Edward Porter Humphrey, b* 18 February,
1873; (living 1903); *m* 25 November, 1902,
Mrs. *Virginia (Brown) Booth,* (living
1903).

(277) *Lewis Craig Humphrey, b* 28 September, 1875;
(living 1903), *unm.*

(278) *Heman Humphrey, b* 15 March, 1880; (living
1903), *unm.*

(279) *Jessamine Humphrey, b* 29 November, 1882;
(living 1903), *unm.*

(280) *Mary Brown Humphrey, b* 21 February, 1885;
(living 1903).

104. Sarah Addie Barkley, *b* 17 August, 1850; *m* 1878,
Nathaniel Lafon.

(281) *Nathaniel Lafon, b* February, 1879; (living
1903), *unm.*

(282) *Alice Lafon, b* September, 1880; (living 1903),
unm.

106. Martha Barkley, *b* 30 November, 1844; (living 1903);
m 25 February, 1875, *Joseph (Henderson) Lane;*
(living 1903).

(283) *Frank Wilber Lane, b* 16 February, 1876;
(living 1903), *unm.*

(284) *Margaret Barkley Lane.*

107. Margaret Clarke Barkley, *b* 1 August, 1847; (living
1903); *m* 21 January, 1868, *John Steele,* (living 1903).

(285) *William Clarke Steele, b* 22 October, 1868;
d 31 August, 1883.

(286) *Hallie Steele, b* 4 August, 1876; *d* 19 August,
1889.

(287) *Addye Mitchem Steele, b* 30 August, 1884;
(living 1903), *unm.*

(288) *Margaret Clarke Steele, b* 4 July, 1891; (living 1903).

112. **Eugenia Barkley,** *b* 23 June, 1862; (living 1903); *m* 9 April, 1887, *George Hutchison,* (living 1903).

(289) *Margaret Hutchison, b* 27 January, 1888; *d* 21 February, 1896.

(290) *Lucille Hutchison, b* 10 May, 1890; (living 1903).

(291) *George Hutchison, b* 3 October, 1892; (living 1903).

(292) *Frank Young Hutchison, b* 29 April, 1895; (living 1903).

113. **William Lucas Barkley,** *b* 31 May, 1865; (living 1903); *m* 22 September, 1886, *Prue Hunt Blackburn, d* 1892.

(293) *Adeline Belle Barkley, b* 15 October, 1887; (living 1903).

(294) *John Steele Barkley, b* 9 March, 1889; (living 1903).

(295) *Lon Crittenden Barkley,* (living 1903).

116. **Stephen Edward Jones,** *b* 23 April, 1833; (living 1903); *m* (1) *Martha McKee, b* 2 August, 1837; *d* 15 November, 1873; *m* (2) *Frances Prevost Breckenridge,* (living 1903).

(296) *Alice Lafon Jones, b* 21 December, 1859; (living 1903), *unm.*

(297) *Hugh McKee Jones, b* 4 September, 1861; *d* 3 October, 1881.

(298) *Annie Barkley Jones, b* 9 December, 1865; (living 1903); *m* 5 October, 1903, *Thomas Hoyt Gamble.*

(299) *Stephen Edward Jones, b* 15 March, 1870; (living 1903).

(300) *Hunt Jones, b* 22 February, 1884; (living 1903).

(301) *Lafon Jones, b* 20 January, 1885; (living 1903).

(302) *Robert Breckinridge Jones, b* 4 January, 1888; (living 1903).

(303) *Richard Cocke Jones, b* 10 March, 1900; (living 1903).

120. **William Benjamin Barkley,** *b* 3 March, 1841; *d* 11 December, 1901; *m Katherine Scott, b* 29 January, 1862; (living 1903).

(304) *William Edward Barkley, b* 28 December, 1882; (living 1903).

121. **Henry Clay Barkley,** *b* 4 March, 1843; (living 1903); *m* 22 October, 1879, *Elizabeth Boggs, b* 18 April, 1853; (living 1903).

(305) *Mary Elizabeth Barkley, b* 8 October, 1880; (living 1903); *m* 27 December, 1899, *William Henry Lowens, b* 8 September, 1881; (living 1903). S. P.

(306) *Joseph Henry Barkley, b* and *d* November, 1881.

(307) *Margaret Butler Barkley, b* 8 December, 1882; *d* 7 March, 1899.

126. **Frank Barkley,** *b* 11 June, 1856; (living 1903); *m* 8 May, 1879, *Leona Doggett, b* 17 March, 1860; (living 1903).

(308) *Mary Louisa Barkley, b* 25 January, 1881; (living 1903), *unm.*

(309) *Elizabeth Davis Barkley, b* 8 September, 1882; (living 1903).

(310) *Roscoe Barkley, b* 12 September, 1888; (living 1903).

(311) *Cora May Barkley, b* 25 March, 1890; (living 1903).

(312) *Annie Barkley, b* 20 July, 1892; (living 1903).

    (313) *John Lewis Barkley,* b 28 August, 1895; (living 1903).

    (314) *Lelia Barkley,* b 27 October, 1899; (living (1903).

    (315) *Frank Crawford Barkley,* b 24 November, 1902; (living 1903).

130. **John James Thomson,** b 21 August, 1850; d 6 March, 1887; m 20 November, 1873, *America Lyons* (living 1903).

    (316) *Sallie May Thomson,* b 17 September, 1875; d 5 December, 1894.

    (317) *John William Thomson,* b 18 August, 1877; (living 1903); m 1 August, 1901, *Hattie Rose.*

    (318) *Amos Herman Thomson,* b 19 April, 1881; (living 1903); m 31 July, 1903, —— *Davenport.*

    (319) *Hattie Lyons Thomson,* b 4 January, 1887; d 11 January, 1894.

132. **Margaret Boyd Thomson,** b 5 June, 1854; (living 1903); m 19 November, 1879, *Monroe Walker.*

    (320) *Henry Means Walker,* b 9 December, 1891; (living 1903).

134. **Thomas Samuel Thomson,** b 1 December, 1861; (living 1903); m 29 November, 1883, *Alverda Lee Boyd.*

    (321) *Alice Catherine Thomson,* b 4 November, 1884; (living 1903).

    (322) *Margaret Boyd Thomson,* b 13 October, 1895; (living 1903).

136. **John Clay Blount,** b 20 April, 1856; (living 1903); m 9 October, 1879, *Sarah Ann Herrin,* b 23 December, 1854; (living 1903).

    (323) *Henry Clay Blount,* b 23 July, 1880; (living 1903), *unm.*

(324) *Mary Jane Blount, b* 31 December, 1881;
(living 1903), *unm.*

(325) *Omar Daniel Blount, b* 29 September, 1883;
d 16 June, 1901.

(326) *Milburn Blount, b* 23 January, 1885; *d* 23
December, 1893.

(327) *Rolla Emmet Blount, b* 1 May, 1886; *d* 29
August, 1886.

(328) *John Sherman Blount, b* 12 September, 1887;
(living 1903).

(329) *Ollie Trigg Blount, b* 27 July, 1889; (living
1903).

(330) *William Russell Blount, b* 28 June, 1892;
(living 1903).

(331) *Elsie Catherine Blount, b* 26 December, 1894;
(living 1903).

(332) *Hobart Blount, b* 14 April, 1896; (living
1903).

137. **Mary Elizabeth Means,** *b* 25 February, 1844; *d* 2 September, 1869; *m* 6 December, 1866, *Madison Monroe Walker.*

(333) *Hattie Means Walker, b* 21 July, 1867; (living
1903); *m* 3 October, 1888, *Charles Clarke
Pearce.*

(334) *Hendrick Monroe Walker, b* and *d* 1869.

138. **George Means,** *b* 26 February, 1846; *d* 20 February, 1877; *m* 14 February, 1869, *Julia Burgess.*

(335) *Annie Conie Means, b* 2 April, 1872; (living
1903).

142. **James Barkley Means,** *b* 12 November, 1857; (living 1903); *m* 17 October, 1894, *Helen Luman, b* 25 January, 1869; (living 1903).

(336) *William Amos Means, b* 14 April, 1896;
(living 1903).

(337) *Walker Wilson Means, b* 7 March, 1898;
(living 1903).

148. **Ella Mae Barkley,** *b* 2 October, 1873; (living 1903); *m* 18 October, 1893, *Robinson Lee Carter, b* 13 September, 1870; (living 1903).

    (338) *Douglas Roscoe Carter, b* 20 April, 1896; (living 1903).

    (339) *Elaine Carter, b* 22 January, 1900; (living 1903).

149. **Mintie Emma Barkley,** *b* 1 April, 1861; (living 1903); *m* 24 September, 1884, *Ellsworth Henderson, b* 1 July, 1861; (living 1903).

    (340) *Harry Bruce Henderson, b* 23 May, 1887; (living 1903).

150. **Mary Belle Barkley,** *b* 1862; (living 1903); *m Jack Hendrickson, b* 1 March, 1860; (living 1903).

    (341) *James Herbert Hendrickson, b* 1883; *d* 1885.

    (342) *Catherine Cassidy Hendrickson, b* 22 October, 1885; (living 1903).

    (343) *Amy Florence Hendrickson, b* 4 June, 1887; (living 1903).

    (344) *George Barkley Hendrickson, b* 29 April, 1889; (living 1903).

151. **George William Barkley,** *b* 1871; (living 1903); *m Frances May Hull, b* 1872; (living 1903).

    (345) *Bruce Hull Barkley, b* 1897; (living 1903).

    (346) *Jennie Louise Barkley, b* 1902; (living 1903).

157. **Isabella Lee Barkley,** *b* 7 January, 1871; (living 1903); *m* 4 October, 1899, *Stanley Simpson Bartlett;* (living 1903).

    (347) *Henry Howell Bartlett, b* 9 December, 1900; (living 1903).

158. **Frank Owens Barkley,** *b* 16 January, 1874; (living 1903); *m* 3 October, 1900, *Roberta Stockton Robinson,* (living 1903).

    (348) *Eugene Robinson Barkley, b* June, 1901; (living 1903).

161. Lucile May Barkley, *b* 27 November, 1867; (living
1903;) *m* 27 December, 1892, *Allen Clement Ater, b* 1
January, 1858; (living 1903).

>   (349) *Mildred Marguerite Ater, b* 19 September,
>   1899; (living 1903).

166. William Thomas Barkley, *b* 13 September, 1867; (living
1903) ; *m* 14 September, 1896, *Marguerite Rudolph,*
(living 1903).

>   (350) *Adonis Rudolph Barkley, b* 1897; (living
>   1903).
>   (351) *William Thomas Barkley, b* 1900; (living
>   1903).

169. Mary Alice Barkley, *b* 25 March, 1876; *d* 4 May, 1903;
m 1897, *John J. Phillips.*

>   (352) *Mary Alice Phillips, b* 1898; (living 1903).
>   (353) *Caroline Barkley Phillips, b* 1903.

170. Mary Amanda Pemberton, *b* 7 June, 1844; *d* 3 June,
1879; *m* (1) 26 May, 1864, *William Joseph Ross, b*
1840; *d* 14 June, 1872; *m* (2) 6 March, 1878, *Hub
Ashbrook.*

>   (354) *Catherine Pearce Ross, b* 30 March, 1865;
>   *d* 15 March, 1896; *m* 13 May, 1886, *Edwin
>   H. Kenner, b* 18 August, 1861. Issue:
>   *Webb Ross Kenner, d* 1887.
>   (355) *Lillie Belle Ross.*
>   (356) *Mary Pemberton Ashbrook, b* and *d* 1879.

172. Henrietta Wadsworth Pemberton, *b* 4 September, 1848;
d 24 March, 1888; *m* 29 December, 1868, *James Robert
Webb, b* 5 December, 1846; (living 1903).

>   (357) *Harriet Ashbrook Webb, b* 15 October, 1869;
>   (living 1903) ; *m* 29 June, 1892, *Walter W.
>   Waldron,* (living 1903). S. P.
>   (358) *Catherine Pemberton Webb, b* 19 March, 1871;
>   (living 1903) ; *m* 27 December, 1897, *Charles
>   Lewis Merrick,* (living 1903). S. P.

      (359) *Abigail Baldwin Webb, b* 28 August, 1876; (living 1903), *unm.*

      (360) *Mary Henrietta Webb, b* 3 March, 1879; (living 1903); *m* 1 June, 1903, *Mathew W. Matticheck.*

177. **John Dillon Bridges,** *b* 13 March, 1849; (living 1903); *m* 20 July, 1881, *Stella Marie Grimes,* (living 1903).

      (361) *William Southerland Bridges, b* 27 November, 1884; (living 1903).

179. **Henry Barkley Bridges,** *b* 19 November, 1859; (living 1903); *m* 19 August, 1890, *Lula Klein, b* 2 January, 1872; *d* 15 June, 1903.

      (362) *Louis Thies Bridges, b* February, 1891; (living 1903).

      (363) *Mary Rice Bridges, b* 11 April, 1892; (living 1903).

186. **James Hickman Barkley,** *b* 20 January, 1863; (living 1903); *m* 15 August, 1886, *Minnie May Martin, b* 9 March, 1862; *d* 4 March, 1903.

      (364) *Crawford Thomas Barkley, b* 17 June, 1887; (living 1903).

      (365) *Margaret Frances Barkley, b* and *d* June, 1888.

      (366) *Gordon Fletcher Barkley, b* 3 March, 1894; (living 1903).

      (367) *Ruth Gretchen Barkley, b* 5 August, 1901; (living 1903).

189. **Lamotie Barkley,** *b* 1 January, 1870; (living 1903); *m* 5 July, 1892, *Gibbons Poteet, b* 30 August, 1866; (living 1903).

      (368) *Barkley Gibbons Poteet, b* 13 May, 1893; (living 1903).

      (369) *Robert Pembroke Poteet, b* 26 September, 1894; (living 1903).

      (370) *Frances Lucretia Poteet, b* December, 1895; (living 1903).

(371) *James Hugh Poteet, b* 1900; *d* 1901.

(372) *Charles Owen Poteet, b* 8 January, 1902;
(living 1903).

191. **Francina Alice Barkley,** *b* 18 September, 1850; (living
1903); *m* 8 October, 1871, Rev. *William Henry Wright,
b* 12 October, 1848; (living 1903).

(373) *Leslie Alban Wright.*

(374) *Ray Barkley Wright* (M.D.), *b* 24 April, 1874;
(living 1903); *m* 26 September, 1900, *Jessie
Neal.*

(375) *James Erwin Wright,* b 11 March, 1876; *d* 20
September, 1877.

(376) *Malinda Alice Wright.*

(377) *Lonnie Joe Wright* (a daughter), *b* 10 October, 1884; *d* 3 February, 1899.

(378) *Rovena Mason Wright, b* 20 January, 1888;
(living 1903).

192. **Leonidas Marue Barkley,** *b* 8 October, 1853; (living
1903); *m* 8 October, 1889, *Laura Hardisty, b* December, 1868; (living 1903).

(379) *Juliet Malinda Barkley, b* 6 October, 1890;
(living 1903).

(380) *Burk Burnett Barkley, b* 9 December, 1895;
(living 1903).

193. **Rovena Gertrude Barkley,** *b* 3 July, 1857; (living 1903);
m ——— *Morgan.*

(381) *Edward Leonidas Morgan,* (living 1903).

194. **Laura Josephine Barkley,** *b* 18 October, 1859; (living
1903); *m* 21 December, 1890, *Thomas J. Wood, b* 29
February, 1860; (living 1903).

(382) *Eula Wood, b* 21 February, 1892; (living
1903).

(383) *Thomas Barkley Wood, b* 24 June, 1896;
(living 1903).

197. **Jesse Crawford Neal**, *b* 23 November, 1846; (living 1903) ; *m* 26 March, 1878, *Mary Land, b* 29 June, 1855; (living 1903).

> (384) *William Land Neal, b* 20 April, 1879; (living 1903), *unm.*
>
> (385) *Perry Mason Neal, b* 29 July, 1882; (living 1903).
>
> (386) *Denver D. Neal, b* 25 October, 1886; (living 1903).
>
> (387) *Harry L. Neal, b* 23 November, 1895; (living 1903).

198. **Charles Waller**, *b* 18 September, 1856; (living 1903) ; *m* 25 April, 1889, *Lula Hamilton, b* 1 May, 1867; (living 1903).

> (388) *Rena Barkley Waller, b* 25 March, 1890; (living 1903).
>
> (389) *Laura Charlie Waller, b* 5 July, 1891; (living 1903).
>
> (390) *Clarence Hamilton Waller, b* 22 January, 1893; (living 1903).
>
> (391) *Mary Nelson Waller, b* 14 May, 1894; (living 1903).
>
> (392) *J. M. Haden Waller, b* 10 October, 1896; (living 1903).
>
> (393) *Martha Frances Waller, b* 16 July, 1898; (living 1903).
>
> (394) *Joseph Gamboe Waller, b* 29 September, 1900; (living 1903).
>
> (395) *Zerelda McKinney Waller, b* 20 May, 1902; (living 1903).

199. **Laura Waller**, *b* 5 July, 1859; (living 1903) ; *m* 19 April, 1892, *Charles Mitchell*, (living 1903).

> (396) *Walter Scott Mitchell, b* 19 February, 1893; (living 1903).
>
> (397) *William Jennings Bryan Mitchell, b* and *d* 1896.
>
> (398) *Frances Louisa Mitchell, b* 18 December, 1899; (living 1903).

203. **Ethelbert Logan Barkley**, *b* 10 July, 1861; (living 1903);
m 15 October, 1884, *Cora Lee Curd*, *b* 17 April, 1864;
(living 1903).

> (399) *Lyda May Barkley*, *b* 2 April, 1887; (living
> 1903).

204. **Francina Mildred Barkley**, *b* 27 October, 1858; (living
1903); *m* 15 October, 1875, *James Harvey Thomas*, *b*
21 May, 1855; (living 1903).

> (400) *Rosie Jane Thomas*, *b* 10 August, 1876; *d* in
> infancy.
>
> (401) *Ola Jay Thomas*.
>
> (402) *Henry Silas Thomas*, *b* 27 August, 1880;
> (living 1903), *unm*.
>
> (403) *William Reader Thomas*, *b* 25 May, 1887;
> (living 1903).
>
> (404) *Sarah Lillian Thomas*, *b* 1889; *d* 1893.
>
> (405) *Evelyn Thomas*, *b* 11 March, 1893; *d* in in-
> fancy.
>
> (406) *Walter Harvey Thomas*, *b* 7 May, 1895;
> (living 1903).
>
> (407) *Velma Barkley Thomas*, *b* 5 October, 1897;
> (living 1903).
>
> (408) *Birdie Thomas*, *b* and *d* in 1902.

205. **Richard Warren Barkley**, *b* 21 February, 1859; (living
1903); *m* 27 September, 1887, *Maria Louisa Henley*, *b*
5 May, 1866; (living 1903).

> (409) *Robert Yates Barkley*, *b* 3 March, 1889; (liv-
> ing 1903).
>
> (410) *Katherine Elizabeth Barkley*, *b* 17 July, 1890;
> (living 1903).
>
> (411) *Dorothy Fleet Barkley*, *b* 30 August, 1892;
> (living 1903).
>
> (412) *Priscilla Meriwether Barkley*, *b* 22 August,
> 1899; (living 1903).

206. **Margaret Francina Barkley**, *b* 10 June, 1863; (living
1903); *m* (1) *Charles Breckinridge Pardonner*, *b* 18

July, 1856; *d* 4 May, 1897; *m* (2) *Charles Robert Curry;* (living 1903).

    (413) *Melinda Rachel Pardonner,* *b* 29 February, 1884; (living 1903); *m* 17 January, 1903, *W. Thomas Foote, b* 12 October, 1880; (living 1903).

    (414) *Jonathan Franklin Pardonner, b* 21 May, 1891; (living 1903).

    (415) *Lillian Marguerite Pardonner, b* 21 May, 1891; (living 1903).

    (416) *Alice Rebecca Pardonner, b* 13 September, 1893; (living 1903).

    (417) *James Richard Charles Pardonner, b* 23 May, 1896; (living 1903).

    (418) *Mary Catherine Curry, b* 4 September, 1900; (living 1903).

    (419) *Margaret Barkley Curry, b* 22 December, 1901; (living 1903).

207. **Margaret Alice Barkley,** *b* 5 January, 1862; *d* 5 November, 1891; *m* December, 1885, *Richard L. Gregory,* (living 1903).

    (420) *Richard L. Gregory, b* 28 August, 1886; (living 1903).

210. **Edward Owen Barkley,** *b* 21 June, 1868; (living 1903); *m* 1893, *Pearl Dyer,* (living 1903).

    (421) *Margaret Dyer Barkley, b* 2 December, 1900; (living 1903).

    (422) *David William Barkley, b* 28 July, 1903.

216. **Harry C. Barkley,** *b* 5 April, 1876; (living 1903); *m* 1 July, 1902, *Ruby Roy,* (living 1903).

    (423) (A daughter), *b* 1903.

236. **Mary A. Barkley,** *b* 7 November, 1858; (living 1903); *m* 18 March, 1881, *Osborn W. Watkins, d* 16 April, 1903.

(424) *Barkley J. Watkins, b* 20 December, 1884; *d* June, 1886.

(425) *Duval C. Watkins, b* 4 July, 1886; (living 1903).

(426) *Ozbert O. Watkins, b* 19 February, 1888; (living 1903).

(427) *William W. Watkins, b* 12 September, 1889; (living 1903).

(428) *Elizabeth M. Watkins, b* 27 March, 1891; (living 1903).

237. **Evelyn L. Barkley,** *b* 22 December, 1860; (living 1903); *m* 15 March, 1879, *Taylor C. Nichols, b* March, 1845; *d* 15 January, 1903.

(429) *Clarence G. Nichols, b* 14 October, 1884; (living 1903).

238. **John O. Barkley,** *b* 14 January, 1862; (living 1903); *m* 19 March, 1891, *Margaret E. Penn, b* 22 October, 1865; (living 1903).

(430) *Evander Penn Barkley, b* 30 December, 1891; (living 1903).

(431) *John C. Barkley, b* 13 December, 1893; (living 1903).

(432) *Mildred M. Barkley, b* 15 January, 1895; (living 1903).

(433) *Atwell S. Barkley, b* 7 September, 1897; (living 1903).

(434) *Frances E. Barkley, b* 12 June, 1902; (living 1903).

244. **Sarah Steele,** *b* 20 December, 1874; (living 1903); *m* 25 February, 1899, *Horace Bruce Taylor,* (living 1903).

(435) *Annie Steele Taylor, b* 15 June, 1901; (living 1903).

270. **Henry Read Barkley,** *b* 2 August, 1868; (living 1903); *m* 20 July, 1899, *Frances Scott Bullock, b* 29 July, 1874; (living 1903).

(436) *Frances Virginia Barkley, b* 5 July, 1900;
(living 1903).

(437) *Elizabeth Rayman Barkley, b* 24 February,
1903.

274. **Catherine Prather Humphrey,** *b* 24 January, 1869; (living 1903) ; *m* 3 October, 1893, Rev. *Benjamin Lewis Hobson, b* 31 July, 1859; (living 1903).

(438) *Martha Barbour Hobson, b* 22 August, 1894;
(living 1903).

(439) *Jessamine Humphrey Hobson, b* 25 August,
1897; (living 1903).

275. **Sally Green Humphrey,** *b* 24 February, 1871; (living 1903) ; *m* 1 June, 1893, *Robert Coleman Price, b* 18 May, 1861; (living 1903).

(440) *Jessamine Price, b* 5 March, 1894; (living 1903).

(441) *Edward Humphrey Price, b* 8 May, 1895;
(living 1903).

(442) *Mary Frances Price, b* 17 June, 1897; (living 1903).

284. **Margaret Barkley Lane,** *b* 29 September, 1879; (living 1903) ; *m* 15 March, 1899, *W. L. Sickles,* (living 1903).

(443) *Lane Barkley Sickles, b* 13 October, 1902.

355. **Lillie Belle Ross,** *b* 26 June, 1868; (living 1903) ; *m* 14 April, 1887, *Jefferson Hall Belt, b* 25 June, 1862; (living 1903).

(444) *Jefferson Hall Belt, b* 10 November, 1888;
(living 1903).

(445) *Catherine Ross Belt, b* 7 March, 1891; (living 1903).

(446) *Lillie Pemberton Belt, b* 27 May, 1894; (living 1903).

(447) *Daisy Elizabeth Belt, b* 27 August, 1900;
(living 1903).

373. **Leslie Alban Wright,** *b* 18 July, 1872; (living 1903); *m* 21 September, 1899, *May Nelson,* (living 1903).

> (448) *Leslie Alban Wright, b* 1 September, 1900; (living 1903).

376. **Malinda Alice Wright,** *b* 24 November, 1877; (living 1903); *m* 14 September, 1897, *Arthur Eames Barrett,* (living 1903).

> (449) *Arthur Eames Barrett, b* 14 June, 1898; (living 1903).
>
> (450) *Irvine Ray Barrett, b* 10 August, 1899; (living 1903).

401. **Ola Jay Thomas,** *b* 21 October, 1878; (living 1903); *m* 21 December, 1898, *Ida Brown Lightner, b* 27 February, 1882; (living 1903).

> (451) *Viola Elma Thomas, b* 21 December, 1899; (living 1903).
>
> (452) *Urcel Byron Thomas, b* 19 July, 1901; (living 1903).

PART XI.

Some Scattered Barclay Records.

(The writer does not claim completeness for what follows. He has simply transcribed here sundry notes which he made during the course of his searches.)

Massachusetts.

Rev. WILLIAM BARCLAY was the Minister of the Church of England at Braintree in New England, between 1702 and 1704. (HISTORY OF OLD BRAINTREE AND QUINCY, by W. S. Pattee, M. D., 1878, p. 246.)

New York.

ROLL OF FREEMEN, NEW YORK CITY (1675-1866).

1765, October 1,—DAVID BARCLAY, Peruke maker (*N. Y. Hist. Soc. Collection of 1885,* p 202).

1769, January 31,—THOMAS BARCLAY, Merchant (*Ibid,* p. 218).

SECRETARY OF STATE'S OFFICE, ALBANY.

Marriage License.

JOSEPH BARCLAY and *Sarah Caduser.* License issued 3 June, 1760. (M. B., vol. III, p. 175.)

SURROGATE'S OFFICE, ALBANY COUNTY.

1802, December 16,—Will proved of MARGARET BARCLAY, widow of John Barclay, late Mayor of Albany. Will dated October 1, 1782. Executors: Tobias ten Eyck (a brother), Conrad Gansevoort (a nephew) and Elizabeth Peebles (a niece). *Witnesses:* James Livingston, Coenrad Scharp, and Abraham A.

Lansing. Bequests or devises to the heirs of deceased sister Gerritie ten Eyck, wife of Peter Gansvoort; to niece Elizabeth Peebles widow of Thomas Peebles of the Half Moon; and to brothers Jacob C. ten Eyck, Anthony ten Eyck, Barent ten Eyck, Tobias ten Eyck, and Andries ten Eyck. Recorded *Lib.* B of Wills, p. 143. (CALENDAR OF WILLS, compiled by Colonial Dames of New York, page 41.)

SURROGATE'S OFFICE, NEW YORK COUNTY.

1778, August 13,—Will proved of JOHN BARKLEY of the City of New York, mariner, and letters testamentary issued to his wife, *Ann Barkley,* to whom he leaves his entire estate. Will dated 1 December, 1775. *Witnesses:* John Young, Jr., and John Henderson, pilot (*Lib.* 31 of Wills, p. 202).

1786, October 28,—Will proved of JOHN BARKLEY, yeoman, of Ulster County, Providence of Montgomery, New York, and letters testamentary issued to James McCardy and Samuel Barkley. Will dated 4 September, 1786. *Witnesses:* Samuel Crawford, David Crawford and Joshua Crawford. Referred to his two sons William Barkley and Nathan Barkley and to his daughter Jean Barkley (*Lib.* 39 of Wills, p. 311).

1787, January 15,—Letters of administration on estate of JOHN BARCLAY, merchant, late of the Island of St. Thomas, deceased, issued to John Ritsen of the City of New York, merchant, a principal creditor (*Lib.* 3 of Adm., p. 11).

1793, July 30,—Will proved of DAVID BARCLAY, of New York, gentleman, and letters testamentary issued to Thomas North and Ezekiel Robins. Will dated at New York June 28, 1792, and witnessed by Maria McKesson, George Lyon, James Boyd, and John McKesson. Gives income of his estate to wife, *Mary Barclay,* for life. Gives to Elizabeth Clinton, daughter of His Excellency, George Clinton, house and lot fronting on William Street which he purchased from some of the Walton family. Upon his wife's death gives to Zalmon Bedient of Canaan, Connecticut, all his lands in the town of Milton, Vermont. Gives legacy to George Garland, of New York, innkeeper. Same to his wife's sister, Ann Betts. Gives residuary estate to Thomas North of Poughkeepsie, mariner, son of Robert North; David Falconer, son of John Falconer; David B. Betts, of New York, bricklayer, son of John Betts; William B. Wood, son of John Wood of New York, schoolmaster; and Thomas Penneyer of Westchester County, tailor. Appoints as executor, in addition to those who qualified as above stated, Melancthon Smith (*Lib.* 41 of Wills, p. 194).

1806, March 11,—Will proved of JAMES BARCLAY, at present of New York, and letters testamentary issued to Abraham B. Martling of New York. Will dated December 4, 1805. Refers to father, *James Barclay,* and mother, *Jane Barclay,* both living in South Shields, Durham County, England. Appoints as executor, in addition to the one who qualified as above, William Hayward of New York (*Lib.* 46 of Wills, p. 237).

Other wills on record in the Surrogate's Office, New York County, are:

Proved 1764, October 1,—HENRY BARCLAY, rector of Trinity Church, dated June 19, 1764 (*Lib.* 24 of Wills, p. 498).

Proved 1776, May 25,—ANDREW BARCLAY, his brother, dated August 12, 1763. (*Lib.* 30 of Wills, p. 184.)

Proved 1783, June 20,—JOHN BARCLAY, Mayor of Albany, dated January 30th, 1779. (*Lib.* 36 of Wills, p. 184.)

Proved 1830, June 1,—THOMAS BARCLAY, British consul-general, dated December 3, 1828. (*Lib.* 66 of Wills, p. 206.)

Proved 1837, July 3,—SUSAN BARCLAY, his wife, dated December 29, 1834; first codicil dated February 18, 1835; second dated November 5, 1836. (*Lib.* 76 of Wills, p. 327.)

Proved 1838, March 2,—THOMAS BARCLAY, (this is Thomas Edmund Barclay), son of Thomas and Susan Barclay above named, dated November 12, 1831. (*Lib.* 78 of Wills, p. 252.)

BOARD OF HEALTH, CITY OF NEW YORK (1798-1856).

DEATHS REPORTED.

Date of death.	Name.	Age.	Place of death.	Where buried.
1803, June 9.	BARCLAY, ANNY,			
Aug. 10.	" ANNE,	25	Mulberry St.	Presb. Cem.
1808, May 8.	" HENRY,	28	N. Y. Hospital.	
1813, April 9.	BARCKLY, GEORGE,	28	Gen'l Rendezvous. Market St. *b* in Ireland.	St. Peter's Cem.
18.	BARCLAY, ISABELLA,	4	Henry St.	St. Peter's Cem.
July 26.	" CATHARINE,	8 mos.	Henry St.	St. Peter's Cem.
Aug. 3.	" JOHN,	14	*b* in New York.	Christ Cem.
1814, Mch. 16.	" THOMAS,	25	John St. *b* in New York.	1st Presb. Cem.
Aug. 13.	" NATHAN,	4 mos.	Grand & Orchard Sts.	Rutgers St. Cem.
1815, April 20.	" MARY,	2	Spring St.	Methodist Cem.
1818, July 5.	" SARAH,	53	45 Market St. *b* in New Jersey.	
1819, Aug. 2.	BARKLEY, DEBORAH,	11 mos. 23 days	Spring St. *b* in Pennsylvania.	Refd. Presb. Cem.
1826, Aug. 3.	BARCLAY, JOHN,	1	23 Lombardy St.	
1827, Oct. 4.	BARKLEY, GEORGE,	4 mos.	67 Christie St.	Methodist Soc'y
5.	" JAMES,	7 mos.	Elizabeth St.	Rutgers St. Presb. Cem.
1828, Mch. 19.	BARCLAY, SARAH,	83	Pump St. *b* in New Jersey.	Methodist Soc'y
Dec. 29.	BARKLEY, MARIA,	21	Elizabeth.	Rutgers St. Presb. Cem.
1829, Dec. 25.	BARCLAY, JAMES,	61	Broome St. *b* in New Jersey.	Rutgers St. Cem.
1830, Aug. 17.	" DEBORY,	32	Broome St.	Rutgers St. Cem.
1831, Mch. 2.	BARCKLEY, SUSAN,	24	Centre St.	St. Phillips Cem.
1832, July 13.	BARKLEY, EBENEZER,	8	Norfolk St. *b* in New Jersey.	Rutgers St.
1834, May 22.	BARKLEY, MARGARET,	1	Delancey St.	Methodist Soc.
1835, Feb. 10.	" MARTHA,	23	Hammond St.	Rutgers St.
Nov. 28.	BARCLAY, CECILIA,	22	*b* in Troy.	
1836, Mch. 3.	BARKLEY, CATHERINE	10 yrs. 1 mo.	East Dey St.	Marble Cem.
June 5.	BARCLAY, ELIZA,	31	*b* in Virginia.	
Aug. 12.	BARKLEY, JAMES,	35	*b* in Ireland.	
Oct. 7.	BARCLAY, JOHN,	25	92 Vesey St. *b* in Philadelphia.	
1838, Jany. 14.	" JOHN,	40	203 Broome St.	
1840, Sept. 3.	" JULIA,	26	123 Thompson St. *b* in England.	Brick Church Cem.

Date of death.	Name.	Age.	Place of death.	Where buried.
1841, Feb. 10.	BARKELEY, ROBERT H.,	3 yrs. 10 mos. 4 days	134 Elizabeth St.	Marble Cem.
May 29.	BARCLAY, STEPHEN,	36	56 Sullivan St. b in France.	Methodist Soc.
1842, April 25.	" ELIZABETH M.	15	24 Rivington St.	West Presb. Cem.
1842, Aug. 5.	" MARY,	40	N. Y. Hospital.	
1843, Aug. 10.	" CATHERINE,	60	205 Mott St. b In Ireland.	St. Patricks
1844, Feb. 19.	BARKLEY, BENJAMIN F.	3	260 Second Ave.	Removed from the City.
May 2.	BARCLAY, DAVID,	38	183 Prince St. b in Scotland.	Methodist.
Oct. 20.	" ELIZABETH,	16 yrs. 11 mos.	18 Sixth St.	Refd. Presb. Prince St.
1846, July 24.	" MARY,	67	48 Hubert St. b in Wales.	Methodist.
1847, May 21.	" BENJAMIN,	35		
1848, Aug. 27.	" DIANA,	30	b in Albany.	
Dec. 8.	" MRS.,	43	11 Oliver St.	Removed from City.
1849, Jan. 10.	" THOMAS,	35		
Aug. 6.	" MARY,	44	137 Pitt St.	Removed from City.
1850, Sept. 28.	" ANN,	30	31 Orange St. b in Virginia.	
1850, Dec. 20.	BARKLEY, ROBERT H.,	1 yr. 2 mos.		Marble Cem.
1851, April 29.	" ELIZA,	37	179 Laurens St. b in Ireland.	4th Cong.
1852, Sept. 2.	BARCLAY, WILLIAM,	1 yr. 8 mos.	54 Tenth St.	Removed from City.
1854, May 26.	BARKLEY, JOHN,	22	b in Ireland.	Ward's Island.
Aug. 30.	BARCLAY, MARY ANN,	5 mos.	2 Jay St.	Calvary.
Nov. 23.	" JULIA,	50	62 Willet St. b in Ireland.	Calvary.
1855, Feb. 24.	BARKLEY, THOMAS F.,	6 mos. 13 days	136 Ninth St.	19th St. M. E.
May 6.	" CATHERINE,	30 yrs. 3 mos. 7 days	190 W. 24th St. b in New Jersey.	New Jersey.
Aug. 7.	BARCLAY, THOMAS,	1	113 Washington St.	N. Y. B. C.
Dec. 19.	" HENRY H.,	24	64 Lispenard St.	Greenwood.

(The records of *Marriages* in the Board of Health of the City of New York, begin with 1847; but they contain very few entries for many years.

The records of *Births* also begin with 1847; but few births were reported until a comparatively recent date.)

TRINITY PARISH RECORDS, NEW YORK CITY.

Burials.

BARCLAY, CAPT. JAMES, December 9, 1805, aet. 28 yrs.
　　Trinity.
"　　(Mr.'s CHILD), August 10, 1780.
"　　MRS., September 6, 1801, aet. 35 yrs.　St. Paul's.
"　　JOHN, October 26, 1826, aet. 38 yrs.　St. Johns.
"　　CHARLOTTE, February 28, 1874, aet. 31 yrs.
　　Greenwood.
"　　JAMES, July 5, 1896, aet. 58 yrs. 6 mos.　N. Y.
　　Bay Cemetery.

Marriages.

1782, February 27, *Richard Steers* and EVE BARCLAY, by Rev. Charles Inglis.

1797, September 24, GEORGE BARCLAY and *Elizabeth Sims,* by Rev. Benj. Moore.

1813, February 27, WILLIAM BARCLAY and *Rosanna McCullough,* by Rev. John H. Hobart.

1885, November 9, *Charles H. Moorehouse* and MARY ANN BARCLAY, by Rev. A. J. Thompson and Rev. Pierre Cushing.

Baptisms.

1783, April 6, BENJAMIN BARCLAY (*b* 20 January, 1783). *Parents:* John and Silvia Barclay.　*Sponsors:* Richard Richards, Elizabeth Richards and Joseph Brown.

1806, January 10, SUSAN MARY BARCLAY (*b* 26 November, 1805).　*Parents:* Philip and Catherine Barclay.

1843, April 7, JAMES HINSON BARCLAY (*b* 23 November, 1842).　*Parents:* James and Elizabeth H. Barclay.　*Sponsors:* George St. John, Henry H. Godet, Eliza St. John and parents.

1854, October 10, THOMAS BARCLAY (*b* 21 July, 1854). *Parents:* Robert and Catharine Barclay.　*Sponsors:* William Cook and father.

1856, May 21, ELIZABETH A. BARCLAY (*b* 6 May, 1856). *Parents:* Robert and Catharine Barclay. *Sponsors:* Mary Ann Barclay and parents.

1858, April 3, CATHARINE BARCLAY (*b* March, 1858). *Parents:* Robert and Catharine S. Barclay. *Sponsors:* Elizabeth and John Barclay.

1860, August 20, ANDREW BARCLAY (*b* 6 January, 1860). *Parents:* Robert and Catharine S. Barclay. *Sponsors:* Parents.

1863, July 30, WILLIAM BARCLAY (*b* 11 June, 1863). *Parents:* Robert and Catharine Barclay. *Sponsors:* William Barclay and Ann Dowling.

1864, November 17, MARGARET LAVINIA BARCLAY (*b* 9 July, 1858). *Parents* and *Sponsors* same as those last mentioned.

1864, November 17, JESSIE HARDY BARCLAY (*b* 20 April, 1860. *Parents:* Thomas and Margaret Lavinia Barclay. *Sponsors:* William D. Elliott and parents.

1865, March 15 LAVINIA BARCLAY (*b* 22 August, 1864). *Parents:* Robert and Catharine Barclay.

1866, December 11, MARY EMMA BARCLAY (*b* 6 October, 1866). *Parents:* Robert and Catharine Barclay. *Sponsors:* Parents.

Inscriptions in Trinity Church Yard.

"In memory of Capt. JAMES BARCLAY, a native of England, who departed this life the 8th of December, 1805, aged 40 years."

CHRIST CHURCH RECORDS, NEW YORK.

Marriages.

1802, March 30, JAMES BARCLAY and Violet Wells.

Baptisms.

VIOLETTE BARCLAY, dau. of James and Violette Barclay, born 19 September, 1806.

ELOISA BARCLAY, dau. of same, born 22 March, 1809.

St. Thomas Parish Records, New York City.

Elizabeth M. Barclay interred in Carmine Street burial grounds, 25 April, 1842.

First and Second Presbyterian Churches, New York City.

Births and Baptisms.

1769, October 28,—Mary, Daugh'r of John Barclay and *Cath'e Murray*, his wife, Born Octo'r 9th, 1769 (N. Y. Gen. & Biog. Rec. vol. VII, p. 172).

1772, March 22,—John, son of John Barclay and Catherine Murray, his wife, born March 3rd, 1772 (*Ibid*, vol. IX, p. 82).

1786, April 26,—Margaret, Dau'r of *William Miller* and Mary Barclay, his wife, born Octo'r 1st, 1785 (*Ibid*, vol. XIX, p. 61).

Marriages.

1763, May 28,—Peter Barclay to *Bell Thompson* (N. Y. Gen. & Biog. Rec. vol. XIV, p. 118).

1774, May 30, Daniel Barclay to *Christian Lasting*, widow (*Ibid.*, p. 170).

1775, Jan'y 30,—John Barclay, mariner, to *Ann Rider*, spinster (*Ibid*, p. 171).

1783, April 14,—John Barclay and *Sarah Logan*, both of New Jersey (*Ibid*, vol. XII, p. 35).

1800, August 17,—James Barclay and *Ann Brower* (*Ibid*, vol. XIV, p. 40).

Miscellaneous.

From the Weekly Museum of Saturday, 30 September, 1797:

"*Married*: On Sunday Evening last" (that is, 24 September, 1797) "by the Rev. Dr. Moore, Mr. George Barkley to Miss *Elizabeth Sims*, both of this City."

From NEW YORK SPECTATOR of 9 November, 1803.

"A list of deaths of those who died of the malignant fever between July 29 and October 29, 1803 * * *

1803, September 14, ELEANOR BARCLAY, 62 Cedar Street."

From NEW YORK GAZETTE of May 20, 1820:

"*Married* at Newburgh" (date not stated) *"Samuel M. Wilson* of Pittsburgh to Miss ANN BARCLAY."

From THE NEW YORK SPECTATOR of Tuesday, 25 October, 1831:
(sub-date, Thursday, October 20th).

"*Died:* Yesterday afternoon" (that is, 19 October, 1831) "after a short but severe illness, GEORGE W. BARKLEY, son of the late James Barkley, in the 17th year of his age."

ALBANY NOTES.

1784, October 18,—"Isaac Arnold and James Stewart returned from a trading expedition to Detroit, having lost three of their companions, Jacobus Teller, DANIEL BARCLAY and Isaac Van Alstyne, who were murdered by four Delaware Indians at a landing place on Lake Erie." (MUNSELL'S ANNALS OF ALBANY, vol. 2, p. 290).

1813, Albany City Directory: BARCLAY, JAMES, City Superintendent, 59 Chapel St (*Ibid,* vol. 5, p. 55).

Presbyterian Burying Ground on State Street,—Inscriptions: JAMES BARCLAY, died November 1, 1814, aged 61. JANET BARCLAY, relict of James Barclay, died May 16, 1818, aged 61 (*Ibid,* vol. 3, p. 230).

Married at Albany, 17 August, 1807, CATHERINE BARCLAY, daughter of James Barclay, to Sylvanus P. Jermain, merchant. (From the "Suffolk Gazette" of Long Island. See N. Y. GEN. & BIOG. REC. vol. XXIV, p. 160).

1821, January 11,—"WILLIAM BARCLAY died at the Island of Bermuda, whither he had gone for the recovery of his health" (MUNSELL'S ANNALS OF ALBANY, vol. 7, p. 154).

New Jersey.

Marriage Licenses.

1749, April 6,—JOHN BARCLAY of Baskenridge and *Catherine Crawford* of Elizabethtown.

1749, November 21,—ANNE BARCLAY of Perth Amboy and *John Craig* of Freehold.

1750, April 9,—SAMUEL BARCLAY[1] of Hunterdon County, and *Anne Reid* of Freehold.

1779, April 18,—ANNE BARKLEY of Somerset and *Andrew Hunter* of Somerset.

Wills and Administration.

1749, February 8,—Will of JAMES BARKLEY (not described as of any place), proved at Burlington and letters testamentary issued to John Kelly and John Todd. The will was not dated and referred to testator's wife, "Jenut Barkley," and to his daughter "Agnis Barkley." No other legatee mentioned (*Lib.* 6, p. 338).

1775, November 16,—Letters of administration granted to Thomas Junk on the estate of JAMES BARCLAY, late of Sussex County, deceased (*Lib.* 16, page 495).

1789, May 12,—Letters of guardianship of the person and estate of Charlotte Mackay, granted to JOHN BARKLAY (*Lib.* 31, page 359).

1790, February 6,—Will of ROBERT BARKLEY of Bedminster in the County of Somerset, proved at Millstone, and letters testamentary issued to *John Barkley* (a son of the testator) *Hugh Barkley* (a brother) and Robert Blair. The will was dated September 10, 1789, and referred to wife, *Christian Barkley;* to son *John Barkley;* to daughter *Isabel Little,* wife of

---

[1] In HISTORY OF HUNTERDON AND SOMERSET COUNTIES, by James P. Snell (Philadelphia: Everts & Peck, 1881), it is stated at pages 722-3 that in January, 1750, SAMUEL BARCLAY was buried in Leamington Churchyard, Bedminster."

Robert Little, and to her son *Samuel Little;* to daughter *Elizabeth Dunham,* wife of Benyon Dunham; to daughter *Martha Dunham,* wife of David Dunham; to daughter *Nancy King,* wife of John King; and to daughter *Rebecca Walker,* wife of Thomas Walker (*Lib.* 31, page 506).

1792, August 27,—Will proved of JOHN BARKLEY, of the Township of Bedminster in the County of Somerset, dated August 8, 1792. The will mentioned wife, *Mary Barkley,* and son *James Barkley* and referred to other children without naming them (*Lib.* 34, page 97).

1794, December 15,—Letters of administration granted to Daniel Lundy and Samuel Lane on the estate of THOMAS BARCLAY, late of Sussex County, deceased (*Lib.* 35, page 178).

1803, July 30,—Will and codicil proved of HUGH BARKLEY, of Bedminster in the County of Somerset. Will dated February 2, 1793. Referred to wife, *Elizabeth Barkley;* to son, John *Barkley;* to son, *Hugh Barkley;* to daughter, *Mary Miller,* wife of Robert Miller; to daughter, *Jeane Robertson,* wife of William Robertson; to daughter *Nancy Dennison,* wife of Andrew Dennison; and to daughter *Sarah Angle,* wife of John Angle (*Lib.* 40, page 446).[2]

CLERK'S OFFICE, MIDDLESEX COUNTY, NEW BRUNSWICK.

Marriages Reported (1795-1860).

1806, January 8,—MARGARET BARCLAY to *James McChesney, Jr.*

1818, September 17,—DANIEL BARCLAY to *Elizabeth E. Voorhees.*

1819, March 3,—THOMAS BARCLAY to *Nancy Van Deshoven.*

---

[2]For the descendants of ROBERT BARKLEY and HUGH BARKLEY of Bedminster Township, see pages 254-5 of EARLY GERMANS OF NEW JERSEY, by Theo. F. Chambers. Dover, N. J., 1895. The author, however, is in error when he says that this family *may* have descended from John Barclay of Perth Amboy.

In HISTORY OF HUNTERDON AND SOMERSET COUNTIES, already referred to, there is stated at page 93 the following list of privates who served in the revolution: JOSEPH BARCLAY; GEORGE BARKLEY; HUGH BARKLEY; JOHN BARKLEY; JOSEPH BARKLEY; and JOHN BARTLEY. This author, too, is in error in his statement at page 706 that the Bedminster family was descended from the Barclays of Ury.

1820, December 27,—CHARLES BARCLAY to *Deborah Storg.*

1822, March 6,—MARY BARCLAY to *Charles Everingham.*

1833, December 18,—MARGARET M. BARCLAY to *George E. Dancer.*

1844, October 26,—PETER BARCLAY to *Jane Mesler.*

1848, February 19,—SUSAN BARCLAY to *Gustus Ryno.*

1860, January 1,—CHARLES H. BARCLAY, of Cranbury, N. J., to *Mary J. Martin,* of Washington, N. J.

PARISH RECORDS OF CHRIST CHURCH, SHREWSBURY.

Baptisms (1733-1809).

1735, July 28,— PETER BARCLAY, son of James [3] and Catherine Barclay at "Topenaizmous" Church.

1752, September 19,— ELIZABETH BARCLAY, daughter of John and Catherine Barclay, of Cranbury.

1753, May 14,—SAMUEL BARCLAY, son of John Barclay, of Cranbury.

1766, July 20,—LYDIA BARCLAY, daughter of David Barclay and Catherine Barclay at the Church at Freehold.[4]

1767, February 15,—JANE BARCLAY, daughter of David Barclay and Catherine Barclay, at the Church at Freehold.[5]

---

[3] The name "James" here written is manifestly a mistake for "John." The Peter Barclay whose baptism is thus recorded was undoubtedly tne fifth child (fourth son) of John Barclay (son of John Barclay and grandson of Col. David Barclay of Ury and Katharine Gordon, his wife), who was born 3 March, 1735. See Part IV above.

[4] Is it not possible that the clergyman who transcribed this record was completely in error as to the names of the child's parents? There are no existing records from which it may be inferred that David Barclay of Freehold had a wife Catherine, or a daughter Lydia. His brother *Charles Barclay* had a daughter Lydia, born 1766; but the name of Charles' wife was Rebecca, not Catherine. It seems more than probable that the child, whose baptism is here recorded in *Shrewsbury* was the fourth child of Charles Barclay (son of John Barclay, grandson of John Barclay and great grandson of Col. David Barclay of Ury) and Rebecca Gordon, his wife. See Part IV above.

[5] Here, too, the name "Catherine" was doubtless incorrectly written. The Jane Barclay whose baptism is thus recorded was beyond question the sixth and youngest child (born 1767) of David Barclay (son of John Barclay, grandson of John Barclay and great grandson of Col. David Barclay of Ury) and Elizabeth Walker, his wife. See Part IV above.

From NEW JERSEY GAZETTE of 20 October, 1779:

In a list of letters remaining at the Post Office, at Trenton, on October 5, 1779, was one for

"*Barclay, Thomas*,—opposite Trenton."

In NEW JERSEY GAZETTE of Wednesday, 28 June, 1780, appears a notice dated at Trenton, June 26, 1780, signed by THOMAS BARCLAY and Samuel Meredith, calling for wagons to convey provisions to the army under Washington's command. The subscribers agree to pay for the wagons, provide fodder and prevent impressment.

Delaware.

JOHN BARCLAY of White Clay Creek Hundred, merchant (White Clay Creek was in the vicinity of Wilmington, Del.), in 1777 married *Eleanor Porter* of New Castle Hundred (Records of Baltimore Yearly Meeting, at Park Avenue Meeting House, Baltimore). For his second wife he married *Mary Searle*. See Part X above.

The original marriage bond given by him on the occasion of his marriage to Eleanor Porter, with David Finney, "of Mill "Creek Hundred," his surety, in the sum of six hundred pounds "good and lawful money of America" is on file at Wilmington, Del., dated June 24th, 1777. It reads, in part, as follows:

"The Condition of this Obligation is such that there shall not hereafter appear any Lawfull Let or Impediment by Reason of any Pre-Contracted Consanguinity, Affinity, or any other just excuse whatever, but that the above mentioned JOHN BARCLAY and *Eleanor Porter* of New Castle Hundred in the County of New Castle County, May Lawfully Marry and that there is not any suit pending before the Judge Ecclesiastical or Civil for or against any such Pre-Conduct, and also if the said Parties, and each of them, are of the full age of Twenty-one, and are not under the Tuition of his or her Parents or Guardians respectively to the said marriage, and if they or either of them are not indentured servants, and do and shall save harmless and kept indemnified the above John McKinley Esq. (President and Commander in Chief of the Delaware State) and his successors, for and concerning the Premises, and that likewise the said parties in Matrimony for or by of so doing, that this obligation to be void, null and of none effect, or else to stand and remain in full Force and Virtue."

ELIZABETH BARCLAY of White Clay Creek in New Castle County, left a will dated 11 May, 1811, proved 11 November, 1811. Bequests were made to Nicholas Van Dyke and to the three children of the testatrix's sister Ann Cloud, namely, Alice Eliza Cloud, Mary Forrest Cloud and Jeremiah Cloud. Executor: Rev. Francis Hindman (NEW CASTLE COUNTY WILLS, Book Q., p. 1).

Pennsylvania.

PROVINCIAL SECRETARY'S OFFICE.

Marriage Licenses.

1748, April 13, ELIZABETH BARKLEY and John Blakely.
1760, February 13, ELINOR BARCLAY and John Chevalier.
1761, December 31, GILBERT BARCLAY and Ann Inglis.
1765, August 24, HANNAH BARCLAY and Richard Palmer.
1766, March 20, MARY BARCLAY and Thomas Barr.
1766, March 29, MARY BARCLAY and Robert Miller.
1766, November 12, JANE BARCLAY and William Craig.
1770, October 18, THOMAS BARCLAY and Mary Hoops.
1772, March 3, ANN BARCLAY and Andrew Denison (PENN. ARCHIVES, 2nd Series, vol. II, p. 24).

PARISH RECORDS OF CHRIST CHURCH, PHILADELPHIA (1709-1806).

Marriages.

1759, February 8, ALEXANDER BARCLAY and *Rebecca Robinson*.[6]

1761, December 31, GILBERT BARCLAY and *Ann Inglis*.

---

[6]This was the *second* marriage of ALEXANDER BARCLAY, Comptroller of Customs at Philadelphia from 1749-1751 (PENN. MAGAZINE, vol. XXV, p. 576), a grandson of the Apologist and the father of *Robert Barclay*, founder of the Bury Hill line. The commission to him as "Comptroller of all the Rates and Duties and Imposcions arising "and growing due to His Majesty at Philadelphia, in Pennsylvania, in America" dated at the Custom House, London, on August 5, 1749, will be found in PENN. ARCHIVES, 3rd Series, vol. VIII, p. 667. The name "Robinson" recorded in the Christ Church records is a mistake for "Robertson." Alexander Barclay's second wife was *Rebecca Evans*, widow of *Peter Robertson*, and daughter of Peter Evans, Sheriff of Philadelphia. (PENN. MAGAZINE, vols. V, p. 96, and VI, p. 256). The following chart shows his family:—

1781, December 11, JOHN BARCLAY and *Mary Searle.*

1786, September 28, GEORGE BARCLAY and *Mary Garette.*

1805, November 11, SARAH MILES BARCLAY and *William Magee.*

(From PENN. ARCHIVES, 2nd Series, vols. VIII and IX).

RECORDS OF SECOND PRESBYTERIAN CHURCH, PHILADELPHIA (1763-1812).

Marriages.

1772, March 3, ANN BARCLAY and *Andrew Denison.*

1779, October 21, ELIZABETH BARCLAY and *George Gregg.*

1810, June 7, RACHEL BARCLAY and *Nathan Beach.*

1811, March 26, ANN BARCLAY and *Andrew Dennison (Ibid).*

RECORDS OF THIRD PRESBYTERIAN CHURCH, PHILADELPHIA (1785-1799).

Marriages.

1785, December 19, JAMES BARCLAY and *Sarah Ross (Ibid).*

ALEXANDER BARCLAY, born in London, 1712, son of David Barclay and Anne Taylor, his wife. Was Comptroller of Customs at Philadelphia, 1749-1751.

Died at Philadelphia, 12 January, 1771 (INSCRIPTIONS, ST. PETER'S CHURCHYARD, Philadelphia, p. 52).

Married (1) *Anne Hickman,* dau. of Robert Hickman and Patience Hickman, his wife (PENN. MAGAZINE, vol. V, p. 96); buried Christ Church, Philadelphia, 28 June, 1753 (*ibid,* vol. I, p. 350).

Married (2) 8 February, 1759, *Rebecca Evans,* dau. of Peter Evans and widow of Peter Robertson (*ibid,* vol. VI, p. 256), born 1717; died 25 April, 1784 (INSCRIPTIONS, ST. PETER'S CHURCHYARD, p. 52).

His children by his first wife were:

I. ROBERT BARCLAY, *b* Philadelphia 15 May, 1751 *bap.* Christ Church 12 June, 1751 (PENN. MAGAZINE, vol. XIII, p. 237); *m* (in England) 1775, *Rachel Gurney,* dau. of John Gurney.

II. PATIENCE BARCLAY, *b* Philadelphia, 1753; *d* 4 January, 1781 (INSCRIPTIONS, ST. PETER'S CHURCHYARD, p. 52).

m (1) 4 August, 1772, *Joseph Worrell.*

(2) 6 June, 1780, *Reynold Keen.*

(PENN. MAGAZINE, vol. V, p. 96).

The following notice appeared in THE PENNSYLVANIA GAZETTE of Thursday, January 17th, 1771:

"Last Saturday Morning died ALEXANDER BARCLAY, Esq., Comptroller of His Majesty's Customs for this Port; a Gentleman who was greatly esteemed by the trading Part of this City as a *good Officer,* and by all his private Acquaintance as a *benevolent* and *honest Man.* He was the Son of the late DAVID BARCLAY, Merchant, in London; and Grandson of the celebrated Apologist, ROBERT BARCLAY of Urie."

RECORDS OF NESHAMINY PRESBYTERIAN CHURCH, BUCKS COUNTY
(1785-1804).

Marriages.

1793, April 3, RICHARD BARCLAY and ——*Smith* (*Ibid*).

RECORDS OF ABINGTON PRESBYTERIAN CHURCH, MONTGOMERY
COUNTY (1716-1821).

Marriages.

1745, October 3, HUGH BARCLAY and *Elizabeth Vandyke.*

1747, October 29, ADAM BARKLEY and *Martha Dickson*
(*Ibid*).

RECORDS OF THE SWEDES CHURCH, PHILADELPHIA (1750-1810).

Marriages.

1794, November 12, MARIA BARCLAY and *John Young.*

RECORDS OF LANCASTER COUNTY, PENNSYLVANIA.

(Lancaster County was set off from Chester County in 1747).

Land Records.

1736, May 13, JOHN BARCLAY procures warrant for 150 acres
on West Branch of Octoraro Creek adjoining lands of James
Purtle and *Hugh Barclay.*

1736, May 13, WILLIAM BARCLAY procures warrant for 150
acres on same branch, next to *John Barclay's* land.

1743, May 10, WILLIAM BARCLAY procures warrant for 100
acres adjoining his other land in Little Britain township.

1748, April 23, HUGH BARCLAY procures a warrant for 30
acres adjoining his other land in Colerain township.

1749, May 17, JOHN BARCLAY procures a warrant for 200
acres in Colerain township next to lands of *Hugh Barclay* and
Robert Allison.

1752, August 5, JOHN BARCLAY procures a warrant for 25
acres next to his other land in Colerain township (patented this
day) and next to land of *Hugh Barclay* and John Gilmore.

1753, March 29, WILLIAM BARCLAY procures a warrant for 25 acres in Little Britain township next to his other land and to that of William Balbridge.

1753, March 29, WILLIAM BARCLAY procures a warrant for 25 acres in Little Britain township next to his other land and to that of John Walker.

1753, March 29, WILLIAM BARCLAY procures a warrant for 80 acres in Little Britain township next to his other land and to that of James Denny.

A warrant for 200 acres on Beaver Creek in Martick township was granted to William Ernest. It was subsequently forfeited and 1742, November 4, was ordered surveyed to one Thomas McCreary who by order dated January 19, 1748/9, assigned it to HUGH BARCLAY. The original order was sent to Philadelphia, 3rd mo., 20th, 1761.

Colerain and Little Britain townships were on the Octoraro Creek near the Susquehanna River, and not far from the border of Cecil County, Maryland.

Deeds.

1759, October 26, HUGH BARCLAY of Colerain township, Lancaster County, to Jacob Bare of Bart Township, Lancaster County, Conveys 200 acres acquired February 21, 1745, from James Murphy and wife.

1770, April 5, WILLIAM BARCLAY and JAMES BARCLAY of Lancaster County, to James Porter. Conveys the tract on which they dwelt in Drumore Township, Lancaster County, adjacent to lands of their father ANDREW BARCLAY, deceased, which he took by warrant from the proprietors on March 1, 1753.

1771, March 28, HUGH BARCLAY of the County of Lancaster, shoemaker, and Henry Small of the Borough of Lancaster, to JOHN BARCLAY of the County of Lancaster, tailor. Conveys for two hundred pounds the two undivided eighth parts of the grantors in a tract of 669 acres on the West branch of the Octoraro Creek, in Little Britain Township.

1773, January 1, JOHN BARCLAY of Little Britain Township, farmer, to HUGH BARCLAY, Joseph Miller, John Williamson and Robert Campbell. Recites that grantor was eldest son of WILLIAM BARCLAY, deceased, who left a widow and seven children, and that the land now conveyed was set apart to the grantor by the Orphans' Court.

Wills and Administration.

On March 26, 1757, ESTHER BARCLAY, of Lancaster County, Penn., filed her bond as administratrix, etc., of WILLIAM BARCLAY, deceased, with James Morrow and *John Barclay* of the same place, sureties.

In 1761 (day and month not stated) she filed her account in which she described herself as "widow and relict" of WILLIAM BARCLAY, deceased. WILLIAM BARCLAY and JOHN BARCLAY are mentioned in the account.

On April 2, 1764, was proved the will of HUGH BARCLAY of Colerain Township, dated March 9, 1754. Mentions son HUGH BARCLAY; son (*sic*) John McConnall; daughter MARY BARCLAY; son WILLIAM BARCLAY; and wife MARY BARCLAY. The children seemed all to be under twenty-one. *Executors:* John McConnall and Joseph Miller. *Witnesses:* Daniel McConnall, MARTHA BARCLAY and MARGARET BARCLAY, of Lancaster County.

On May 6, 1765, was proved the will of JOHN BARCLAY of Colerain Township, Lancaster County, dated December 22, 1764. Mentions wife, MARTHA BARCLAY; also a "Miss MARTHA BARCLAY," without stating the relationship, if any; cousin, Mary Allison; nephew, JOSEPH BARCLAY; brother HUGH BARCLAY's son, HUGH BARCLAY; JOHN BARCLAY and HUGH BARCLAY, sons of testator's brother, WILLIAM BARCLAY; and makes bequests to John McConnall, Daniel McConnall and Alexander McConnall. Executors: wife MARTHA BARCLAY, Daniel McConnall and HUGH BARCLAY.

On June 8, 1765, were filed the accounts of John McConnall and Joseph Miller as executors of the last will and testament of HUGH BARCLAY late of Colerain Township, Lancaster County, deceased. Recite that deceased was the guardian of one William Turner.

On March 3, 1769, JAMES BARCLAY, of Lancaster County, Penn., filed his bond as administrator, etc., of ANDREW BARCLAY, deceased, with James Marshall and James Porter of the same place, sureties.

On the same day WILLIAM BARCLAY filed a renunciation, dated February 27, 1769, of the right to administration on the estate of "my father" ANDREW BARCLAY, in favor of "my brother" JAMES BARCLAY.

On October 27, 1769, were filed the accounts of JAMES BARCLAY as administrator, etc., of ANDREW BARCLAY, late of the Township of Drewmore in Lancaster County, yeoman, deceased.

On December 2, 1769, were filed the accounts of MARTHA BARCLAY, Daniel McConnall and HUGH BARCLAY as executors of the last will and testament of JOHN BARCLAY, late of Colerain Township, Lancaster County, deceased.

On April 21, 1778, was proved the will of JOHN BARCLAY, yeoman, of Little Britain Township, Lancaster County, dated 1773 (day and month not stated). Mentions wife JEAN BARCLAY, and two children (both seemingly under ten years of age) MARY BARCLAY and JOHN BARCLAY, and brothers HUGH BARCLAY, STEPHEN BARCLAY and JOSEPH BARCLAY. Executor: brother HUGH BARCLAY. *Witnesses:* John Allison and Hugh Quigley.

On June 24, 1816, was proved the will of WILLIAM BARCLAY, yeoman, of Colerain Township, Lancaster County, dated May 11, 1816. Mentions wife ELIZABETH BARCLAY; son STEWART BARCLAY; daughters, ANN BARCLAY, ELIZABETH BARCLAY, MARY BARCLAY and MATILDA BARCLAY; and three grandchildren, "heirs" of his daughter Mary,—William S., Louisa and Henrietta Louise (last names not stated). *Executor:* wife ELIZABETH BARCLAY.

On August 24, 1836, was proved the will of WILLIAM BARCLAY, of Colerain Township, Lancaster County, dated July 21, 1836. Mentions wife SARAH BARCLAY; daughter SARAH BARCLAY who married Alexander Campbell; daughter ANN BARCLAY who married James M. Kilpatrick; grandson James Kilpatrick;

grandson William Galbraith, son of testator's daughter Eliza Galbraith; grandsons Alexander Campbell and James Ross Campbell; son-in-law Ross Campbell. *Executors:* Dr. Robert Agnew and Hugh Andrews.

On September 21, 1849, was proved the will of ROBERT BARCLAY of Martic Township, Lancaster County, dated July 26, 1849. Mentions son WILLIAM S. BARCLAY and daughter Julia N. Duckel. Executor WILLIAM S. BARCLAY.

From PENNSYLVANIA ARCHIVES, 3rd Series.

Warrantees of Land.

			Acres.	Surveyed.
Luzerne Co.	HANNAH	BARCLAY,	400	Sept. 3, 1792.
"	GEORGE	"	400	"
Bucks Co.	JAMES	"	50	March 12, 1750
"	"	"	50	"
Cumberland Co.	"	"	300	Sept. 10, 1762
Lancaster Co.	WILLIAM	BARCLAY	100	May 10, 1743
"	JOHN	"	200	May 17, 1749
"	HUGH	BARCLAY	30	April 23, 1748
"	JOHN	"	150	May 13, 1736
"	WILLIAM	"	150	"
"	JOHN	"	25	Aug. 5, 1752
"	WILLIAM	"	80	March 29, 1753
"	"	"	25	"
"	"	"	25	"
Cumberland Co.	WILLIAM	"	40	July 7, 1815
Huntingdon Co.	HUGH	BARKLEY	100	June 24, 1788
"	JOHN	"	400	July 27, 1792
Northumberland Co.	GEORGE	BARCLAY	400	June 13, 1792
Bedford Co.	GEORGE	"	400	July 19, 1793
"	HUGH	"	400	January 22, 1794
"	HUGH	"	300	Dec. 21, 1785
"	HUGH	"	177	Dec. 28, 1793
"	GEORGE	"	400	July 19, 1793
"	HUGH	"	400	January 22, 1794
"	JOHN	"	400	February 10, 1794
"	HUGH	"	400	"
"	MAY	"	400	February 11, 1794
"	HUGH	"	100	April 10, 1794
Franklin Co.	JAMES	"	400	September 6, 1792
"	JOHN	"	400	"
"	"	"	400	December 6, 1792
Northumberland Co.	"	"	400	July 27, 1787
"	"	"	400	July 31, 1792
"	"	"	400	March 22, 1793
"	"	"	400	"
Bedford Co	"	"	400	May 16, 1794
"	JOSIAH E.	"	60	February 29, 1820
"	JOSIAH E. Ex BARCLAY		25	June 18, 1847
"	SAMUEL M. "	"	42	August 12, 1847

			Acres.	Surveyed.
Bedford Co.	ROBERT BARCLAY		310½	May 9, 1774
"	"	"	412.138	"
"	"	"	297	"
"	SAMUEL M.	"	100	July 8, 1834
"	" "	"	2	September 11, 1869
"	WILLIAM M.	"	300	February 23, 1871
"	" "	"	18	January 12, 1874
NorthumberlandCo.	THOMAS	"	300	March 17, 1774
"	"	"	300	June 15, 1774
Northampton Co.	JAMES	"	400	March 7, 1793
"	JOHN	"	400	"
"	"	"	400	June 19, 1793
Westmoreland Co.	THOMAS	"	300	February 28, 1774
"	SAMUEL	"	400	January 15, 1794
"	THOMAS	"	400	February 4, 1794
"	JOHN	"	157.156	February 12, 1794
"	"	"	243.162	"
"	"	"	310.140	"
"	"	"	100	February 15, 1825
"	"	"	50	January 19, 1828
Washington Co.	THOMAS	"	250	August 28, 1792

(Vols. xxiv, xxv and xxvi).

Assessments and Taxes.

(From *Penn. Archives,* 3rd Series).

CHESTER COUNTY:

For 1766 West Nottingham...JAMES BARCLAY, 100 acres 1 horse 3 cattle (vol. XI, p. 165)

" 1767 " " .....JAMES BARCLAY, 200 acres 2 horse 3 cattle 3 sheep (*ibid*, p. 377)

Lower Chichester...THOMAS BARCLAY, 14 acres (*ibid*, p. 265)

" 1768 " " ......MARY BARCLAY, 16 acres (*ibid*, p. 463)

West Nottingham..JAMES BARCLAY, 150 acres 2 horses 4 cattle 4 sheep (*ibid*, p. 422)

LANCASTER COUNTY:

For 1771 Little Britain ......JOHN BARCKLEY, 200 acres 2 horse 2 cattle 1 servt. Tax 5:6 (vol. XVII, p. 69)

HUGH BARCKLY, freeman. Tax 15:0 (*ibid*, p. 72)

Colerain ....WIDOW BARCLAY, 200 acres 1 horse 1 cattle Tax 10:0 (*ibid*, p. 20)

" 1772 Little Britain ......STEPHEN BARCLY, freeman. Tax 15:0 (*ibid*, p. 206)

HUGH BARCLAY, freeman. Tax 15:0 (*ibid*, p. 206)

JOHN BARCLAY, 200 acres 2 horse 2 cattle. Tax 5:6 (*ibid*, p. 204)

Colerain ....WIDOW BARCLEY, 100 acres 1 horse 1 cattle. Tax 9:0 (*ibid*. p. 183)

For 1773 Little Britain ......STEPHEN BARCLY, freeman. Tax 15:0
(*ibid,* p. 372)
HUGH BARCLY, freeman. Tax 15:30
(*ibid,* p. 372)

NORTHAMPTON COUNTY:
For 1772 Mount Bethel.......JAMES BARCKLEY. Tax 8:16.0 (vol.
XIX, p. 31).

CITY OF PHILADELPHIA:
For 1774 Dock Ward.........THOMAS BARCLAY, merchant, 1 servt.
Tax 119:2:0 (vol. XIV, p.
225)
REBECCA BARCLAY, widow. Tax
13:0:0 (*ibid,* p. 232)
MARY BARCLAY, widow. Tax 24:6:0
(*ibid,* p. 239)
Manor of Moreland..ALEXANDER BARCLAY.

LANCASTER COUNTY (Effective Supply Tax):
For 1779 Colerain............WIDOW BARCLAY, 250 acres 2 horses 2
cattle 1 sheep (vol. XVII,
p. 634)

CITY OF PHILADELPHIA (Effective Supply Tax):
For 1779 South Ward.........THOMAS BARCLAY'S EST. Tax 15:0
(vol. XIV, p. 496)

CITY OF PHILADELPHIA (State Tax):
For 1779 Dock Ward, South
Part ....MARY BARCLAY, widow. Tax 7:10:0
(*ibid,* p. 751)
REBECCA BARCLAY. Tax 2:10:0 (*ibid,*
p. 753)
South Ward........THOMAS BARCLAY'S EST. Tax 3:15:0
(*ibid,* p. 772)

COUNTY OF PHILADELPHIA (State Tax):
For 1779 Southwark.........WIDOW BARCLAY (vol. XV, p. 150)

COUNTY OF PHILADELPHIA (Effective Supply Tax):
For 1779 Southwark.........WIDOW BARCLAY (vol. XIV, p. 709)

CITY OF PHILADELPHIA (Effective Supply Tax):
For 1780 Dock Ward, South
Part ....THOMAS BARCLAY (vol. XV, p. 207)
REBECCA BARCLAY, widow. Valuation
20,200. Tax 50:10:0 (*ibid,*
p. 219)
Mulberry Ward, East
Part ....JOHN BARCLAY S EST. Valuation 18,-
000. Tax 63:0:0 (*ibid,* p.
338)

For 1781 Dock Ward, South
Part ....JOHN BARCLAY. Valuation 782. Tax
8:19:9 (*ibid,* p. 744)
WILLIAM BARCLAY. Tax 6:0:0 (*ibid,*
p. 744)
Mulberry Ward, East
Part ....THOMAS BARCLAY'S EST. Valuation
600. Tax 6:18:0 (*ibid,* p.
635)

For 1782 Dock Ward, South
    Part ....JOHN BARCLAY. Valuation 356. Tax
          1 :19:5 (vol. XVI, p. 315)
        WILLIAM BARCLAY. Tax 1 :10 :0 (*ibid*,
          p. 315)
       WIDOW BARCLAY. Valuation 700.
         Tax 3 :17 :7 (*ibid*, p. 330)
  Southwark, East Part.WIDOW BARCLAY'S EST. Valuation
         120. Tax 12 :8 (*ibid*, p. 378)
       WIDOW BARCLAY'S EST. Valuation
         170. Tax 19 :2 (*ibid*, p. 378)
    West Part.SAMUEL BARCLAY. Valuation 33.
         Tax 3 :6 (*ibid*, p. 393)
   North Ward.......DOCTOR BARCLAY. Valuation 225.
         Tax 1 :14 :9 (*ibid*, p. 428)
  Mulberry Ward, East
    Part ....THOMAS BARCLAY'S EST. Valuation
         600. Tax 3 :2 :6 (*ibid*, p. 486)

BUCKS COUNTY (State Tax) :

For 1779 Falls Township......THOMAS BARCLAY, 220 acres 8 horses
         9 cattle (vol. XIII, p. 19)
 " 1781   "   ......THOMAS BARCLAY, 220 acres 6 horses
         6 cattle 6 servts (*ibid*, p. 126)
       BARCLAY & MITCHELL, 672 acres (*ibid*,
         p. 126).
 " 1783 Warwick ....JAMES BARCLAY. Tax 3 :14 :0 (*ibid*,
         p. 357)
   Springfield ....JOHN BARCLAY. Tax 2 :2 :9 (*ibid*, p.
         396)
 " 1784 Falls Township......BARCLAY & MITCHELL, 672 acres, 3
         dwellings, 1 outhouse, 20
         white inhabitants (*ibid*, p.
         494)
 " 1785 Durham ....JOHN BARCLAY, 98 acres (*ibid*, p. 567)
   Springfield ....JOHN BARCLAY, 110 acres 3 horses 3
         cattle (*ibid*, p. 600)
 " 1786 Durham ....JOHN BARCLAY. Tax 4 :8 (*ibid*, p.
         696)
   Springfield ....JOHN BARCLAY. Tax 9 :9 (*ibid*, p.
         698)
 " 1787 Durham ....JOHN BARKLY. Tax 3 :0 (*ibid*, p. 804)
   Springfield ....JOHN BARCLAY. Tax 10 :0 (*ibid*, p.
         806)

CUMBERLAND COUNTY :

For 1781 Middleton..........MILES BARCLEY, 1 horse 2 cattle (vol.
         XX, p. 462)

BEDFORD COUNTY (State Tax) :

For 1783 Bedford Township..HUGH BARCLAY. Single freeman. 1
         horse. Tax 1 :2 :1 (vol.
         XXII, p. 208)
 " 1784 Dublin Township...HUGH BARCLAY. Single freeman
         (*ibid*, p. 284)

FAYETTE COUNTY (State Tax):

For 1785 Springhill...........JOHN BARCKLEY, Sr. Tax 4:11 (*ibid*, p. 564)

JOHN BARCKLEY, Jr. Tax 6:9 (*ibid*, p. 564)

JAMES BARCKLEY. Tax 15:0 (*ibid*, p. 564)

NORTHUMBERLAND COUNTY (State Tax):

For 1785 Bald Eagle Township ....ROBERT BARCLAY (non-resident), 271 acres. Tax 9:2 (vol. XIX, p. 618)

" 1786 " ROBERT BARCLAY (non-resident), 271 acres. Tax 10:1 (*ibid*, p. 715)

" 1787 " ROBERT BARCLAY (non-resident), 270 acres. Tax 7:0 (*ibid*, p. 797)

HUNTINGTON COUNTY (State Tax):

For 1788 Non-residents......A. BARCLAY, 297 acres. Tax 7:6 (vol. XXII, p. 366)

ALEXANDER BARCLAY, 412 acres. Tax 10:2 (*ibid*, p. 366)

ALLEGHENY COUNTY (State Tax):

For 1791 Elizabeth Township..JOSEPH BARCLAY. Single man. Tax 3:9 (*ibid*, p. 685)

SOLDIERS WHO SERVED AS RANGERS ON THE FRONTIERS (1778-1783).

(From *Penn. Archives*, 3rd Series, vol. XXIII).

Westmoreland County,—ELIJAH BARCLAY (p. 284).

Northumberland County,—GEORGE BARCLAY (pp. 263, 347).

Cumberland County,—HUGH BARCLAY, Adjt. (p. 258).

PENSIONERS OF THE REVOLUTION.

(*Ibid*).

Westmoreland County,—STEPHEN BARCLAY. Private in Sampson's 1st Regt. of riflemen (p. 489).

MUSTER ROLLS, CUMBERLAND COUNTY MILITIA.

(*Ibid*).

HUGH BARCLAY, private, second class, in Capt. William Lay's Company, 8th Battalion, 4th Co., on first call, 23 October, 1777 (p. 617).

JOHN BARCLAY, private in Capt. Alexander Peeble's Company under Col. James Dunlap (p. 710).

From RECORDS OF THE REVOLUTIONARY WAR by
W. T. R. Saffell.

SAMUEL BARCLAY was a private at Mt. Independence on November 26, 1776, in Company No. 1 (Samuel Hay, Captain) of Col. William Irwin's Pennsylvania Regiment. He enlisted January 30, 1776.

JOSEPH BARCLAY was a private in Company No. 7 (Moses McLain, Captain) of the same regiment, and was taken prisoner June 21, 1776.

RECORD OF TROOPS IN PROVINCIAL SERVICE.

(Penn. Archives, 2nd Series, vol. II).

1756, ROBERT BARCLAY, a private in the Independent Company of Foot, Philadelphia (p. 522).

1756, ALEXANDER BARCLAY, the same (p. 523).

1756, GILBERT BARCLAY, the same (p. 524).

1756, JOHN BARCLAY, an ensign in the associated Companies of Lancaster County (p. 530).

FROM THE COLONIAL RECORDS.

1722, April 16, GEORGE BARCLAY was clerk to the Governor of the Province (PENN. COLONIAL REC., vol. III, p. 243).

1765, October 31, JOHN BARCLAY was licensed as a trader (PENN. ARCHIVES, 2d Series, vol. II, p. 623).

1772, June 20, JOHN BARCLAY was licensed as a trader (Ibid, p. 662).

MISCELLANEOUS.

1777, February 19, THOMAS BARCLAY appointed by the Council of Safety, Philadelphia, a member of the Navy Board (PENN. COLONIAL REC., vol. XI, p. 127).

1777, June 24, THOMAS BARCLAY took oath of allegiance to Commonwealth of Pennsylvania (PENN. ARCHIVES, 2nd Series, vol. III, p. 8).

1777, July 22, THOMAS BARCLAY sells a cargo of salt then at Tom's River, N. J., to the Council of Safety at ten dollars per bushel (PENN. COLONIAL REC., vol. XI, p. 127).

1782, December 21, JOHN BARCLAY obtains commission as Justice of the Peace for Bucks County (*Ibid*, vol. XIII, p. 454).

1783, December 1, HUGH BARCLAY obtains same for Town of Bedford, Bedford County (*Ibid*, p. 760).

1782, June 27, THOMAS BARCLAY writes from Amsterdam to William Moore, Pres. of the State of Pennsylvania (PENN. ARCHIVES, 1st Series, vol. IX, p. 563).

1784, May 17, THOMAS BARCLAY writes from Paris to John Dickinson, at Philadelphia (*Ibid*, vol. X, p. 267).

1786, November 14, JOHN BARCLAY and Samuel Caldwell write to Hon. Charles Biddle, claiming title to Hog Island under purchase of the forfeited estate of Joseph Galloway (*Ibid*, vol. XI, p. 89).

From PENNSYLVANIA PACKET of Saturday, April 13, 1782.

"To BE SOLD by Public Vendue, on Tuesday the 16th instant, at Summerset (where THOMAS BARCLAY Esquire lately resided, near Trenton-ferry), SOME HOUSEHOLD FURNITURE and a Variety of farming Utensils. Attendance will be given and the terms made known by

JOHN BARCLAY."

From NEW YORK GAZETTE of Thursday, 19 March, 1801:

"*Married:* Last Thursday evening" (that is, March 12, 1801) "by the Rev. Dr. Linn, Mr. JAMES BARKLEY, Merchant of Philadelphia, to Miss *Finlay.*"

Died at Philadelphia, June 9, 1806, JAMES BARCLAY, JR.

From MARYLAND JOURNAL AND BALTIMORE ADVERTISER of Friday, February 13, 1789:

JOHN BARCLAY of Philadelphia, joins in a petition of upwards of 2,000 respectable citizens of Philadelphia, to the General Assembly, praying a repeal of any law or part of a law which prohibits the exhibition of Dramatic Entertainment.

From New York Gazette of Saturday, 13 January, 1819:

"Married, at Philadelphia" (date not stated) *"John Jarden* to Miss Grace Barclay."

From New York Gazette of Thursday, 2 December, 1819:

"Died, at Philadelphia," (date not stated) "Mrs. Catharine Barclay, aged 28."

Maryland.

Rev. John Barclay (*d* September 9, 1772), rector of St. Peter's Church in Talbot County, Maryland, son of *David Barclay* of Kincardine, Scotland, and *Christian Barclay,* his wife, *m* March 4, 1768, *Rachel Goldsborough,* dau. of Nicholas Goldsborough and Sarah Jolly Turbutt, his wife; *b* January, 1735, *d* September 18, 1796.

They had one child, Sarah Barclay, *b* August 1, 1771, *m* October 23, 1788, *Joseph Haskins,* for many years Cashier of the Farmers Bank of Maryland, at Easton, Talbot Co., *b* February 28, 1762 (Records of St. Peter's Parish, Talbot Co., Md., and "Old Kent," by George A. Hanson, M. A.)

The children of Joseph Haskins and Sarah Barclay Haskins, his wife, were (1) *John Barclay Haskins, b* October 3, 1789; *d* August 1790 (Records of St. Peter's Parish, p. 318); (2) *Barclay Haskins m (1)* 1842 Elizabeth Robins Hayward; *m (2)* Mary Trippe, dau. of Richard Trippe of Baylies Neck; and (3) *Ann Haskins* who *m* John Bowie and had children, *John Haskins Bowie, Louisa Bowie, Emily Bowie, Isabella Bowie, Dallas Bowie,* and *Josephine Haskins Bowie* ("Old Kent" by George A. Hanson, M. A., page 295).

The will of Rev. John Barclay, dated July 6, 1772, was proved November 22, 1772, and recorded at Annapolis, Md. He makes reference in his will to his two married sisters, *Elizabeth Walker* and *Anne Keth* (Book No. 38 of Wills, p. 983).

Thomas Barclay, *m* March 26, 1763, *Margaret Cole* at St. Paul's Parish, Baltimore County, Md. The church now stands at the corner of North Charles and Saratoga Streets, Baltimore (Records of St. Paul's Parish, Baltimore).

JOHN BARCLAY (or Barkley), late of Edinburgh, North Britain, but now of Annapolis, Anne Arundel County, Md., left a will dated October 13, 1732, proved November 28, 1732, and recorded at Annapolis. He appoints his wife, *Grace Hay Barclay,* his executrix and, in her absence from the province, appoints his friends Robert Gordon and William Tweedie of Annapolis, executors for the purpose of disposing of his property and turning the proceeds over to his wife. No children are mentioned and the testator describes himself as "being distant from my wife and family." *Witnesses:* William Cumming, George Stewart and Burgis Copner (Book No. 20 of Wills, p. 484).

Accounts were rendered by Robert Gordon and William Tweedie on May 16, 1735 (*Liber* 13 of Accounts, fol. 67).

Inventory was filed as of the Estate of "Capt. John Berkley," and recites "Kindred nine" (*Liber* 17, fol. 442).

JOHN BARCLAY (or Barkley) of Somerset County, Md., left a will in the record of which his name and the name of his children are written "Barklett." The will was dated February 21, 1753, was proved November 18, 1756, and recorded at Annapolis. He gives all his real estate to his youngest son *Alworth Barclay* (or Barkley), and mentions two other sons *John Barclay* and *Abraham Barclay,* a daughter *Alice Barclay,* and wife *Ann Barclay. Witnesses:* John Wallace, Bloyce Harris and Joseph Dashiell (Book No. 30 of Wills, p. 215).

In the record of the inventory of his estate the name is written indifferently "Barkely" and "Berkley." *Ailworth Barkley* appears to have been the executor and the only next of kin mentioned are *Abraham Barkley* and *Alice Barkley* (*Lib.* 62, fol. 256).

JOHN BARCLAY (or Barkeley) of Somerset County, Md., left a will dated August 30, 1774, proved April 6, 1775, and recorded at Annapolis. In the record of this will the name of his son *Charles Barclay,* whom he appoints executor, is written "Charles Barklett," while the names of his sons *Henry Barclay* and *John Barclay* are written "Henry Berkley" and "John Berkley." He refers to a wife, without naming her, and to a friend Ephraim King. He also mentions a grandson *Elijah Bar-*

clay (recorded as "Elijah Barklett,") seemingly the son of Charles. *Witnesses:* Martha Kemp, *Rachel Barkley* and *Sarah Barkley* (Book No. 40 of Wills, p. 386).

In Testamentary Procedure Book No. 46, fol. 300, the filing of this will is noted, and *Henry Wallace Barkley* and *J. Joseph Barkley* are recorded as sureties on the executor's bond.

SARAH BARKLEY, dau. of Thomas Barkley and Margaret Barkley, his wife, *b* December 14, 1724 (Records of STEPNEY PARISH, Somerset County, Md., p. 40).

JOHN BARKLEY *b* January 3, 1799 (*Ibid,* p. 183).

FROM LAND RECORDS OF KENT COUNTY.

THOMAS BARKLEY of Kent County, Merchant, is described, July 10, 1747, as being the owner of 275 acres in Kent County known as "Blays Range" and "Blays Addition" (J. S. No. 26, page 50).

On March 3, 1749, he takes from Peregrine Brown, of Kent County, gentleman, in consideration of £305, current money, a tract of six acres at the mouth of Turner's Creek called "Jarman Point" (J. S. No. 26, page 321).

("Turner's Creek" was in the vicinity of Galena P. O. in Kent County, and took its name from a family of Friends who lived in that vicinity until a comparatively recent time).

On June 9, 1749, he conveys the tract last mentioned to Thomas Crosby, of Philadelphia, merchant, for £408 (J. S. No. 26, page 323).

On April 7, 1750, for the consideration of £350, current money of Maryland, he takes from Samuel Milborn of Kent County, Planter, a parcel of 200 acres being part of a tract called "Suffolk" (J. S. No. 26, page 303).

On May 4, 1750, he conveys the tract last mentioned to James McLaughlin and Alexander Lunan of Cecil County, Maryland, for £450 (J. S. No. 26, page 316).

On October 3, 1750, he conveys to William Rasin, of Kent County, gentleman, all the real estate in Kent County which he held in right of his wife or of which she was possessed when he married her (J. S. No. 26, page 324).

FROM THE RECORDS OF SHREWSBURY PARISH, KENT COUNTY.

(Shrewsbury Parish was near Turner's Creek,—a branch of the Sassafras River which divides Kent and Cecil Counties).

THOMAS BARKLEY and *Mrs. Isabella Wethered* were married January 23, 1746/7 (p. 264).

Mrs. Isabella Wethered's maiden name was Isabella Blay. She was the youngest daughter of Col. William Blay, of Blay's Range, the only son of Col. Edward Blay and Ann Blay, his wife, who was for many years a vestryman of Shrewsbury Parish and represented Kent in the Legislature of Maryland during the sessions of 1714 and 1715. Col. William Blay married Isabella Pearce, daughter of Judge William Pearce and Isabella Pearce, his wife. Their children were: John Tilden Edward Blay, *b* January 31, 1707; William Blay, *b* October 22, 1714; and Isabella Blay, who first married Richard Wethered, son of Samuel Wethered and Dolly Lewin, his wife (OLD KENT, p. 316).

FROM THE RECORDS OF ST. JOHN'S OR PISCATAWAY PARISH, *Prince George County, Maryland.*

MARY WELLING BARKLEY, dau. of *Rodman Barkley* and *Virlinda Barkley,* his wife, *b* October 13, 1791.

FROM THE STATUTES OF THE PROVINCE OF MARYLAND.

A private act, passed at the October, 1753, Session of the Maryland Legislature, was entitled: "AN ACT for the relief of "THOMAS BARKLEY, a languishing Prisoner in Kent County "Gaol."

Recites that for four years and upwards THOMAS BARKLEY, of Kent County, had been closely confined for debt and that the sheriff as well as the principal and greatest number of his creditors were willing to release him, and then

Enacts that unless within thirty days some creditor should give security for the payment of the future imprisonment fees and for meat, drink and clothing during his future imprisonment, he be discharged from custody. An oath was required from the debtor that he owned absolutely nothing, real or personal, and he was granted three years immunity from prosecution by the sheriff for imprisonment fees.

From the Records of Harford County.

' (N. B. Harford County was established in 1773. Prior to that its limits were included in Baltimore County).

Land Records.

JOHN BARCLAY, on December 28, 1788, was surety with one William Whiteford on the bond of Thomas Steel as administrator of Capt. James Steel of Harford County, Md. (Book 1, p. 274).

JOHN BARCLAY petitioned the County Court for the issuing of a commission to mark and bound a tract that he was possessed of called the "Grove," which he apprehends from original location thereof. The prayer of the petition was granted and the commission met September 7, 1788, and again October 21, 1788. The principal witness was a man who testified that he had carried the Surveyor's chain on a survey 27 years before and the bounds seem largely to have been determined by his recollection. Final report of commission March 21, 1798.

1808, March 23, JOSHUA BARCLAY, legatee of *John Barclay,* deceased, conveys to ELIZABETH R. BARCLAY all his interest in his father's estate.

1815, March 6, JOHN BARCLAY and *Mary Barclay,* his wife, convey to John McCauseland a tract in Harford County called "Barclay's Slope" and another called "Barclay's Dream," and all the share of the grantor in lands of which his father JOHN BARCLAY died seized.

1815, March 6, JOHN BARCLAY, son of *John Barclay,* conveys to George McCauseland all his interest in his father's estate.

1820, September 15, ROBERT BARCLAY, of Lancaster County, Pennsylvania, conveys to George McCauseland, of Harford County, his undivided right in 392 acres called "Prospect," and a tract of 33 acres which his father *John Barclay*, deceased, had purchased from Joseph Miller.

Wills and Administration.

Will of JOHN BARCLAY of Harford County, Md., dated October 12, 1799; proved June 23, 1800. Mentions wife, *Elizabeth Rogers Barclay*, and his six sons, *John Gill Barclay, James Barclay, William Barclay, Joshua Gill Barclay, Robert Barclay* and *George Washington Barclay*, the last three of whom are described as his "three youngest sons." Witnesses: John Weeks, Robert M. Fadin and James Kilpatrick.

Will of JOHN BARCLAY of Harford County, Md., dated May 14, 1833; proved June 4, 1833. Mentions mother, *Mary Barclay*, grandfather, *Joseph Stokes*, and sisters, *Elizabeth Forwood* and *Hannah Barclay*. Refers to land devised to him by his grandfather as being part of a tract called "Clark's Den, Merry in Antrim." Witnesses: Harvey Stokes, Isaac Pyle and John H. Stokes.

FROM RECORDS OF CECIL COUNTY.

(N. B. Cecil County was organized in 1674).

Wills and Administration.

1750, April 2, Bond of Richard Price as administrator, etc., of GEORGE BARKLEY, late of Cecil County, deceased. John Holland and Isaac Hamm were sureties on the bond.

1781, December 10, Bond of WILLIAM BARKLEY, Gentleman, as executor of JAMES BARKLEY, late of Cecil County, deceased. Richard Hall and Andrew Work were sureties on the bond.

Executor's accounts filed February 11, 1782. Among the debtors to the estate were *John Barkley* and *James Barkley*.

Land Records.

1787, December 10, WILLIAM BARCLAY of Cecil County takes from Richard Hall of the same place, title to one negro boy as security against liability on a bond to Archibald Job which William Barclay signed as surety at Richard Hall's request.

1790, January 12, WILLIAM BARCLAY, of West Nottingham Hundred, Cecil County, Md., and *Sarah Barclay,* his wife, convey to JOSEPH BARCLAY of the same place, 122 acres of grantor's tract known as "Barclay's Square."

1794, December 18, JOSEPH BARCLAY, of West Nottingham Hundred, Cecil County, Md., conveys the 122 acres last described to Abraham Trump of the same place.

From "NOTES AND QUERIES" by William Henry Egle, M. D., M. A.

WILLIAM BARCLAY died previously to 1761. At that time his widow *Esther Barclay* had married one McIntire. He had eight children: *John Barclay, Hugh Barclay, Stephen Barclay, Joseph Barclay, Mary Barclay, Margaret Barclay, Martha Barclay* and *Esther Barclay* (page 137).

FROM RENT ROLLS OF TALBOT COUNTY.

On March 12, 1662, NICHOLAS BARKLEY, together with one John Alley, caused a survey to be made by one Richard Neck of 300 acres on the North side of the Choptank River in the dividing creek, possessed by Robert Martin.

On December 28, 1665, NICHOLAS BARKLEY caused a survey to be made by one Petty French of 150 acres on the North side of Choptank River at the head of the Northeast branch of Treadavon (Trade Haven?) Creek, possessed by John Sherwood for the heirs of James Berry.

FROM SUNDRY PARISH RECORDS OF MARYLAND.

Zion German Lutheran Christ Church of Baltimore.

MARRIED: "1788, Ausen Gemeinde 4," GEORGE D. BARKLEY and *Sophia Warwick* (p. 388).

BAPTIZED: 1792, September 7, MARY BARKLEY, child of GEORGE BARKLEY and *Sophia Barkley, b* August 11, 1792 (p. 30).

First German Reformed Congregation of Baltimore.

MARRIED: 1789, January 19, JEMIMA BARKLEY and *James Gormley* (p. 192).

First Presbyterian Church, Baltimore.

MARRIED: 1798, November 1, THOMAS BARKLEY and *Jane McCormick.* (p. 3).

BORN: 1816, November 2, REBECCA BARKLEY, dau. of JOHN BARKLEY and *Ann Barkley.*

1817, December 3, SARAH JANE BARKLEY, dau. of JOHN and *Ann Barkley.*

1819, February 19, JAMES BARKLEY, son of JOHN BARKLEY and *Ann Barkley.*

William & *Mary Parish* (Popular Hill Church),
St. Mary's County.

In January, 1808, a Rev. FRANCIS BARCLAY applied for the rectorship and was accepted and continued rector until March 7, 1810, when he resigned. His letter of resignation is spread at length upon the vestry minutes at page 20. He states therein that he has been called to "the church of Alexandria," and refers to his children as orphans and as "without relatives."

FROM THE MILITARY RECORDS OF MARYLAND SOLDIERS IN THE REVOLUTIONARY WAR.
(*Maryland Archives,* vol. XVIII).

JAMES BARCLAY (or Barkley) enlisted May 20, 1776, in the 6th Co. of Maryland Volunteers, commanded by Capt. Peter Adams; 1st Lieut. Nathaniel Ewing; 2nd Lieut. Alexander Murray; Ensign, John Jordan.

JAMES BARCLAY is recorded in June, 1778, as a deserter from the 1st Reg't. Maryland Troops, commanded by Lieut. Peter Brown.

JOHN BARCLAY (or Barkley) appears in the Muster and Pay Roll of 1780 among the men "passed by Thomas Rutter, Baltimore County," on April 11th, 1780.

THOMAS BARCLAY (recorded "Bartcly") was enrolled from St. Mary's County by Capt. Uriah Forrest, and was received and passed as a member of the "Flying Camp," by John A. Briscoe, on July 12, 1776.

From the Muster rolls of Major Archibald Anderson's 3rd Maryland Regiment for December, 1779, it appears that THOMAS BARCLAY (here recorded "Barkly") had enlisted for "during the war," but was at that time absent on furlough.

Among the certificates received from John White, Adjutant's Commissioner, it appears that THOMAS BARCLAY (here recorded "Barckley") served from August 1, 1780, to November 15, 1783.

From the Rolls of Escaped and Exchanged prisoners, 1781-1782, it appears that THOMAS BARCLAY (here recorded "Barkley") was on November 2, 1781, exchanged from Charles Town.

From the Muster Roll of Troops of the Maryland Line, it appears that THOMAS BARCLAY (here recorded "Bartley") enlisted as corporal, March 17, 1777, joined the army in August, 1778, and was a prisoner on May 12, 1779.

From the same Muster roll it appears that THOMAS S. BARCLAY (here recorded as "Bartley") enlisted April 25, 1778, and was discharged (or missing) August 16, 1780.

MISCELLANEOUS.

From MARYLAND JOURNAL AND BALTIMORE ADVERTISER of Tuesdays, April 22 and 29, 1783, HUGH BARKLEY appears to have been Clerk to the Commissioners of the Tax, in Baltimore.

From MARYLAND JOURNAL of January 19 and 23, and February 13, 1781:

"Notice is hereby given to all Persons, not to take an Assignment of a Bond I gave to a certain *Jacob Coble* in November last, for *Forty Pounds* payable in hard money or other money at the Exchange, as I am determined not to pay the same, for sufficient reasons which can be made appear, if the payment should be insisted on, from

MATHIAS BARCKLY."

From MARYLAND GAZETTE of Thursday, May 23, 1776:

"List of letters brought by the last Packet from Falmouth and now in the possession of Henricus Boel, in Crown Street, near the North River, New York:—

...........WALTER and WILLIAM BARCLAY, Baltimore."

Virginia.

FROM CALENDAR OF VIRGINIA STATE PAPERS, by Palmer.

THOMAS BARCLAY, with others, appointed "at a meeting of a number of respectable Inhabitants of the City of Philadelphia" held Friday, May 20th, 1774, a committee "to correspond with our Sister Colonies" (vol. VIII, p. 45).

He writes from Paris, under date of August 23rd, 1785, relative to a bust of Lafayette (vol. IV, p. 49).

On December 6, 1782, he acknowledges the receipt of his appointment as "Agent at the Court of France for the State of Virginia" (vol. III, p. 390).

He writes under date of January 5, 1783, of the unwillingness of France to make loans to the separate States, etc. (vol. III, p. 416).

He writes under date of January 27th, 1783, advising receipt of news from Benjamin Franklin that preliminary articles of peace had been signed between France, Spain and Great Britain (vol. III, p. 422).

He writes from Paris under date of May 17, 1784, enclosing a decree of his French Majesty's Council (vol. III, p. 583).

He writes from Paris under date of October 12, 1785, about the price of arms and advises that he will wait to see Lafayette before closing contract, etc. (vol. IV, p. 59).

He writes from Paris under date of January 16, 1786, concerning arms and ammunition, and adds that the first bust of Lafayette will be finished in about two months and the second in four (vol. IV, p. 81).

JOHN BARCLAY writes to Gov. Nelson under date of August 25, 1781, offering his services as agent for the State of Virginia, Congress having commissioned him to attend to certain commercial matters in France in which the country was about to embark (vol. II, p. 86).

A reward of $500 offered November 3, 1859, for the apprehension of BARCLAY COPPIE for complicity in the Harper's Ferry raid. He is described as "about 20 years old, is about 5 ft. 7½ "inches in height with hazel eyes and brown hair, wears a light "moustache and has a consumptive look" (vol. XI, p. 90).

FROM THE EPISCOPAL THEOLOGICAL SEMINARY AT ALEXANDRIA.

CAPT. EDMUND BARKLEY and *Lucy Barkley,* his wife, had the following children baptized:

> EDMUND BARKLEY, *bap.* December 12, 1704.
> LEWIS BARKLEY, *bap.* January 19, 1706.
> LUCY BARKLEY, *bap.* May 17, 1709.
> MARY BARKLEY, *bap.* May 11, 1711.

RECORDS OF ABINGDON PARISH, GLOUCESTER CO., VA.

(Now in the Theological Seminary at Alexandria, Va. In these records the name is spelt indifferently "Barkley" and "Berkley").

SARAH BARKLEY, dau. of MAJOR EDMUND BARKLEY and *Lucia Barkley,* his wife, was born September 9, 1713.

(and then, seemingly the next generation):

EDMUND BARKLEY (or Berkley) and MARY BARKLEY, his wife, had the following children baptized:

> LUCY BARKLEY *b* January 5, 1729; *bap.* January 10, 1729.
> EDMUND BARKLEY *b* December 5, 1729; *bap.* January 14, 1730.
> NELSON BARKLEY *b* May 16, 1773; *bap.* June 3, 1733.
> SARAH BARKLEY *b* January 27, 1741/2; *bap.* February 28, 1741/2.

FROM RECORDS OF LOUISA COUNTY.

(N. B. Louisa County was set off from Hanover County in 1746).

Marriage Licenses (1781-1853).

1790, December 23, ELIZABETH BARCLAY and *William Gillian.*

1791, November 10, LUCY W. BARCLAY and John *Wells.*

Land Records.[7]

Marriage Settlement, dated *August 12, 1742,* between PAT-

---

[7] For note upon the state of preservation of the various County records of Virginia, see *Appendix F* hereto annexed.

RICK BARCLAY, of the County of King & Queen, Va., Merchant, of the first part, *Col. John Martin,* of the second part, and *Elizabeth Martin,* spinster, his daughter, of the third part.

Recites intended marriage between PATRICK BARCLAY and *Elizabeth Martin;* that Col. Martin had settled on his daughter in fee-tail about 600 acres on the James River in Goochland County, Va., together with certain slaves; and that he had agreed to give to Patrick the sum of £400 sterling as a marriage portion with his daughter.

In consideration of which PATRICK BARCLAY conveys to Col. Martin about 900 acres in Hanover County, Va., which he had purchased of the executors of William Johnson, deceased, together with twenty slaves which he names.

Witnessed by *Andrew Barclay,* Mird. Throckmorton, Francis Jardine, Archibald Gordon and John Martin.

1795, October 3, PATRICK BARCLAY of Trinity Parish, Louisa County, Va., conveys to James Dickinson of St. Martin's Parish, about 300 acres at the head of Rocky Creek. No wife joins in the deed.

1795, October 3, PATRICK BARCLAY, of Louisa County, conveys to William Armstrong, 131¾ acres on a branch of Elk Creek in Louisa County, Va. No wife joins.

1796, September 15, PATRICK BARCLAY, of Louisa County, for an expressed consideration of one dollar, conveys to John Wells, of Fluvanna County, Va., all the land owned by the grantor in Louisa County, containing about 1312 acres and bounded by lands of William Cooke, Mrs. Hannah Tober, James Overton and James Dickinson. These lands are composed of three tracts formerly the property of GEORGE BARCLAY, the grantor's father, and inherited by the grantor as his heir at law.

The deed also recites that the grantor's mother was now Mrs. Mary R. Dickinson.

No wife joins in the deed.

GEORGE BARCLAY and *Mary Barclay,* his wife, by deed (with defeasance) dated March 26, 1764, convey about 414 acres with house and outbuildings to Thomas Johnson, gentleman (sheriff) and John Marshall, to secure payment of £500.

GEORGE BARCLAY (written "Berkley") and *Mary Barclay,* his wife, of St. Martin's Parish, Louisa County, by deed dated March 10, 1768, convey to Griffith Dickinson about 96 acres on the North branch of Elk Creek, bounded by lands of James Overton, George Barclay (written "Berkley") and Griffith Dickinson, and formerly owned by William Sexton.

Court Records.

1742, February Term, SAMUEL BARCLAY recovers judgment against one Sexton.

1770, May Term, GEORGE BARCLAY brings suit against John Fait.

FROM RECORDS OF ALBEMARLE COUNTY.

(N. B. Albemarle County was established in 1744).

Wills and Administration.

Report of Commissioners, dated November 6, 1822, on division of the estate of ROBERT BARCLAY. Sets off to John D. Moon and wife three slaves, valued at $850; to THOMAS BARCLAY four slaves valued at $820; to JAMES BARCLAY four slaves valued at $810; and to ANNE MARIA BARCLAY three slaves valued at $800.

Court Records.

ANDREW BARCLAY seems to have brought a number of suits, mostly for small debts:

1746, May 28, against John Henson.
September 13, against Sacheveral Whitehead.
November 15, against Edward Watts.

1748, June 10, against Andrew McGuire.
And many others.

From Records of Orange County.

(N. B. Orange County was organized in 1734).

Wills and Administration.

JAMES BARCLAY (written "Bartley") of Orange County makes a will dated September 23, 1756, and mentions his two daughters *Martha Barclay* and *Jane Barclay* (both written "Bartley").

Land Records.

WILLIAM BARCLAY and Samuel McKean, trading in Baltimore as "Barclay & McKean" make two deeds of land in Orange County, the one in 1811 and the other in 1812.

From Henning's Statutes of Virginia.

On December 11, 1790, an act was passed authorizing the establishment of a ferry in the County of Harrison (now in West Virginia) across the West Fork of the Monongahela River to land of WILLIAM BARKLEY (vol. 13, p. 131).

By act passed November 25, 1791, WILLIAM BARKLEY was constituted a trustee of Randolph Academy (vol. 13, p. 293).

1758, September 23, paid for provisions furnished to the militia of the County of Augusta.

To GEORGE BARKLEY £1:3:0 (vol. VII, p. 198).

From Record of Patents, 1623-1774, at State House, Richmond.

On May 12, 1770, a patent was granted to HUGH BARKLEY of 95 acres in Augusta County (Book No. 39, p. 82).

From Records of Land Grants, 1779-1803, at State House, Richmond.

On December 20, 1784, a grant issued to THOMAS BARKLEY of 328 acres in Monongahela County (now West Virginia) "including his settlement made there in 1773" (Book M, p. 623).

On the same date another grant of 400 acres on the West fork of the Monongahela River in the same County issued to him, as assignee of the grant to John Simpson (Book N, p. 425) ; and

On the same date a third grant of 311 acres in the same locality issued to him (Book N, p. 425).

MISCELLANEOUS.

Marriage Bonds in Goochland County.

"1766, August 6, GEORGE BARCLAY to *Mary Cole,* daughter of James Cole, gentleman. Security William Thurston. Witness: Val. Wood" (WILLIAM & MARY COLLEGE QUARTERLY, vol. 7, p. 101).

THOMAS PAXTON (of the Marshall family) *b* in Ireland 1719; *d* in Rockbridge Co., Va., in 1788; *m* (2) MARY BARCLAY by whom he had seven children. He had eight by his first wife (*Ibid,* vol. 10, p. 207).

Unclassified.

Married at London, December 12, 1820, T. B. BARCLAY to *Sarah,* daughter of Henry *Peters,* of Belchworth Castle, in the Co. of Surrey, England.

From PENNSYLVANIA GAZETTE of Wednesday, March 5, 1788:

"On the 18th of December last" (that is, December 18, 1787), "died, at his house at Hackney, near London, in the 59th year of his age, JOHN BARCLAY (son of David Barclay, late of that City, and grandson of Robert Barclay, who wrote the Apology for the Quakers). His loss will long be severely felt, not only by his immediate connections, but by numbers who have experienced the spirited efforts of his active friendship. His benevolence was so universal, his desire of doing good was so ardent and invariable, that, instead of making a long confinement to his house and a weak frame of body a plea for declining to promote the welfare and success of those who applied to him for his assistance, he cheerfully and zealously undertook their case, though often to the detriment of his health; and he cordially relieved the distresses of the necessitous, and those who were ready to perish. In an age when the property of the rich is wasted on the most contemptible trifles, and exhausted merely in selfish gratifications; when the number of those who seek occasion to do good is so confined; the death of such a man as John Barclay is and should be considered and lamented as a public loss."

From NEW YORK COMMERCIAL ADVERTISER of Friday, 3 March, 1848.

"*Died:* In the City of Mexico, on the 9th of January last, Captain JAMES BARCLAY of Company C of the New York Volunteers.

"The subject of the above notice was a native of the city of Albany, the only child of William Barclay, deceased, formerly connected with the Bank of Albany. He was in service at the siege of Vera Cruz, and took part in all the great battles in which the American army, under General Scott, was engaged, from that of Vera Cruz to the storming of the City of Mexico. In the battle of Chepultepec he was second in command to Lieut. Col. Burnham, commanding officer of the U. S. Regiment of New York Volunteers, and won for himself a military distinction of no ordinary grade, as will appear from Col. Burnham's report of the part taken in these engagements by the New York Volunteers. He was slightly wounded in the arm during this engagement. Spared by a protecting Providence from an impending death during so many sanguinary battles, he has fallen a victim to the typhus fever now so prevalent, from the last accounts, among the troops in the City of Mexico."

From NEW YORK HERALD of Sunday, August 9, 1903:

"JAMES EDWARD BARCLAY, a portrait artist, formerly well known in this city, Washington, D. C., and Boston, died of pulmonary disease in Edinburgh, Scotland, July 27 last. He was born in London fifty-seven years ago, studied in Italy and spent most of his later years in this country. For several years he had a studio in the Alpine Building, New York, but went from here to Washington, where he resided until two years ago. At the time of his death he was engaged on a portrait of the Lord Mayor of Edinburgh. He painted many well-known people in this city, Washington and Boston."

From COLLECTANEA GENEALOGICA by Joseph Foster (London: Privately printed, 1883) :[8]

"An obituary of the Nobility, Gentry, etc. of England, Scotland and Ireland, prior to 1800, collected by Sir William Musgrave, Bart."

BARCLAY, DAVID, son of the Apologist, in Cheapside, 18 March, 1769, aet. 88 (*London Magazine,* 333).

"   GEORGE, Jamaica, Merchant, 7 June, 1756 (*ibid* 301).

"   JOHN, son of the Apologist, 8 June, 1751. (*Gentleman's Magazine,* 284).

"   PRISCILLA (Mrs.), 12 October, 1769. (*London Magazine,* 544).

"   ROBERT, son of the Apologist, at Ury, 28 March, 1747 (*ibid* 198).

"   ROBERT, at Madras, 6 October, 1786. (*Gentleman's Magazine,* 274).

---

[8] A copy is on file at the Astor Library, New York.

PART XII.

Sundry Records of the Barclays in Ireland, other than of the Ury Family.

In the Dublin searches recently made for the writer, a number of records were noted and returned which are here cited in the hope that they may prove of some use to those who are interested in tracing a descent from one or more of the many families of Barclay in Ireland. It is not claimed that these records are all that may be found in any of the localities named, for the search was not directed against the name of Barclay, generally; but it is believed that what is here given may be relied upon as acccurate, so far as it goes.

Among the original wills proved in Killaloe Diocese and preserved in the Record Office, Dublin, is that of "DAVID BARCLAY, Clerk." Will dated July 18, 1715; proved March 15, 1715/16. The probate of the will describes the testator as "late Incumbent of Killmurry McMahon,"—which was in County Clare, on the Shannon River. The will refers to testator's wife, without naming her, and to his sons *David Barclay, Harey Barclay* and *Andrew Barclay.*

In P. Dwyer's printed "Diocese of Killaloe, 1550-1700" this cleric is referred to a number of times and at page 401 is given a photograph of his portrait. It is also there stated that during the troubles of 1689-1691 he remained at home, and held a valuable farm under the See of Killaloe. His family in 1878 still held Ballyartney.

At page 326 of Dwyer's "Diocese of Killaloe" it is stated that a Mr. Barclay, son of Rev. GAWIN BARCLAY, both before and after 1660 was tenant of Ballina, owned by Major Thompson after forfeiture by Sir T. O'Brien; and at page 395 LADY BARCLAY of County Clare is enumerated among the refugees in England in 1689.

The Subsidy Roll of County Down for the year 1663 recites among those who owned property of the yearly value of £3 or more.

NINIAN BARKLY, of Ralph Gill, in Bangor Parish, Ardes Barony.

NINIAN BARKLY, of Benash, in Killkeell parish, Newry and Mourne.

THOMAS BARKLY, of Ballygonne in Upper Iveagh Barony.

Wills proved in Down Diocese, County Down:

1683, WILLIAM BARKLEY of Rathgill.

1711, JANE BARKLY al. Pollock of Killyleagh.

1713, ELIZABETH BARKLEY of Ballysallogh.

1729, ANDREW BARKLEY of Donaghadee.

Wills proved in Raphoe Diocese, County Donegal:

1754, JOHN BARCLAY of Drumbo.

1768, THOMAS BARCLAY of Ballybofey.

1776, JAMES BARKLY of Fiquart.

1786, WILLIAM BARCLAY of Figart.

1787, GEORGE BARCLAY of Drumbo.

1792, JAMES BARCLAY of Figart.

1795, ROBERT BARCLAY of Letterkenney.

1796, JOSEPH BARCLAY of Ballybofey.

1798, JAMES BARCLAY of Figart.

1855, ANDREW BARCLAY of Figart.

Wills proved in Derry Diocese, Counties Londonderry, Donegal and Tyrone:

1724, JAMES BARKLEY of Ardervar.

1769, SAMUEL BARKLEY of Desertmartin, Co. Londonderry.

1773, JAMES BARKLEY of Maghera, Co. Londonderry.

1776, ROBERT BARKLEY of Desertmartin, Co. Londonderry.

Wills proved in Killaloe Diocese, Counties Clare and Tipperary:

1753, ANDREW BARCLAY of Newmarket, Co. Clare.

1854, MILLICENT BARCLAY of Kilkee.

Wills proved in Waterford and Lismore Diocese, Counties Waterford and Tipperary:

1678, MARGARET BARKLAY al. Cleland.

Wills proved in Connor Diocese, County Antrim:

1686, HUGH BARKLEY.

1696, WILLIAM BARKLIE, Ballywillin.

1766, GEORGE BARCLAY, Belfast.

1835, JAMES BARCLAY, Connor.

1835, WILLIAM BARCLAY, Ballyclug.

1844, WILLIAM BARCLAY, Carncastle.

And twenty-two other Barclay wills between 1700-1858.

Will of JOHN BARCLAY of Lambeg, County Antrim, dated March 23, 1797, proved January 31, 1798, mentions wife *Isabella Barclay*, nephews John Logan and William Logan, sisters Marian Baily and Eleanor Baily and niece Elizabeth Renfrew.

Irish Prerogative Grant Book, Intestate Grants:

1760, JOHN BERKELEY, M. D., Limerick.

1760, JOHN BERKELEY, Lieut. in Effingham's Foot Reg't.

1777, THOMAS BARKLAY, Ballyarny, County Clare.

1837, RICHARD BARCLAY, Bartney, County Clare, Ballyartney.

IRISH PREROGATIVE WILLS:

MARY COPE al. BARKLY. Dated December 14, 1670. Proved May 26, 1671. Mentions deceased daughter Katherine Cope, daughter Elizabeth Cope, son Henry Cope, and father Dean *Robert Barkly*.

(N. B. *Robert Barclay*, Dean of Clogher, married Elizabeth Maxwell, daughter of Dr. Robert Maxwell, Dean of Armagh,—

Brit. Museum ADD. MSS. No. 4820. This *Robert Barclay* died April 1, 1654,—Ulster Office. In 1642 he was son-in-law to Sir William Cole of Enniskillen,—Sir F. Hamilton's Pamphlet in vol. 3 of the "Thorpe Collection").

DOROTHY BERKLEY, of Glasnevin, County Dublin, widow. Dated August 18, 1724. Codicil signed August 3, 1727. Proved May 4, 1727. Refers to her marriage settlement dated March 7, 1680. Mentions son *Maurice Berkley*, daughter *Elizabeth Berkley* and daughter *Dorothy Charlton*, wife of Job Charlton.

ROBERT BARCLAY, of Ballyshannon, County Donegal, merchant. Dated June 3, 1783. Proved December 3, 1783. Mentions wife *Margaret Charlotte Barclay*, daughter of Elizabeth Crofton, wife of Henry Crofton, grandson James Buchanan, son *John Barclay* (to whom the testator leaves a farm on the Basil estate "if he returns home to demand it in person"), son *Robert Barclay*.

ANN BERKELEY, widow of Dr. *George Berkeley*, late Bishop of Cloyne. Dated April 22, 1781. Proved in London June 16, 1786. Mentions son Dr. *George Berkeley* who proposes to reside for the next four years at St. Andrew's to superintend the education of testatrix's grandson. Refers to her son's house at Canterbury and her own estate and lands at Ballysinagh, County Tipperary.

ANN BERKELEY of Dublin and of Middleton. Dated April 6, 1796. Proved November 6, 1799. Refers to her father and mother as buried in Middleton churchyard. Mentions sisters *Elizabeth Berkeley* and Arabella Hamilton, brothers *George Berkeley, Joshua Berkeley* and *William Berkeley*, nieces *Anne Berkeley* and Catherine Atterbroy, and nephew *Joshua Berkeley*. Executor: Sackville Hamilton. Affidavit of Joshua Berkeley of Rockville, in the South Liberties of Cork, that the entire will was in the handwriting of the testatrix.

(Note. Sackville Hamilton, grandson of the first Viscount Boyne, married *Arabella Berkeley*, daughter of Rev. Dr. *George Berkeley*, Bishop of Cloyne).

ORIGINAL DUBLIN WILL preserved at the Record Office, Four Courts, Dublin:

JOHN BARKLEY of Mark Street, Dublin City, gentleman. Dated February 20, 1810. Proved March 19, 1811. Mentions wife *Catherine Barkley* and refers to interests received by him under will of Lawrence Lawrenceson, deceased.

REGISTRY OF DEEDS OFFICE, Henrietta Street, Dublin.

Marriage Settlement of JOHN BARCLAY of Ballybofey, County Donegal, gentleman, and *Elizabeth Curry,* spinster, of Londonderry City, daughter of Samuel Curry, of the same place, merchant. Mentions *Joseph Barclay,* of Ballybofey, brother of said John and eldest son and executor of Joseph Barclay of Ballybofey, deceased. Also mentions *Robert Barclay* of Strabane, County Tyrone. Dated November 16, 1774 (Transcript of Memorial, vol. 307, p. 396, No. 204,720).

Declaration of Trust by JOHN BARCLAY of Strabane, County Tyrone, that he holds certain lands in Strabane in trust for Rev. Andrew Thomas Hamilton of Donagheady. Dated November 16, 1785 (Transcript of Memorial, vol. 369, p. 449, No. 249,037).

Deed from ROBERT BARCLAY and Andrew Carson of Strabane, merchants and others, of certain lands in Longfield parish, County Tyrone. Dated May 22, 1740 (Transcript of Memorial, vol. 100, p. 354, No. 70,771).

Marriage Settlement of Richard Chadwick of Dublin City, counsellor at law, and BRIDGET BARCLAY, spinster, daughter of *Thomas Barclay* late of Ballyarney, County Clare, esquire, deceased, and *Anne Barclay,* his widow, now of Limerick City. Dated January 5 and 6, 1785 (Transcript of Memorial, vol. 370, p. 559, No. 253,601).

Sale of rent charge from JOHN BARKLEY of Limerick City, gentleman, son and heir of *John Barkley,* Doctor of Physic, late of the same place, deceased, and *Abigail Barkley* al. Craven, widow of said John Barkley, deceased, to Anthony Parker of Castlelough, County Tipperary, esquire. Dated January 4, 1755 (Transcript of Memorial, vol. 174, p. 228, No. 115,946).

Deed from JOHN BARCLAY of Strabane, County Tyrone, esquire, to William Law of Edenmore and James Johnston of Stranorlar, both in County Donegal, gentleman, of certain lands used by said *John Barclay* as a bleach green and bounded on the East by the bleach green of *Joseph Barclay,* on the West, etc., etc. Witness: *George Barclay* of Stranorlar. Dated February 14, 1786 (Transcript of Memorial, vol. 380, p. 112, No. 252,964).

EXCHEQUER BILL BOOKS 1719-1820:

July 12, 1723, Bill of GEORGE BERKELEY and Robert Marshall against Peter Partington and others.

July 4, 1724, Bill of GEORGE BERKELEY and Robert Marshall against Bartholomew Partington Vanhomrigh.

June 24, 1726, Bill of ROBERT BARKLEY against Crain Brush.

February 7, 1728/9, Bill of MAURICE BERKELEY, clerk, against John Morris.

June 29, 1729, Bill of ROBERT BARKLEY and *Mary Barkley,* his wife, against John Potts and others.

December 23, 1731, Bill of JOHN BARKLEY, Doctor of Physic, against Richard Craven.

February 8, 1731/2, Bill of MAURICE BERKELEY, clerk, against William Gardiner.

June 16, 1732, Bill of MAURICE BERKELEY, clerk, against John Maxwell, Judith Maxwell, Robert Curtis, *Elizabeth Berkeley,* Dorothy Charlton and Mary Deane.

December 3, 1735, Bill of same against *Elizabeth Berkeley,* Dorothy Charlton and Henry Napper.

May 11, 1739, Bill of JOHN BARKLEY against Richard Craven and Anthony Copley.

May 20, 1739, Bill of Rev. GEORGE BERKELEY, Dean of Derry, and Robert Marshall, against Thomas Pierson.

February 27, 1749/50, Bill of DAVID BARCLAY against Rice, Carrique & Philips.

April 17, 1751, Bill of LOFTUS BERKELEY against James Nugent and Thomas Hart.

December 3, 1751, Bill of MAURICE BERKELEY, clerk, executor of *Dorothy Berkeley*, against *Elizabeth Berkeley*, Dorothy Charlton and others.

December 27, 1753, Bill of ROBERT BARCLAY, executor of Hugh Brown, against William Newton and others.

November 2, 1754, Bill of JAMES BARCLAY against Anthony Short.

February 9, 1759, Bill of JOHN BERKELEY against Joseph Henry and others.

December 17, 1759, Bill of DAVID BARCLAY and others as creditors of Anthony Hickman against William Finch, Henrietta Hickman and others.

April 10, 1764, Bill of THOMAS BARCLAY as executor of *David Barclay,* and others against Jonathan Ashe, Henrietta Hickman and others. (The names of both plaintiffs and defendants seem to be County Clare and Limerick names.)

November 7, 1772, Bill of ROBERT BERKELEY, clerk, against Edmund Fowler.

March 9, 1776, Bill of WILLIAM BARKLIE and William Ferguson against *Thomas Barklie, John Barklie* and others.

April 21, 1780, Bill of JOHN BARCLAY against Samuel Price. Complains that Lawrence Lawrenceson of Dublin City, gentleman, by his will dated October 15, 1766, left certain property to *Mary Crowley,* who was plaintiff's mother, and to James Crowley, her husband, etc., etc.

June 5, 1782, Bill of ROBERT BARCLAY, as executor of John Henry, deceased, against Anthony Coane and others.

April 28, 1792, Bill of ANNE BARCLAY, widow and administratrix of Thomas Barclay, against John Miller and others. (Three actions were commenced by this plaintiff against different sets of defendants. The plaintiff was evidently of Ballyartney, County Clare.)

November 18, 1796, Bill of JOHN BARCLAY of Lambeg, County Antrim, Linendraper, against Letitia Maxwell and others on a real estate transaction.

CHANCERY BILL BOOKS 1720-1812:

May 18, 1723, Bill of Rev. HENRY BARCLAY, clerk, against Edward Daton.

November 24, 1731, Bill of JOHN BERCLY against *Humphrey Bercly* and others.

October 27, 1739, Bill of WILLIAM LORD BERKELEY against Robert Percevall and others.

September 8, 1740, Bill of JOHN BERKLAY against Richard Hughes and others.

December 5, 1754, Bill of DAVID BARKLEY of Konigsberg in Prussia, merchant, against John Scott and others of Newry in County Down, relative to a cargo of 1,000 barrels of flaxseed.

February 16, 1758, Bill of JOHN BERKELEY, gentleman, against Jonathan Short and others.

June 12, 1761, Bill of JOHN BARKLEY, gentleman, against Jonathan Short and others.

November 3, 1766, Bill of JOSEPH BARCLAY and others as executors of Joseph Neily, against Robert Ewing.

1797, Bill of THOMAS BARCLAY against John Scott.

1810, Bill of GEORGE BARCLAY against John Fenton.

1812, Bill of GEORGE BARCLAY against James Young.

APPENDIX A.

EXTRACT FROM RECORDS OF THE MONTHLY MEETING OF FRIENDS AT AMBOY (now, 1897, kept at the Friends Meeting House at Plainfield, N. J.).

"The 3d of the 8th Month, 1686.

"Friends at Amboy agreed to have a monthly meeting * * * the first to begin the second 4th day of the 9th month 1686.

"At the monthly meeting held in Amboy the 10 day of the 9th month 1686, agreed that all friends belonging to this monthly meeting bring minits of births & burials (since they first came into this place) that they may be recorded." (No such records are found prior to 1705.)

*   *   *   *   *   *   *

"At the monthly meeting held in Amboy the 12th of the 11th month 1686/7 *Miles Forster* & *Rebecca Lawry* proposed to the meeting their intention of marriage. The meeting appoints *John Mill* & *William Bethell* to inquire into the matter and see if all things be clear with these persons in order to there marriage & to make report thereof against next monthly meeting."

"At the Monthly Meeting held in Amboy the 9th of the 12th month 1686/7 *Miles Forster* & *Rebecca Lawry* came the second tyme to the meeting expecting friends answer. The meeting being satisfied had nothing to object against there marriage & yrfore allowed them to appoynt a meeting of friends, wherein to solemnize the same."

*   *   *   *   *   *   *

"At the Monthly Meeting held at Amboy the 11th of the 3d month 1687, enquiry being made if any have to offer to the meeting. Its thought fit that JOHN BARCLAY receave the contribution for the formes[1] and pay for the same. * * *

---

[1] *i. e.*, 6 formes for seats in the meeting house.

"Friends appoint *Andrew Hanton & John Wrane* to speak to *widow Mitchell* that she do not talk of *Peter Sonmans* as it seems shee doth, rather wish her to come to the meeting and if yr be difference lay it before friends according to the order of truth."

"At the Monthly Meeting held in Amboy the 8th of the 4th Month 1687, *Peter Sonmans & Mary Mitchell* refer'd the whole matter in difference betwixt them unto *Miles Forster,* JOHN BARCLAY, *Benjamin Griffith & Edward Grig* to determine the same & does promise to agree unto there decision."

"JOHN BARCLAY gives an account that he has receaved the contribution for the formes & payed for them."

"Friends desire *John Neill & Benjamine Griffith* to speak to *Benjamine Clerk* about his absenting himself from friends meetings & to desire him to come to next Monthly Meeting."

"At the Monthly Meeting held in Amboy the 13th of the 5th month 1687, the friends appoynted to speak to *Benjamine Clerk,* brought his answer, which was, that he would not come because *Governor Lawry* called him a divil (as he sayes), wherewith friends not being satisfied, desires *George Keith* & JOHN BARCLAY to speak to him again."

"At the Monthly Meeting held in Amboy the 10th of the 6th month 1687 JOHN BARCLAY brought *Ben. Clerk's* answer, being the same with what he sayd before."

"At the Monthly Meeting held in Amboy the 14th of the 7th month, 1687, *William Bethell* having a desyne to marry a woman who lives in Philadelphia, desr'd a certificat from this meeting which accordingly was granted."

"At the Monthly Meeting held in Amboy the 9th of the 9th month 1687, *John Lufborrow* and *Gartrüd Holland* proposed there Intention of marriage to the Meeting, who apoynts them to come next monthly meeting to receave there answer."

"At the Monthly Meeting held at Amboy the 14th of the 10th month 1687, *John Reid* who hitherto kept the book for this meeting being now removed with his family to another County, desr'd friends to order another in his stead, whereupon the Meeting apoynt'd *Ben. Griffith* to keep the book & receave the contributions."

"*Mary Forster,* Daughter of *Miles Forster* and *Rebeckah Forster,* was born the 18th of the 8th month, 1687."

"At a monthly meeting held in Amboy the 11th day of the 11th month 1687, It being proposed to bring Contributions towards the Rent of the Meeting House, JOHN BARCLAY inform'd that the yearly rent was 3£ and that therof thirty shillings theroof paid. 10s by *James Millow,* 10s by *John Reid* and 10s by JOHN BARCLAY. *John Lufburry* promised to contribute a bushell of wintow wheat—*John Sim* the like, JOHN BARCLAY Dr for *John Laing* 4s *Miles Forster* 10s."

"At a Monthly Meeting held at Amboy the 11th day of the 4th month 1688,

"JOHN BARCLAY informed the meeting he had discharged the money due to the *Widdow Bunn* for nursing *Widdow Mills* child viz £2:6:0- Towards which *Miles Forster* promised to pay 10s *John Reid* 10s JOHN BARCLAY 6s *John Laing* 4s *Ben Griffith* 6s."

A monthly meeting was held in Amboy 14th day of 9th month, 1688.

The next Monthly Meeting was held in Woodbridge the 17th day of the 8th month, 1689, the entry being:

"It was agree'd that the monthly meeting should be kept, the third fifth day in every month, at *Benjamin Griffith's* in Woodbridge. That friends of the ministry coming to visit us should be taken care of."

Then, in another handwriting:

"The above said monthly meeting fell from ye year 1689 to ye year 1704 by reason of *George Keith's* separation which was 15 years, and then was appointed to be kept at Woodbridge first by a preparative meeting, and abt 2 years after kept a monthly meeting."

The next entry was of a quarterly meeting, following the yearly meeting in Shrewsbury, held at the meeting house 24th 8th month 1704.

APPENDIX B.

Act of Parliament (private bill, not printed.) 45 Geo. III.
Ch. 88, 1805.

An Act for settling and securing certain Parts of the Lands of
Redcloak and Findlayston, lying in the Parish of Fetteresso
and County of Kincardine, upon, and to, and in favor of
Robert Barclay Allardice, of Urie, Esquire, and the same
series of Heirs, and under the same Conditions and Limitations, as are mentioned and contained in a Deed of Entail
made by Robert Barclay, of Urie, deceased; and for vesting in the said Robert Barclay Allardice, and his Heirs
and Assigns in Fee Simple, certain Parts of the Barony of
Urie, lying in the said County of Kincardine.

WHEREAS by a Disposition and Deed of Entail bearing
date the ninth day of October in the year one thousand seven
hundred and twenty-two, and registered in the register of Tailzies
in *Scotland* upon the sixth day of February, in the year one thousand seven hundred and twenty-three, and in the books of Council and Session upon the twenty-eighth day of November one
thousand eight hundred and one, Robert Barclay, of Urie, deceased, settled, conveyed, and disponed, heritably and irredeem-
ably, to and in favour of Robert Barclay his eldest lawful Son,
and the heirs male lawfully to be procreated of his body, which
failing, to David Barclay, his second lawful Son, and the heirs
male of his body, which failing, to the heirs male to be procreated of his own body, which failing, to David Barclay his
Brother-german, and the heirs male of his body, which failing,
to his Brother John Barclay and the heirs male of his body,
which failing, to his Uncle John Barclay and the heirs male
of his body, which failing, to his heirs and assignees whatsoever,
without division, all and whole the Lands of Urie, the Mains
thereof, with the Manor Place, the Salmon Fishing at the mouth
of the Waters of Cowie and Carron, both in fresh and salt water,

betwixt the shore of Stonehaven and the shore of Cowie, and all and whole the Town and Lands of Megray, Woodhead, Powbear, Balnagight, Glethnoe, and Cairnton, Mill of Cowie, Mill Plough, Mill Lands, Multures, Sequels, and Knaveships of the same, including the Multures of the said Hail Lands, as also the Multures of the Town and Lands of Redcloak and Findlayston, and of those Lands which sometime belonged to the Earl of Errol, lying in and about the Town of Cowie, and the Multure of the Walkmill Lands of Urie, with the Pertinents for payment of the Multures and Knaveship used and wont, comprehending also the Multures of Easter and Wester Logies, with the Pertinents for the payment of Outsucken Duty; and all and whole those Parts and Pendicles of the Lands of Montquich called Trees, Burnhaugh, Rothnick, and Corseley, with the Mill of Montquich, Mill Lands, Multures, and Sequels of the same, comprehending the Multures of the whole twelve Ploughs of Montquich, with the Parts, Pendicles, and Pertinents of the same, with Houses, Biggings, Yards, Orchards, Outsets, Insets, Mosses, Muirs, Commonties, Common Pasturages, Dependencies, Tenantries, Service of Free Tenants, Tofts, Crofts, Parts, Pendicles, and Pertinents of the said whole Lands above mentioned, all lying within the Parish of Fetteresso and Sheriffdom of Kincardine, together with the Teinds of the said whole Lands, both Parsonage and Vicarage included; and that as principal and certain other Lands therein mentioned in special warrandice thereof, all annexed and united in one Free Barony called the Barony of Urie, but with and under the following Provisions and Declarations; that is to say, that it should not be lawful to the said ROBERT BARCLAY (the Son) or any of the heirs of tailzie above mentioned, to alienate or dispone either the Fee or the Life Rent of the said Estate so disponed, or any part thereof, to any Person or Persons, or to contract any Debt or do any Deed whereby the said tailzied Estate might be evicted or burdened further than it stood burdened by the said Disposition and Deed of Tailzie, excepting by granting Jointures to their Wives suitable and competent to the tailzied Estate, and Portions to their Children not exceeding twenty thousand pounds Scots, and that the said ROBERT BARCLAY (the Son) and his foresaids, nor any of the heirs of tailzie above mentioned, should not suffer diligence to pass by adjudication or otherways upon the tailzied Estate, for any of the Debts or Deeds of the said ROBERT BARCLAY (the Grantor) so as that the property thereof might be carried off, declaring all Deeds by the said ROBERT BARCLAY (the Son) or his foresaids, or any of the heirs of tailzie, contrary or prejudicial thereto, to be in themselves void and null, and that the next heir of tailzie or provision might immediately upon contravention pursue Declarators thereof, and serve themselves heirs to him who died last infeft in the Fee, and did not contravene without necessity to represent the Contravener by fulfilling his deeds contrary to the true meaning of the said Deed of Entail:

AND WHEREAS the said ROBERT BARCLAY the Disponee in the said Deed did make up in his person a complete feudal Title to the said tailzied Lands and Estates under the said Deed, and having departed this life he was succeeded therein by ROBERT BARCLAY ALLARDICE, late of Urie, Esquire, his eldest Son, who was duly served heir in special to his said Father and infeft in the said tailzied Lands and Estate, and he having also died was succeeded by ROBERT BARCLAY ALLARDICE, now of Urie and of Allardice, his eldest Son, who stands duly infeft and seised in the said Lands and Estate as heir of tailzie and provision, subject to the conditions and provisions in the said Deed of Tailzie above mentioned:

AND WHEREAS the Lands after mentioned, part of the said Barony of Urie, and comprehended in the said Deed of Entail, lie disjoined from the bulk of the Estate, and at a greater distance from the Mansion House of Urie than those Lands which are proposed to be substituted in lieu of them, and are otherwise inconveniently situated for the Holder; that is to say, all and whole those Parts and Pendicles of the Lands of Montquich called Trees, Burnhaugh, Rothnick, and Corseley, with the Mill of Montquich, Mill Lands, Multures, and Sequels of the same, comprehending the Multures of the Hail, twelve Ploughs of Montquich, with the Parts, Pendicles, and Pertinents of the same, with Houses, Buildings, Yards, Orchards, Outsets, Insets, Mosses, Muirs, Commonties, Common Pasturage, Dependencies, Tenantries, and Service of Free Tenants, Tofts, Crofts, Parts, Pendicles, and Pertinents of the said Hail Lands above mentioned, together with the Teinds of the said whole Lands, both Parsonage and Vicarage included, all lying within the Parish of Fetteresso and Sheriffdom of Kincardine, the present annual Rental of which Lands so lying disjointed amounts to the Sum of two hundred and sixty-five pounds eighteen shillings and one penny sterling, according to the Schedule hereunto annexed (marked A):

AND WHEREAS the said Robert Barclay Allardice, now of Urie and of Allardice, stands seised and possessed in fee simple of the following Lands and Premises which lie adjacent to and intermixed with the said entailed Estate of Urie, and near the Mansion House thereof (that is to say) all and whole those Parts of the Lands of Redcloak and Findlayston, lying in the County of Kincardine and Parish of Fetteresso, bounded and described as follows: *videlicet:* Beginning upon the south at the junction of the Burn of Maxie with the Water of Cowie, and following up the channel of the said Burn in a westerly direction, until it is intersected by the Turnpike Road leading from Stonehaven to Bridge of Fough by the Slugmouth, from thence keeping the line of the said Turnpike Road in a northerly direction, until it is intersected by a straight line drawn from the point of junction of the Marches of the Estates of Findlayston and Urie at the stone wall inclosing the field called Balnagight, from the plantation thereof; from said point in said Turnpike Road, going in an easterly direction along said line, to the beforementioned point of junction of the Marches of the Estates of Findlayston and Urie, from thence keeping a southwesterly direction along the line of Marches between the said Estates of Findlayston and Urie, until it joins the Water of Cowie, and from thence holding down the course of said Water in a southeasterly direction to the mouth of the Burn of Maxie, at which this description commences, with Houses, Biggings, Yards, Orchards, Woods, Plantings, Fishings, Mosses, Muirs, Meadows, Commonty, Common Pasturage, Tofts, Crofts, Parts. Pendicles, and Hail Pertinents of the same whatsoever, together with the Teinds, both Parsonage and Vicarage, of the Lands and others above mentioned, and Hail Desks, Seats, Rooms, and Burial Places belonging to the said Lands, within the Church and Church Yard of Fetteresso,

the present annual Rental of which Lands amounts to the Sum
of three hundred and fifty-one pounds seventeen shillings and
tenpence sterling, according to the Schedule hereto annexed,
marked (B):

AND WHEREAS it would be convenient, on account of
the situation, for the said ROBERT BARCLAY ALLARDICE, and the
heirs of entail entitled to succeed to him in the said Barony and
Estate of Urie, if the Lands and Hereditaments immediately
before mentioned, parts of the Lands of Redcloak and Findlayston, so held by the said ROBERT BARCLAY ALLARDICE in fee simple,
were annexed to the said entailed Estate of Urie in lieu of and
in exchange for the said parts thereof disjoined and inconveniently
situated, and it would likewise be advantageous for the said
heirs of entail because the said Lands so proposed to be annexed
to the entailed Estate are of greater value than the said Lands
proposed to be taken therefrom; But as such Exchange, by reason
of the limitations and prohibitions of the said Deed of Entail,
cannot be effectuated without the aid and authority of Parliament;

MAY IT THEREFORE PLEASE YOUR MAJESTY,

Upon the Humble Petition of your Majesty's dutiful and
loyal Subject the said ROBERT BARCLAY ALLARDICE, now of Urie
and of Allardice in the County of Kincardine, Esquire, That it
may be Enacted;

AND BE IT ENACTED by the King's Most Excellent
Majesty, by and with the Advice and Consent of the Lords
Spiritual and Temporal, and Commons in this present Parliament
assembled, and by the Authority of the same, That from and
immediately after the passing of this Act, the said ROBERT BAR-
CLAY ALLARDICE, and failing of him by decease, the heir for the
time being, seised and in possession of the Lands and Hereditaments before mentioned, shall be at liberty to apply to the Court
of Session in Scotland, and by and with the direction and approbation of that Court to make, grant, and execute a disposition
and Deed of Settlement of the said Lands and Hereditaments
particularly before described, parts of the Lands of Redcloak and
Findlayston, and which at present belong to the said ROBERT

BARCLAY ALLARDICE in fee simple, in such form and manner as shall appear to the Judges of the said Court proper for effectually settling and securing the said Lands and Hereditaments, free of all Debts and Incumbrances, to and in favour of the said ROBERT BARCLAY ALLARDICE, and the other heirs entitled to take under the before recited Deed of Entail of the Estate of Urie, and with and under the conditions, limitations, and irritancies therein expressed; which settlement of Tailzie shall be so framed as to bind the Person executing the same, as well as the succeeding heirs of entail.

AND BE IT ENACTED by the authority aforesaid, That after the said Disposition or Deed of Settlement shall be so made and executed in manner and to the effect aforesaid, a Charter or Charters shall or may pass and be obtained thereupon, and Infeftment taken by virtue of the Precept of Sasine therein contained, agreeably to the forms of the Law of Scotland; and that the said Disposition or Deed of Settlement shall be recorded in the register of entails for Scotland, and of that of the Court of Session for preservation, for the benefit of all and every Person or Persons interested therein, to all which the said Judges of the Court of Session shall interpone their authority.

AND BE IT ENACTED, That from and immediately after the granting and executing the aforesaid Disposition and Deed of Settlement, the recording the same in manner above mentioned, the passing the Charter, and completing the Infeftments in the said Lands and Hereditaments above mentioned, and the authority of the Court of Session being interponed thereto, all and whole the said Parts and Pendicles of the said Lands of Montquich, called Trees, Burnhaugh, Rothnick and Corseley, with the Mill of Montquich, Mill Lands, Multures, and Sequels of the same, with the Parts and Pertinents before described; together with the Teinds of the said Lands, both Parsonage and Vicarage included, lying within the Parish of Fetteresso and Sheriffdom of Kincardine, and hereinbefore described as being parts of the entailed Estate of Urie, but lying at a distance from the Mansion House thereof, and proper to be exchanged for the said parts of the Lands of Redcloak and Findlayston before described; together with all Right, Title, and Interest, Claim of Right, Property, and Possession, which the said ROBERT BARCLAY ALLARDICE, his predecessors or authors, or heirs or successors, had, have, or anyways might pretend to the said Lands, or to the Teinds, Parsonage and Vicarage, in any manner or way comprized in Fee Tail by the aforesaid Deed of Entail of the ninth day of October one thousand seven hundred and twenty-two, and Investiture thereupon, shall be, and the same are hereby settled and vested in the said ROBERT BARCLAY ALLARDICE, his heirs and assignees, in fee simple; and the same shall from thenceforth be freed and absolutely acquitted, released, exonerated, and discharged of and from the conditions, provisions, declarations, limitations, and irritancies, in and by the said Deed of Entail limited, provided, expressed and declared, of and concerning the said Premises, or any of them, which from thenceforth shall be at the free disposal of the said ROBERT BARCLAY ALLARDICE, and his heirs and assigns.

SAVING AND RESERVING to the King's Most Excellent Majesty, his Heirs and Successors, and to all and every other Person and Persons, Bodies Politic and Corporate, his, her, and their Heirs, Executors, and Successors (other than and except the said ROBERT BARCLAY ALLARDICE, and the Heirs under the aforesaid Entail of the said Barony or Estate of Urie) all such Estates, Rights, Titles, Interests, Claims, and Demands of, in, to or out of all or any of the Lands, Estate, and other Premises aforesaid, as they, every, or any of them, had before the passing of this Act, or could, should, or might have had, enjoyed, claimed, or demanded, in case this Act had never been made.

SCHEDULE (B).—RENTAL of Parts of the Lands of REDCLOAK and FINDLAYSTON, contiguous to the House and Estate of URIE belonging to Robert Barclay Allardice, Esquire, over which the Entail of URIE is proposed to be extended, in place of certain other Lands contained in the said Entail.

Tenants' Names.	Possessions.	Term of Entry.	Endurance of Leases.	Expiry.	Money Rent. £ s. d.	Total Rent, Sterling Money. £ s. d.
1. REDCLOAK.						
1. John Milne	Part of Redcloak called Burnshol.	Marts, 1790	19 Years	Marts, 1809	4 5 ..	
2. John Melven	do	do 1804	19	do 1823	4 12 3	
3. Alexander Macbane	do	......	......	Whit. 1807	49 5 ..	
4. Robert Caird	do	......	......	do 1807	8 5 ..	
5. George Walker & Co	do	Marts, 1802	21 Years	Marts, 1823	7 9 ..	
6. Mrs. Smart	do	do 1793	19	do 1812	4 1 ..	
7. James Cruickshank	Lochfield	Whit. 1804	19	Whity, 1823	20 2 6	
8. Proprietor	Boddomley, &c				161 10 ..	
9. Roger Chapman	Chapman Farm	Marts, 1788	19 Years	Marts, 1807	5	
10. John Beattie	Bleachfield	do	19	do	22 6 1	286 15 10
2. FINDLAYSTON.						
1. John Milne	Part of Nether Findlayston	Whity, 1790	19 Years	Whity, 1809	15 6 ..	
2. Alexander Marr	Part of Whitefield	......			31 16 ..	
3. William Stuart	Part of Balnagight	......			18	65 2 ..
						351 17 10

The Value of Wood upon this Estate is Fifteen Hundred Pounds.

JOHN INNES, Land Surveyor.

SCHEDULE (A).—RENTAL of certain Lands contained in the Entail of the Estate of URIE belonging to Robert Barclay Allardice, Esquire, from which the Fetters of the Entail are proposed to be transferred to certain unentailed Lands also belonging to him.

Tenants' Names.	Possessions.	Term of Entry.	Endurance of Leases.	Expiry.	Meal.	Swine.	Fowls.	Money Rent.	Total Rent, Sterling Money.
								£ s. d.	£ s. d.
1. ROTHNICK & CORSELEY.									
1. James Morison	Part of Rothnick	Whity, 1804	19 Years	Whity, 1823				17	
2. Alexr. Law	do called Keelsgreen	Marts, 1789	19 do	Marts, 1808				8 15 ..	
3. Andrew Lawson	do	do	16 do	do 1805				5	
4. William Leiper	do							8	
5. James and William Scorgies	do	Whity, 1790	19 Years	Whity, 1809				22 8 ..	
6. Mrs. Robertson	do Carrick Greens							2 2 ..	
7. George Leiper	do	Whity, 1795	19 Years	Whity, 1814				24	
8. Joseph Jameson	do	do 1786	19 do	do 1805				7 10 ..	
9. Alexr. Bowman	Corseley	do 1795	19 do	do 1814				14	
10. John Smith	do	do 1795	19 do	do 1814				9	
11. John Finlay	do	do	19 do	do 1815				15	
12. George Strachan	Leys Croft of Rothnick	do 1796	19 do	do 1815				2	134 15 ..
2. MONTQUICH, BURNHAUGH, TREES.					BOLLS.				
13. Alexr. Walker	Mill of Montquich	Whit., 1798	19 Years	Whit., 1817	40 a. 16/.	1 a. 30/.	36at/1od.	35	
do	do							20	
14. William Lyal	Burnhaugh	Whit., 1797	19 Years	Whit., 1816				12	
15. George Smith	do	do 1789	19 do	do 1808				14	
16. William Ogg	Part of Trees and Scanderbeg	do 1802	19 do	do 1821				40	
17. John Walker	Part of Trees	do 1786	19 do	do 1805				7	
18. John Keith	Eddieslaw	do 1787	19 do	do 1806				3 3 1	131 3 1
									265 18 1

There is no Wood on this Estate.

JOHN INNES, *Land Surveyor.*

APPENDIX C.

The Ancestry of Lady Katharine Gordon.

In an article by the late Rev. Beverley Robinson Betts, entitled "The Heraldry of St. Paul's Chapel, New York," published in volume III of the New York Genealogical & Biographical Record, at page 21, a genealogical table is given which purports to show the descent of Col. Thomas Barclay,—first British Consul in New York,—from Henry III, King of England, and from Robert Bruce of Scotland. This table is certainly erroneous in three particulars, first, in that it recites Rev. Thomas Barclay of Albany as a son of John Barclay, brother of the apologist, and thus seeks to connect Col. Thomas with the Ury line, whereas he was *not* a descendant of the Ury family; secondly, in that it describes John Barclay, the apologist's brother, as "of New York," whereas he never was of New York, but always (in this country) of East New Jersey; and, thirdly, in that it names "Cornelia Van Schaick" as the wife of John Barclay, the apologist's brother, whereas John Barclay's wife was *not* named Cornelia, but Katharine, and probably was not a Van Schaick; and it may be erroneous in many more particulars.

As showing the probable ancestry of Lady Katharine Gordon, however, the table is entertaining, and is reproduced below (in abbreviated form) for what it may be worth. The writer has not deemed the matter of sufficient importance to check the accuracy of the table from Lady Katharine Gordon to Henry III and Robert Bruce, and assumes no responsibility for any inaccuracies which may appear therein. As a matter of amusement he has carried the table on beyond Henry III, and he gives Hume as his authority for the statements made in such further portion.

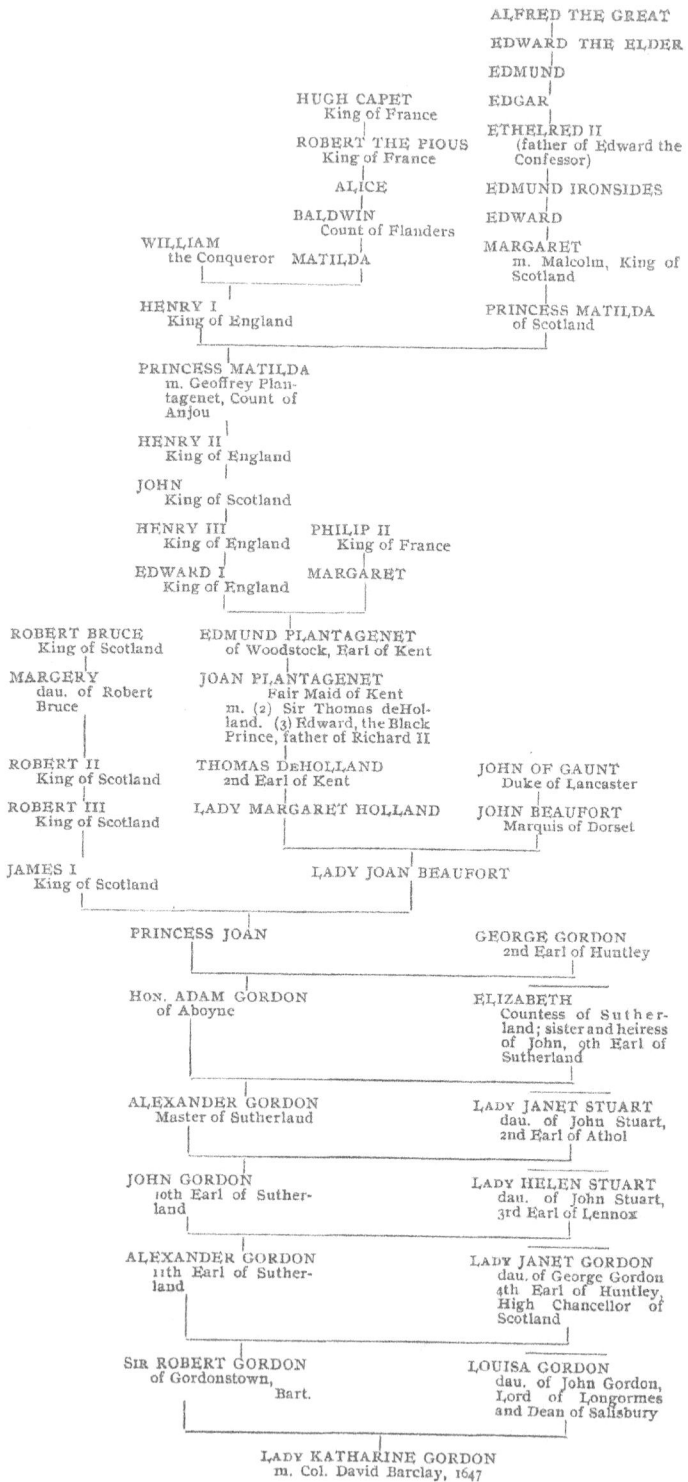

ALFRED THE GREAT
|
EDWARD THE ELDER
|
EDMUND
|
EDGAR
|
HUGH CAPET   ETHELRED II
King of France   (father of Edward the
| Confessor)
ROBERT THE PIOUS
King of France   EDMUND IRONSIDES
| |
ALICE   EDWARD
| |
BALDWIN   MARGARET
Count of Flanders m. Malcolm, King of
WILLIAM   Scotland
the Conqueror MATILDA
| | PRINCESS MATILDA
HENRY I   of Scotland
King of England

PRINCESS MATILDA
m. Geoffrey Plan-
tagenet, Count of
Anjou
|
HENRY II
King of England
|
JOHN
King of Scotland
|
HENRY III   PHILIP II
King of England King of France
| |
EDWARD I   MARGARET
King of England

ROBERT BRUCE   EDMUND PLANTAGENET
King of Scotland of Woodstock, Earl of Kent
| |
MARGERY   JOAN PLANTAGENET
dau. of Robert   Fair Maid of Kent
Bruce   m. (2) Sir Thomas deHol-
| land. (3) Edward, the Black
| Prince, father of Richard II
ROBERT II   THOMAS DeHOLLAND   JOHN OF GAUNT
King of Scotland 2nd Earl of Kent   Duke of Lancaster
| |
ROBERT III   LADY MARGARET HOLLAND JOHN BEAUFORT
King of Scotland   Marquis of Dorset
|
JAMES I   LADY JOAN BEAUFORT
King of Scotland

PRINCESS JOAN   GEORGE GORDON
                 2nd Earl of Huntley

HON. ADAM GORDON   ELIZABETH
of Aboyne   Countess of Suther-
              land; sister and heiress
              of John, 9th Earl of
              Sutherland

ALEXANDER GORDON LADY JANET STUART
Master of Sutherland dau. of John Stuart,
              2nd Earl of Athol

JOHN GORDON   LADY HELEN STUART
10th Earl of Suther- dau. of John Stuart,
land   3rd Earl of Lennox

ALEXANDER GORDON LADY JANET GORDON
11th Earl of Suther- dau. of George Gordon
land   4th Earl of Huntley,
           High Chancellor of
           Scotland

SIR ROBERT GORDON LOUISA GORDON
of Gordonstown,   dau. of John Gordon,
      Bart.   Lord of Longormes
           and Dean of Salisbury

LADY KATHARINE GORDON
m. Col. David Barclay, 1647

APPENDIX D.

The Arms of the Barclays of Pierston and of the Barclays of Mather and Urie.

In an article entitled "The Heraldry of St. Paul's Chapel, New York," by the late Rev. Beverley Robinson Betts,[1] the tablet is described which was erected in St. Paul's to the memory of Col. Thomas Barclay, the first British Consul in New York (grandson of Rev. Thomas Barclay of Albany), and his arms are stated to be:

> "Gules a chevron or between three crosses patée argent.
> *Crest:* A sword erect argent, hilt and pomel or
> *Motto:* Crux Christi nostra Corona."

"By some oversight," wrote Mr. Betts, "doubtless of the engraver, the chevron is given *or* whereas it should be *argent.*

"The arms of the ancient family of Barclays of Urie," he goes on to say, "are

> "Gules a chevron between three crosses patée argent,

and they were so borne by Col. Barclay in his lifetime."

But the Rev. Mr. Betts was mistaken in his description of the arms of the Barclays of Ury, whatever may have been the arms borne by Col. Thomas Barclay in his lifetime. The crest and the motto above described have come down to Col. Barclay's descendants, beyond any doubt, for they are used by them to-day; but they are not the crest or motto of the Ury family, as we shall presently see, but *are* approximately the crest and motto of Sir Robert Barclay of Pierston. Nor, as we shall also see, were the arms described by Mr. Betts the arms of the Barclays of Mather and Ury.

---

[1]N. Y. Gen. & Biog. Rec., vol. III, p. 21.

The arms of Sir Robert Barclay of *Pierston,* were:

Azure a chevron betwixt three crosses patée or
Crest: A sword in pale ppr hilt and pomel;
Motto: Crux Christi nostra Corona;"[2]

while the arms of the Barclays of Mather and *Ury* originally were, as recorded in the Lyons Register:

Azure a chevron and in chief three crosses patée argent.[3]

In the appendix to the second volume of Nisbet's "System of Heraldry,"[3] page 241, the following appears as a part of the genealogical account of the Barclays of Mather and Urie, written in 1725, and apparently by one of the family:

"Their armorial bearing was formerly *three crosses patées with a* "*cheveron, and a mitre for a crest.* But the present Barclay of Urie, "anno 1725, after the example of Struan Robertson, threw out the "cheveron, as being by some thought a mark of cadency; though, as Sir "George Mackenzie observes in his Heraldry, it was anciently esteemed "an ornament; so their present bearing is
"Azure three crosses patée in chief argent with a dove and olive "branch in its mouth for a crest. In an escrol above 'Cedant Arma' and "below 'In hac vince,' as extracted from the Lyon's books 1725."

A steel plate showing the arms will be found on page 6 of the plates immediately following the appendix.

In Stodart's "Scottish Arms," the writer says:

"In 1725 Robert Barclay of Urie as representing Barclay of Mathers, "registered (in Lyons Court)
"Azure, three crosses patée in chief argent.
"*Crest:* A dove with an olive branch in its mouth, all ppr.
"*Motto:* Cedant Arma, and In hac vince.
"The direct line having ended in an heiress, Mrs. Margaret Barclay "Allardice (Ritchie), the heir male, Arthur Kett Barclay of Bury Hill, "co. Surrey, in 1858 recorded arms with alterations, and was allowed sup-"porters which had been previously borne by the Barclays of Urie, but "not registered:
"Azure a chevron and in chief three crosses patée argent.
"*Crest:* A bishop's mitre affrontee with tassels flottant upward or
"*Motto:* In cruce spero.
"*Supporters:* Two old savage men, wreathed about the loins with oak leaves, holding in their exterior hands clubs erect, all ppr."

---

[2]See BURKE'S ENCYCL. OF HERALDRY; PEERAGE OF SCOTLAND, by Sir R. Douglas; Sir James Balfour MMS. OF BLAZONS IN LYONS COURT; and Stodart's SCOTTISH ARMS.

[3]A SYSTEM OF HERALDRY, by Alexander Nisbet, Gent., Edinburgh: William Blackwood, 1816.

In Burke's LANDED GENTRY, edition of 1852, the arms of the Barclays of Urie and of Bury Hill are given as above described in Stodart's SCOTTISH ARMS; and the same arms are given in the edition of 1871.

Whether Mr. Betts' description of the arms borne by Col. Thomas Barclay as being gules in the field, was an error of the sculptor, or is indicative of a descent of Col. Thomas from some family other than either the Pierston or Ury family, the writer is not in a position to form any opinion. Certain it is that the arms described by Mr. Betts are not the arms of either Pierston or Ury, although the crest and motto inscribed in St. Paul's are practically the same as those of Sir Robert Barclay of Pierston.

It is an interesting fact to note in this connection that most of the English Berkeleys, as a research will show, bore gules in their fields while most of the Scottish families had azure fields. And yet in 1247, according to Sir James Balfour in his MMS. OF BLAZONS IN LYONS COURT, the surname of Berkeley carried "gules a chevron between ten crosses patée argent, six in chief and four in base." While this blazon was generally that used by the Berkeleys for a considerable period, several of the branches of the family found it more in accordance with the usages of heraldry and more agreeable to arms to reduce the number of crosses to three and have altered the tinctures in their several bearings.

Sir Robert Barclay of Pierston, Ayres, Knt., was created Baronet of Nova Scotia, October 22nd, 1668, with remainder to the heirs male of his body. He died in 1694-5, having married (1) August 4th, 1653, Catherine, dau. of Alexander Lochhart of Edinburgh, merchant (of the Carnwath family) by whom he had three sons and a daughter, and (2) September 28th, 1659, Barbara Deans, by whom he had eight sons and three daughters.[4]

---

[4]See THE PEERAGE, BARONETAGE AND KNIGHTAGE OF THE BRITISH EMPIRE for 1881, by Joseph Foster. Westminster: Nichols & Sons.

APPENDIX E.

"In the name of God, Amen:

I, John Barclay, of Perth Amboy in County of Middlesex, being of perfect mind and memory, thanks be given to Almighty God for the same, and calling to mind the mortality of my body do make and ordain this to be my last will and testament. And as tutching such wordly estate wharewith it hath pleased God to bless me with in this life, I give and bequeath and dispose of the same in manner and form following,

First, I give to my loveing wife Jane, the sum of teen pounds an addityon to a sum of money I did agree to give her by a Contract between my Wife and my selfe before we was married if I should dye before her which she did agree to except of in leu of her Dowry and quitt all my estate both real and personal I give to my wife my Negro gerl Esie so long as she remains my widow, I give to my wife wife (*sic*) any room in my dwelling house and one of my Milch Cows all which I give to my wife in leu of her Dowry agreeable to the above recited contract.

And whareas I have given a deed to my son John for one half of all my lands lying on Matcheponix Neck, I give and bequeath to my son Robert Barclay and to his heirs and assigns all the other half of my lands lying on said neack in consideration my son Robert delivers a bond which I gave him payable after my decease to my son John. If Robert refuses or neglects to deliver s'd bond, I do Ipower and athorise my sons John and Charles to sell as much of the land I have willed to Robert as will amount to the sums due on s'd bond and my will is that my son Robert must pay to Archable Craige, son of Samuel Craige, deceased, when he arrives to the age of twenty-one years and to no other person, the sum of teen pounds.

I give to my son Robert my great Armd Chair and one paire of hand Irons, and my chest which stands in my room.

I give to my son Charles my desk.

I give to my son Peter and to his heirs and assigns all my land lying at Cranbury meadows which was in partnership with Laurence Dey, but we have devided and given releases to each other the boundres of my part is in Laurence Dey's release to me. I give to my son Peter all my waring cloaths and opperl, and my saddles I give to my daughter Lydia.

My bead and furniture and half my puter I give to my daughter Katharine. The other half of my peuter, my bilsted Cubbart my looking Glass, my round table and stand, six chairs, my iron Kittel which I bought at Mrs. Tenent's Vendue, my small small (*sic*) tongues and tribet Iron and one iron trammell, I give to my granddaughter Jane Barclay, daughter of my son David deceased, the sum of twenty pounds and one Cow to be paid to her when she is married. If she dyes before she is married, I givn her legasay legasey (*sic*) to her three sisters, share and share alike.

My will is after my funeral charges and just debts are all paid and all the aforesaid leageses are all paid in currant money of this province or state, I give and bequeath to my son John, all the remainder of my moveable estate, if my executors should receive part of the money due to me by the bank of Notes, if it doth not amount to one hundred and fifty pounds they are to pay all they receive to Lydia and Katharine, share and share alike, their two sisters, according to this my will, but if they receive more than one hundred and fifty pounds the remainder after they have paid one hundred and fifty pounds to their two sisters, share and share alike, is to be devided amongst my three sons John, Charles and Robert and all the children of my son David deceased, share and share alike by my executors according to this my will.

And I do nominate constitute and appoint my three sons John, Charles and Robert my executors to execute this my last will and testament.

In witness whereof, I have sett my hand and seal and declared this to be my last will and testament this twenty-sixth day of May and in the year of our Lord one thousand seven hundred eighty and two 1782. I give to my aforesaid granddaughter four sheep to be delivered to her when she is married.

JNO. BARCLAY. (L. S.)

In the presence of us witnesses:

> *John Forman,*
> *William Vanderipe,*
> *Duncan Campbell,*
> *Archebald Gordon."*

CODICIL.

"There is several leigeses forgot to be mentioned in this my will for which reason I make this codesell.

I give to my grandson George Barclay, the son of my son David, deceased, the sum of five pounds, and whereas it has been said by the widow of my son David that I am indebted to his estate, if she receives any money of my executors my will is that so much as she receives must be reducted out of the leigesey I left to her daughter Jane, the leagisey left to my granddaughter Jean is to be paid to her when she is Married if she doth not marry till she arrives to the age of twenty-five years the sd legisey is to be paid to her then.

I give to my daughter Lydia my yallow and blew coverled, made in my first wife's time.

I give to my daughter Katharine my case and the bottles.

In witness whereof I have set my hand and seal this ninth day of June in the year 1782. I give to my Daughter Katharine one of my linnine wheels.

JNO. BARCLAY. (L. S.)

In the presence of us witnesses

> *John Forman,*
> *William Vanderipe,*
> *Archebald Gordon."*

The foregoing will and codicil were proved at New Brunswick by William Vanderipe and Archibald Gordon, as witnesses, before Jona. Deare, Surrogate, on December 24th, 1790.

APPENDIX F.

Memorandum on the State of Preservation of Sundry Records in Virginia and Maryland.[1]

I.

County Records of Virginia.

FREDERICK COUNTY was established from Orange County in 1738, and from 1743 the records, including marriage licenses, for all Northern Virginia were kept in the court house at Winchester. The records are well cared for and are in good condition.

LOUDON COUNTY was taken from Fairfax County and was established in 1757. Its wills and deeds from 1757, and marriage licenses from 1793, are preserved in the court house at Leesburg.

FAIRFAX COUNTY was established in 1742 out of Prince William County, and its records are complete from that date with the exception of a few books that were lost during the civil war. The marriage licenses date back only to 1856. All records are preserved at Fairfax Court House, and among them the original will of George Washington. The record of this will covers twenty-two pages and includes his observations upon the value of his properties in Virginia, Maryland, New York, and other localities.

PRINCE WILLIAM COUNTY was established out of Stafford County in 1730. The county seat is at Manassas and the records are in good condition.

FAUQUIER COUNTY was taken from Prince William County and was established in 1759. Its wills, deeds and court records

---

[1]The contents of this Appendix, with the exception of the notes on the parish records of St. Mary's and Charles Counties, Maryland, were prepared by KIRK BROWN, professional genealogist, of 1813 North Caroline Street, Baltimore, from memoranda made by him on the different occasions of his searches for the writer and for others.

from 1759, and its marriage licenses from 1798, are preserved in good order at the court house at Warrenton.

CULPEPPER COUNTY was established out of Orange County in 1778. The records are preserved in good condition at Culpepper Court House, and are well indexed.

ORANGE COUNTY was taken from Spottsylvania County and was established in 1734. Its records are preserved in good order at Orange Court House.

STAFFORD COUNTY was erected out of Westmoreland County in 1666. Its records at Stafford Court House are in poor condition and but little cared for, and many were lost or destroyed during the War of the Rebellion. Conveyances, wills, administrations, appraisals and other public papers are recorded promiscuously in the same volumes. Those that remain at the Court House, however, are indexed and include the years 1699-1709, 1748-1763, 1809-1813, and 1839 to date.

The old church records in Stafford County, with the exception of a portion of the records of Overwharton Parish, seem also to have been destroyed during the civil war. "OVERWHARTON PARISH REGISTER, 1720 to 1760" is the title of a neat little volume of 195 pages by William F. Boogher.

KING GEORGE COUNTY. The records at King George Court House commence with 1721 and are complete,—with the exception of Will books, from 1721 to 1744, which are said to have been carried away by a soldier during the civil war and to be still in existence somewhere in the City of New York.

The records of Lambs Creek Parish, King George County, were destroyed during the war.

SPOTTSYLVANIA COUNTY was established in 1720 out of King George, Essex and King William Counties. Its records date from 1722, with the exception of marriage licenses subsequently to 1750, which were destroyed during the civil war, and are in fair condition. They are preserved at Spottsylvania Court House. The records of the old church of Spottsylvania were destroyed during the war, as were also the records of St. George's Parish, of Fredericksburg.

At Fredericksburg may be found the record of wills, administrations, conveyances, etc., from 1782, the year of the incorporation of the city.

LOUISA COUNTY was set off from Hanover County in 1742, and the records, including marriage licenses from 1781, are preserved at Louisa Court House.

ALBERMARLE COUNTY was established in 1744. Its records, including orders and judgments, are preserved in good order at Charlottesville.

AUGUSTA COUNTY was set up out of Orange County in 1738. Its records of wills and deeds from 1745 and of marriage licenses from 1785 are preserved in good condition in the court house at Staunton.

HANOVER COUNTY was established out of New Kent County in 1720. Its records of wills, administrations, deeds and mortgages from 1733 to 1865,—with the exception of two old books of general entry,—were sent from Hanover Court House to Richmond for preservation during the War of the Rebellion, and were destroyed by fire when Richmond was burned. The two books preserved contain general entries from 1733 to 1792.

The records of St. Stephens Parish, Hanover County, were also destroyed during the war.

CAROLINE COUNTY records are kept at Bowling Green and date from 1727, when the County was established. During the civil war they were sent to Richmond for safe keeping, and a portion of them, including wills from 1727 to 1814 and land records from 1727 to 1836, were destroyed in the burning of Richmond.

The only *old* records at Bowling Green are some old Order and Judgment books from 1732 to 1740, which are in fair condition, and are indexed. Those from 1740 to 1759 are simply a mass of waste paper with indices gone, and are of little or no practical use to the genealogist. Those from 1759 to 1772 are in hopeless confusion, and many of the indices are missing. It is impossible to gain any continuous knowledge of their contents. The books from 1781 to 1800 are indexed and are available for general use, as is also the record of marriage licenses from 1786 to 1846.

WESTMORELAND COUNTY was established in 1663 and its records date from that year. They are extremely interesting, and are preserved in fair condition in the court house at Montross.

KING AND QUEEN COUNTY was established in 1691 out of New Kent County. Its records were sent to Richmond for preservation during the civil war and were there destroyed by fire.

GLOUCESTER COUNTY was established out of York County in 1652. Its county seat is Gloucester Court House. All records were sent to Richmond for preservation during the civil war, and were there destroyed in the burning of Richmond.

ACCAMAC COUNTY records date from 1663 and are preserved in good condition at Accamac Court House. They are among the most interesting in Virginia.

YORK COUNTY was one of the original counties into which Virginia was divided in 1634. Its records are preserved at York-town. Wills from 1633 and deeds from 1645 are complete to date. They are, generally speaking, in good condition and are among the most reliable records in Virginia. They remained in the old court house at Yorktown through the Revolutionary struggle, the war of 1812 and the civil war.

JAMES CITY COUNTY was also one of the original counties in Virginia. Its records, however, were sent to Richmond for safe keeping during the civil war and were there destroyed by fire. Its county seat is Williamsburg.

NEW KENT COUNTY was established out of York County in 1654. Its records were all destroyed in the burning of Richmond, to which city they had been sent for preservation during the war.

HENRICO COUNTY was another of the original counties in Virginia, and dates from 1634. All county records prior to 1810 and all records of the city of Richmond were destroyed by fire when Richmond was burned, except that the general records of patents granted from 1623, may still be found in that city. A large number of these patents issued to soldiers of the Revolution by way of bounty, and were generally located in what are now the States of Ohio and West Virginia. They contain much genealogical information.

HAMPSHIRE COUNTY (West Virginia) was established in 1754 from Augusta and Frederick Counties, Virginia. Deeds from 1757 are in the court house at Romney; but all wills, excepting a few originals, were destroyed during the War of the Rebellion. There are no marriage licenses.

HARDY COUNTY (West Virginia) was taken from Hampshire County and was established in 1786. Its records, including some marriage licenses, are in good condition at the court house at Moorefield.

II.

Parish Registers at the Virginia Theological Seminary near Alexandria.

Register of Abingdon Parish, Gloucester County, 1677-1761.
    "   " Christ Church, Middlesex Parish, 1663-1812.
    "   " Lunenburg Parish, Richmond Registry, 1792-1799.
    "   " St. Peters Parish, New Kent Register, 1690-1784.
    "   " St. Charles Parish, York County Register, 1648-1800.

There are also a number of parish vestry books, not indexed, which contain but little genealogical information.

III.

County Records of Maryland.

At *Annapolis,* in Anne Arundel County, are preserved the records (presumably for the entire State) from 1635 to 1777.

They include wills, administrations, deeds, patents, certificates, land warrants and similar records.

An abstract of each will, as recorded in the will books of the Prerogative Court of the Province, has been taken from those books now on deposit in the vault connected with the office of the Register of Wills of Anne Arundel County, by Mrs. JANE BALDWIN COTTON, and is being printed under the title: "*The Maryland Calendar of Wills:* Wm. J. C. Dulany Co., Publishers, Baltimore, Md., 1901." This publication, if completed, will be an extremely valuable addition to the genealogical literature of Maryland.

While many wills of the provincial period are also recorded in the several counties of the State, the records at Annapolis are believed to be more complete and more accurate.

BALTIMORE COUNTY has its records of wills, administrations and deeds from 1664, and marriage licenses from 1776. They are all preserved at Baltimore and are in good condition.

CAROLINE COUNTY was established in 1773. Its county seat is Denton.

CALVERT COUNTY was established in 1654. Its county seat is Fredericktown.

CECIL COUNTY was established in 1674. Its records of wills, deeds and administrations date from 1773 and are preserved in good condition at Elkton, the county seat.

CHARLES COUNTY records are intact from 1655 and are carefully preserved in a modern well-arranged court house at the county seat, La Plata.

DORCHESTER COUNTY was established about 1669. Its county seat is Cambridge. All wills prior in date to 1854 and marriage licenses prior to 1780 have been destroyed by fire.

FREDERICK COUNTY was set off from Prince George County in 1748. Its records are preserved at Frederick, the county seat, and date from 1743 excepting the marriage licenses which date back only to 1782.

HARFORD COUNTY was set off from Baltimore County in 1773. Its records are kept at Bel Air, the county seat, and are in good condition. Wills, deeds, and administrations date from 1773, and marriage licenses from about that time.

HOWARD COUNTY was taken from Anne Arundel County in 1850. Wills, administrations and deeds date from that year. Ellicott City is its county seat.

KENT COUNTY originally included the whole of the Eastern shore and was under the government of an officer styled the "Commander of the Island of Kent." Its deeds date from 1749 and its wills from 1669. They are on record at Chestertown, which is the county seat.

MONTGOMERY COUNTY was set off from Prince George and Frederick Counties in 1786. Its records date from that year. Its county seat is Rockville.

PRINCE GEORGE'S COUNTY was established in 1695. Its county seat is Marlboro Station.

QUEEN ANNE'S COUNTY was established in 1706. Its county seat is Centerville.

SOMERSET COUNTY was established in 1666. Its records are preserved at the county seat, Princess Anne, and consist of wills from 1685, deeds from 1665, and one book of records from 1670 to 1700 containing births, deaths, marriages, cattle marks, and other interesting matter.

ST. MARY'S COUNTY, one of the oldest in the State, has its county seat at Leonardtown. All its records, excepting marriage licenses from September, 1794, and wills from 1658, were destroyed with the burning of the court house about 1832. The records of wills and marriage licenses had previously been saved when the court house was burned by the British in 1814.

TALBOT COUNTY was established in 1661. Its records are preserved at the county seat, Easton. The wills date back to 1667, deeds to 1721 and marriage licenses to 1774.

WORCESTER COUNTY was established in 1742. Its county seat is Snow Hill.

IV.

Parish Records of Maryland.

The Maryland Historical Society has copied and indexed and has on file in its library in Baltimore, the following parish records:

ANNE ARUNDEL COUNTY:

St. Anne Parish, Annapolis, from 1712 to 1777. Births, deaths, marriages, baptisms and vestry proceedings.

All Hallow Parish, from 1689 to 1854. Births, deaths, marriages, baptisms and vestry proceedings.

St. Margarets, Westminster Parish, from 1673 to 1809. Births, deaths, marriages and baptisms.

St. James Parish. Births, deaths, marriages, baptisms and vestry proceedings.

Christ Church, Queen Caroline Parish (now in Howard County, which was established in 1850), from 1736 to 1854. Births, deaths, marriages, baptisms and vestry proceedings.

Rock Creek Parish (now in Frederick County, which was established in 1748), from 1726 to 1854. Births, deaths, marriages, baptisms and vestry proceedings.

BALTIMORE COUNTY:

St. Paul's Parish, Baltimore, from 1715 to 1796. Births, deaths, marriages and baptisms.

St. James and St. Johns Parish, Baltimore from 1782 to 1815. Births, deaths, marriages and baptisms.

First Presbyterian Church, Baltimore, from 1768 to 1819. Births, marriages and deaths.

First German Reformed Congregation, Baltimore, from 1779 to 1851. Births, marriages and deaths.

Zion German Lutheran Christ's Church, Baltimore, from 1786 to 1834. Births, marriages and deaths.

CALVERT COUNTY:

All Saints Parish, from 1707 to 1753. Vestry proceedings.
Christ Church Parish, from 1707 to 1813. Births, deaths, marriages, baptisms and vestry proceedings.

CAROLINE COUNTY:

St. Johns Parish, from 1752 to 1799. Births, baptisms, marriages, deaths and vestry proceedings.

CARROLL COUNTY:

Jerusalem Lutheran Church, from 1783 to 1853. Births, marriages and deaths.

CECIL COUNTY:

St. Mary Anne's Parish, from 1742 to 1799. Births, baptisms, marriages, deaths and vestry proceedings.
St. Stephens Parish, from 1694 to 1837. Births, baptisms, marriages and deaths.

CHARLES COUNTY:

Durham Parish. Vestry proceedings.
See also "Register of Births, Marriages and Deaths in Charles County from 1654 to 1726," transcribed by Philip D. Laird, Commissioner of the Land Office in 1895, and filed in the Land Office of Maryland at Annapolis.

DORCHESTER COUNTY:

Dorchester Parish, from 1743 to 1770. Births, baptisms, marriages and deaths.

FREDERICK COUNTY:

All Saints Parish, from 1727 to 1862. Births, baptisms, marriages, deaths and vestry proceedings.

KENT COUNTY:

St. Pauls Parish, from 1693 to 1800. Births, baptisms, marriages, deaths and vestry proceedings.
Shrewsbury Parish, from 1745 to 1882. Births, baptisms, marriages, deaths and vestry proceedings.

MONTGOMERY COUNTY:

> *Prince George's Parish,* from 1792 to 1845. Births, baptisms, marriages and deaths.

PRINCE GEORGE COUNTY:

> *Queen Anne Parish,* from 1705 to 1773. Births, deaths, marriages, baptisms and vestry proceedings.
>
> *St. John's or Piscataway Parish,* from 1695 to 1774. Births, deaths, marriages and vestry proceedings.

QUEEN ANNE COUNTY:

> *St. Paul's Parish,* from 1693 to 1818. Vestry proceedings.

SOMERSET COUNTY:

> *Stepney Parish,* from 1724 to 1889. Births, baptisms, marriages, deaths and vestry proceedings.
>
> *Coventry Parish,* from 1750 to 1866. Births, baptisms, marriages, deaths and vestry proceedings.

ST. MARY'S COUNTY:

> *All Faith Parish,* from 1693 to 1817. Vestry proceedings.

TALBOT COUNTY:

> *St. Peter's Parish,* from 1681 to 1805. Births, baptisms, marriages, deaths and vestry proceedings.

V.

The Parish Records of St. Mary's County, Maryland.

The three original parishes of St. Mary's County were:

1. *William and Mary Parish,* in the South and East;
2. *King and Queen Parish,* in the West; and
3. *All Faith Parish,* in the North.

In 1750, a new parish was created out of William & Mary, known as *St. Andrew's* parish, which included the Easterly part of the County, and one hundred years later, 1850, a new parish was set off at the extreme South, called *St. Mary's* parish.

At a comparatively recent date, King & Queen parish has been divided into *Chaptico* and *All Saints* parishes.

William & Mary Parish was founded in 1650. The church was formerly called "St. George's" but for more than a hundred years has been known as "Poplar Hill." It is out in the country, about sixteen miles from Leonardtown. All parish records prior to November 10, 1798, have been destroyed, part with the burning of the Court House between 1826 and 1832, and part with the burning in 1829 of the house of a vestryman, Dr. Broome, in St. Mary's City.

St. Andrew's Parish. The church at Leonardtown is a chapel of this parish. The church had no incumbent in 1897 and the records were in the possession of the register of the parish, Mr. Walter H. Briscoe, whose house is on the Patuxent River, near Hollywood P. O. They include births, marriages, burials and vestry proceedings, and date from November 27, 1753.

King and Queen Parish. Prior to the division of this parish, the parish church was situated in the village of Chaptico. The rector (in 1897), Rev. James L. Smiley, and Mr. George R. Garner, one of the vestrymen, are authorities for the statement that *all* the parish records prior to 1832 disappeared during a controversy between the then rector and the vestry, and have never since been found. A single leaf, covering births, marriages and burials, 1772-1774, may be found in the Whittingham Episcopal Library at 1108 Madison Avenue, Baltimore.

All Faith Parish has its parish church at Mechanicsville. Its vestry minutes from 1692 to 1800 have been copied and may be found at the Historical Society in Baltimore. The rector's record of births, marriages, burials, etc., seems to have disappeared.

VI.

Parish Records of Charles County, Maryland.

Trinity Parish has its parish church at Charlotte Hall. Its records had been lost for many years, but were recently found. The records of births, marriages and burials date from 1756.

Port Tobacco Parish was laid out in 1692. The (1897) rector, Rev. James E. Poindexter, of La Plata, is authority for the statement that *all* records prior to 1869 have completely disappeared.

Durham Parish. The original records which still exist are at the Whittingham Library in Baltimore. They are chiefly vestry minutes, and contain no record of births, deaths, marriages or confirmations.

VII.

Records of Early Quaker Meetings in Maryland and Virginia.

The early Meetings of Friends in MARYLAND were the *West River* Monthly Meeting, on the Western Shore of Chesapeake Bay, and the *Third Haven* Monthly Meeting on the Eastern Shore.

The former dates back to 2nd mo. (i. e. April O. S.), 1672, and was composed of (1) *West River,* (2) *Herring Creek* and (3) *Indian Springs* in Anne Arundel County, and *The Cliffs* in Calvert County.

The *Third Haven* (sometimes called "Trade Haven") Meeting, dates back to 8th mo. (i. e. October, O. S.) 3rd, 1672.

In the Northern part of the State was the *Nottingham* Monthly Meeting, dating from 1730, *Gunpowder,* dating from 1739, *Deer Creek* from 1765, *Pipe Creek* from about 1767, and *Baltimore* from 1793.

Hopewell Monthly Meeting was established in 1732 as a part of the Nottingham Monthly Meeting, and became a Meeting of Record in 1735. The first volume of records, 1735 to 1759, was destroyed by fire. The records from 1759 are preserved in the vault at the Park Avenue Meeting House, Baltimore.

Fairfax Monthly Meeting (Loudon County, Virginia), was established in 1745, and its records from that date are preserved at the Park Avenue Meeting House, Baltimore, as are also the records of the *Crooked Run* Monthly Meeting (of the same County) established 1783 and abandoned 1807. *Goose Creek* Monthly Meeting (Loudon County, Virginia), was established in 1785 and its records, together with those of the *Alexandra* Monthly Meeting, near Washington (which date from 1805), are preserved in the same vault as are the records above mentioned.

Further information concerning these meetings may be had by consulting Janney's "History of Friends," or Weeks' "Southern Quakers and Slavery;" or by addressing KIRK BROWN (Custodian of the Records, Park Avenue Meeting House, Baltimore), who has made a complete index of the contents of these records. Mr. BROWN also has extensive notes compiled by him from the records of the *South River* Monthly Meeting in Bedford County, Virginia, 1757-1878; of the *Henrico* Monthly Meeting, in Henrico County, Virginia, formerly called *Curls*, 1698-1755; and of the *White Oak Swamp* Monthly Meeting in the same locality, 1792-1837.

INDEX I.

Surname Barclay.

INDEX II.

Surname Barkley.

INDEX III.

Surnames other than Barclay or Barkley.

www.ingramcontent.com/pod-product-compliance
Lightning Source LLC
Chambersburg PA
CBHW071825270326
41929CB00013B/1900